Instructor's and Counselor's Guide for
Career Choices

An Interdisciplinary Curriculum for High Schools and Colleges

by Mindy Bingham

Contributions by:
Tanja Easson
Rochelle Friedman, Ed.D.
Kenneth B. Hoyt, Ph.D
Laura Light, M.Ed.
Sandy Stryker

and the
generous Career Choices *instructors*
noted throughout this text

Completely revised and updated

Academic **Innovations**
Santa Barbara, California

        Published by Academic Innovations
        Tel: (800) 967-8016   FAX (800) 967-4027
        www.academicinnovations.com
        careerchoices@academicinnovations.com

Manufactured in the United States of America

Foreword

Changing Attitudes, Changing Lives...

In four words, that sums up the goal of the *Career Choices* curriculum. What began as a passion in 1990 for Mindy Bingham, has grown into a mission for the nearly 20 individuals who write, administer, support, and train in this curriculum.

To date over 3,800 schools and programs with roughly a half million students have used *Career Choices*. Throughout this manual you'll find the thoughts, ideas, and creative energies of some of the hundreds of educators who have embraced and championed this concept.

When *Career Choices* was first published in 1990, it was considered a cutting edge curriculum because it integrated the theme of career and life planning into the traditional subjects of English/language arts, math, and social studies. Using an interdisciplinary approach grounded in real-life activities, students find the answer to the age-old question: 'Why is education important?'. Now, with the addition of its technology-based enhancements, Academic Innovations continues to provide educators with the latest and best strategies for motivating and educating our young people.

If you want to make a major difference in the lives of your students, read on. Then pick up the phone and call our curriculum and technical support department. Our job does not stop when you order your classroom sets of these textbooks. It only begins. We are devoted to your success and the success of your students.

Contents

Section Four   Lesson Plan Suggestions

Section Five   Specialized Lesson Plans

Section Six   Special Teaching Tips and Strategies

Section Seven   Integrating Technology into Your Classroom

Section Eight   Resources and Curriculum Support

Section Nine   Start-Up Strategies

Section Ten   Getting the Community and Parents Involved

Introduction

Integrating Career Guidance into Academics to Create Motivated Learners

To prosper in the 21st century workplace, an exceptional education is critical. Gaining such an education requires work, effort, and striving. However, many students do not understand the link between life satisfaction and academic achievement; thus, they fail to make the necessary personal investment.

An old adage says, "you can lead a horse to water but you can't make him drink." Educators know all too well, *you can sit a child in the classroom but you can't make him think*. Motivating the unmotivated is, perhaps, the greatest challenge educators face.

Academic teachers across the country are meeting this challenge by "repackaging" their traditional disciplines. By infusing real-world themes and issues, the core content is delivered with a fresher, more relevant slant.

The advent of Tech Prep and School-To-Work programs helped educators identify the need for comprehensive guidance. After all, students are being asked to make important, sophisticated choices at increasingly younger ages. These choices are to be made in a world where many parents are less accessible and school guidance counselors have less time to spend with each individual student. These conditions may cause new programs with higher academic standards to fail. This failure will not necessarily be a result of poor teaching; more likely, students' immaturity, lack of motivation, and insufficient exposure to the real world will be factors.

Award-winning author Fox Butterfield (American Book Award) probed the underlying reasons Asian students achieve higher academic goals than Americans did. He found two important differences. First, young Asians had a clear vision of their adult roles and their future lives. Secondly, they embraced the concept that hard work—not innate talent or intelligence—was the key to success.

If academic success lies in the ability to visualize the future and set goals aimed at achieving that vision, why have so many students yet to develop these all-important skills? The answers shouldn't be too startling. After all, long-range planning can be a frightening notion. Not surprisingly, many families simply refuse to discuss the future. This attitude has helped to create a society accustomed to instant gratification. Our societal credos? *Just charge it. Just fax it. Just do it.* As a result, the average savings rate in the United States is less than half that of other industrialized nations.

Our society's attitude regarding the future may have a greater impact on our youth than we often realize. According to researcher Michael Resnick, Ph.D., author of one of the most respected studies on teen pregnancy prevention, students who have no vision of their future are far more likely to become teen parents. The director of the Girls Incorporated National Resource Center, Dr. Heather Johnston Nicholson, states, "There is little evidence that sex education by itself makes any difference in the adolescent pregnancy rate." Conversely, research does show a strong relationship between a girl's career aspiration and the prevention of adolescent pregnancy.

The ability to project into the future and understand the consequences of today's actions is equally critical to dropout prevention for students of all ages. In fact, studies show that college students who have clear career goals as entering freshmen are far more likely to graduate than those who do not.

What can secondary schools do to help a student become a distance thinker in a society focused on sprinting? Long-range thinking and planning can be taught, and the best place to teach these skills is in the academic classroom. Curriculum, classroom discussions, and academic projects can present themes that help students visualize their adult lives and understand the aftereffect of today's choices.

The best guidance curriculums are delivered in the academic classroom. By incorporating a career and life-planning theme into academic subjects, teachers find students are motivated by topics relevant to their developmental needs. This helps to achieve several important goals:

Students recognize the value of education. When students see a link between staying in school and their future happiness, they devote more focused energy to their education. Therefore, comprehensive guidance is an important component of Tech Prep, School-To-Work, and college-prep programs.

Students become identity-achieved, which builds self-esteem and character. Young people with high self-esteem are more likely to persevere in today's rigorous academic and technical education settings. Therefore, a comprehensive guidance program will increase the motivation to stay in school.

Students learn a life and career planning process they can use again and again. In a complex and ever-changing world, this process empowers students. Knowledge of the importance of long-range planning helps students expand and revise their goals as they move through school and into careers.

Academic subjects take on new meaning. A guidance curriculum can enhance rather than displace existing disciplines. By integrating career guidance into the core curriculum using self-discovery themes, reading, writing, and computation assignments build skills and create motivated learners at the same time.

Career Choices: A Guide for Teens and Young Adults, Who Am I? What Do I Want? And How Do I Get It?, used in over 3,800 schools nationwide, is a proven curriculum designed to meet these needs. The resources, strategies, and ideas throughout this manual will help you implement this exciting curriculum, and may change the way you approach teaching.

How to Use This Guide

The *Career Choices* curriculum is a flexible program that can be used in many ways. Although this guide presents a number of possibilities, we encourage you to use your creativity to make the curriculum relevant and stimulating for your own classes.

Courses based on this curriculum may run anywhere from six weeks to an entire school year. Most often, however, it is used over a nine-week quarter or an 18-week semester. Since text materials build on skills learned in previous chapters, we urge you to follow the sequence of the books.

The *way* you use the materials, however, can vary greatly. Many schools are currently restructuring, working with interdisciplinary education, teaching teams, Tech Prep and School-to-Work programs, and more. You will find that this curriculum can easily be adapted to meet your particular needs. For instance, you may choose to use only the *Career Choices* text with the *Workbook and Portfolio for Career Choices*, or you may choose to include the *Possibilities* and/or *Lifestyle Math* texts. You may choose to use all the texts within one course or team teach the materials across a number of disciplines.

The core of this *Instructor's Guide* includes chapter-by-chapter, exercise-by-exercise learning objectives, presentation suggestions, and, where appropriate, exercises and activities. There's also room for you to add your own notes, comments, and ideas. Because more and more schools are incorporating interdisciplinary teaching teams into their restructuring plans, this curriculum can be used in a variety of configurations in traditional academic classrooms.

On pages **2/8** to **2/14** you'll find an overview of how to incorporate the anthology *Possibilities* for those of you who plan to use this optional literature component. Then, throughout Section Four, beginning on page **4/1** you'll find suggestions about where each literature selection could be assigned to reinforce both the understanding of the activity and the meaning of the literary work.

Information regarding *Lifestyle Math* is also included. The majority of the problems in *Lifestyle Math* augment the activities in Chapter Four of *Career Choices*. This text can be used by either math instructors in an interdisciplinary model, or by instructors from other disciplines who enjoy math, financial planning and economics. See page **5/3** for one example of an interdisciplinary approach.

In the past, in order to make the correction process feasible for busy instructors, students completed irrelevant problems with only one answer. Today, Internet technology has made grading a personalized and relevant "math problem" like *Lifestyle Math* possible. Since the nature of each student's portfolio depends on his or her personal goals and plans, there is rarely a "right" answer. The online correction tool available at <u>www.lifestylemath.com</u> enables you—or your students—to correct these personalized computations easily and effectively.

The Internet has made the process of researching what was once hard-to-come-by data much more accessible to everyone. Now with the *Career Choices* Internet site, www.careerchoices.com, you and your students will have at your fingertips the best resources the Internet has to offer around the topics of career and life planning. By adding this optional element to your *Career Choices* lesson plan, you'll compound your students' enthusiasm and increase their understanding of this critical material. See pages 7/6 to 7/14 for details, or visit www.careerchoices.com.

Obviously, a language arts instructor will use the books differently than a math or career education teacher or a guidance counselor. Likewise, you will use the materials differently when working with gifted, mainstream, at-risk, Tech Prep, or School-To-Work students. We have, therefore, incorporated hints that may be helpful under a variety of different circumstances. Throughout the *Guide*, you'll find numerous resources that will be valuable as you begin planning your strategy for bringing *Career Choices* into your classroom. Throughout Section Four, beginning on page 4/4, we've dropped in classroom ideas and comments from teachers who use one or all of the *Career Choices* textbooks. In Section Six, you'll find a variety of supportive materials you may find useful as you build your program.

In addition, since the books present excellent exercises for hands-on learning and group discussion, we have included sections on group dynamics and classroom techniques.

We know you are capable, but we also know you are very busy! Therefore, we have included charts and worksheets that can be helpful. While the materials in *Career Choices*, the *Workbook and Portfolio for Career Choices*, *Possibilities*, and *Lifestyle Math* are copyrighted materials and may not be photocopied or reproduced in any fashion without the written permission of the publisher, you are granted permission to photocopy pages 4/26, 4/35, 4/97, 4/98, 4/99, 4/100, 4/105, 5/2, 5/3, 6/14, 6/15, 6/17, 6/19, 6/20, 6/21, 6/22, 6/38 and 6/39 from this *Instructor's and Counselor's Guide for Career Choices* for your own classroom use.

We are committed to your success. Therefore, we have on-staff curriculum specialists who are available to provide technical support as you incorporate this program into your school. Do not hesitate to pick up the phone and call us at (800) 967-8016 between 9:00am and 3:00pm MST. We stand ready to help in any way we can.

Connect Online with Academic Innovations

http://www.academicinnovations.com

Would you like to access teaching strategies proven successful by your colleagues? Are you interested in a discussion group for teachers using the *Career Choices* curriculum in classrooms across the country? Would you like to ask Mindy Bingham, the co-author of *Career Choices*, questions about the curriculum?

You can do all these things and more by visiting the Academic Innovations' home page. Log on to find ideas for using the curriculum, resources to enhance your program, articles from past newsletters, a schedule of upcoming workshops, funding suggestions, and much more.

 Each time you see this logo, you'll know you can find a variety of additional resources by visiting the URL (Internet address) noted.

Question	Go to URL:	You'll find:	Helpful hints & tips
How would I approach a business in our community for help with funding our Career Choices program?	http://www. academicinnovations.com/ corpfun.html	A detailed explanation of how to approach the business community for funding	*Print out this page plus the text from all the hyperlinks in this section. Form a committee to strategize a plan using this information.*

You'll find similar charts sprinkled throughout this guide. In addition to the URL where you'll find the answer to your question, the chart provides helpful hints on how best to use the material.

Let Us Hear from You!

Would you care to reveal your observations and ideas in future editions of this guide? What has worked well for you? What innovations have you made? What additional information or resources could we provide?

Let our Curriculum and Technical Support department know what you think!
    Call us with your thoughts: (800) 967-8016, ext. 677
    Fax your comments: (800) 967-4027
    E-mail your suggestions: academic@academicinnovations.com

We'd like to thank the numerous dedicated and innovative educators who have given us feedback and shared their exceptional teaching strategies with us. You'll find comments and recommendations from these teachers throughout this guide.

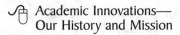

Academic Innovations—
Our History and Mission
http://www.academicinnovations.com/
company.html#profile

Meet our staff and consultants
http://www.academicinnovations.com/staff.html

Do you want to be included
on our mailing list?
http://www.academicinnovations.com/news.html

Here's What We're Hearing...

It Works

The counselors reported a real difference when my students went to register for next year's classes: they knew what they wanted.

— Elizabeth Farris
English teacher
San Gabriel High School
San Gabriel, California

After utilizing Career Choices as a counseling instrument and a career cluster selection, less than 5% of our students are changing programs. This evidence supports our belief that the program is a key to career decision-making.

— Jim Campbell, Ph.D.
Executive Director of
Delaware Tech Prep
Recipient of Dale Parnell Outstanding
Tech Prep Program Award

It's Easy to Use

Career Choices is great for the classroom teacher who doesn't know that much about career guidance.

— Ernie Gomes, Science Chair
Casa Roble Fundamental
High School
Orangevale, California

It has been easy to fit in other projects and lessons with Career Choices. They are the best career education materials I've used in 18 years. Thank you!

— Bonnie Morris
Business and careers instructor
Anacortes High School
Anacortes, Washington

It Motivates Students

[As a result of this text] many students recognized the need to buckle down more to reach their goals. Others made decisions regarding a career possibility or interest they had.

— Linda Wolverton
9th grade English
Milford High School
Milford, Ohio

I wanted to thank you for the enlightening course, Career Choices...I know now that school really does pay off and that the longer I stay in school, the more likely I am to have a high paying job.

— Thank you letter to the authors
from a California student

It's Ethnic and Gender Fair

My students are 80% non-white minority students. The selections in [Career Choices and Possibilities] make them feel OK about themselves.

— Julie Vetica
8th grade Language arts
Hargitt Middle School
Norwalk, California

The first year, my biggest success was when students of different races found common ground and learned a language to talk to each other.

— Susan Henneberg
9th grade English
Milford High School
Milford, Ohio

The results of this project were extraordinary. Participants were exposed to the writings of poets, visionaries, and other great authors. They learned the practical applications of math. For the first time, these students began to understand the correlation between knowledge, employment, and education. The success of the program amazed even the teachers, many of whom had dual master's degrees . . . By the fourth week, many parents had called to thank me for the changes they'd seen in their children. In previous years our dropout rate averaged 40%, this year it was only 3%.

— Joe Werner, JTPA Administrator
Monterey County, California

Before this class I thought everything would just fall into place. Now I realize that I have to make my future happen, it won't just work out good by itself. So how I do now will not only affect me for the rest of my life, it will also affect my children.

— Student in Dee Fay's class
Ukiah High School
Ukiah, California

[Young] women who never dreamed of higher education saw possibilities and opportunities. Many…were excited about going to college and spoke of the decision with bright eyes.

— C. Sue Waldfogel Huff
Administrative Assistant
Silverado High School
Mission Viejo, California

Career Choices *received a Promising Intervention Award form the U.S. Department of Education in recognition of its effectiveness in reducing dropout rates and supporting higher achievement in reading and math.*

— Techniques magazine — March 2001
published by the
Association For Career and
Technical Education (ACTE)

The year 2000 results are spectacular . . . [there was] significant improvements in reading and math. The utilization of **Career Choices** *. . . facilitates learning and increases the awareness of the relationship between academic achievement and work. Students continually comment that learning in this manner is fun.*

— from the independent
evaluation report of the
UAW-Diamler Training Center
Delaware School-To-Work Program 2000

What educators are saying about
the *Career Choices* curriculum

http://www.academicinnovations.com/
whatsay.html

Career Choices *is definitely "politically correct" in terms of race, gender, etc.*

— Linda Wulff
Chairperson, Communications Dept.
Waupun High School
Waupun, Wisconsin

SECTION TWO

Overview of the Curriculum

What Is the
Career Choices Curriculum?

The *Career Choices* curriculum is an academically based program, repackaged as a career guidance and self-discovery experience. The overlying theme of the course provides students the opportunity to uncover their own unique answers to three important questions: Who am I? What do I want? How do I get it? By exploring their own particular abilities, ambitions, and dreams, students learn not only how this knowledge can help them plan for a future career and successful life, but the importance of being able to read, write, speak and compute well.

The *Career Choices* materials are based on the premise that everyone has strengths and we each must be given the chance to use these strengths to succeed. Although the student is responsible for doing the work, the teacher plays a vital role in facilitating learning success. With *Career Choices*, an ardent teacher, and a supportive environment, any student can flourish!

Encouraging group input and hands-on learning, these course materials foster warm relationships within the class. A "we're all in this together" approach cultivates group support and cooperative learning. If student volunteers are willing to share personal dilemmas, the class can practice the decision-making and problem-solving skills they are developing.

At the same time, the contemplative nature of what is viewed by the students as vital personal information, nurtures a high level of self-reflection, which is critical to the successful transition from child to adult, student to worker. As the adolescent works through their self-discovery process, they develop a vision for their future and begin developing realistic life plans. As we ask young people to make important life path decisions at a younger and younger age, this early maturation is crucial not only to the success of programs such as Tech Prep and School-To-Career, but also for the college-bound.

The *Career Choices* materials are markedly different from those traditionally used; however, they offer an effective and creative way to promote authentic learning. For example, as a language arts course, *Career Choices* invites students to look at fiction from a new perspective as they begin to identify with the characters. Optional components of the program help young people become comfortable using computers and turning to the Internet for information they'll use in their daily lives.

And, because the course framework is flexible, with a variety of resources and structures, the instructor's creativity can come into play, making the experience more meaningful for teacher and student alike.

Career Choices also affords a channel for school and community linkage. As the kind of program most business leaders and employers have sought in their community schools, this innovative approach readily gains recognition and public support. Here is an ideal opportunity for teachers to showcase creative solutions to tough educational problems.

Much as we would like students to learn for the love of learning, most young people today need the stimulation that comes from seeing how the subject at hand relates to them and to their place in the world. *Career Choices* offers that stimulation. In addition, it graphically illustrates personal benefits—what they have to gain from staying in school and putting forth their best effort.

An Academically-Based Guidance Curriculum

The *Career Choices* curriculum provides a quality comprehensive guidance program that works because:

1. **It is classroom based**, providing between 45 to 180 hours of activities, discussions, and research opportunities in a sequential format.

2. **It is integrated with academics**, making it possible to provide quality career guidance and maintain academic rigor for students at all levels of achievement.

3. **It has scope and sequence**, modeling a self-discovery and decision-making process students can use throughout their lives—whenever they make important decisions.

4. **It helps students develop self-awareness** by answering critical questions: Who am I? What do I want? How do I get it? And why do I need a good education? Students become "identity achieved;" learn progressive decision-making techniques and skills; become critical thinkers in relation to their future lives; complete quantitative plans; and discover reality-based options for their adult lives.

5. **It exposes students to the skills of personal success:** goal setting, decision making, budgeting, resource management, and overcoming fears and personal resistance.

6. **It exposes students to the realities and responsibilities of the adult world**, providing opportunities to discuss and explore various aspects of adult life. Young people can then better define the kind of life they want and, thereby, make wise educational decisions today.

7. **It helps students learn to project themselves into the future and understand the consequences of their actions today.** Studies show students who can visualize their future and understand how today's choices impact future happiness are far less likely to drop out of school, become a teen parent, or abuse drugs.

Career Choices: A Guide for Teens and Young Adults

A large, beautifully illustrated text, *Career Choices* is more journey than book. Masquerading as an attractive journal, *Career Choices* is actually a carefully designed, self-paced, easy-to-follow program that learners find visionary and logical—inspiring and, at the same time, matter-of-fact. In addition to realistic anecdotes, it contains a variety of questionnaires, self-evaluation quizzes, and exercises that empower individuals to think seriously about their aptitudes and inclinations.

The concept behind the *Career Choices* curriculum works because most adolescents have at least one thing in common: an avid interest in themselves and their futures. When classroom assignments help answer students' most urgent questions (Who Am I? What do I Want?), their attitudes toward writing, reading, and math assignments improve. Consequently, the motivation to practice these basic skills is elevated.

Career Choices has all of the expected career research information. It's the unexpected aspects that make this book exciting and unique. *Career Choices* augments traditional career planning topics with practical advice on overcoming obstacles and fears; solving problems; dealing with rejection and anxiety; and recognizing and using mentors.

This interactive book guides the reader toward greater self-knowledge, enabling them to make intelligent, well-thought decisions about their own futures. *Career Choices* helps students identify their own passions, values, personality styles, skills, and aptitudes. This knowledge then leads them to investigate careers that match their strengths and desires. As the "fit" becomes more apparent so does the motivation to strive to prepare themselves for a desirable future.

Most importantly *Career Choices* is a carefully crafted step-by-step process that, if learned, can be used over and over again throughout an individual's life as they make important decisions. As they grow and mature, and as the world changes around them, this dynamic process will be one of their most meaningful life lessons.

The culmination of the book is the development of a doable ten-year plan for realizing their dreams. Equipped with their life vision and action plan, their chance of a successful transition to adulthood is greatly enhanced.

Perhaps the reason teenagers think they know all the answers is because they haven't heard all the questions yet.

The *Workbook and Portfolio* for *Career Choices*

Ideally, every student would be given a copy of the *Career Choices* text to complete and take with them into the world. However, in reality many schools simply don't have the funds to make this possible. For this reason the *Workbook and Portfolio* was created. The *Workbook and Portfolio* is an inexpensive compilation of the activities contained within the *Career Choices* text, and it should be an integral part of any program.

What makes the *Workbook* so important?

1. The *Workbook and Portfolio* contains all the exercises found in *Career Choices*. Using the *Workbook* young people can review the key concepts as they revise and refine their plans. The ultimate goal of *Career Choices* is not for students to create a final agenda for their lives, but for them to learn a process. Then, as their interests, abilities, and ambitions expand, or as new challenges or opportunities arise, they can repeat the process.

2. The *Workbook and Portfolio* grows with the student. Your students will grow and mature both intellectually and emotionally as they move through school (and life). The portfolio aspects of the *Workbook* allow students to review and implement the main concepts from *Career Choices* as their understanding of themselves and the world increases. For instance, learning to overcome stumbling blocks may not seem important to a teen that has faced few challenges. However, with their workbooks in hand, students will have someplace to turn for help and be ready to face obstacles as they arise.

3. The *Workbook* is a permanent record. How many of your students take notes thorough enough to still make sense two months later, much less two years? This is precisely why providing each student with a *Workbook* is so important. Loose papers and notebooks are not viewed with the same importance and respect afforded a printed text. Furthermore, the *Workbook and Portfolio* is part book, part journal, so students tend to keep it and treasure it for years to come.

4. The *Workbook and Portfolio* can be extremely helpful to guidance counselors. The time counselors have with each student is often limited. A completed workbook quickly gives them insight into each student's aspirations. Counselors are then better able to steer students toward the right classes, the right programs, or the best college. Students who have been through a *Career Choices* program are more aware of their own needs and desires. Thus, they can present their own interests and plans more clearly and assertively.

Are you considering omitting the *Workbook* because your budget is stretched? Before you make that decision, weigh the possibility of asking students to pay for their own copy. Because the *Workbook and Portfolio* is "consumable" (like an art project), many states allow for this arrangement. Teachers have succeeded using this strategy to help fund their *Career Choices* programs. Some have even found that students have more "ownership" in the program and are more devoted.

If student purchase is not a viable option, consider turning to the community for help. Dozens of programs have found that community service organizations or local businesses are happy to help out with this expense. See pages **9**/12 to **9**/13 and **10**/1 to **10**/5 for guidance on this process.

Career Choices and Changes

The adult version of *Career Choices*

Career Choices and Changes brings the same self-discovery process found in *Career Choices* to a more mature audience: college students, people re-entering the workforce, individuals changing careers—anyone wrestling with the important questions of identity, life satisfaction, and future planning.

Adapted from the original, *Career Choices and Changes* covers all the topics in *Career Choices* but is written on a slightly higher level, with age-appropriate stories and examples. *Career Choices and Changes* also includes an additional chapter. Providing a comprehensive discussion of change, this addition helps readers decide not only what to change, but how and when to make their move.

Ideal for:

- Parent and student workshops
- College career planning classes
- Career center counseling sessions
- Job re-entry and retraining programs
- Corporate development programs
- Individual self-discovery

Instructor's Guide adaptation for *Career Choices and Changes*

Turn to Section Four of this manual for activity-by-activity instruction. The page numbering and activity format in *Career Choices* are the same as *Career Choices and Changes* through page **4/149** of this manual. At that point an extra chapter entitled "Making Changes, the inevitable process" has been added to *Career Choices and Changes*. For an instructor's guide to this additional chapter, see pages **4/171** to **4/178** of this manual. The last two chapters of *Career Choices* and *Career Choices and Changes* are again an adaptation of each other, and the lesson suggestions beginning on page **4/151** of this manual can be used.

Possibilities: A Supplemental Anthology for Career Choices

Career advice from John Updike and Robert Frost? Pep talks from Emily Dickinson and Albert Camus? Unusual perhaps, but not surprising when your goal is academic integration. When you combine *Career Choices* and *Possibilities*, a language arts class becomes an ideal place to teach problem solving, risk taking, and the work ethic.

Most of the literature contained in *Possibilities* appears on recommended reading lists across the country. However, the selections included in the anthology are flexible enough to be used in a variety of situations and with students of varying abilities.

There are 50 essays, short stories, poems, speeches, and plays from poets, authors, and statesmen. More importantly, the *Possibilities* selections reinforce the themes and lessons in *Career Choices*.

Use *Career Choices* and *Possibilities* together as:

- A semester or year-long class in the English department

- A team teaching opportunity for the English department and the school counselor, career technician, or family and consumer science instructor

- A team teaching opportunity for the English department and the math and/or social studies department

- Two fully integrated classes (for example, a freshman orientation class coupled with 9th grade English)

See the following pages of this manual for more detailed information about integrating *Career Choices* and *Possibilities* into the core English curriculum.

3/5, 3/9–11, 6/3–6, 6/55–61, 7/2–5, 9/27–34

A Literature-Based Curriculum

Possibilities reflects a literature-based approach to teaching English/language arts. Various teaching strategies are employed to help address the different learning styles found in any group of students.

Throughout *Possibilities* the "into, through, and beyond" format helps students relate the themes found in the literature to their lives. With assignments that are relevant to the students' real world, this approach builds on what students already know and what they are working on in their own life planning process.

The "into" activity (journal entries) helps get the students started and prepares them for the material they are about to read. After they have read "through" the material, the "beyond" questions and activities help students discover the meaning of the work and apply that data, theme, advice, or information to their lives.

Finally, the *Career Choices* curriculum achieves the goals of integrating academics with vocational/career education. The themes woven through the curriculum help students understand the need to prepare for a satisfying and fulfilling life. The literature selections in *Possibilities* underscore these themes, giving students the motivation to see their education as an essential component for reaching their dreams and ambitions.

More specifically, *Career Choices* with *Possibilities* is an ideal launching course for Tech Prep and School-to-Work programs. This integrated curriculum helps adolescents enthusiastically assess and select a path or course of study that meets their various interests and aptitudes. At the same time, they develop an appreciation for the literature of our culture.

> *We look at the poems as advice and lessons of life...They write poetry and essays following the same themes.*
>
> — Susan Adams
> English Teacher
> Parkersburg South High School
> Parkersburg, West Virginia

> *A cutting edge curriculum....It is an outstanding and unique example of how core academic subjects can work together with vocational-technical education to create a new and exciting synergy in education.*
>
> — Association for Career and Technical Education,
> formerly American Vocational Association

> *I am using the **Possibilities** anthology in the English component of the Automotive Integrated Curriculum at my school. This is the material that I have been waiting for. In the past, I would spend many hours analyzing materials for school to work applications. Thanks for a useful, innovative tool.*
>
> — Rosetta B. Tetteh
> English Teacher
> Senn Metropolitan Academy
> Chicago, Illinois

Career Choices/Possibilities Cross Reference

The following is a suggested cross reference guide. It is designed to assist you in deciding when to incorporate the stories, poems, essays, plays, or speeches found in *Possibilities* with the corresponding activities and exercises in *Career Choices*.

Career Choices is a sequential curriculum. This outline assumes you are working through the *Career Choices* textbook from beginning to end in the order presented.

Chapter 1
Envisioning Your Future

The Secret Life of Walter Mitty (page 11)
  Read after reading pages 10–13 in *Career Choices*

Psalm of Life (page 19)
Dreams (page 24)
I Have a Dream . . . speech by Martin Luther King, Jr. (page 27)
  Read after completing page 14 in *Career Choices*

Work, an excerpt from *The Prophet* (page 33)
  Read after completing pages 15–17 in *Career Choices*

Richard Cory (page 37)
  Read after completing pages 18–21 in *Career Choices*

Question	Go to URL:	You'll find:	Helpful hints & tips
I'm an English/language arts teacher. Are Career Choices *and* Possibilities *appropriate for my classes?*	http://www.academicinnovations.com/indepth.html	A variety of stories about educators' experiences in a variety of disciplines.	*Choose the hyperlinks to Phyllis Stewart of IN, Doug Campbell of CA, Mary Ellen Fowler of FL, Roberta Freed of MN, Priscilla Gregory of TN, and Scott Hess of WA.*
AND...	http://www.academicinnovations.com/ela.html	Comments from English/language arts teachers using *Career Choices*.	*Print out for later reading.*
AND...	http://www.academicinnovations.com/English22.html	Resources to help you evaluate the *Career Choices* curriculum for your English/language arts classroom.	*Explore the hyperlinks to better understand how Career Choices can enhance your current curriculum without sacrificing academic rigor or content standards.*

Chapter 2
Your Personal Profile

Sonnets From the Portuguese (page 40)
Read after completing pages 28–29 in *Career Choices*

Alice in Wonderland (page 43)
Read after completing pages 28–45 in *Career Choices*

I Know Why the Caged Bird Sings (page 47)
Sympathy (page 57)
Read after completing pages 28–49 in *Career Choices*

Life (page 61)
Read after completing page 52 in *Career Choices*

Self-Reliance (page 64)
Read after completing page 53 in *Career Choices*

Chapter 3
Lifestyles of the Satisfied and Happy

Growing Older (page 69)
Read as an introduction to the "Looking into the Future" exercise on page 4/41 in the *Instructor's and Counselor's Guide*

I Shall Not Pass This Way Again (page 72)
Read after completing pages 60–61 in *Career Choices*

Red Geraniums (page 74)
Read after completing 66–69 in *Career Choices*

I feel the usage of these materials helped my students to see the relevance of English to their lives and helped them formulate a more mature career plan. These materials, I think, have also caused them to be more conscious of the quality of their assignments and the importance of doing well in school.

— Amy S. Heaton
Applied Communications/
Creative Writing Teacher
Horn Lake High School
Horn Lake, Mississippi

*The writing was revealing and showed positive growth.
They showed me how much they really know and that they
are further ahead than we usually give them credit for.*

— Jose E. "Tito" Chavez
   English Department Chair
   West Las Vegas High School
   Las Vegas, New Mexico

Chapter 7
Decision Making

The Monkey's Paw (page 127)
Read after completing pages 168–174 in *Career Choices*

The Road Not Taken (page 139)
Read after completing page 177 in *Career Choices*

To Build a Fire (page 142)
Read after reading page 179 in *Career Choices*

Chapter 8
Goal Setting

Uphill (page 164)
Read before beginning Chapter 8

The Myth of Sisyphus (page 166)
Read after completing pages 182–185 in *Career Choices*

Prince of Tides (page 178)
Read after completing pages 182–191 in *Career Choices*

Chapter 9
Avoiding Detours and Roadblocks

Hope (page 172)
Read after completing pages 194–199 in *Career Choices*

A Dream Deferred (page 212)
Read after completing pages 214–215 in *Career Choices*

Mother to Son (page 214)
Read before completing pages 196–197 in *Career Choices*

A Noiseless Patient Spider (page 216)

All I Really Need to Know I Learned in Kindergarten (page 216)
Read after completing pages 216–217 in *Career Choices*

Over the Hill to the Poor-House (page 221)
Read before completing pages 208–209 in *Career Choices*

George Gray (page 225)
Read after completing pages 216–221 in *Career Choices*

Chapter 10
Attitude is Everything

Chapter 11
Getting Experience

Chapter 12
Where Do You Go from Here?

I found all the selections to be very helpful. This book provided creative involvement which revealed a key ingredient in understanding the emotional component of career choices and well being. Students were challenged to develop their own personal values, goals and individual philosophy which will give meaning and value to their lives.

— Doris R. A-Martinez
  Community and Student Services
  Los Angeles Trade-Tech College
  Los Angeles, California

Lifestyle Math:
Your Financial Planning Portfolio

Lifestyle Math is a wonderful way to deliver personalized math. It effectively and dramatically debunks many of the myths that hinder students in achieving math excellence. *Lifestyle Math* makes math exciting and pertinent, proving to students that they can do math if they try. Perhaps its greatest benefit, *Lifestyle Math* demonstrates to students the personal relevance math has in daily life—their daily lives—today and in the future. This, in turn, motivates them to apply themselves to their math studies.

The cornerstone of the module is an extension of the budget exercise found in chapter four of *Career Choices*. Working on the same premise, young people begin to think about and plan for the kind of life they want to have by age 29. As students move through the budgeting process, they build more than math skills. Step by step, the exercises increase motivation and commitment to prepare for the future by doing well in school today.

With *Lifestyle Math* basic math practice comes in the guise of party planning, buying a dream car or home, vacation planning, and much more. Students find that math is important to their happiness and, because of the personal interest, it provides the realization they can do it!

The innovative optional internet enhancement strengthens *Lifestyle Math*'s overall effectiveness. (You'll find more information about these on pages **2/19** to **2/20**.)

I love this text. **Lifestyle Math** *presents down-to-earth material in a fashion that stimulates students to participate. It is the most practical, useful text we use in the BST class.*

— Sara L. Carter
Business Teacher
Garden City High School
Garden City, Michigan

The Key to Success

Studies suggest that in order for students to be successful at math:

1. **They must see themselves as successful in math.**

    Lifestyle Math addresses student attitudes and math anxiety, and offers ongoing support and encouragement. With some initial help from you in these same areas, your class will soon view itself as quite capable of doing the work.

2. **They must have support and high expectations from family, teachers, and peers.**

    Again, the program is designed so that you and your students can support and encourage each other.

3. **They must understand what's in it for them, why math is important to their future success and satisfaction in life.**

    Lifestyle Math makes this abundantly clear. You'll never have a more engaged class, and you may play a rewarding part in helping some students chart entirely new courses for their lives.

Career Choices instructors from all disciplines enjoy teaching this unit. They include:
- Career educators
- Teachers of freshman orientation courses
- English/language arts instructors
- Business and economics teachers
- Family and consumer science professionals
- Special population instructors and program directors

A Supplemental Text for Students at All Levels of Math Proficiency

Lifestyle Math...is an excellent supplementary resource for math classes at all levels, including algebra, pre-algebra and basic skills.

— Association for Career and Technical Education, formerly American Vocational Association

Lifestyle Math can be used in conjunction with the *Career Choices* curriculum or as an ideal supplemental activity for math classes at all levels. *Lifestyle Math* clearly demonstrates the link between education and life satisfaction, making math relevant, essential, a subject to be mastered.

Algebra and more advanced math students should be able to complete the portfolio in 15 to 20 hours. The text provides an excellent review of basic skills, teaches important economic and financial formulas, and demonstrates how continuing math education in college will pay future dividends in job and career satisfaction.

There are several ways to use the materials with your Algebra students. You may want to spend a week or two on *Lifestyle Math* at the beginning of the term, reviewing basic skills and starting students thinking about the value of math in their lives. You might allow students to work through the text alone or in small groups, as an extra credit project. You can effectively use *Lifestyle Math* as an energizer, or you might allow time each week for students to work on their portfolios after they complete a quiz or test. You'll find they look forward to working on this project and will view this as a reward.

Pre-algebra students may need up to a quarter to complete the *Lifestyle Math* module. They, too, will be reviewing basic skills and applying them to real-life decisions. Students will have an opportunity to practice sophisticated problem-solving techniques relating to their own future expectations of success.

Young people still struggling with basic skills may need a full semester or even a full school year to complete the program. For this group of students, you will want to supplement *Lifestyle Math* with more traditional lessons and drills. The good news is they will want to complete the work, and will come to realize how math relates to all other aspects of their life, present and future. This should prove motivational and may be the key to their future math success.

The Key Principles of *Lifestyle Math*

1. *Lifestyle Math* helps students take responsibility for their own learning by demonstrating the value of applying themselves to their math education.

2. *Lifestyle Math* emphasizes the need for mastering basic skills by showing how math skills are used everyday—from determining take home salary to planning an entertainment and vacation budget to saving for a comfortable retirement.

3. *Lifestyle Math* exposes students to important mathematical formulas they will use throughout their lives (figuring mortgage payments, buying a car, preparing budgets for food, child care, health care, vacations, and so on).

4. *Lifestyle Math* encourages critical thinking and problem-solving skills for all individuals and demonstrates the value of teamwork when used with small groups.

5. *Lifestyle Math* suggests possible reasons why students might be resistant to math, and helps them understand the payoff for time and energy invested in their math work.

6. *Lifestyle Math* encourages students to enroll in upper division math classes by providing them with reasons to apply themselves and struggle with difficult concepts. Otherwise, they might drop out of math.

7. When used with optional technology supplements (see the following pages), *Lifestyle Math* helps students become comfortable using computers in their daily lives. The *optional* internet correction key, www.lifestylemath.com, allows young people to quickly check the financial consequences as they change career and educational plans. When used in conjunction with www.careerchoices.com, students can gather pertinent, current facts and figures from the Internet to use in formulating their budget.

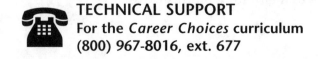

TECHNICAL SUPPORT
For the *Career Choices* curriculum
(800) 967-8016, ext. 677

Correcting *Lifestyle Math* Using Technology

www.lifestylemath.com

Because of the individualized nature of the *Lifestyle Math* workbook, correction and assessment can be challenging. To help make that task as easy as possible, we've created an optional technology component.

The *Lifestyle Math Correction Key Online*

www.lifestylemath.com is made up of 47 mathematical problems and activities from the *Lifestyle Math* workbook. Until now, math problems have needed to be uniformly designed with one answer for each problem so instructors could check student work against a written answer key. This internet site allows students to quickly correct their own personalized math computations from their *Lifestyle Math* workbook.

LifestyleMath.com (www.lifestylemath.com) gives the dream of effortless correction embodiment, delivering a quick and easy tool to your students to use at school or home, over the Internet. After completing their computations the old-fashioned way (with paper and pencil in their workbook), students can go online with their password and check their answers digitally. Using the online correcting format, students are alerted to any errors and encouraged to rework their computations. Once students arrive at the correct solution, they can print out their work and turn it in to you for credit. For more information see page 7/15.

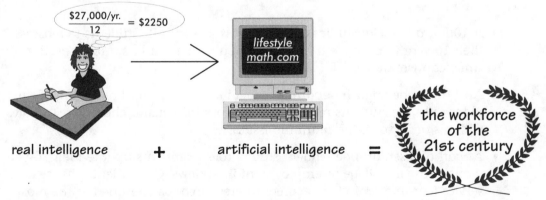

real intelligence + artificial intelligence = the workforce of the 21st century

[I particularly liked] the web site [and] the practical math.

— Louis Fleming, Tech Teacher
Andrews High School
Andrews, TX

My10yearPlan.com — A Powerful Online Enhancement for the *Workbook & Portfolio*

My10yearPlan.com provides an online planning area where students can store and update the 10-year plans they develop as they complete their *Career Choices Workbook & Portfolio*.

With password-driven access to these plans, teachers, advisors, and counselors are better equipped to mentor students on their best educational path and provide support when academic effort doesn't match lifestyle aspirations.

How Does It Work?

Step one: Students work through *Career Choices*, completing the activities and recording their plans in their own copy of the *Workbook & Portfolio*

Step two: Students then enter select data from their workbook into the secure forms on their password-protected area of My10yearPlan.com

Once the entry of their data is complete, the site compiles a summary 10-year plan that makes it easy to share goals, dreams, and plans with teachers, counselors, parents, and friends. And, because it's online, they have access to review and revise their plans throughout high school—an important step in maintaining the motivational momentum started by your *Career Choices* course.

With inter-departmental support at all grade levels, students can revisit and revise their online 10-year plans during their sophomore, junior, and senior years.

For example:

- A 10th-grade social studies department works with its students to reassess their 10-year plans once they study globalization and its impact on the American workforce.

- An 11th-grade English department facilitates the annual re-editing of the plans once the students read a literary work in which a character struggles with his or her own life-planning issues.

- As part of a senior independent study project, students update their 10-year plans to use in college or employment interviews. Or, students choose a service learning project in a career interest area, as identified in the most current version of their plan.

For detailed information, visit www.My10yearPlan.com.

Internet Enhancement— www.careerchoices.com

"Now is the time to look at content."

— Linda G. Roberts
Director, Office of Technology
US Department of Education

"But selecting which content to use for a particular lesson can be a daunting task."

— Education Week
Annual report, Technology Counts '99

With the launch of www.careerchoices.com, we've made a "daunting task" easier for teachers and students. This easy-to-use web site can deliver exciting digital content to even the most novice computer user.

CareerChoices.com (www.careerchoices.com) is a subscription site with over 80 web links (and growing) tied directly to the *Career Choices* curriculum. The links we've chosen provide students with the means to complete the research and activities in *Career Choices*. Detailed instructions, learning objectives, and lesson plans for each web link are supplied for both teachers and students. See pages 7/6–7/14 for detailed information and license fee schedules.

Career Choices and www.careerchoices.com allow for virtually effortless integration of technology, career education, and core academics by providing:

A ready-made Internet enhancement—www.careerchoices.com has easy-to-follow lesson plans for teachers and step-by-step instructions for students. This Internet link allows for uncomplicated integration without endless Internet surfing.

A proven guidance and career planning model for the academic teacher—Each activity in *Career Choices* and www.careerchoices.com motivates students to excel by demonstrating the relationship between their present classroom studies and their future lives. As they practice reading, writing, and computation, students learn about themselves, build crucial life skills, and become competent Internet users.

The best the Internet has to offer—www.careerchoices.com was developed only after extensive research. It enhances the entire *Career Choices* experience, providing a safe environment in which to build critical skills—for students and teachers alike.

Whether you use this resource in English, math, or as a stand-alone career guidance component, *Career Choices* and www.careerchoices.com will re-energize and re-focus the classroom experience.

Frequently Asked Questions

1. Most of my students are headed for college. Why do they need career guidance?

Studies clearly show that college freshmen who have a career in mind are more likely to graduate than classmates who haven't made a career choice. A career focus is the best indicator for academic success and matriculation for college students.

2. I teach English! Why should I get involved with career and life planning?

A career-planning theme in an English classroom—or any other academic classroom—adds instant relevancy, capturing the imaginations of even hard-to-motivate students. Students are engaged because the reading and writing assignments address the identity issues most important to adolescents. The *Possibilities* anthology includes many required pieces, but encourages students to view the literature from a new point of view.

3. I just don't have the time to learn a whole new curriculum?

You don't have to learn an entirely new curriculum! You simply enhance what you're already doing. *Career Choices* has ready-made English and math components, complete with lesson plans. It's integration made easy!

4. My students complete a computer-based interest inventory. Isn't that enough?

Career choice is the second most important decision students will ever make. This requires personal reflection, discussion, contemplation, decision making and goal setting. Students who complete the *Career Choices* curriculum learn a career and life planning process they can use over and over again throughout their lives.

5. The kids I work with are still struggling with basic skills.

Career Choices is academically based, providing basic skill practice disguised as self-discovery. What was once viewed as "drill and skill" is now camouflaged in meaningful personal exercises and activities. By the end of the class, attitudes about education will dramatically change as students realize how being able to read, write and compute impacts their futures.

6. I work with 9th graders. Aren't they a little too young to make a career choice?

Career Choices teaches a proven career and life planning. While most students will not make a final career choice in the 9th grade, this course will help them envision a future that is realistic. Armed with that information they will be less likely to drop out of school, engage in destructive behavior or scale down their academic goals. In four years you'll find most *Career Choices* students entering post-secondary education or training.

Now you're ready to take the Quick Tour of the curriculum.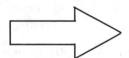

A Quick Tour

We've designed this tour—an overview of the *Career Choices* curriculum—to save you time. The textbooks before you are your ticket to a unique educational experience, so gather them up and let's get started!

pages **1/8–9**
pages **1/2–4**

Instructor's Guide

This essential first stop on pages **1/8–1/9** gives you a brief but comprehensive outline of the curriculum and the ways it is most often used. You may want to linger here a few minutes, until you get a feel for the territory.

Next stop: the table of contents on pages **1/2–4**. Here you'll get a better idea of the range and scope of information available in this *Instructor's Guide*. While the contents in other guides may read like historic markers, ours is clearly mapping out new territory.

page **5**

Career Choices

Another table of contents for your review. Examine this one and you'll see that the *Career Choices* course was designed to follow a particular sequence, each new topic building on and reinforcing skills and information from preceding chapters. The entire text is laid out to help you teach a critical-thinking process students can use throughout their lives.

page **3**

Workbook Portfolio

Think of this as a travel diary or low-cost souvenir. Long after the course is over, this consumable workbook allows students to hang on to hard evidence of self-knowledge gained and plans developed. It can also be enlightening for counselors and other instructors when students share the materials in their portfolio.

pages **5–7**

Possibilities

A welcome sight for English and language arts instructors! Take a few minutes to review some of your favorites from this impressive list of literary selections.

pages **3 & 8**

Lifestyle Math

An unexpected stop, perhaps. Review these pages to quickly see how you can improve your students' math skills while providing important career guidance.

One of the greatest strengths of this curriculum is a format that encourages class discussion, team projects, peer learning groups, and experiential learning. As a quick side trip, leaf through the texts, paying particular attention to the number of activities, exercises, discussion questions, writing assignments, surveys, math problems, and other vehicles for interactive learning.

An educational stop. Since some instructors may feel they lack experience with the latest strategies and techniques for group learning, the *Instructor's Guide* explains some of the best ones, then connects them to activities in *Career Choices*.

pages **6/23–35**

Take a moment to focus on the following examples of interactive learning:

Move on to the books themselves for a better understanding. For instance, turn to pages 182–185 in the main text, or page **4/118** in the *Instructor's Guide*, for examples of activities that could be enriched by using buzz groups. You'll find a good sample of a model on pages 44–45 of *Possibilities*, and pages 98–99 of *Lifestyle Math* offer an appropriate opportunity for peer learning groups.

pages **182–185**   *page* **4/118**   *pages* **44–45**   *pages* **98–99**

Career Choices Lesson Plan Suggestions

You are now entering a world of ideas: more than 150 pages of guidance, activity by activity! No need to take them all in now, but you'll find yourself returning here again and again. Note how many additional suggestions were provided by classroom teachers using the curriculum. We hope you'll join this group!

begins on page **4/1**

A Sample 180-Hour Lesson Plan

No tour would be complete without a stop at the sample 180-hour lesson plan. Even if your class runs only 30 hours, you're sure to find plenty of useful ideas here.

pages **5/15–33**

If you're interested in interdisciplinary education, these pages should be at the top of your "must see" list. You'll find descriptions of a dozen possible ways to use *Career Choices* in your school. (On page **3/8**, take a moment to note the directions to further information on our web site on the Internet. You may want to expand your tour to include a stopover in cyberspace!)

ages **3/8–13**

For instance, the English/Language Arts instructor could team with a guidance counselor, career educator or family and consumer science instructor to teach a dynamic course.

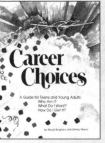

Career Choices/Possibilities Cross Reference Guide

Here is one example of how the texts work together:

Note how questions 6, 7 and 9 on page 17 of *Possibilities*, following "The Secret Life of Walter Mitty," relate to and reinforce the messages on pages 13 and 14 of *Career Choices*. Teachers who use these books in their English/Language Arts classes tell us they're amazed at how well the two textbooks compliment each other. Many are gratified to see students excited about and responding to literature for the first time in their young lives.

ages **4/4–5**   *page* **17**   *pages* **13–14**

Combining Math with Guidance:

The budget exercise in *Career Choices* is greatly expanded in *Lifestyle Math*, making it an appropriate addition to any math or consumer education class. Here, too, the relevance of the material greatly increases student interest and motivation, which eventually leads to increased skills and ability.

pages **78–79**   *pages* **14–31**

Nine-Week Interdisciplinary Lesson Plan:

A map to interdisciplinary education! This complete 9-week interdisciplinary lesson plan tracks both vertically (the traditional way) and horizontally so that, for example, what is being taught in English on any given day will relate to what is learned that same day in math.

NOTE THESE SIGNS. You'll find these icons, added to alert you to interdisciplinary opportunities, throughout Section Four of the *Instructor's Guide*, beginning on page **4/1**.

ages **5/5–14**

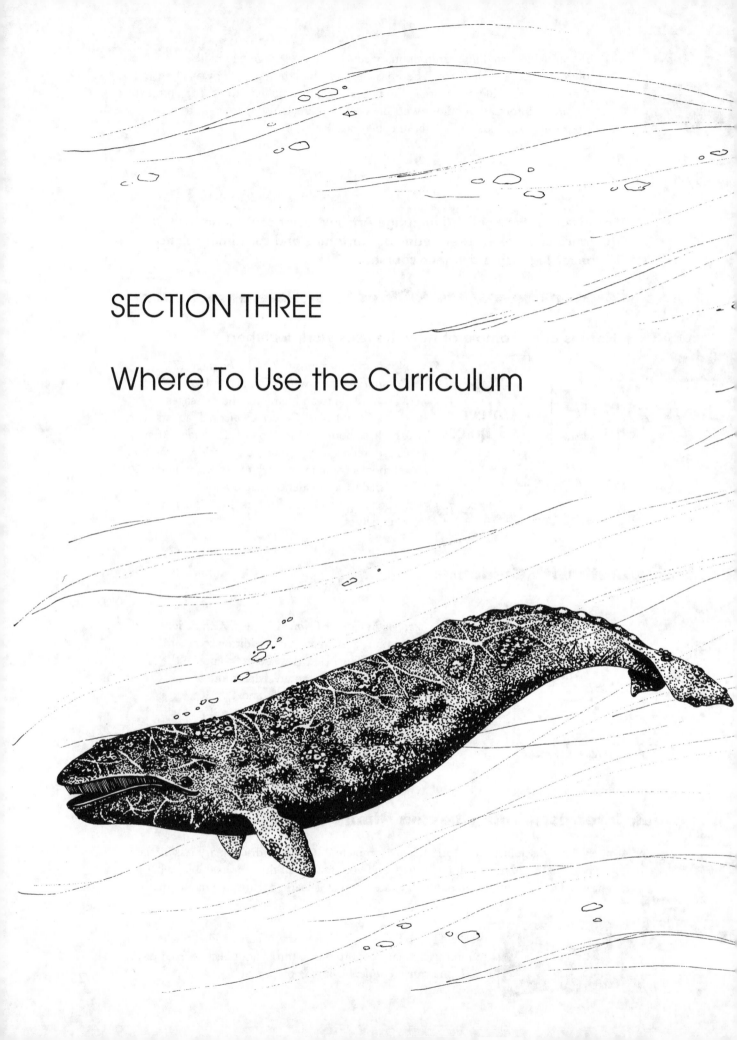

SECTION THREE

Where To Use the Curriculum

I found these materials adaptable to both my gifted and talented students and to my non-motivated students.

— Kathryn T. Harcum
English Chairperson
North Caroline High School
Ridgely, Maryland

Designed for All Students

Experience has taught educators that certain types of information are essential for all students. With this in mind schools have been reinventing themselves in an attempt to better meet the needs of all students—not just those headed straight from graduation to college.

All young people will be making the same kinds of decisions, just at different stages in life. Many teens are making potentially life-altering decisions at earlier ages. Because of this it is imperative that students learn about making good decisions, setting goals, solving problems, taking initiative and calculated risks, overcoming anxieties, and peer pressure.

Career Choices delivers this critical educational information and should be part of every young person's school experience. However, it is up to each school to determine the most appropriate way to deliver its wisdom. Whether the text is used in language arts or family life courses, in employment seminars or freshmen orientation, this *Instructor's Guide* offers enough suggestions that teachers can work with it creatively and comfortably, knowing they are meeting the needs of their students.

Question	Go to URL:	You'll find:	Helpful hints & tips
My state framework calls for competency in goal setting, decision making, critical thinking and problem solving. Where and how does the Career Choices curriculum address these skills?	http://www. academicinnovations.com/ workport.html	A list of hyperlinks about how *Career Choices* meets a variety of learning objectives	*Surf through the hyperlinks with a copy of Career Choices beside you so you can review each noted exercise.*

Urban Students Get 36 Weeks of Career Guidance

At San Gabriel High School on the border of inner city Los Angeles, students in speech and communications classes are also receiving a full year of career guidance. The program, called Directions, draws on the activities in *Career Choices* for speech assignments, class discussion topics, group projects, and more.

Doug Campbell, Chair of the Communications Department, recommended that all teachers go through the complete *Career Choices* textbook in sequence. This not only helped keep a uniform focus for all the classes, but also allowed students to build their awareness of the central issues—who am I, what do I want, and where am I going—in a natural progression, much like peeling the layers of an onion. At the center students discovered their true identity and were thus able to make better choices for their lives and their futures.

"Guidance counselors reported that students who had taken the Directions class seemed to have a plan when they came in at scheduling time," according to Doug. "They were clearly more involved in choosing their classes, rather than simply accepting the schedule given to them by the counselor. Students were actually seeing that there is a purpose for being in school."

The class also helped students get ready for success in the workplace by teaching such skills as working cooperatively, setting goals and making decisions. Class members teamed up to do mock interviews and practiced expository speaking by presenting reports they researched on careers. "This built up students' self-image and gave them more confidence to eventually enter the workplace," Doug said.

Most importantly, perhaps, he adds that "The one thing everyone learns in my class is that they always have a choice in life, and that they are always responsible for the choices they make. All of our freshmen (600 students) take the course."

Student quotes from our evaluations:

"Life really is one choice after another."
"I learned I was smarter than I thought."
"I discovered skills I didn't know I had."
"I learned life (growing up) isn't so easy. I'm not so anxious."
"Now I know how hard it is for my parents."

— Elizabeth Farris
English Department Chair
San Gabriel High School
San Gabriel, California

For Use with College-Bound and Gifted Students

Career Choices allows instructors to personalize the academic rigor of the language arts curriculum for gifted students. These high achievers and academically motivated students are often as socially insecure, unhappy, and unsure about their future as other students. What's more, they may be reluctant to admit their insecurities and talented enough to conceal them.

Before you begin, you might want to hold a parents' meeting (with your principal's permission). Reassure the parents that you know the importance of the academic mission. These students, however, are probably capable of carrying on much of that work on their own. As parents and teachers, you want to be sure that they also have the personal skills they need to be happy and satisfied individuals. By discussing the importance of problem solving, decision making, and long-range planning with parents, you should be able to demonstrate that, while their children's academic talents will get them into college, these practical skills will determine whether they stay there and thrive.

Studies clearly show that students who enter college with a specific career or career area in mind are far more likely to graduate four years later. It is the strongest indicator of success in college and in an individual's future work life.

Gifted students are often programmed to believe their talents should be applied in a particular direction. Or, because they are used to having things come easily to them, they may tend to give up at the first sign of difficulty. They may also be overwhelmed by the sheer number of choices available to them. It is very important, therefore, that they develop the skills and attitudes (decision making, anxiety tolerance, overcoming fears, and so on) needed to be their own best and happiest person.

Comprehensive Career Guidance for College-Bound Students

There are several unusual things about the *Career Choices* class Career Counselor Ruby Takebayashi teaches at the Mid-Pacific Institute in Honolulu, Hawaii. Perhaps most unusual is the fact the Ruby teaches at a private school, where 100% of the students are considered "college-bound." That doesn't reduce their need for career guidance, according to Ruby. "It's not just about making *Career Choices*, it's making life choices." That's why Ruby's class is a graduation requirement.

Ruby started using *Career Choices* back in 1990, and has been hooked ever since. During the nine-week course she and her students work through the entire *Career Choices* text. She also brings in selections from *Possibilities* and a variety of her own activities. These enhance the text and take school "out of the realm of the mundane and into possibilities."

Besides a love for learning and a plan for the future, Ruby wants her students to leave *Career Choices* with an understanding that "life is terrific and the challenges are enormous, but it's our responsibility to prepare for it and live it the very best we can."

I've been reading all your information on career development on the web for the past half hour and must admit I am impressed with your correct approach to today's unmotivated youth. Unfortunately, I can identify with those without direction all too well. I am a 23-year-old recent college graduate and have little motivation towards a specific career path. With each passing day, I increasingly yearn for a passion in some specific vocation but am continually lost...I can relate to your claim that a person must know themselves before they can correctly choose a career and felt that I never achieved this identification when I should have many years ago.

— Response to Academic Innovations' web site via e-mail

English/Language Arts Curriculum

When *Career Choices* is paired with *Possibilities*, there is a very natural fit for providing career guidance through the language arts department. In fact, this approach is often used to help ensure that all students are exposed to the *Career Choices* materials.

Because the selections in *Possibilities* are drawn from recommended reading lists, English teachers can easily cover the required literature and add relevancy to class discussions.

The flexibility and variety of the *Career Choices* materials allow instructors to use *Career Choices* and *Possibilities* with general, honors, and even special education students.

Career Guidance Integrated with English

Liz Lamatrice, a Career Coordinator, wanted career development integrated with all academic subjects. She was thrilled to discover the *Career Choices* curriculum at an Academic Innovations workshop in Columbus, Ohio. Liz took her full set of books and passed them on to Elizabeth Truax, a guidance counselor at Edison High School in Richmond, Ohio.

What timing! Edison needed a way to support the district-wide Individual Career Plan (ICP), a process which began in the 8th grade and culminated in the 12th grade with a Career Passport. Teachers wanted an emphasis on career exploration, decision making, and self-awareness for 10th graders. With a strong literature component, English teacher Cathy Miles saw the fit right away. "Having a proven curriculum like [Career Choices] gave us a foundation on which to build our own unique program." She and another English teacher, Rosann Lauri, developed a program and took it into the classroom for Tech Prep and college-bound students.

Edison High School recently graduated the first class to experience this model English program. Of the 221 graduates, 70% went on to pursue further education, generating over $1 million in academic scholarships (nearly double the year before). Cathy attributes the increase to a rise in ambition on the part of students who set goals for their future while sophomores. Now, Cathy and Rosann give talks and workshops for other teachers, and their model program has spread from school to school, with some 1,500 students receiving career guidance through academic classes.

Career Education or Freshman Orientation

Comprehensive guidance is a vital experience for students to have early in their high school career, especially if they will be entering an academy program. One way to ensure that all students receive the necessary career guidance is to implement the *Career Choices* materials in a required career planning or freshmen orientation course. This might also be the only opportunity your students have to obtain the critical information they need to answer three pressing developmental questions: Who am I? What do I want? How do I get it?

A freshman orientation class will help students make better selections as they plan their high school curriculum and better choices as they plan their life beyond high school. While teaching important goal setting and decision-making skills, *Career Choices* will walk students step-by-step through the development of their own comprehensive graduation plans. Because *Career Choices* offers in-depth career interest and aptitude surveys, you can reduce "horizontal movement" between pathway offerings and ensure that students develop a much greater interest in pursuing post-secondary education or training.

You'll want to review the Tennessee and Texas State Standards for their career and freshman orientation classes begin on page 8/15. A quarter, semester, or yearlong class focusing on life skills, study skills, decision making and career planning is an ideal way to start incoming freshmen down the path to a successful high school career—and future.

Creative Scheduling for all Students

During the first year of implementation, students at Dover-Eyota High School in Eyota, Minnesota were offered *Career Choices* as an elective. The problem with that, reports family/consumer science teacher Julie Gergen, was that many of the students were already juniors and seniors. The goal of the program was to help young people select the high school courses needed to pursue their dream career; if students took the class their junior or senior year, they were getting the information too late. Another problem, Julie says, was that the class just wasn't long enough to get through the entire *Career Choices* curriculum.

As a solution to both dilemmas, a Career Exploration class is now required for all ninth graders. Students work through approximately the first half of *Career Choices* during this course. Then, in high school, they work through the remainder of the text in a class called Career Horizons.

Math or Consumer Math Class

Whether *Career Choices* and *Lifestyle Math* are used in a math class or the math teacher works as a team member with the career counselor, English teacher, or family and consumer science teacher, *Lifestyle Math* lends an obvious link to the relevancy of math education.

The expanded budget exercise found in *Lifestyle Math* makes *Career Choices* suitable for use in the math or consumer math classroom.

Interdisciplinary Combinations

For those who prefer a team teaching/interdisciplinary approach, the *Career Choices* program offers outstanding potential, both for structured schools and less traditional settings.

A language arts instructor and guidance counselor make an extremely effective team, with the counselor coming in once a week to lecture, facilitate discussion, or provide small group counseling or support. School counselors usually have a wealth of experience in dealing with people, yet their more customary duties do not permit them to fully utilize their talents. If your counselors would like to participate but just don't have the time, point out that they can accomplish many of their counseling and class scheduling goals more effectively by using this curriculum in your classroom.

Many successful programs bring together language arts and technology teachers. Students learn about computers by using them to complete their language arts assignments. More ambitious programs have involved setting up and computerizing mock businesses, videotaping student job interviews, and using graphics programs to design brochures to promote a book instead of the traditional book report.

Lifestyle Math is designed for use in the math classroom as a supplemental text for all math levels, or by the consumer education, business, or economics instructor. However, it can also be used to enhance the use of *Career Choices* in any other setting. You may want to bring in the math teacher to talk about those exercises involving numbers and calculations. This is a good way to both integrate learning and illustrate what we can do in the real world.

You may find other team members among the career education, family and consumer science, and social studies teachers.

Question	Go to URL:	You'll find:	Helpful hints & tips
Our interdisciplinary team is studying ways to structure our classes using the Career Choices curriculum. I need some ideas.	http://www.academicinnovations.com/indepth.html	Hyperlinks to a variety of stories about 20 educators along with a summary of their creative approaches	*Choose the hyperlinks to Phyllis Stewart of IN, Robert Freed of MN, Scott Hess of WA, Barbara Larson and Peg Slusarski of NE. Print and share their stories with your teammates.*
AND...	http://www.academicinnovations.com/interdis.html	A variety of interdisciplinary academic combinations for *Career Choices*	*Print, share and discuss these various possibilities with your teammates.*

The Career Choices curriculum offers many integrated course structure options:

Career Choices and the *Workbook/Portfolio* is an ideal combination for:

- *career education classes*
- *freshman orientation courses*
- *the guidance component for Tech Prep/School-To-Work programs*

Use both *Career Choices* and *Possibilities* as:

- *a semester or year-long class in the English department*
- *a team teaching opportunity for the English department and school counselors, careers instructors or family and consumer science department*
- *two integrated classes; for example, a freshman orientation class coupled with 9th grade English*

Use *Career Choices*, *Possibilities* and *Lifestyle Math* as:

- *a semester or year-long interdisciplinary course taught by the English, Math, and Social Science counseling departments*
- *a fully integrated academic course taught by one instructor within an academy, school-within-a-school or special populations program*

Add over 80 Internet lessons to any of these winning combinations.

New! www.careerchoices.com

Students will learn the powerful Internet processes for:

- ❏ **researching careers online**
- ❏ **locating and applying for jobs**
- ❏ **finding mentors, job shadows and interviews**
- ❏ **researching colleges and vocational schools**
- ❏ **applying for financial aid**
- ❏ **comparing salary levels of various careers**

Go online to the visitor's section of careerchoices.com to learn more about this exciting and timely curriculum enhancement.

Some Sample Combinations

English/Language Arts or Communications

In many of the schools currently using the *Career Choices* curriculum, it is the English teachers who teach the course. Some instructors use only the *Career Choices* text with the *Workbook and Portfolio*, and some use the *Career Choices* text and *Possibilities*.

English/Language Arts and Guidance Department

Many English/language arts teachers have teamed with the Guidance department to enrich the curriculum by having a guidance counselor come in at specific points to lead the lesson for the day. We have noted some particular activities in Section Four of this guide. At the end of the course, students schedule planning sessions with their guidance counselor and use their *Workbook and Portfolio* as an integral part of the planning process.

Family and Consumer Science and English/Language Arts

Because of the guidance and career and family living expertise of the instructors in the Family and Consumer Science department, some schools have used this model. The family and consumer science teachers use the *Career Choices* text, while the English teachers use *Possibilities*. This is usually accomplished in a block format.

English/Language Arts, Math and Social Studies

Schools using this format are usually divided into "houses" or clusters and work with block scheduling. The material in the *Career Choices* text is presented by the social studies instructor, *Possibilities* by the English teacher, and *Lifestyle Math* by the math teacher. Usually this course is a quarter or semester in duration, at the 8th, 9th, or 10th grade level.

Tech Prep/School-To-Work

Tech Prep and School-to-Work programs are using the *Career Choices* texts as one of their cluster options in the beginning of the program. The course is designed to help students choose a career path. A variety of instructors from different disciplines have chosen to teach this cluster.

Career Education

A career education instructor can effectively present the materials from *Career Choices* with the *Workbook and Portfolio* or use all the texts of the series.

Career Education and English/Language Arts

This combination of disciplines works especially well. The career educator presents the *Career Choices* text along with the *Workbook and Portfolio*, and the English/language arts instructor teaches from *Possibilities*.

Business Education and English/Language Arts

Many business education instructors are right at home with the material in *Career Choices* and *Lifestyle Math*. Teaming with the English/language arts department, using *Possibilities*, makes for an effective interdisciplinary approach to learning.

Technology Education and English/Language Arts

Because communication and computer skills are indispensable in the workplace and in post-secondary education, these instructors can combine to form a powerful program for all students.

Freshman Orientation Class

This can be accomplished in a single class at the beginning of the 9th grade year, using the main text, or as a block-scheduled course, using all the texts within an interdisciplinary team.

A Guidance Class: Counselor in the Classroom

In some schools, the counseling staff finds that one of the most efficient and effective ways to provide comprehensive guidance to students is in the classroom. Quarter and semester courses are designed and taught by the counselor using a combination of texts.

A School-Wide Class: All Students Take the Course

At one school, in San Juan, California, the whole school took the *Career Choices* course over a one-year period. Class periods were adjusted so that once per week, at the same time, every instructor in the school taught from the *Career Choices* text along with the *Workbook and Portfolio*. Because the workbook is consumable, the students bought their own books.

Our guidance counselors met with our freshmen classes once a month to present various ideas and units presented in **Career Choices***.*

— Linda Wulff
Chairperson, Communication Department
Waupun High School
Waupun, Wisconsin

Whole School Takes Career Choices

Starting a brand new comprehensive guidance program for freshmen only can present a dilemma for a school. Why not students in the sophomore, junior, and senior classes? Don't they need this critical information, too? Casa Roble Fundamental High School in Orangevale, California came up with a unique way in which to address this concern.

A recipient of one of the state's five-year restructuring grants, Casa Roble had identified comprehensive career education as critical to its success. A special period was added at the end of the day to accommodate a career course. The implementation year saw every one of the 1,800 students experiencing comprehensive career guidance with *Career Choices*. The course was scheduled one hour per week in every classroom. The fact that every teacher in the school taught the course presented a challenge. But, as Ernie Gomes reports, "*Career Choices* is great for the classroom teacher who doesn't know that much about career guidance."

During the course of the year, all students who completed their own copy of the consumable *Workbook* and *Portfolio* were exposed to a wide variety of guest speakers, and participated in a day-long career fair. The following year all freshmen were divided into houses, with each house completing a one-quarter course in *Career Choices*.

School-within-a-School Concept Works

Mission Bay High School in San Diego was chosen as a California Investment High School. The faculty set out to test various alternatives for meeting their goal: improving the educational climate on campus. Piloting a school-within-a-school program, they assigned 100 high-risk students to a "house" to be taught by a team of teachers. They hoped this team concept would enable teachers to give more attention to each individual, while allowing students to develop a feeling of community and commitment. Each of the 100 students would also work through the *Career Choices* textbook.

School Counselor and Magnet Coordinator Steve Stangland reported: "…our pilot group of 100 students had better attendance, high grades, reduced dropouts, and fewer suspensions." The success of the pilot program encouraged all staff to make a commitment to restructure with or without additional funds. The following year the entire 9th grade was divided into four houses and the *Career Choices* program was adopted for use in all houses.

Putting the Counselor in the Classroom

"As a guidance counselor—certified in both elementary and secondary schools—I commend you on dealing with the 'whole child,'" Wendy Hanslovan wrote us recently from St. Mary's, a public high school in St. Mary's, Pennsylvania, where she teaches a mandatory *Career Choices* class for freshmen. "Your multidimensional approach, I am sure, is the reason for the universal appeal of this curriculum."

Hanslovan and her colleagues in the counseling department are the exclusive instructors for the St. Mary's High School class, which includes four or five sections each semester. Although some teachers from other departments would like to teach the material, the counselors are determined to remain in the classroom, believing fervently that this is vital information for their students and a quality guidance opportunity.

"Students are typically unassertive about choosing a career direction," says Hanslovan, noting that in the past, counselors often couldn't take the time to help each young person plan wisely for the future. And she knows how important the process is. "I knew I was going to college, but beyond that I had no clue. My counselor was no help and that is precisely why, eventually, I ended up in this career. I think it's important to our country, our society, and it's important to individuals, as well."

At St. Mary's, the primary focus is on helping students choose an appropriate course from among six different career clusters and eventually find a satisfying career. *Career Choices* is extremely helpful in this process, Hanslovan says, because it helps young people clarify their thoughts about who they are and what they want before they begin making career decisions. "The students are relating to it," she states. "I cannot say enough good things about *Career Choices*."

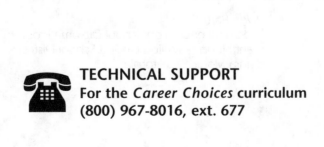

TECHNICAL SUPPORT
For the *Career Choices* curriculum
(800) 967-8016, ext. 677

Tech Prep and School-To-Work Programs

The U.S. Departments of Education and Labor joined together in an effort to better serve the 75 percent of students who will not graduate from college. They hoped to also provide a more skilled workforce for the nation. The Tech Prep and School-To-Work (School-To-Career) programs were the result. The funding for School-To-Work has twilighted, but the goals of these two initiatives remain priorities for many programs.

The Tech Prep and School-To-Work programs have much in common. For instance, both programs are designed to prepare students for skilled, high-paying jobs; both require cooperation between educators and employers; and both ask students to make important decisions about their future at an age when many do not have the level of maturity or self-knowledge necessary to choose wisely.

After years of experience one thing is clear: Comprehensive guidance is essential for student success in programs such as Tech Prep and School-To-Work—and the earlier the better. Students entering these programs are often asked to make sophisticated choices that many adults still struggle with. Fifteen minutes with a guidance counselor or a couple of hours with a computerized interest inventory simply is not enough to help guide these young teens or build the enthusiasm necessary for them to adapt to the rigor required.

To further complicate matters, students are often not educationally motivated to begin with. They need to understand the relationship between their academic subjects and their future success. Only then will they be motivated to put forth the effort required.

We have 23 sites using this curriculum with great success. As we focus more and more on School-To-Work, this curriculum will become even more essential.

— Lynn Porter
Coordinator of High School Diploma Program
Santa Monica-Malibu Unified School District
Santa Monica, California

Delaware School Receives State and National Awards

Sussex Technical High School, a Tech Prep school in Georgetown, Delaware, received a Presidential Blue Ribbon Award from the Department of Education as one of the top ten schools in the country. It also received the McGraw-Hill Award as one of the ten most innovative schools in the United States, and was honored as a Top Level Performance School by the Delaware Department of Public Instruction. However, things weren't always so at Sussex.

The school had no problem attracting students, but many arrived with little focus and no clear ideas about their future. They received little career counseling and, not surprisingly, from about 25 percent to almost 40 percent of the students changed their career majors each year. According to Dr. Jim Campbell, Delaware Director of Tech Prep, Sussex revamped its program after attending a *Career Choices* workshop he sponsored. After the workshop, teachers and administrators decided to implement a mandatory new program: Ninth graders would complete the *Career Choices* curriculum, receive vocational counseling, and testing prior to choosing a career major.

The results speak for themselves: Now, fewer than five percent change majors over the course of a year. Dr. Campbell is particularly pleased that many students are deciding to attend four-year schools, not to mention the fact that the dropout rate at Sussex is now less than one-half of one percent!

Three-Way Winner: Career Guidance, Vocational Training, and Community Support

Plantation High School, located just north of Miami, Florida, offers students many magnet choices: business, finance, travel and tourism, horticulture, and auto mechanics to name a few. It is in this Tech Prep/School-To-Work program that English Teacher Mary Ellen Fowler teaches a class called Career Decision-Making and Critical Thinking Skills. She uses a three-part approach: technical classes, career guidance, and community involvement. *Career Choices* and *Possibilities* are the foundation for the career guidance component.

Mary Ellen found *Career Choices* at the Association for Supervision and Curriculum Development conference. She brought the materials back to her school, where they have been used ever since. "Life isn't so simple anymore, that you can train for one profession, and that's it for the rest of your life," she told us. "Today, we have to teach students how to think and how to make decisions on their own, because the world they are entering will require this of them."

Students have responded so positively to the class that recently, when the air conditioning went out due to a renovation, they came to class even though they didn't have to. "It was amazing—there were no absences! Students actually like coming to school because they find the material relevant and are doing something they really want to do: discovering themselves and exploring their opportunities."

Youth Employment Programs under the Workforce Investment Act of 1998

Some of the most gratifying reports of success with *Career Choices* have come from educators using the materials in summer and year-round programs funded through the Job Training Partnership Act (JTPA). However, in August of 1998 the Workforce Investment Act of 1998 (WIA) was signed into law. The Workforce Investment Act replaces JTPA, which officially expired on June 30, 2000.

Among the key principles driving WIA is a desire to improve youth services, including the youth programs formerly provided for under JTPA. Eligibility for youth programs under WIA is based on age (14–21 years of age), economic opportunities (low income), and at least one barrier to employment. The Act identifies youth with barriers to employment as falling into one or more of the following classifications:

- Basic skills deficient;
- School dropout;
- Homeless, runaway, or foster child;
- Pregnant or parent;
- Offender; and/or
- Requiring additional assistance to complete education programs, or to secure and hold employment

The youth programs designed under WIA require ten essential elements similar to those of JTPA programs, including:

- Preparation for post–secondary educational opportunities
- Alternative secondary school services
- Summer employment opportunities
- Paid and unpaid work experience
- Occupational skills training
- Leadership development opportunities
- Adult mentoring
- Comprehensive guidance and counseling
- Supportive services
- Follow-up services

Because of these similarities, instructors in WIA programs can expect to face many of the same challenges faced by JTPA instructors. Many of the young people participating in the youth programs are frustrated and turned-off by education. While there are a variety of reasons for their frustration, some are directly related to the type of learning experienced in school. Success will depend on an ability to make these programs look different from school while maintaining strong academic linkages.

What JTPA coordinators have found is that the *Career Choices* curriculum is an effective way to face this challenge. It not only meets the federal guidelines, but it is also a big hit with employers, instructors, and young people.

The SCANS skills are essential to youth programs run under the Workforce Investment Act. *Career Choices* addresses the SCANS competencies and foundation skills in an effective and user-friendly manner.

Career Choices also helps in addressing each of the 10 essential elements outlined under the WIA.

1. Preparation for post-secondary educational opportunities:

- *Career Choices* engages students in a process of self-discovery. By demonstrating the impact education and training will have on their future life, *Career Choices* effectively motivates young people to apply real energy to their studies.

- Completion of *Career Choices* means completion of a comprehensive career and life planning process, making completion of high school and the pursuit of post-secondary training far more likely.

2. Alternative school services:

- Alternative schools services were developed to prepare young people for a traditional world in a nontraditional way. *Career Choices* can help do this.

- *Career Choices* is not a traditional textbook; it's a covert learning experience. By engaging students in a process of self-discovery, you have automatic relevance—Who am *I*? What do *I* Want? How do *I* get it?

3. Summer employment opportunities:

- *Career Choices* has been successful in JTPA and WIA programs across the country, touching the lives of thousands of students.

- By teaching students skills that are essential for success in the workplace, *Career Choices* can enrich any summer job.

4. Paid and unpaid work experience:

- *Career Choices* discusses the process by which young people can obtain work experience—both paid and unpaid.

- *Career Choices* also encourages young people to "network" with adults in the local business community, thereby helping them find appropriate mentors and work experience opportunities.

5. Occupational skills:

- Goal setting and decision making are essential occupational—and life skills. *Career Choices* gives students practice in applying both.

- Equally important skills include attitude (yes, having a good attitude is a skill), avoiding roadblocks, and getting back on track if you're derailed, all of which are covered in *Career Choices*.

6. Leadership development opportunities:

- Many of the occupational skills discussed above are also important elements of leadership.

- *Career Choices* is filled with cooperative learning activities that give young people a chance to uncover and build their own leadership abilities. Whether through group discussions, small group projects, or building effective teams, *Career Choices* provides practice of practical leadership skills.

7. Adult mentoring:

- In addition to the mentoring and job shadowing activities outlined in this *Instructor's Guide* (pp. **4**/94–**4**/100), *Career Choices* encourages young people to work with adults in the community. For example, as students work on their budgets (Chapter 4) and begin their career research (Chapter 6), they are urged to interview adults as a source of vital information.

- Instructors are also prompted to invite adults to class as guest speakers, giving students additional access to potential mentors from the community.

8. Comprehensive guidance and counseling:

- Each activity in the *Career Choices* texts motivates students to sharpen academic skills by demonstrating the relevance of present studies to their future lives. At the same time they practice reading, writing, and computation, students learn to identify interests, explore career options, and build decision-making skills.

9. Supportive services:

- *Career Choices* builds conscientious consumers. Young people are taught not only to find appropriate services, but also how to identify the need for these services.

- Students are also taught that planning and goal setting can often help avoid the need for state-supported services.

10. Follow-up:

- This *Instructor's Guide* includes a pre/post-testing instrument that can be used to effectively measure attitudinal change. Also outlined is the process for measuring gains in skills/academics.

- Completion of *Career Choices* means completion of a comprehensive career and life planning process. The *Workbook/Portfolio* is designed to facilitate follow-up, providing counselors/advisors with a written record of dreams, goals, and plans so they can better counsel the participants.

More information on WIA is available in Section Eight of this guide, or by visiting www.academicinnovations.com/wia.html

Two words: Common sense.

— Coordinator John Gill on why JTPA youth
benefit from Career Choices
Hempstead, New York

*The children that we started with seven weeks ago are
not the kids we have now. They look different, they act
differently, they hold their heads up, they speak
distinctly. . . [and it all happened] in seven weeks.*

— Anne Swygert, coordinator
Greensboro, North Carolina

*We had kids from two different sides of town, two different
ethnic backgrounds, two different gang mentalities. We had not
one fight.*

— Deb Mumford, JTPA coordinator
Denver, Colorado

*The program did provide 90 hours of quality instruction for the
youth which produce significant improvement in academic Basic
Skills as well as positive attitudinal changes towards learning.
The vast majority of participants did connect academic learning to
practical life skills and the majority of participants' self-concepts
as learner did improve.*

— report by Dr. Charles Branch
external evaluator for Denver, Colorado JTPA

*Sixty-four percent reported they would be or probably would
be in the program even if they were not being paid, and 93
percent of the 42 subjects interviewed would recommend the
Academic Enrichment Program to friends.*

— Dr. Branch's report above

*They did some wonderful math they weren't supposed
to be able to do. [While pre-tests in math and reading
showed students performing at levels from fourth grade,
fourth month to sixth grade, seventh month] when we
finished the program I had quite a few of them jump all
the way up to the 12th grade level.*

— Jessy James, instructor
Marshall, Minnesota

Using *Career Choices* with Special Populations

Who Is At-Risk?

From a traditional viewpoint it's not difficult to recognize the students who are "at risk." They are failing or dropping out of school. They spend more time in the parking lot than the classroom. They abuse drugs and alcohol. They can't read. They don't care.

The above description is the obvious. We would broaden this definition to include anyone not living up to his or her potential. The young woman who sits quietly in the back row using her 140 IQ to earn Bs and Cs is at risk. The student who's attended six different schools in as many years is at risk. The abused student is at risk. The troublemaker is at risk. The child living in poverty is at risk. The student whose family is in a state of crisis is at risk. The young woman who is pregnant or already a mother is at risk. Any student with physical or emotional problems is at risk. Any student who can't seem to "get it together" or who lacks the discipline to make use of their abundant talents is ultimately at risk.

Students need to experience success and feel empowered. Success follows self-esteem, and empowerment follows success. Those students whose only point of reference is failure will inevitably fail.

The strength of the *Career Choices* curriculum is that it empowers students, allowing them to feel in control of their lives. This empowerment serves to motivate them. By providing a learning environment that focuses on individual strengths rather than weaknesses—real or imagined—students are given the chance to succeed at what they do best. It speaks to those students who need just a little more support and attention to see how they fit in and how education is relevant to their lives. With *Career Choices* you can deliver what these students need, to the benefit of us all.

One student talked another student (who had dropped out of school) to come back because of what she learned in the program.

— Tim Bridges
Social Studies Career Education Teacher
Lanesville Community School Corp.
Lanesville, Indiana

For Use with At-Risk Students

Career Choices is the ideal central text for an integrated career education/language arts program targeting at-risk students. It makes education relevant to students who have been turned off by academics, allowing them to see themselves as successful individuals with potentially satisfying futures.

The career education/language arts combination provides ample opportunity for cooperative learning, hands-on activities, self-analysis, autobiographical reading and writing, and role-playing; these strengthen academic skills as well as self-awareness. The life skills taught (decision making, problem solving, and overcoming obstacles) are especially critical for this population. In addition, the career education component teaches essential job preparation skills: filling out job applications, writing resumes, and being interviewed for work.

It's important that classes for at-risk students be kept small, so that they can be known as individuals who matter, and who have a future. Within these small groups instructors should focus on the question "Where do you want to be in ten years?" From that vantage point it's not difficult for students to determine what might stand in the way of achieving that goal or if the possibility of reaching it makes staying in school worthwhile.

Journal writing is essential; it can often act as an effective vehicle when young people are crying out for help. You may learn more about your students and their special needs or problems from this ongoing activity than from other sources.

At-risk students also benefit greatly from getting out into the world (see the shadow program described on pages **4/94–4/100** of this guide). You might wish to take this one step further by having students become unpaid interns for longer periods of time. This not only allows students to observe or take part in work that might interest them, but it also reinforces what is taught in school: the importance of being on time, getting along with others, following directions, and so on.

Local Business Adopts Alternative High School

In Great Falls, Montana, one local business "adopted" an alternative education high school. Using the Personal Profile System test (mentioned on pages **4/22**, **4/23** of the text) for its own workers, the employer first helps the students identify their work behavioral styles, and then places them in intern positions that match their strengths and work styles. The employer believes that this process gives students better opportunities for success and they will therefore be more motivated to apply themselves as a result of the assessment.

Life 101: Career Guidance for At-Risk Youth

When STW Coordinator Teri Redl started with Medina County School District in Ohio, she was handed a failed training and employment program for at-risk youth. Her directive: Get it up and running on all seven of the district's high school campuses. The students in her charge needed academic tutoring to get through school, a system of support to deal with their lives outside of school, and guidance in making decisions about their futures. Teri needed a curriculum flexible enough for the all the settings encountered as she traveled from school to school: classroom, one-on-one, and group situations. The *Career Choices* curriculum fulfilled the needs of her embryonic program, and a *Career Choices* workshop in Columbus, Ohio showed her how the books could be integrated. She decided to use all five books with her students.

Career Choices helped Teri's students get a handle on their personal lives. *Lifestyle Math* reinforced math skills and helped them realize the economic benefit of further education. Many students had levels too low to do silent reading, so they read out-loud from *Possibilities* each day. By following along and receiving extra prompting, they could understand the selections and participate in meaningful discussions, all while improving their reading skills. "They didn't even realize they were reading the best authors—the classics!" Teri exclaimed.

Did *Career Choices* help Teri's students stay in school and look towards more realistic futures? "Absolutely! It has helped make life more manageable for them, especially their personal lives, which is so often where the real problem is. *Career Choices* gave them the chance to say: 'Here is something I can do!' It's truly geared for life—Life 101!"

For Use within the
Juvenile Justice System

Today many young people are out of control, in trouble with the law, or, in some other manner, limiting their own chances for a satisfying future—or any future at all. Often those people who aren't succeeding think of themselves as victims. Something has been "done to" them and there's nothing they can do about it.

In some cases, they are partially correct. Youngsters who are abused or neglected are certainly victims. Disadvantaged children have little recourse concerning their plight. But, having come to an age where they are able to make their own decisions, all these young people have choices. They can choose to give up all power over their own futures and continue to be victims, or they can choose to get on with their lives.

With its emphasis on accountability, problem solving, and decision making, *Career Choices* is valuable in demonstrating that the past is behind us. Students must naturally take responsibility for past decisions. However, they must also be taught see they are working with a fresh slate and are in a position to make choices that will determine their future satisfaction.

Many youth corrections programs have educational instruction, allowing youth to earn school credit or their GED. The young people in these programs need materials that will help them prepare for a traditional world in a nontraditional way. With a flexible and engaging format, *Career Choices* is not a traditional textbook; it's a covert learning experience. By engaging students in a process of self-discovery, you have automatic relevance—Who Am I? What Do I Want? How Do I Get It?

Federal money is available for juvenile justice programs. You may wish to take advantage of this situation by having someone from juvenile justice work with teachers on this project. Contact your local law enforcement agency or conduct research on the Internet for appropriate funding.

For Use with Pregnant Students or Teen Parents

With *Career Choices*, parenting or pregnant students are taught to look at their current situation objectively. The course encourages them to believe that obstacles can be overcome, that doors are not permanently closed to them because of a single mistake. *Career Choices* encourages them to ask what they want now, and how they can go about reaching those goals, rather than dwelling on the past.

In schools with a comprehensive high school program for pregnant teens or parenting teens, *Career Choices* can be used successfully within the language arts curriculum. In other schools, it can be the core of a childcare, future planning, career skills, or life preparation course. It should be offered for credit.

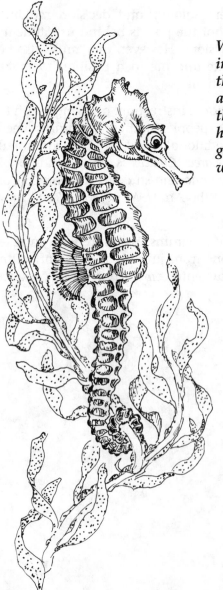

Working with a group of pregnant/parenting teens in a program called "Young Families Can—Jobs," the groups became bonded and shared hopes, fears and dreams for their futures…. They didn't want the program to end. This group of young women had transformed from street smart, tough, gang-girls into talking about freedom, justice and wanting to be president.

— Tamara Luckett
Career Educator
Parents Anonymous
Phoenix, Arizona

I am gratified to see an awareness of the girls' self-worth. Low self-esteem is the norm for our students. They really have trouble seeing past their pregnancy. We have had some students who just blossomed here, and as a result, went on to college and earned a degree.

— Jean A. Granger
Career Exploration Teacher
School Age Parents Program
Waukesha, Wisconsin

For Use with
Special Education Students

Often overlooked, students in special education programs are among those for whom comprehensive guidance is most important. These are students who may believe their choices are very limited; this mindset only increases their need for good decision making and life planning skills.

There is a somewhat natural tendency among young people to focus on past failures rather than future opportunities for success. This can certainly be seen among special education and other at-risk students. All too often frustration leads to an "I just can't do it" attitude, which, in turn, fosters failure. *Career Choices* works against this cycle, providing students with an opportunity to discover their own unique strengths and abilities. By building self-esteem and furnishing students with the chance to succeed, *Career Choices* assists students in uncovering their value as members of society, all while helping them find their place in the world.

Vocational Guidance for the Special Education Classroom

Roberta Freed teaches a unique class at Little Falls Community High School in Little Falls, MN. The class, which combines English with career and employability skills in a two-hour block, is for special education students. Some students are going to work right after graduation, while others are headed for college or technical training. All have some form of learning disability or mild mental retardation, and all have jobs or are in the job-search process.

Roberta teamed up with the OJT (On-the-Job) teacher, Ron Hanenkamp, and the result is a fully integrated English OJT class where students can earn credits for both subjects. She uses all the *Career Choices* materials because the progression of the curriculum parallels the topics covered in OJT, providing reinforcement.

Roberta believes that special education students can benefit from vocational and career guidance—and *Career Choices* can deliver it. "It's easy when you use a curriculum like *Career Choices*…and satisfying when your students come back to share, not only with you, but with your class, that they are making it, thanks to your efforts."

SECTION FOUR

Lesson Plan Suggestions

For *Career Choices and Changes*, use the lessons in page number order for Chapters 1–10 of this manual (pages **4**/2 to **4**/149). Then, because an additional chapter was added to this adult version, you'll need to turn to page **4**/171 for these lessons. Once that chapter ("Making Changes") is completed, turn back to page **4**/151 of this manual for the balance of the lessons. For these last two chapters, use the activity headling for page guidance rather than the logo page number at the top of each page.

These chapter-by-chapter, exercise-by-exercise classroom suggestions should be helpful as you develop your lesson plans. Each exercise has a learning objective with presentation suggestions. In addition, many have suggestions for optional activities, resources, and suggested reading and writing assignments.

The *Energizers* are special activities which students particularly enjoy. Their activity-oriented design facilitates a high level of student participation.

As you experiment with what works best with your population, make notes in the margins of the *Guide*. Please remember to share your ideas so we can consider including them in a future version of this *Guide*.

 Throughout this section of the manual, you'll see this logo at the bottom of certain pages. This indicates Internet enhanced lessons are available on www.careerchoices.com.

Before you begin, it's important that you understand copyright. This briefly explains what can and can't be done with the **Career Choices** curriculum materials in the name of education and why. However, copyright law is very precise and technical and, therefore, it can confusing. For more extensive information, review *The Copyright Handbook, How to Protect and Use Written Works,* 8th Edition by Stephen Fishman (Nolo Press 2004) or the online information provided by the United States Copyright Office.

What is a copyright?

Copyright is the legal device that gives the creator of a work of art, literature, or software, the right to control how and when that work is used. It grants the author a number of exclusive rights to reproduce, adapt, perform, and display their works.

Copyrighted material is **intellectual property** and an asset of the owner. Like other forms of property, it may be used for the economic benefit of the owner. The owner must give permission, usually for compensation, for the use of their property. If someone uses the property in a way not granted by the owner, the owner may use legal recourse to recover damages.

When you purchase a book, you purchase the right to read the book, and even pass the book on to someone else in the form in which you purchased it. However, you have not purchased the right to copy the material from the book **in any way** and then pass it on in another format (e.g., photocopy, electronic transfer, digital transfer).

What about "fair use" and don't teachers have certain rights?

Yes, teachers have a **limited** right to copy materials under **very strict** guidelines. However, as outlined in *Marcus v Crowley*, 695 F. 2d 1171 (9th Circuit court. 1983)

"Multiple copies may not be made to substitute for the purchase of books,. . . or to substitute for or replace 'consumable' works such as workbooks, exercises, standardized tests, test booklets and answer sheets."

This ruling makes it clear that photocopying, digitally copying, or storing the "exercises" or any of the consumable workbooks in the *Career Choices* curriculum digitally is prohibited under all circumstances without written permission from the publisher.

We know budgets are tight and funding is often in a flux; however, there are a variety options available. Please call our office for funding ideas and strategies.

Introduction

Presentation suggestions:

Ask a student to read the introduction aloud in class. Have each student explain how he or she would have completed the flight assignment. Note the variety of responses.

Emphasize the last paragraph of the introduction. It is not the purpose of this course to have students make a final career choice. They should, however, learn a process for making rewarding life choices in the future.

Activities:

To help the class get acquainted, ask students to write several things about themselves on nametags. Students may want to note a particular talent or skill they are proud of, an interest area or favorite hobby, a place they most like to visit, the most important people in their lives, an important achievement, or even something personal no one else in the room knows. Then, have students move about, silently reading other student's tags.

As with all activities of this nature, if an individual does not want to share information, respect that student's privacy.

Chapter 1

Envisioning Your Future

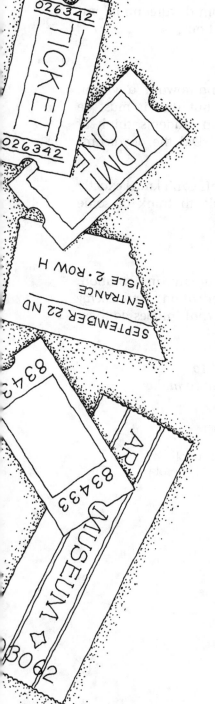

As you move into Chapter 1, have students read the opening stories aloud.

The overall goal of this course is to help each student become aware of his or her own identity and ambitions, and to develop an action plan for realizing these dreams. The basic purpose of the first chapter is to start students thinking about an ideal future. It also provides you with some baseline information on how much thought they have given this topic previously and whether their ambitions are relatively high or low. This information should be taken into account as you plan the remainder of the course.

As you begin, be careful not to step on anyone's dreams. A goal may seem unrealistic for a particular student, but many, many people who demonstrate little potential in high school go on to excel in their future careers. You may need to remind some students from time to time that success requires action in addition to vision. It may also be appropriate to encourage some students to aim higher if you sense they lack confidence in their own capabilities.

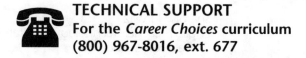

TECHNICAL SUPPORT
For the *Career Choices* curriculum
(800) 967-8016, ext. 677

Vision Plus Energy
Equals Success

Page 13   Page 5

Learning objective:

To help students realize that success does not come just from daydreaming, but from combining a vision with appropriate and necessary actions.

Presentation suggestions:

Discuss the difference between daydreaming and working toward a vision. Emphasize that daydreaming is an important first step, but that it must be followed by action if dreams are to become reality. Can students think of daydreams they've had that they did not work to realize? Did the daydreams come true?

As a class, work through the charts on page 13. While students can't know exactly what actions these people took, the class should be able to think of some reasonable steps based on their accomplishments.

Activities:

Ask the class to think of synonyms for the words *vision* (dream, imagination, conception, creation, inspiration, invention, fantasy, fabrication) and *energy* (activity, liveliness, spirit, vivacity, eagerness, zeal, vigor). What images do these terms suggest?

I invited a Native American artist to my class to teach my students how to make "DreamCatchers."

— Barbara Muir
Teacher
North High School
Minneapolis, Minnesota

Distribute short magazine articles on the visions of famous people. (Newsweek, Parade magazine, etc.) As a small-group activity, have students write a phrase explaining the vision of each celebrity.

— Sharon Hurwitz
English Teacher/Technology Facilitator
Bethel High School
Hampton, Virginia

The Secret Life of Walter Mitty
by James Thurber
Read after completing pages 10–13 in *Career Choices*

I learned a variety of things. The most important words that I learned were "vision + energy = success." I think those words are very important to a person who tries to figure out his/her own career. . . . I know now that I have to plan my career. I can't just jump into anything, I have to plan out my career first. I have to do research on what job I would like to do.

— Student in Linda Costello's class
ASA Learning Center
San Bernadino, California

The following is a copy of the invitation Arlene Bowman of William Penn High School in New Castle, Delaware, hands out to her 9th grade English students at the beginning of Chapters 1 and 2:

Join the Celebration!!
Let's celebrate ourselves and each other . . .

Who: Everyone in this classroom
When: Friday, September 8th through Wednesday, September 13th
What: Creating a community of learners

Celebration Preparation:

1. I will bring the balloons, markers, glue, and ideas . . .
2. You bring your "open mind" and then be prepared to . . .
   a. Go someplace you've never been before.
   b. Write down the things (at least 10) you feel you would need in this place to feel at home in it (bring list Friday).
   c. Bring three symbols to class on Friday that reflect what you value about yourself and your life.

Envisioning Your Future

Page 14   Page 6

Learning objective:

To have students begin imagining the kind of future they would find most satisfying.

This provides the instructor with a pre-assessment survey and establishes baseline information that can be used to measure growth and learning.

Presentation suggestions:

After reading the introductory material for this exercise, ask students to close their eyes and imagine their ideal future lives. Allow several minutes for the vision to appear, then have students write about what they imagined. You may want to have students share their visions as a way of getting to know each other better (and to help you know what their thoughts are at this point). You should ask to see everyone's description, whether it is shared with the class or not. This will help you gauge how much progress individuals are making as they proceed through the class.

This will be a difficult exercise for some people in the class. After they have attempted this task, reassure them that even if they had no vision at all, it's okay. They will develop a vision soon enough.

Refer again to the previous exercise, emphasizing that energy must match vision in order to achieve success.

This may be a good time to bring the school counselor into the class as a resource person and facilitator.

> *I added musical selections to enhance my program.*
> *For example, for Martin Luther King's "I Have a*
> *Dream," I used Garth Brooks' "We Shall Be Free."*
>
>   — Belinda Boyce
>   English Teacher
>   Buckeye Local High School
>   Rayland, Ohio

Optional

Pages 19–32

A Psalm of Life
by Henry Wadsworth Longfellow
Dreams
by Langston Hughes
I Have a Dream . . . (speech)
by Martin Luther King, Jr.
Read after completing page 14 in *Career Choices*

Linda Paulson's "Visualizer" Activity

The idea for "visualizers" or "fantasy tuner-inners" came to Linda Paulson, 9th grade language arts teacher in Grafton, North Dakota, one day in class when students couldn't seem to grasp the meaning of James Thurber's story, "The Secret Life of Walter Mitty" (*Possibilities*, pages 11–18). Clearly, the students needed a way to get in touch with their hopes and dreams.

Paulson asked each student to bring a wire coat hanger (you may want to substitute pipe cleaners) to class the following day, and the first "visualizers" were born. The hangers were bent any way the students chose. The main requirement was that they were to be worn on their heads in order to receive visions of their future.

Today, class members plan ahead and bring all sorts of materials to school to decorate their vision receivers, which have become much more sophisticated. Paulson's only stipulation is that only found objects can be used; nothing can be bought.

Students wear their new head gear for an entire day (they get points for doing so). In Paulson's English class, they get time to fantasize about possibilities for their own lives—living somewhere else, holding a particular job, or whatever—and then write about that fantasy (*Career Choices*, page 14). In other classes, teachers allow five or ten minutes on that day to pose a question related to their subject, and students again imagine a solution and write it down. They receive credit for their work in every class.

Although the hats are formally used only on this day, Paulson keeps them in her classroom. Students have permission to wear them "whenever they feel the need." It gives them "a right to be playful," Paulson says, and also breaks down barriers that can hold a young person's imagination in check.

What a wonderful way to help students begin to get in touch with their own visions of their future. Congratulations, Linda, on a fabulous idea!

Why People Work

Page 15   No Workbook
                        Page

Learning objective:

To illustrate that work is not just a way to earn a living, but an important part of most people's identity.

Presentation suggestions:

Review the reasons why people work listed in the book. Write them on the board. Ask the class if they can think of other possible reasons. Why do they think their parents work? Students will probably come to the conclusion that people work for a combination of all of these reasons.

When we studied "The Prophet," we divided our students into 6 groups with each group writing a section in their own words. As a large group we put all 6 parts together and the end result was fantastic!

— Lisa Demuth
Special Education Educator
Walnut Creek Campus
West Des Moines, Iowa

Optional

Work, **an excerpt from** *The Prophet*
by Kahlil Gibran
Read after completing page 15 in *Career Choices*

Pages 33–36

Everybody Works

Page 17   Page 7

Learning objective:

To help students recognize the scope and diversity of every individual's accomplishments on a daily basis.

Presentation suggestions:

Discuss work in terms of the things students do every day and ask them to answer the questions on page 17. Follow with class discussion. How do students feel about their accomplishments (proud, intelligent, resentful, satisfied, talented, lucky, relieved)?

Be sure to emphasize that everything we "do" is work. A student is a worker; unpaid, perhaps, but still a worker.

Activity:

Because students are going to be asked how they "feel" about something throughout this course, define emotions and feelings.

Brainstorm with the class a list of emotions and feelings. Are they adjectives or verbs? You might debate this issue. Noted psychologist Dr. William Glasser argues that emotions and feelings are verbs because you choose them (e.g., you choose to be angry).

Defining Success

Career Choices
Pages 18–19

Workbook and Portfolio
Page 8–9

Learning objective:

To help students see that individuals have personal definitions of success and that the only one they need to meet is their own.

Presentation suggestions:

In contemporary American society, success is often seen in terms of money, power, or material possessions. Assure students that while these things may make them appear successful to the rest of the world, they hardly guarantee a life of contentment. Everyone must define success personally. It is only by living up to that definition that people feel truly successful. Have students individually read the statements on the chart and mark whether they strongly agree, agree, are not sure, disagree, or strongly disagree with each definition. There are no right or wrong answers. The point is to help students sort out their own feelings on the topic. They should write their own definition of success on page 21 and sign it.

Allow plenty of time for students to think about the quotations or assign this exercise as homework. In your discussion emphasize, too, that their own definitions are likely to change, depending on what's going on in their life. A new parent who formerly defined success as getting ahead at work may decide that raising a healthy, happy child is far more important. Someone taken seriously ill might redefine success as getting and staying well.

Activities:

Ask students how they think certain well-known individuals [Abraham Lincoln, Shaquille O'Neil ("Shaq"), Whoopi Goldberg, Ann Landers, Steven Spielberg, Gloria Estefan, Amy Tan, Howard Stern, Venus Williams] would define success, based on their actions.

Have students view the movie *Forrest Gump* for your first Video Book Club discussion (see listings beginning on page 6/41). Did Forrest have a vision of success? What energy did he display? How does the class think he would define success for himself? Is Forrest a good role model for the class? Why or why not?

Reading assignment:

Bless the Beasts and the Children, by Glenden Swarthout

This book centers around a group of young "misfits" who have been sent to camp to be "straightened out." The group comes together as one by one they are rejected by the other groups in camp. The boys go on an unusual quest to see a herd of buffalo sentenced to a cruel death by the park service and, in so doing, find a measure of their own worth and freedom. An excellent starting point for discussions on setting and achieving goals and defining and attaining personal success, this book is high-interest reading with a strong message.

Course Wrap-Up

Ask students to write their own definitions of success entitled "Success Is…" Refer them to the Robert Louis Stevenson quotation at the bottom of page 283 in *Career Choices*. Throughout the course, there will be a great deal of discussion and debate as to what success is. By the end of the course, each student should have a more complete personal definition. Allow at least a couple of days for completion of the assignment; they will need time to think about it. This is not an activity that should be done as a group. Explain that the personal nature of the task requires individual contemplation.

Energizer:

Once their expanded definition is complete, turn it into an art project by neatly lettering it on a large piece of art paper. The computer lab can be utilized along with a laser printer to produce high-quality lettering. The italic setting usually adds interest to a quotation. Remind the students to "sign" their quotation similar to the style used for quotes in *Career Choices*.

Ask the students to complete a color border around their quotation using watercolors, felt pens, tissue paper collage, or even color pictures from magazines. We suggest using this activity as a celebration. Perhaps some students will bring in refreshments. Play instrumental recordings in the background.

Once the projects are complete, post them around the room for everyone to share. If there are appropriate display areas in the school, why not share the project at a PTA meeting, a school board meeting, or with other students?

At the time you make the assignment, why not share your own success quotation and art project?

The Stevenson quotation written in calligraphy with completed art would make a lovely classroom decoration. Collaborate with your art department on this.

The writing activities were most appealing to the students. For example, writing the last page of Richard Cory's diary.

—— Belinda Boyce
English Teacher
Buckeye Local High School
Rayland, Ohio

Optional

Pages 37–39

Richard Cory
by Edwin Arlington Robinson

Read after completing pages 18–21 in *Career Choices*

Making Career Choices

Page 20–21

Page 9

Learning objective:

To help students identify their own decision-making patterns and evaluate their effectiveness.

Presentation suggestions:

Read the stories about the various decision-making patterns aloud in class. Ask students to evaluate and discuss which patterns are likely to lead to the most desirable results, which patterns are likely to lead to the least desirable results, and which patterns they use most often. Let students know they will learn much more about decision making as they work through *Career Choices*.

While students are entering the room, have the Simon and Garfunkel song "Richard Cory" playing. Then have the students read the poem "Richard Cory" in **Possibilities** *and answer the questions following the work.*

— Sharon Hurwitz
English teacher/Technology Facilitator
Bethel High School
Hampton, Virginia

Career Portfolio

A career portfolio is an intentional collection of the records, work samples and certificates that demonstrates an individual's qualifications, skills, experience and achievements. The most effective portfolios are organized from a career development perspective. It is not only a product used to demonstrate competencies to a potential employer or college recruiter; it is also a process. A career portfolio is a way to track what an individual has accomplished and plan for the skills still needed—all in the context of the careers that will meet both an individual's emotional and financial needs.

How to Assemble a Career Portfolio

Encourage each student to get a three-ring binder with a 2- or 3-inch spine and a packet of tabbed notebook dividers. This format allows students to update and customize this notebook throughout their lifetime.

Sections one and *two* are the planning portions of their portfolio. Label the first tab *Career Exploration Activities* and the second tab *Your Professional Development Plan*. Include the documents listed below in the appropriate section.

Section One—Career Exploration Activities

Activity	*Career Choices* Page	Workbook/Portfolio Page
Envisioning Your Future	14	6
Your Personal Profile bulls eye chart	27	11
Components of Lifestyle	63	28
Your Budget Profile for your desired lifestyle at age 29	92–93	42
Your Chart describing your ideal career characteristics	134	62
Career Interest Surveys	150–155	68–73
Career Decision-Making Chart	177	83

Section Two—Your Professional Development Plan

Activity	*Career Choices* Page	Workbook/Portfolio Page
Goal Setting Chart	189–190	87
Transferable Skills Chart	246	101
Career Alternatives Ladder	227	109
Job Application and Interview Questions	257–259	112–113
Your Education and Training Plan	270–273	116–118
Your Plan—Goals for education/training, living arrangements, employment and finances for the next 10 years	278–282	121–124

Section Three—Documentation of Competencies

In addition, create a tab sheet for each of the bulleted topics listed below. Review what should be included behind each tab and encourage students to make it a habit to place these important documents in their portfolio as they are completed or acquired. That way, when an opportunity arises for an important interview, the documents are readily available.

- Your resume
- Work or project samples
- Letters of recommendation
- Certificates, diplomas, awards
- Records of work experience (paid and unpaid)

Gathering the Documents for a Career Portfolio
Sections One and Two

On page 6 of the *Career Choices Workbook and Portfolio* is a list of the activities we encourage students to include in their Career Portfolio. You'll want to point this page out to your students in the beginning of the course. Students may either add these completed surveys, charts and activities to their three-ring binder as they complete them or at the end of the course. Suggest they keep their completed *Workbook and Portfolio for Career Choices* in the back cover pocket of their three-ring binder for review in the future. Remind your students they will want to continually update these charts and surveys as they mature, gain experience and change their goals.

Section Three

This will be an ongoing process over the course of their lives, and it is rewarding for an individual to watch this section grow. For instance, whenever they receive a letter of recommendation (from a teacher, counselor, employer, or community source) they'll want to keep a copy in their portfolio. The same is true for copies of certificates, diplomas and awards. Employers and colleges like to see samples of an individual's writing and technical skills. Written reports or photographs of completed projects should also be included. A resume, work history or vita is a dynamic document that should be revised with each new position, promotion or volunteer activity.

How to Use the Career Portfolio

- **Career exploration and planning**—Encourage students to take their notebooks with them whenever they meet with their school counselors, mentors, teachers and career advisors.

- **Employment and college interviews**—At the time of an interview, the documents in section three should be removed from the three-ring binder and placed in an appropriate jacket or folder for a more professional appearance.

- **Career changes**—If future workplace conditions or personal desires dictate a career change, the notebook provides the framework for creating a new vision and plan for the future. The individual will want to follow the process they learned in their *Career Choices* course and re-exam these questions: Who am I, what do I want and how do I get it. Their *Career Choices Workbook and Portfolio* will come in handy for this project.

Chapter 2

Your Personal Profile

The purpose of this chapter is to help students answer the question "Who am I?" Without a basic understanding of their own personality, values, skills, and passions, they cannot hope to make wise career and life decisions. Yet, in most career education courses, the subject is touched on only superficially, if at all.

For the teacher, this material offers some unique opportunities and a few potential problems. Identity, after all, is a very personal matter. Some students will be reluctant to share their innermost thoughts and desires with the class. These feelings must be respected. It is much more important for the individual to discover his or her own unique qualities than it is for the class to hear about them.

On the other hand, some students may need to overcome a bit of discomfort in order to begin thinking about these important concepts. Many young men, for example, will be unfamiliar with identifying and talking about their feelings. Until they can articulate their emotional responses—either verbally or in writing—their lives are likely to be less satisfying.

You are in the best position to judge the activities that will best serve your class. Some groups will be open to lively class discussions. Others may feel more comfortable—or be more honest—in writing. In all cases, students should be assured of confidentiality, if they so desire.

The activities in chapters 2, 3, 4 and 5 constitute a formal career interest and aptitude assessment. The information collected provides the personalized data necessary to begin researching career opportunities that match a student's traits and desires. With this information they can analyze the affect personal interests and aptitudes have on educational and career planning.

Bull's Eye Chart

Page 24–27   Page 11

Learning objective:

To help students discover the many layers of qualities and characteristics that make up their unique identity, and to help them appreciate how knowing their identity is a necessary and ongoing part of any rewarding life.

Presentation suggestions:

Before you begin, review the definitions on page 26 with the class. Then, together, try to complete a chart on the board. You may use yourself as the example, if that feels comfortable. Or, you might try to make a chart for a celebrity or historic figure the class feels it knows well (Examples: George Washington, Connie Chung, Bill Cosby, Ricky Martin, Michael Jordan, Eleanor Roosevelt).

Begin with the outer circles of the chart, working your way toward the center.

Activities:

Ask students to make a collage representing their own passions, values, personality traits, strengths, skills and aptitudes, roles, occupations, and vocations. If you want to do this in class, bring in large pieces of paper or poster board, scissors, glue, and an assortment of recycled magazines. Have students find images they feel represent their own identity, cut them out, and glue them to the large pieces of paper. You may wish to assign this activity as homework.

Have students "define" themselves audio-visually with a collage of photos, words, songs, or whatever comes to mind. Then, as a class, try to identify which project matches which student.

Energizers:

Ask students to complete their own charts but not to share them with anyone. Then have class members choose a partner they feel they know well and complete a chart for him or her. Ask them to compare the second-party chart with the original. In most cases, students will find it relatively easy to complete the outer rings of the chart. However, they are unlikely to do as well with the inner ring topics.

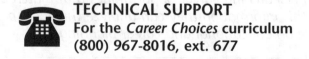

TECHNICAL SUPPORT
For the *Career Choices* curriculum
(800) 967-8016, ext. 677

Follow-up at the end of the course:

When the class has completed the book or the course, ask students to go back and update their charts with new information they have gained. These newly discovered qualities and traits should be entered in a different color ink. Then assign a one-page essay on the topic "Self-Discovery: A Life-long Process." If students are willing to share, you might post charts and essays around the room. Then, allow time for students to read them and follow with a group discussion.

Reading assignment:

The Diary of Anne Frank by Anne Frank

After discussing values, passions, roles, vocations, etc. [Bull's Eye Chart, chapter 2], I show the movie Mr. Holland's Opus. Students can clearly see all of the concepts in that film.

— Julie Gergen
Family and Consumer Science Teacher
Dover-Eyota High School
Eyota, Minnesota

The Personality Profile helped them see themselves as well-rounded, complex and unique individuals.

— Bonnie Morris
Business and Careers Instructor
Anacortes High School
Anacortes, Washington

Chapter two was wonderful! The students enjoyed determining their values, passions, and work styles. The activities in the guide were fun and easy to incorporate into regular class discussion and activities. This chapter was a wonderful "ice breaker."

— Kyra Krause
Special Education teacher
Lubbock-Cooper High School
Lubbock, Texas

Identifying Your Passions

Page 28–29   Page 12

Learning objective:

To help students learn to identify and articulate those things that are extremely important to them on an emotional level.

Presentation suggestions:

We thought about substituting another word for *passion* but, after lengthy debate, decided it was the most appropriate term. You are likely, however, to get some snickering from a few students. Be prepared. Use the situation to demonstrate how the things that matter most to an individual can elicit feelings of excitement similar to those usually associated with romantic or sexual passion.

Begin by writing the two definitions on page 28 in *Career Choices* on the board. Then have students brainstorm and write their own definitions, sharing them with the class. When someone alludes to the romantic overtones in the term, ask him or her to describe the feeling. List these on the board and then use them to help the class identify other passions. "What else makes you grin? What other situations make your heart race? What else do you do that makes you lose track of time?" And so on.

Activities:

As a group, think of words that could be substituted for *passion* or that convey the same feelings. Examples: Rapture, bliss, ecstasy, euphoria, exaltation, something that makes you go "aha!" Learning to recognize the objects, events, or situations that make you feel like this is an important step toward self-knowledge.

English/Language Arts:

Have students use the list of passions they identified on page 29 to write an essay on their ideal day—one that involves as many of their favorite experiences as possible. Letitia's day, for example, might include winning a political debate while wearing her red shoes; hearing *The Star-Spangled Banner* at the start of a Lakers' game; eating chocolate during a sad movie; and walking home in a thunderstorm.

Follow-up:

Occasionally, throughout the course, ask students at the beginning of class, "Did anyone discover a new passion recently?" Be prepared for blank stares and even giggles the first few times you ask this question. Share an experience or feeling you have had or someone has shared with you. You might start this conversation in the staff lunchroom to gather stories and examples, being sure to protect confidentiality. Soon students will start sharing their experiences and ideas. The importance of this is that they will start recognizing the feeling and evaluating what is happening at the time. This simple skill will help with lifelong happiness.

When students began to see themselves for what they wanted instead of what other people expected, it was remarkable.

— Lauren K. DeLay
Family and Consumer Science Teacher
Conestoga Public School
Murray, Nebraska

Optional

Excerpt from *Sonnets From the Portuguese*
by Elizabeth Barrett Browning
Read after completing pages 28–29 in *Career Choices*

Pages 40–42

Work Values Survey

 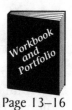

Page 31–37   Page 13–16

Learning objective:

To help students clarify which work values are most meaningful in their own lives.

Presentation suggestions:

Read the directions on page 31 aloud. Allow about 45 minutes for students to complete the survey and score their answers. Stress the importance of answering from their own perspective since there are no right or wrong answers. Remind the class that values (what is important to you) can change over the course of one's life. Periodic re-evaluations are helpful.

To make scoring easier, you may wish to prepare an answer sheet which will eliminate the need to turn pages back and forth.

After students have finished scoring their surveys, have class members identify their top three values. Review the definitions on pages 36 and 37. Remind students that a combination of their values must be considered when choosing a career.

Activities:

In a dialogue with friends and families, students begin to learn their values and passions.

Gender equity activity:

Poll the class to see if there seems to be any relationship between gender stereotypes and values identification. How many males included helping others in their top three values? How many females? How many females had power as their top value versus the males? What about money?

If any trends are evident, discuss why this might be. Young women, for example, are more likely than young men to value helping others. And, quite often, young men will be more comfortable saying they value power than will young women. Why do students think this is so? Is it biological? Societal conditioning?

Is there any relationship between power and helping others? Who would be in a position to help more people, a nurse's aide or a chief surgeon?

To carry this concept further, read the children's picture book *My Way Sally* to the class. Winner of the 1989 Ben Franklin Award, this story is an allegory in which a compassionate foxhound learns that power and leadership can be used to help others. The issues addressed in the Afterword on page 47 of *My Way Sally* would make for lively class discussion.

Follow-up:

Suggest that students have their parents, siblings, or boy/girlfriend also take the work values survey (on a separate piece of paper). Do they have the same work values? Different ones? This can open new fields of communication. It is also interesting to discuss in class how students' values compare to those of these "significant others." Quite often, brothers and sisters have very different work values, even though they were raised by the same parents in the same household. Why do students think this is so?

> *Students created "value totems" and then orally presented their belief systems. Many of the totems were works of art.*
>
> — John Fishburne
> Teacher
> Cascade High School
> Leavenworth, Washington

Of Special Note:

This Work Value Survey is an activity that helps students identify and evaluate the kinds of preferences they have in relationship to career or work choice. For instance, some students will find they value independence, while other may value security. The individuals who value independence will not want to work in an environment that is too restrictive or set-in-its-ways. On the other hand, the student who values security would probably want to find a career where the work is steady and predictable. A Work Value Survey merely helps an individual measure his or her priorities, predilictions, and inclinations.

If you are questioned about teaching "Values," the following quote from *Newsweek* magazine may be helpful:

> *For the ordinary citizen, virtue is easily confused with "values." Since personal values differ, Americans argue over whose values ought to be taught. But "values" is a morally neutral term that merely indicates preference and can be quite banal. To choose vanilla over chocolate is not the same as deciding how to raise children though both express values. A virtue, by contrast, is a quality of character by which individuals habitually recognize and do the right thing. "Instead of talking about family values," says James Wilson of UCLA, "everyone would be better off talking about virtues that a decent family tries to inculcate.*
>
> — Kenneth L. Woodward
> Newsweek magazine, June 13, 1994

Strengths and Personality

Page 38–43   Page 17–19

Learning objective:

To help students identify and understand their work behavioral style as an important trait to consider when evaluating their interests and career options.

Presentation:

You may need to review the definitions on page 39 before students complete that exercise. A number are included in the vocabulary list for this chapter.

Once they have completed the exercises on pages 39, 41 and 42, ask each "style" to go to a different corner of the room. For example, all the students whose style is (a) are dominant, the (bs) are influencing, etc. Then read the descriptions on page 43 together. Many students will nudge each other as they agree with these very basic descriptions.

Point out that the higher the number of responses in each of the letters the more prominent those characteristics might be. Also be sure to remind the students that there are 19 different profiles in this assessment system. Very few people are pure dominance or pure steadiness. Each person has varying degrees of each of these characteristics. Without taking the actual assessment tool (a self-scoring seven-minute activity) it would be hard to know just what your real profile is. The purpose of the activity is to introduce the student to another dimension of personality that should be taken into account when choosing a career and aiming for the highest level of life satisfaction.

For further applications of this theory, see pages 162–165 in *Career Choices* and pages 4/102–105 in this *Instructor's Guide*.

The actual assessment instruments and training are available through Academic Innovations. For more information, you can contact Academic Innovations at (800) 967-8016.

For ordering information on the Personal Profile System, see page 10/17–19 of this *Guide*.

Resources:

William Moulton Marston, *Emotions of Normal People*. Persona Press, Inc. Minneapolis, MN.

Author's Note

In 1983, I attended a week-long training seminar for community agency leaders. During that week, which was sponsored by the IBM Corporation, we were introduced to the latest systems and management techniques. These tools would help us better manage our charitable agencies. Of particular interest to me was the Personal Profile System assessment tool, which major corporations were using to help them determine what jobs employees fit best.

For more than a dozen years, I have used this instrument with my staff, our local Junior League, and in various consulting and personal situations. It is one of the most usable and powerful assessments I have ever seen.

Of particular interest to me was how people dissatisfied in their work were able to change either their job or job description to better fit their own work behavioral style. When this took place, I saw greater job satisfaction and, therefore, higher productivity.

Pretty soon I became somewhat intuitive as to a person's style, which impacted who I hired for specific jobs in my agency. As I counseled young people on career choice, this factor was an important component when suggesting different careers for possible research.

It would be an understatement to say I was "excited" when the Carlson Corporation gave me permission to adapt their research into a simplified evaluation exercise. I feel that this information is extremely important to young people and will give them another means of knowing themselves and making the right choices. Major corporations have used the assessment as an important management tool for 20 years; it is exciting to see it now available to young people.

I recommend that you consider giving the actual assessment to your students. Academic Innovations distributes these assessment tools. For ordering information see page **10**/17–19.

I would also like to recommend use of the Personal Profile System assessment tool (the one used by corporations) for staff development and team building activities with faculty and school personnel. It will be one of the most productive staff training and sharing sessions you have ever conducted. As your team begins understanding everyone's strengths (and weaknesses, too), task force assignments and committee work will become more productive and satisfying for everyone.

And, yes, I have a dream. It is my hope that once instructors learn their own personal style of working and communicating, they will use the assessment tool to identify the style of each of their students. Then, teachers will better understand how each student learns and works and, therefore, be better able to nurture and reward those individual strengths in the academic setting.

— Mindy Bingham
Author, Career Choices

Your Strengths

Page 44–45   Page 20

Learning objective:

To help students identify their strengths and understand how those capabilities can be combined with the strengths of other individuals to create an effective team.

Presentation suggestions:

Review the list of possible strengths and ask the class to add any other traits. Divide the class into groups of four, asking group members to help each other identify their strengths. Then have students individually complete the chart on page 45.

Activities:

Write the list of adjectives from page 44 of *Career Choices* on slips of paper. Cut up with one word per piece of paper. Have each student draw three slips. Using each adjective, students complete the following statement (in writing):

I am _____ when I _____.
       (chosen adjective)

Examples:

I am decisive when I choose my wardrobe.

I am spontaneous when I play with my little brother.

I am sensitive when I help my friends with a problem.

Ask students to share one of their statements at the next class meeting. This exercise should help them realize that, in some circumstances, they are capable of displaying almost any character trait. This knowledge helps to build their confidence and self-esteem.

I had students ask adults at home to list their child's strengths and weaknesses, while I wrote each student a letter telling him or her what I thought their strengths and one of their weaknesses were—in a very positive vein, of course. The students seemed to appreciate the interest, and several had a chance for good interaction at home because of this activity.

— Mary Nan Johnson
9th grade English teacher
Lake Brantley High School
Altamonte Springs, Florida

Teamwork Energizer:

Divide the class into the same groups of four. Make copies of the situations on page **4/26** of this guide and give one copy to each group. Ask them to choose one of the problems described. Then, based on their individual strengths, students must decide who would play what role and what their solution would be.

Ask each group to report back to the class.

This exercise should be useful for getting across the concepts of (1) how various kinds of strengths have different values and (2) the importance teamwork—and shared responsibility—play in occupations in our changing society.

Another Energizer:

Joyce Huff, School-To-Work Coordinator from Montgomery, Missouri enhances her class discussion of teamwork with an activity known as the Egg Drop. The class is divided into teams and each team is directed to deliver a valuable product (an egg) to a customer. Their delivery company is located at the top of a ladder and the customer is located at the bottom. Each team is given the same resources and 10 minutes to prepare their product for delivery. After the activity the class discusses the different delivery methods; the positive and negative team behaviors that are exhibited; and how teams might improve performance and the probability of success.

After either of the above energizers, ask the class to brainstorm the characteristics of an effective team member and list these traits on the board. (Their list will grow throughout this course as they participate in the team-oriented activities).

Once the class finalizes this list, ask each student to evaluate their strengths and characteristics that match those from the list and complete an "effective team member" profile to place in their *Career Portfolio*. Employers are looking for individuals who are good "team members". This profile will come in handy when an employer asks the standard interview question: Describe your strengths.

Using Langston Hughes' poem "Dreams," I have the students replace lines 3 and 4 and lines 7 and 8 with their own creations. Then after they've written their Acrostic Poem, I have them place them back-to-back on construction paper; attached to a wire coat hanger with red yarn and we hang them as mobiles around the room.

— Felicity Swerdlow
    9th Grade English Teacher
    Duarte High School
    Duarte, California

Optional

Pages 43–46

Alice in Wonderland
by Lewis Carroll
Read after completing
pages 28–45 in *Career Choices*

Class Exercise

Before choosing a situation, review the four top strengths of each group member.

Record below.

Name   Strengths

_____   _____

_____   _____

_____   _____

_____   _____

Situation 1

Your group is stranded behind enemy lines. You need to cross five miles of dangerous terrain in order to get back to your side. You are likely to be stopped. The enemy speaks English. What would your group do, and what roles would each group member play?

Situation 2

Your boss has assigned your group to develop a new product and a plan for selling it. What would the product be, and who would be in charge of what?

Situation 3

An industrial polluter is dumping the wastes from its factory into the river that flows through the middle of your lovely city. Your group decides to expose the company's illegal activities and force it to stop poisoning the water supply. What would your group do, and what jobs would you assign to each group member?

Situation 4

Your group decides to hold a fundraiser for the new homeless shelter in your town. What would your group do, and what jobs would you assign to each group member?

Name That Skill

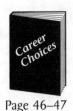

Page 46–47   Page 21

Learning objective:

To help students begin identifying the skills they have developed and to begin the process of developing a skills inventory list.

Presentation suggestions:

Be sure that the class understands the difference between an aptitude, an interest, and a skill.

An "aptitude" is best thought of as potential for being able to do something. A "skill" is competence in doing something. An "interest" is a desire to do something. Some aptitudes, however, especially among young people, may not have been tapped. For example, a student may have an aptitude for math, but, if he or she has not taken the necessary classes, that aptitude is probably not yet a skill. An interest is something a person enjoys, but it does not necessarily involve an aptitude or skill. Millions of people, for example, have an interest in professional football, but few have the necessary aptitude or skills to take part.

Divide the class into small groups where individuals can help each other identify their skills following the exercise on page 47.

Students with low self-esteem may have trouble identifying any of their skills or accomplishments. As a class, identify things any class member could accomplish and break them down into the skills involved.

Also point out that each student does excel in some things.

> *Example*: Getting to school on time may involve coordinating a wardrobe, compiling books and papers, making breakfast or fixing lunch, and negotiating a ride with one's older sister.

If your class is mature and supportive enough, you might try a "hot seat" exercise in which class members take turns voicing the skills of a particular student. Unkind remarks—or deafening silence—can be devastating to the student's self-esteem, so judge your group carefully. It's also helpful to allow a few minutes for the class to consider its answers.

Throughout your course, encourage your students to add to their list of skills as they learn or discover something new. For instance, when you notice a particular skill in a student (someone has convinced you to change a B to an A), be sure to comment—i.e., *Amanda, you are a particularly good persuader. You'll want to add that skill to your skills list.*

This list will help your students develop their transferable skills chart (page 247 of *Career Choices*), an important tool for their career exploration process and strategizing their education and training plan.

Skills Identification

Page 48

Page 22

Learning objective:

To help students identify and understand standard skills categories so they can
a) group skills for the purpose of investigating career alternatives and
b) identify transferable skills.

Presentation suggestions:

Write the list of skills on page 48 on the board and discuss them to make sure students understand the meaning of each term.

Have the class try to think of ways in which each of these skills might be used in a certain activity, such as giving a party.

Once they understand the basic skills, have students add the skills they have from the list at the top of the page to the chart at the bottom of page 48 in the appropriate column.

You might recommend students create an electronic spreadsheet of skills, grouping their skills based on the three categories: data, people and things. That way trends may become apparent that will help students narrow their search for the best careers for them.

To demonstrate that all skills are necessary and valuable, have the class consider all of the skills that go into a project: building a house or publishing a newspaper. The plumber and the painter are as essential as the architect. The reporters may get more glory, but where would they be without the typesetters, truckdrivers, and press operators.

Remind the class that they will continue to acquire new skills throughout their lives.

Activities:

List the skills of several student volunteers on the board. Ask the class to brainstorm potential careers for someone with these skills.

Examples:

Drawing, computing, instructing, reading
Math, persuading: business executive, sales representative, math teacher

Math, persuading, analyzing, playing the saxophone
Small business owner, sales associate in a music store, math/band teacher, real estate agent.

In a rapidly changing workplace understanding the application of transferable skills as it relates to career planning is important. Many workers will have sequential careers (a series of different careers throughout a lifetime). To demonstrate this, share this scenario with your students.

Robin (the student in the second example above) was a sales associate in the local music store while working her way through college. Upon graduation she took a job at the local high school as the music and band teacher. Unfortunately, the music program was cut due to budget deficits. Luckily, because of her excellent math, Robin was able to transfer into the math department. Upon retirement from education she studied for her broker's license and started her own real estate company.

Look again at the students' brainstorming session. Choose one of the examples and ask small groups to create a scenario similar to the one above.

Follow-up:

Interest and aptitude tests can be helpful in skills identification. If your school does not provide them, you may at least want to inform students that they are available elsewhere. Young people can especially benefit from these tests since they may open up whole new fields for exploration.

Mental aptitude tests usually measure verbal, math, and reasoning abilities. Physical aptitude tests measure things like finger dexterity and manual dexterity.

The Kuder interest inventory helps determine suitable career categories by asking students to identify which of three items they like most and which they like least. COPs, another interest inventory, asks students to indicate their feelings about given statements ("like a lot" to "don't like at all"). In addition to determining job categories, this inventory lists specific jobs for which the student may be suited.

Resources:

Kuder: Science Research Associates, 1540 Page Mill Road, Palo Alto, CA 94304.

COPs: California Occupational Preference System, Edits, P.O. Box 7234, San Diego, CA 92107.

Other well-known career interest inventories include:

Harrington-O'Shea Career Decision-making System: American Guidance Service, Publishers' Building, Circle Pines, MN 55014.

Ohio Vocational Interest Survey: Psychological Corporation, 555 Academic Court, San Antonio, TX 78204.

Strong-Campbell Interest Inventory: Consulting Psychologists Press, 577 College Avenue, Palo Alto, CA 94306.

Roles, Occupations, and Vocations

Page 49

No Workbook
Page

Learning objective:

To help students identify and evaluate their roles, occupations, and vocations.

Presentation suggestions:

With the class, review the definitions for each term on page 49. Point out that this may be the easiest ring to complete on their charts, since what you do is much more obvious than who you are.

Activities:

Divide the group into pairs and have them introduce each other to the class without using roles, occupations, or vocations. Instruct the rest of the class to respond with whistles or boos if any titles (student, sister, basketball player, or whatever) sneak into the introduction. It sounds easy, but it's not. When a hundred highly educated, professional people came together and tried this experiment, they found it extremely frustrating. If it seems more appropriate in your classroom, you could have students introduce themselves instead of dividing into pairs.

Even though we usually define ourselves by what we do, it is important that students realize this is only a portion of who we are. It is a measure of self-esteem to be able to identify and value the traits that make us unique. Then, no matter what a person's occupation, he or she will feel confident of holding a special place in the world.

I had students make a dream catcher to go along with chapter 2. They enjoyed this project and I learned a lot about their dreams and what is important to them.

— Kathy Yesensky
JTPA Coordinator
Camp Fire Boys and Girls
San Bernardino, California

Chapter Follow-up:

Once this exercise is complete, ask the students to turn back to page 27 in *Career Choices* and, in a different color ink, write the additional characteristics they've identified while working through Chapter 2.

As a homework assignment, ask each student to choose three heroes/heroines (present-day or historical figures). In class, ask them to complete a bull's eye chart for one figure they've chosen. When the chart is complete, ask the students to underline characteristics that parallel their own chart and to circle those characteristics on the hero's or heroine's chart they would like to acquire as they mature and gain experience.

Once this is done, write this statement on the board:

> *"The people we admire most are a reflection of our inner selves."*
>
> — Joseph Campbell

Do your students agree or disagree with this statement? If many of the characteristics on their hero's or heroine's charts are either underlined or circled, this could be accurate.

I have students identify their heroes after the section on values. Then we compare to determine if their values coincide.

— Marianne Bryan
Science Teacher
Thomas Jefferson Middle School
Jefferson City, Missouri

With our theme, "Search for Identity," we use the mandala to show each student's "sun side" and "shadow side." After that search for self, they can better understand characters such as Mitty ("The Secret Life of Walter Mitty") and Loisel ("The Necklace"). Also, their identity poems were great and their poetry was so beautiful that some were published.

— Claudia Gerhardt
English Department Chair
Hillside Junior High School
Boise, Idaho

Message Center

Page 50–53   Page 23–24

Learning objective:

To make students more aware of the messages—verbal and otherwise—they get from society and from significant people in their lives, and to help them understand how these messages can affect the way they feel about their future or their potential.

Presentation suggestions:

If students become aware of the messages they are getting from their friends, family, or the world at large, they will be better able to base decisions about their future on their own desires and abilities. Discuss this concept and then ask students to complete the exercise on their own.

Activities:

Ask a school counselor or psychologist to talk with the class about this topic.

Invite a panel of parents to complete the exercise. Then have the panel tell the class how the messages they were given had an impact on their career and life choices.

Discuss in class the messages society gives individuals based on their gender, race, age, physical appearance, physical ability, social status, economic status, intellectual capacity and educational achievement.

Compositions:

"The Person Who Has Most Affected My Life."

"The Brainwashing of the American Mind: How Media Impacts Our Culture."

Debate:

"Does society give girls and boys different messages?"

If you ask a group of students to debate this question, do not put all boys on one side and all girls on the other. Be sure each side is co-ed.

Optional

Pages 61–68

Life
by Nan Terrell Reed
Read after completing page 52 in *Career Choices*

Excerpt from *Self-Reliance*
by Ralph Waldo Emerson
Read after completing page 53 in *Career Choices*

Understanding Others

Learning objective:

To help students learn to differentiate between individuals based upon their traits and motivations. At the same time to help students understand that employers are evaluating them on these topics as well.

Presentation Suggestions:

Success in the workforce not only requires understanding ourselves but understanding the traits and motivations of others. Now that your students have completed an identity inventory for themselves, remind them they have the tools for evaluating friends and associates.

Activities:

Ask your students to brainstorm situations when the ability to evaluate traits and motivations is valuable.

> Hiring of employees
> Choosing a boyfriend/girlfriend
> Making committee assignments

We've included a *Character Analysis Worksheet* on page 4/35 that can be copied for a variety of classroom projects. Suggest students use this as a prompt to help them get to know someone better. They'll want to ask questions and observe an individual's actions as they relate to the rings of the bulls eye chart and the six questions below.

Energizer:

Divide the class into pairs. Ask each pair to roleplay a dialogue between two individuals considering going into business together. Point out that choosing the right business partner may be as important as selecting the right marriage partner. Suggest that students refer to the *Character Analysis Worksheet* on page 4/35 for ideas about the type of questions to ask. You may want to brainstorm how the questions could be rephrased to elicit a certain response. This could be assigned as a written follow-up assignment.

Another Energizer:

Ask a mature student population to complete a *Character Analysis Worksheet* for a hypothetical drug dealer. When completed, review the worksheets in class and ask if this is the type of individual they want to have in their life? Explain that while this is an extreme example of a negative and destructive personality, it is worth analyzing in writing because the facts are glaring.

Optional

I Know Why the Caged Bird Sings
by Maya Angelou
Sympathy
by Paul Laurence Dunbar
Read after completing pages 28–53 in *Career Choices*

Pages 47–60

Character Analysis

English/Language Activity:

Throughout the course, you might include the *Character Analysis Worksheet* on the following page with each reading assignment. It can be used in a variety of ways:

a. Ask students to complete the worksheet for their favorite character.

b. Choose three to five main characters. Divide the class into small groups to analyze one or all of them using the worksheet.

Writing Fiction:

When asking students to write fiction, suggest they use the worksheet to develop their character(s) before they begin to write.

For explanations of each of the concepts on the Character Analysis Worksheet refer to the following pages in the text Career Choices:

Bull's Eye Chart: *page 27*
Question 1: pages 15–16
Question 2: pages 18–21
Question 3: page 20
Question 4: pages 66–71
Question 5: pages 196–227
Question 6: pages 60–61

For the author, character analysis is an essential task. Most great stories and screenplays have wonderful character development. However, remind students it is a vital skill for everyone to have as we choose our friends and associates.

Brainstorm relationships that require this in-depth analysis.

Examples:	Employer	Employee
	Spouse	Mentor
	Best friend	Business partner

Character Analysis Worksheet

Character _____ Story _____

```
                    ┌─────────────────────┐
                         Name

                        Passions

                        Values

                  Personality and
                     Strengths

                  Skills and Aptitudes

                  Roles, Occupations
                    and Vocations
```

1. Why do they work?

_____

2. How would they define success?_____

_____

3. How do they make decisions?_____

_____

4. How balanced is their lifestyle?_____

_____

5. What limitations, either self-imposed or societally imposed, do they face? _____

_____

6. What is their mission in life?_____

_____

Instructor's Notes:

Chapter 3

Lifestyles of the Satisfied and Happy

The next five chapters of this book are meant to help students answer the question "What do I want?" It's not an easy task. Perhaps that is why most career and life planning books devote more time to getting what you want than to determining what that is.

Establishing and consolidating identity, and then setting goals based on that identity, are essential parts of making a career choice. Without these preliminary steps, it is impossible to choose wisely. Students are likely to base their decisions more on what their friends or parents want them to do or what their favorite TV character does than on what will be most satisfying for them.

In this chapter, students are asked to consider their ideal lifestyle. While career, family, leisure activities, friends, and spiritual concerns are part of everyone's lifestyle, each element's importance is something the individual must determine for him—or herself.

Career choice has a huge impact on the other aspects of lifestyle. In fact, for many people, lifestyle is determined in large part by career. Therefore, we think it is essential that students give careful consideration to the way they want to live before deciding on a career path.

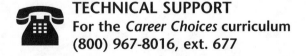

TECHNICAL SUPPORT
For the *Career Choices* curriculum
(800) 967-8016, ext. 677

Maslow's Triangle

Page 56–59   Page 26

Learning objective:

To teach students Maslow's hierarchy of needs and help them understand its impact on their identity and self-esteem.

Presentation suggestions:

Offer an overview of Maslow's triangle, explaining how survival needs must be met before a person can be concerned about safety; how people must feel safe before they can care about social needs; how they seek esteem when their social needs have been met; and how, finally, they can become self-actualized.

Discuss the difference between a *want* and a *need*. Many people, especially those with low self-esteem, do not see anything beyond the most basic means of survival as legitimate needs for themselves. Explain that everyone needs—and has a right to expect or ask for—respect, compassion, companionship, enjoyable experiences, acceptance by others and by oneself.

Activities:

Have students complete the exercise on page 59 on their own. Once they have identified where they are on Maslow's triangle, ask them to begin thinking how they can continue to move up the triangle. What support can they seek? What action can they take? The rest of this course should help them identify possibilities.

Note of caution:

If you are dealing with a high-risk population, it will become very apparent to the learners that they are stuck at the bottom rungs of the triangle. Take extra time with this group or these individuals. Talk about possible plans for feeling safe and secure, getting support, and gaining control over their lives. If appropriate, suggest privately that some students might like to see a school counselor.

Since this section has the potential to identify individuals who may need extra counseling and support, discuss how you should handle this with your principal and counselor ahead of time so you can respond to a student's needs immediately.

Reading assignment:

The fable *Pandora's Box*. Afterward, discuss how hope drives us to improve our lives.

How Do You Want To Be Remembered?

Career Choices
Page 60–61

Workbook and Portfolio
Page 27

Learning objective:

To help students identify an overall goal or mission for their lives.

Presentation suggestions:

Explain to the class that people have a strong need to be identified with something that is "bigger than themselves." Allow students two or three days to think about this assignment. It's something that requires some thought. Remind students that this is a very personal assignment, not something they should decide with a group of friends. Remind them, too, that their goal or mission may change over time.

Activities:

Invite three "self-actualizers" from the community—preferably senior citizens—to talk with the class about their mission in life; how and when they chose it; the sacrifices they've made as a result; and how they would advise a young person. Be sure to tell the guests what you want them to talk about a few days ahead of time so they can be prepared. If possible, invite a variety of people as your guests: an activist, someone with a high profile in the community, a successful businessperson, and a private person with a satisfying personal life.

English/Language Arts:

Complete the activity described on page 4/41. Ask for volunteers to share their letters. Take a poll. What percentage of students wrote about something they did or something they accomplished? What percentage wrote about an accomplishment in a career sense?

> *One success we have had is with "How Do You Want to be Remembered?" in Chapter 3. In addition to talking about the epitaphs, we have a picture of an ancient Memory Bottle that was discovered in China. After looking at the picture and trying to identify the items in the bottle, we discussed the different ways that different cultures have to remember themselves after their death. Students are then asked to reflect on what they would like their descendants to remember about them. After listing the items vertically on a sheet of paper, they are given the homework assignment to create a memory bottle (either visual or written).... The "bottles" brought in by most students were far beyond my expectations. Some students used arts and crafts tools to create a masterpiece.*

— Sharon Hurwitz
English Teacher and Technology Facilitator
Bethel High School
Hampton, Virginia

Follow-Up:

Students will be asked to reiterate their mission in life at the very end of the book. At that time, turn back and again administer the exercise that follows, *Looking into the Future.*

I began my unit, "My Dream: Why and How?" by doing a hands-on activity. My students developed huge collages or posters to represent their dreams for their lives, and because I do a unit on aging (using the poem "Warning" from When I Grow Old, I Shall Wear Purple as a springboard) I ask them to project dreams for an entire lifetime. I display these and refer back to them for the entire year. At the end of the year, we discuss these initial dreams and note any changes. The dreams are also identified in terms of the Maslow hierarchy. Are the students closer to self-actualization now? Usually the answer is yes! My students' most common observation: "For the first time, I feel a class actually relates to me. I can use this 'stuff' in my life..."

— Sarah Marsh
12th grade Applied English teacher
Burley High School
Burley, Idaho

When using "I Shall Not Pass This Way Again" we had our students write their own version as suggested on page 73 of **Possibilities.** *Then the students prepared illustrated posters with their poem and we put them up around the room to remind them of the goals they were setting for the year. We extended the activity by recognizing the uniqueness of each student and the student of the week program.*

— Suzanne M. Reese
Teacher/Gifted Liaison
R.L. Turner High School
Carrollton, Texas

Optional

Possibilities

Pages 69–71

Growing Older
by R.G. Wells
Read as an introduction to the activity on
page 169 of this *Instructor's Guide*

I Shall Not Pass This Way Again
Read after completing pages 60–61 in *Career Choices*

Looking into the Future

Allow an entire class period for this exercise. Ask students to have paper and pens on their desks before you begin.

Turn down the lights and close the doors and windows. If your room is unavoidably noisy, try to find a quieter one.

Speak slowly and quietly, pausing where indicated. Read the following script aloud.

> Relax and settle into your chair. Place your feet flat on the floor. Close your eyes. Clear your mind by imagining the space between your eyes. (Pause at least 15 seconds)

> Pay attention to your breathing. (Pause) Inhale slowly, filling your lungs with air. (Pause) Exhale slowly. (Pause) (Repeat two more times)

> Take a few slow, deep, deliberate breaths. As you exhale, tell yourself to relax and let go. (Pause long enough for three or four deep breaths)

> Feel your body relax (Pause) from your face all the way down to your legs and toes. (Pause) Feel the pleasant warm and tingly feeling of relaxed muscles. (Pause)

> Now project yourself into the future. (Pause) You see calendar pages flipping. (Pause) It's 2004. (Pause) The year 2005. (Pause) 2010. (Pause) 2020. (Pause) 2030. (Pause) How old are you now?

> The calender continues to flip. Stop the calendar at the year you plan to retire.

> You are there now. Take a look around. (Pause) Where are you? What is the setting? (Pause) Who is there with you? Who are the important people in your life? (Pause) Look in a mirror. What do you look like? (Longer pause)

> You hear the doorbell ring. When you go to the door, a mail carrier hands you a letter. You open the letter. It is from someone important to you, commending you, thanking you, and praising you. You feel very good about this letter. (Pause) You feel successful, (Pause) fulfilled, (Pause) and acknowledged. Enjoy that good feeling for a moment. (Pause 30–60 seconds)

> What does the letter say? (Pause a minute or two)

> Now open your eyes and, without saying a word, pick up your pen. . .(Wait until everyone picks up their pen) and write that letter. Begin now.

Note to Teachers: Many authors and writers put themselves into a trancelike state in order to create. They become immersed in the time and place they are writing about, closely identifying with their characters. This exercise may provide your students their first experience with this "altered," creative state. After the students have turned in their letters, discuss this part of the creative process. Ask students how they felt during the exercise, and whether they have ever experienced this "altered," creative state before.

Components of Lifestyle

Page 62–63   Page 28

Learning objective:

To teach students to project into the future and to realize the diverse lifestyle options open to them.

Presentation suggestions:

The necessity of projecting into the future and realizing how today's actions may have long-term consequences is a major theme of this curriculum. This ability has been shown to be a key factor in preventing teen parenting, dropping out of school, and drug use. The present exercise provides another opportunity for students to practice this skill.

Explain the importance of defining their desired lifestyle before choosing a career —careers can dictate lifestyles. This will not be an easy exercise for most students; explain this *after* they have attempted completion. Instruct them not to be frustrated if they cannot finish in one sitting. Students may need to come back to this as they work through the remainder of the book, adding elements or readjusting their plans. Stress, too, that it is a good idea to re-evaluate their lifestyle goals throughout their lives.

You may need to remind students that they'll need to draw on their fantasies and imaginations to complete this exercise. This is the first step in creating a vision. (Remember the formula for success: Vision plus Energy equals Success.)

Composition:

Once the chart on page 63 is complete, ask them to write an essay *"A Day in My Life in _____" (year)*. Choose a year when students will be between the ages of 30 and 45.

Debate:

Which should come first—lifestyle choice or career choice?

Happiness is a
Balanced Lifestyle

Page 64–65

No Workbook
Page

Learning objective:

To help students identify the components of a balanced lifestyle.

Presentation suggestions:

Discuss the various concepts of a balanced lifestyle as described on pages 64 and 65.

Gender equity activity:

The class debates which worker would have the most options for parenting, someone in a structured job with specific hours or someone who is self-employed and directs their own hours.

Reading Assignment:

Having Our Say: The Delany Sisters' First 100 Years, by Sarah and A. Elizabeth Delany with Amy Hill Hearth, Dell Publishing, New York, NY 1994.

In *Having Our Say*, Bessie, age 101, and her sister Sadie, age 103, share humorous and poignant anecdotes of the last 100 years. This inspiring memoir offers a rare glimpse into the early Civil Rights movement and the lives of women of achievement and wisdom.

The Modified Maslow Triangle

Career Choices

Page 66–69

Workbook and Portfolio

Page 29

Learning objective:

To help students understand and identify their needs and to appreciate the desirability of having a balanced internal and external, personal and professional, private and public life.

Presentation suggestions:

Present the modified triangle as described in the book. If students grasped the meaning of the Maslow triangle discussed earlier, this new concept should not be too difficult. Make sure they understand the difference between external and internal needs. Emphasize that it is quite possible to be at different levels on each side of the triangle. That, in fact, is how to determine if a life is out of balance.

Break the class into small groups. Ask each group to discuss Emma's and Isaac's problems and try to find solutions for them. Then have the groups evaluate Joanie's lifestyle, discuss what she might do to bring her life back into balance, and determine the trade-offs she might have to make.

Resources:

Mindy Bingham and Sandy Stryker, *More Choices: A Strategic Planning Guide for Mixing Career and Family.* Advocacy Press, 1987. See ordering information on page 10/17–19.

Throughout the curriculum we've adopted social studies lessons in anthropology, geography, sociology, psychology, etc. to enhance the text work. For example, in the "Who Am I?" unit, we explored personality theories in addition to the Maslow's Triangle activity.

— Mark Yanowsky
Social Studies/Careers Instructor
North Monterey Co. High School
Castroville, California

Optional

Possibilities

Red Geraniums
by Martha Haskell Clark
Read after completing pages 66–69 in *Career Choices*

Pages 74–75

What About Your Life?

Page 70–71   Page 30

Learning objective:

To personalize the balanced lifestyle evaluation process and help students realize the effect outside forces can have on a person's life.

Presentation suggestions:

Ask students to review the questions at the top of the page and write a paragraph about their current situation before shading the triangle to represent the balance in their own lives.

Activities:

Have students interview a parent or another adult, then write a paragraph about this person's lifestyle and shade in a triangle to represent the balance.

As a class, talk about the chart for a homeless person. Obviously, he or she must be solely concerned with basic survival needs. What causes homelessness? There are both personal (drug abuse, emotional illness) and societal causes. Have the class discuss some of the latter.

Examples:

Lack of educational opportunities

Welfare "reform

Scarcity of unskilled jobs

The minimum wage as it relates to the cost of housing

Inadequate facilities or programs to deal with the chemically addicted or the emotionally ill

Decreasing numbers of low-cost rooming houses because they are torn down to make room for office buildings

Can the class imagine how societal issues could have an impact on their lifestyle?

What happens when a pregnant woman works for a company that does not offer extended maternity leave?

What if a working single parent can't find affordable, competent childcare?

What happens if someone who can't afford or doesn't qualify for medical insurance becomes seriously ill?

What if a person working at the best job he or she can find doesn't earn enough to rent an apartment?

English/Language Arts:

After the above discussions, ask students to write a fictional account in the first-person narrative form of a homeless individual's typical day.

Instructor's Notes:

Chapter 4

What Cost This Lifestyle?

Students are likely to know that any given lifestyle has financial costs. Like many adults, however, they have probably not considered the psychological costs, or the costs in terms of commitment to a given career. The goal of this chapter is to instill an understanding of *all three* costs. Emphasis should be on the importance of finding the balance best suited to each individual.

Working through the exercises in this chapter, students should begin to see the relationships between these different aspects. For example, someone wanting a career that will support a lavish lifestyle must usually be willing to make huge commitments in terms of time and/or education.

Similarly, a career that offers a great deal of psychological satisfaction may not always be the one with the biggest financial payoff.

As we move into a new century, many people are finding that financial success alone is not all it was promised to be.

Optional

An expanded version of the Budget exercise from *Career Choices* text

Pages 12–88

Optional

The Mills of the Gods
Read after reading the Ivy Elms' story on pages 74–75 in *Career Choices*

Pages 76–79

Your Budget

Page 77–94   Page 32–43

Learning objective:

Before they can make a wise career decision, students must take into account the cost of living. This exercise should give them a realistic view of the financial considerations that will be important when deciding on a career path. It should also start them thinking about their own financial priorities. Do they really want that expensive sports car? How important are exotic vacations? If they had to choose one or the other, which would it be? Are they willing to work hard enough to have either or both?

Presentation suggestions:

This exercise can be approached in different ways. If you have the time, it is well worth doing a thorough, investigative job in which students come up with their own figures. If time is at a premium, however, students can simply use the charts provided to come up with generally accurate figures.

Go over the exercise in class beforehand to make sure students understand what they should do and how to go about it. As an example, it may be helpful to complete the exercise as a class, creating a composite family, otherwise known as budget-by-consensus. To do this, complete each section, soliciting input from the class, and try to come up with figures that represent the average lifestyle expectations of the class.

Then, as students complete their own budget, you may want to review them section by section, stopping each time to discuss and brainstorm possibilities.

This is an extremely important assignment. Budgets are much more realistic and manageable when presented and communicated in written form. Once students have experienced this written activity, they are going to be much more adept at it as adults.

If you do decide to take the more thorough route, you will probably want to bring in classified sections from local newspapers, catalogs from major department stores, utility bills, and other resources for class reference. Students can use these to determine the cost of appropriate housing, transportation, equipment, furnishings, and the like. They may get other figures by asking parents or other adults, and checking prices in stores.

Having calculators available would also be helpful.

Optional

Pages 12–88

For the most detailed version of the budget exercise, you will want to use *Lifestyle Math: Your Financial Planning Portfolio.*

Lifestyle Math:
Your Financial Planning Portfolio

We hope you think this budget activity is a critical component to your course efforts. Educators and parents alike tell us this is a life altering activity for most young people. Attitudes improve. Students become more focused and motivated. Math studies take on new meaning, and, education as a whole becomes a desired and valued commodity. Your students will no longer have to wait to experience the costs of living on their own to understand how important a good education is today.

If you have the time and the resources, we recommend the addition of the workbook, *Lifestyle Math*, for each of your students. This expanded version of the budget exercise clearly demonstrates the link between education and life satisfaction, thus making math a relevant and essential subject that must be mastered. This one hundred-page math problem walks students through the process of developing a budget for their desired lifestyle when they are 29 years old. Along the way, students learn important economic formulas and mathematical equations they will use throughout their lives.

You can team with the math department to present this important material or you can present it yourself. Instructors of all disciplines who teach *Career Choices* find they enjoy teaching this unit. They include:

- Careers educators

- Teachers of freshman orientation courses

- English language arts instructors

- Business and economics teachers

- Family and consumer science teachers

- Special populations instructors and program directors

For more details on *Lifestyle Math* and its internet enhancement turn to pages **2/15** to **2/20**.

Internet Enhancements for the Budget Exercise

Better yet, on www.careerchoices.com you'll find a variety of resources that will help your students with their budget planning. This Internet enhancement to the *Career Choices* curriculum includes links and lessons for each of the following pages of the textbook:

PPage 78—Housing

- *Table:* Today's home mortgage interest rates
- *Calculator:* Factoring your monthly mortgage payment
- *Calculator:* Factoring how much house you can afford
- *Calculator:* An individualized estimate of the cost of homeowners insurance
- *Calculator:* An individualized estimate of the cost of renters insurance
- *Calculator:* Should you buy a home or should you rent? (basic)

Page 80—Transportation

- *Search:* Finding the "blue book" value of a particular car
- *Calculator:* Finding the current auto loan interest rate
- *Calculator:* Factoring your monthly payments on a car loan
- *Table:* Side-by-side comparisons of any four new car models
- *Commentary:* The pros recommendations among used car models based on vehicle type
- *Informational:* Weigh the pros and cons of purchasing a new vs. used car
- *Table:* Environmental Protect Agency's (EPA) listing of the 20 best models of cars based on miles per gallon (MPG) and the 20 worst
- *Table:* The operating costs of the 10 top selling cars
- *Interactive Quiz:* Help with learning the terms related to auto insurance

Page 83—Clothing

- *Database:* Sample costs from online catalogs of various children's clothing manufacturers
- *Database:* Sample costs from online catalogs of various adult clothing manufacturers

Page 88—Childcare

- *Calculator:* The cost of raising a child to young adulthood based on lifestyle projections (includes childcare figures in the calculations)

Page 89—Savings

- *Calculator:* How much do you need to save to send your child to college (basic)
- *Calculator:* How much do you need to save to send your child to college (advanced)
- *Calculator:* How much do you need to fund your retirement account in order to live the lifestyle you envision at retirement

Page 93—What Salary will Support this Lifestyle?
- *Tables:* Comparison of wages between different occupations
- *Tutorial:* Information on federal tax withholding
- *Calculator:* Calculating take-home pay
- *Tutorial/Calculator:* Estimate taxes due based on income, deductions, etc. Learn important financial terms related to the tax structure (advanced)

Page 116—An Investment in Education . . . Yields Dividends for a Lifetime
- *Tables:* Charts comparing salary levels with education levels
- *Calculator:* How does your earning potential compare with the "power players"

Page 120—Ask Someone Who's Been There
- *E-mail Interview:* Seek out career information by communicating with an expert in your interest area via e-mail
- *Tables*: Charts comparing salary levels with education levels

And best of all, students can use this Internet site at school or at home, as long as they have an Internet-connected computer available. You'll want to check out the latest resources by visiting www.careerchoices.com and signing in as a visitor. The index has over 80 lessons and activities. You'll find more detailed information beginning on page 7/6 of this manual.

 Throughout this section of the manual, you'll see this logo at the bottom of certain pages. This indicates Internet enhanced lessons are available on www.careerchoices.com. For a detailed index of the lessons at the time of the printing of this *Instructor's Guide*, see page 7/11. You'll want to go online to see the most current index because of the growing and changing nature of the Internet. As we find new and better resources, we include them or substitute them for current lessons. Go to the Visitor Section for information about membership and licensing fees.

Checklist of Resources for Budgeting Exercise

Depending on how extensive you want to make this exercise, the following items will be helpful:

☐ One complete classified section from the newspaper for each student in the class

☐ Sample utility bills

☐ Catalogs of major department stores, such as Sears

☐ Sample weekly food bills for families of various sizes

☐ Vacation brochures

☐ Calculator(s)

☐ Internet access

Author's Note

Between 1976 and 1983, I taught evening classes at a local private college for soon-to-graduate seniors. One of the activities I used was a version of this budget exercise. I was always struck with the response I got from my students. It was usually one of shock and, because they were just completing a degree in a lower-paying helping profession, sometimes anger. "Why didn't someone do this with us before?" they'd ask bewildered. They had just completed a degree yet, for many of them, the average salary of their chosen profession could not meet their lifestyle expectations.

This is one of the most critical exercises you can do with your students...the younger the better. We have successfully completed a version of this activity with students as early as the sixth grade. Make it interesting, hands-on, and fun. Don't hurry through it. It will probably be one of the favorite activities of the course and, perhaps, one of the most important.

— Mindy Bingham
Author, Career Choices

USB Bank in Washington State sent a package containing checks, deposit slips, check registers, lists of bills, etc. for the students.

— Alyson Washington
Teacher
Chewelah Alternative School
Chewelah, Washington

Instructor's Notes:

Family Profile

Before they begin to develop their budgets, students must project themselves into the future. After all, the exercise is intended to help them make career decisions. Emphasize that this budget should be based on the way they would like to live after they have completed their education and are working at the job of their choice. Students should assume they are at least 29 years old for the purposes of this exercise.

The cost of living also depends to a large extent on the number of people in the household. Do students plan to be married? Will they have children? How many? What ages?

Finally, since costs vary greatly depending on where they will be living (the budget of an executive in Manhattan will be very different from that of a farmer in Iowa, for example), students must also consider this aspect of their future lives.

Encourage students to fantasize a bit here. They should consider the way of life they think would be most rewarding, not simply the lifestyle they think is most probable for someone in their circumstances. Where would they really like to live? What would be their ideal family? What kind of home would they have? Where would they vacation?

A word of caution before you begin. Because the lifestyles of the most visible individuals tend to be lavish, try to encourage students to be somewhat realistic in their projections. At the same time, respect the students who insist they are going to have a lifestyle very different from their family's. One of the purposes of this total curriculum is to show how, with education, planning, and hard work, individuals can realize their dreams.

Once students decide on their future families, you may choose to introduce a hitch into the planning process. Tell them that, for whatever reason, they are suddenly single. In most cases, they will find themselves single parents. If they look at you aghast, remind students that nearly 50 percent of today's children are raised in single-parent families at some point in their lives.

This aspect of the exercise is of particular importance to the females in your class. Otherwise, many will complete the exercise assuming they will be married when, in reality, a high percentage will be the sole support of their families.

> *When starting the budget section, the kids picked out where they wanted to live in the U.S. (p. 77, **Career Choices**). Then they wrote to that city's Chamber of Commerce asking for info on that city. We went to the computer lab, they typed it up, and I mailed them. They loved receiving the responses. I loved it—it combined formal letter writing, computer skills, civics, and careers.*

— Debra Kuperberg
Special Education Teacher
San Gabriel High School
San Gabriel, California

Housing

Ask students to consider their ideal living situation. Would they own or rent? Have a mansion or a modest apartment? Once they've decided, have them go to the classified ads to find something suitable and see how much it costs. The charts on page 79 will be helpful.

To figure utility costs, ask students to brainstorm with you all the expenses that fall into this category. As a homework assignment, ask them to bring in sample utility bills from their own families.

Sample utility categories:

Gas	Water
Electric	Trash
Heating fuel	Cable
Phone	

www.careerchoices.com

You'll want to review the various online mortgage calculators and tables available through www.careerchoices.com. Turn to page 4/50 and examine the list under *Page 78—Housing* for those available at the time of printing of this guide. To see the most current enhancements, you can sign in as a registered user or visitor. Click on *Teacher* and once you sign in, click on *Index to all Lessons* on the sidebar.

Note the CareerChoices.com Logo in the bottom corner of this page. You'll see these throughout the budget exercise (pages 4/55–64). When you do, review the available Internet resources on www.careerchoices.com and build them into your lessons. This dynamic resource will not only motivate your students but also provide an important lesson on the availability of quality information on the Internet. Information is power!

Activity:

Invite a realtor or mortgage broker to speak to the class on the costs of housing in the community and how to finance the first-time purchase of a home.

Optional

 Pages 14–31

Transportation

Students should choose their desired mode of transportation, considering their living situation as well as their dreams. If they're planning to live in an area without much public transportation, for example, some kind of vehicle is probably necessary. City dwellers with access to taxis, buses, or subways, on the other hand, might not want or need to own a car.

If they feel the need to own a car, once again refer them to the classified section of the newspaper. Ask them to choose a make and model and figure the monthly payments.

What do they project will be their mileage per month? Once they have an idea of this figure, the chart on page 81 should help with factoring estimated gas and maintenance costs.

We had loan officers from local banks take students through the loan process after they had chosen a car, house, and occupation they'd be interested in pursuing. This was extremely beneficial.

— Linda Wulff
Chairperson, Communication Department
Waupun High School
Waupun, Wisconsin

Optional

Pages 32–42

Clothing

Students are probably more aware of clothing costs than they are of any other expense. However, their present wardrobes may not be appropriate for the kinds of jobs they hope to hold. They must take into consideration whether they'll need a uniform, special work clothes, or professional clothing. They may not have any idea how much children's clothing costs, or how quickly a child can outgrow a pair of shoes. You may be able to provide some of this information, or perhaps students with younger brothers and sisters or nieces and nephews can get figures to share with the class.

For their own clothing, remind students that they will not need to buy an entire wardrobe each year.

Activity:

This is an opportunity to talk about workplace dress codes, what is appropriate to wear to work, and what to wear to an interview. Business and professional magazines will provide examples for those working in offices and for interviews. You'll want to talk about personal grooming issues as well. Perhaps someone from your Family and Consumer Science department can provide props or advise.

After this discussion, schedule a day where everyone is encouraged to dress as they would for a job interview. Recognize those in class who have made particularly good choices.

Writing assignment:

Ask students to break down their personal annual clothing budget item by item. Have them use either a current budget or their projected budget for this exercise.

Optional

 Pages 43–47

Food

Food costs vary widely, depending on the size of the family, ages of children, and personal preferences. You might ask for volunteers from families of different sizes to bring in grocery receipts to share with the class.

Activity:

Ask students to plan a week's worth of menus for their fictional family. Then prepare a shopping list item by item. As a homework assignment ask them to go to the store and price the items on their shopping list.

> *When students were preparing their budgets (p. 84, Career Choices),*
> *I brought in fliers from the local supermarkets. They first had to*
> *prepare a weekly menu, then price out the ingredients using the flyer*
> *(or, for some, a trip to the supermarket). Most appreciated their*
> *mother's efforts and many had to "pare down" their menu selections*
> *(steaks were replaced by Hamburger Helper).*

— Sue Butler
English Teacher
Branford High School
Branford, Connecticut

Sundries

Variations are also possible in this category. You might ask students to consider how much they spend now for such items as deodorant, shampoo, makeup, and how often they get their hair cut. They might ask their parents how often they need to buy toilet paper, soap, laundry detergent, and other sundries.

Activity:

An activity similar to the one in the food section could be completed for sundries, with one change: ask students to complete it for a month's worth of supplies and services.

Optional

Pages 43–63

Entertainment and Recreation

This item can be easily overlooked or carried to an extreme. Ask students to think seriously about the "extras" that they would find most satisfying. What are their hobbies? Their passions?

Optional

Pages 64–67

Vacations

Around this point, students start becoming more cautious as their expense figures begin adding up. So many say, "We don't need a vacation!" This is the time to remind them that vacations are important for their physical and psychological health.

Activity:

Ask a travel agent to visit the class and talk about vacation expenses.

Invite someone to speak to the class about how he or she went to Europe on $50 a day.

Brainstorm as a class ways to have economical vacations such as:

> Camping
>
> Hosteling
>
> House swapping
>
> Visiting friends and relatives

Optional

Pages 68–70

Child Care

Ask students to research monthly costs for each of the childcare arrangements listed on page 88 of *Career Choices*. You may want to divide the class up and give each small group a category to research.

It is important to point out that students should not assume "Grandma" will take care of their children. Failure to budget for this important expense could be disastrous.

Invite a panel of working parents to speak about their strategies for childcare. One panel member should be single so students understand the unique childcare challenges of one-parent households.

Optional

Pages 71–73

Health Care

Refer to the chart on page 94 of *Career Choices* for average healthcare costs for families of various sizes.

Invite an insurance agent in to discuss healthcare costs, pensions, and savings plans.

> *Many of my female students planned not to get married ("didn't want the commitment"), but they also planned children out of wedlock. After the budgeting exercise many said, "I don't think I can afford to have a baby."*

— Linda Fraser
Instructor, Tech Prep program
Edison High School
Minneapolis, Minnesota

Optional

Pages 74–75

Furnishings

Refer students to catalogs of large department stores to get sample costs of furnishings. Students will want to add the computer and electronic equipment they plan to own to this line item.

Activity:

This is a good time to discuss how each new electronic device adds a burden to household budgets. As a group research and brainstorm the 'must have' electronic appliances available in each decade in the last 50 years. Write the following dates on the board. Under each date, write the electronics that the **majority** of households had in that year.

1950	1960	1970	1980	1990	2000
radio	radio				
	TV				
	Hi Fi				

Students will notice that the lists grows longer and longer as the years progress. What has this phenomenon done to household budgets? How have families compensated for the increase in costs? Could this be one of the reasons many households require two incomes to survive? Is there just much to buy?

Savings

Refer to the charts on page 91 of *Career Choices*.

Important: Planning for retirement is important and should be encouraged among young people. You will be doing your students a great service by spending time on this concept.

Activity:

You'll find the retirement calculators on www.careerchoices.com particularly intriguing for your students (or yourself). The magic of compounding interest tax-free over 20, 30 and 40 years is very motivational when viewed as a teenager. Do your students a favor and devote one whole class period in the computer lab to this important experience. Create a couple of scenarios for your students to research, varying when an individual starts making retirement account deposits, the rate of return and the amount deposited each month. See page 100 of *Lifestyle Math* for an example of what depositing $100 per month would earn.

Optional

Pages 80–86

The Savings Book
by Gary Soto

Read after completing page 89 in *Career Choices*

Optional

Pages 76–84

Recommended Reading

The Millionaire Next Door, The Surprising Secrets of America's Wealthy by Thomas J. Stanley, Ph.D., and William D. Danko, Ph.D. Longstreet Press, Atlanta Georgia, 1996

This best seller is a fascinating study of the characteristics and behaviors displayed by individuals and families who are able to amass net assets of at least one million dollars. As to who these people are, the title says it all. Many "millionaires" in the United States don't necessarily live in luxury communities, they are our neighbors and friends; blue collar as well as white collar. The text is easy to read and chock full of interesting details students will love. It will be a launching point for lively discussions and energizing debates.

Miscellaneous

Ask the class to brainstorm other items that might go in this miscellaneous category. See page 84 of *Lifestyle Math* for examples.

Your Budget Profile

Career Choices
Page 92

Workbook and Portfolio
Page 42

Students will total their figures from the previous pages to get the average monthly expenses for their desired lifestyle.

Writing assignment:

Have students write a budget narrative describing, explaining, or justifying each of their line items. *For example:*

Housing:

The cost of a three-bedroom, two-bath home in a nice area of the city is $259,000. Amenities include fenced yard, fireplace, and large family room. It is located in one of the best school districts. Utilities are a moderate expense because of the conservation efforts of my family. The only high expense in this category is the phone bill. My best friend and my mother live out of the state.

Once these papers are complete, ask the students to share their budget figures (pages 92 and 93) and their budget narratives with their parent(s). Some teachers share these documents at a parent teacher conference. With this information, parents can reinforce the next phase of the course: How to prepare for a career that will support this lifestyle.

> *My favorite unit is Chapter Four, "What Cost This Lifestyle?" Your process is easy to understand with brief explanations, and I found your tables to be very realistic. Because this is an English class, I had the students write a paper at the end of the unit explaining what they had learned from the process. Some were wonderful!*

— Dorette Kanengieter
11th and 12th grade English/Language Arts
and Applied Communications instructor
Owatona High School
Owatona, Minnesota

Optional

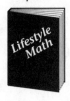

Page 85

What Salary Will Support This Lifestyle?

Page 93   Page 42

Learning objective:

To help students recognize the impact career choice has on personal lifestyle. This activity will help them begin selecting careers that most closely match their personal lifestyle budget.

Presentation:

One final step is required before monthly expenses can be transposed into the salary required to support this lifestyle. Students must factor in taxes withheld from their paycheck to arrive at a figure that equals their gross income. Gross income is the amount listed as salary on career research sites.

The last figure on the page will be very important as they continue the career research process.

Activity:

Spend one or two class periods conducting research at the career center or online. Students will need to compile a list of all the careers and jobs they can find that are interesting and also will support their desired lifestyle. They will want to add this list to their *Career Portfolio* notebook for reference.

My students play a simulation game called "Living On Your Own." They get a job, pay a deposit on an apartment, pay their deposit on utilities, etc. Students clock in each day. A class period is worth eight hours of work. They learn to budget their money because they must pay out-of-pocket, and emergencies each week along with monthly and weekly bills. We devote one day a week to this activity although my students would like to do it every day.

My students can't believe these activities are really English. I remind them that the skills learned in English (reading, writing, speaking and listening) are the skills we are using.

Optional

Pages 86–91

— Linda Spriggs
English Department Chairperson
Lithia Springs High School
Lithia Springs, Georgia

Hard Times Budget

Page 96

Page 43

Learning objective:

To learn to budget the more common way—by having a total figure available and allocating that figure among the line items.

Presentation:

Ask students to review the figure they arrived at on page 93. If this seems beyond what they think they will earn in a year, ask them to research that more appropriate figure and enter it on line (b). Now they must figure their net pay (take home) from this figure. The formula is as follows:

$$\underline{\hspace{3cm}} \div 12 = \underline{\hspace{3cm}}$$
$$\text{(b) monthly salary}$$

$$\underline{\hspace{3cm}} \times 80\% = \underline{\hspace{3cm}}$$
$$\text{(b) monthly salary} \qquad \text{net or take home pay}$$

Depending upon the population you are working with, you might choose to assign this exercise using the figures for the following:

A person earning the minimum wage

A single-parent family living on AFDC
(Aid to Families with Dependent Children)

A single-parent family living on unemployment insurance

I do a scenario unit. Students pick a real life situation from a hat which may involve a single parent, a drop out, a college student, or a lawyer. Each must locate a job in the employment listings of a newspaper, prepare a budget, and go through an interview with me. By starting with real life situations, students realize they don't want the handicap of being a single parent or high school drop out.

— Dana L. Mayers
English teacher
Sequoyah Middle School
Edmond, Oklahoma

Optional

Pages 93–94

Some Sample Budgets

Page 97–101   Page 44–45

Learning objective:

To have students learn to budget the way most people do—by taking a given income and deciding how it should be allocated. An added observation will be the impact of career choice on lifestyle.

Presentation suggestions:

The earlier budget exercise gave students a chance to dream about their future lifestyle, an extremely important thing for them to do. In the real world, though, budgets do not determine income. Instead, it is quite the opposite. In this exercise, students can begin doing something they are likely to become very familiar with later in their lives: deciding how to live within a fixed income. We have presented five stories, each representing a fairly common situation.

> Phyllis is a single parent supporting her two children and herself on her income alone.

> Will is a single person living in subsidized housing provided, in his case, by the military.

> Jeff and Francie are a typical blue-collar couple.

> Carl and Ruth head a double-income professional household.

> Ben and Lynn represent the two-parent, single-income family.

There are two ways to assign the exercise. You could ask students to complete it on their own, or you might break the class into groups and assign a particular budget to each. Group members can spend time discussing how the money should be allotted, and doing necessary research (don't forget the extensive resources on www.careerchoices.com). Then, when the class comes back together, each group can present its budget to the class.

Follow-up:

This is a good time to talk about dual earner families (both individuals work in low skill jobs without a career plan) versus dual career families (each individual has a career plan that focuses on the acquisition of additional skills to upgrade their desirability as an employee).

A Few Words about Poverty

Page 102–103   Page 46

Learning objective:

To recognize the causes of poverty and to reduce the chances of becoming a poverty statistic.

Presentation suggestions:

Review the materials presented in the book in class. Then have students study the statistics on poverty. Ask them to select the statistic they found most startling and write a paragraph suggesting why this condition exists. Have students share their writings with the class. On the board, list any statistic mentioned by a student to see if there is a consensus concerning which facts are most disturbing.

Ask students to answer the questions on page 103, 'Could You Become a Poverty Statistic?'

A word of caution: Be particularly sensitive to students who may be living in poverty. If you think this might present a problem, ask the school counselor to help facilitate this discussion. The important theme of the follow-up discussion should be that planning, energy, and a vision can enable individuals to work their way out of poverty.

Activities:

At the beginning of class, ask students to list the factors they think cause poverty. (Examples: lack of education, too few jobs, high cost of housing, inflation, the changing economy, lack of opportunity to succeed, inability to budget or to live within one's means)

Gender equity activity:

Ask a single parent on AFDC or a panel of single mothers living in poverty to talk with the class about such things as what they thought they were going to be when they were growing up, how they got into their present situation, and, if appropriate, what their plans are for the future.

This activity could be especially powerful for young women in the class. Some may not think it's necessary to prepare for a career—there will always be someone else willing and able to support them. Students of both sexes may feel that poverty is something that happens to other people, never to anyone they know. This activity could be both a cautionary tale and a lesson in empathy.

Composition:

Poverty Is Only a Divorce Away: A National Crisis for Women and Children.

Ask students to come up with recommended solutions.

After this assignment, brainstorm reasons men end up as poverty statistics. One example is that they are replaced in industry by automated machinery or robots.

Debate:

Do men and women experience poverty differently?

One student, who was doing the grocery shopping required for the budget, saw a woman with her child at the store. The student's scenario, chosen in class, seemed similar to this woman. As they both shopped for bargains, the student became aware that the scenario was real. The next day she shared the experience and cried in class. She described the clothing and attitude of the woman. She said she never wanted that scenario for herself, therefore she was never quitting school or having children too soon.

— Dana L. Mayers
Sequoyah Middle School
Edmond, Oklahoma

Optional

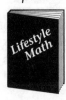

Pages 95–97

Optional

Pages 87–94

Miss Rosie
by Lucille Clifton

Christmas Day in the Workhouse
by George R. Sims

Read after completing page 103 in *Career Choices*

Money Isn't Everything

Page 104–105   No Workbook
Page

Learning objective:

To explore the myth that money can make you happy.

Presentation suggestions:

It's a very common perception among young people: life would be perfect if only they were rich and famous. Statistics and anecdotal evidence, however, indicate that this is not so. Present the information to the class and have them discuss why they agree or disagree with the evidence. Ask students to list rich people or celebrities who have been in the news in recent years because of personal problems that would seem to indicate they are not entirely happy. Examples: Kelsey Grammer (chemical dependency), Darryl Strawberry (chemical dependency), Princess Stephanie of Monaco (divorce), Prince Charles and Princess Diana (adultery and divorce), Elizabeth Taylor (alcoholism and divorce), Kurt Cobain (suicide), Leona Helmsley (felony conviction).

Activities:

Bring in magazine articles or ask students to research and write a short paper based on an interview with a wealthy person who has recently had problems. Have them share their reports in class. The same phrase will probably turn up in interview after interview: money isn't everything.

If you know of a wealthy person in your community who has had to overcome personal tragedy, or who has given up "life in the fast lane" to do meaningful but unglamorous work, you might ask him or her to talk on this subject with the class.

Reading assignment:

The Gift of the Magi, by O. Henry

In this story of a young couple who sacrifice their most precious possessions for each other, how is happiness defined? Students will argue this one!

Optional

Pages 95–102

Gift of the Magi
by O. Henry
Read before you assign *Money Isn't Everything* on pages 104–105 in *Career Choices*

Psychological Costs— Sacrifices Versus Rewards

Page 106–110   Page 46–48

Learning objective:

To help students learn that there are sacrifices and rewards associated with every job and every lifestyle. This exercise should help them evaluate both aspects of any career they are considering, and to decide whether or not it would be a wise choice.

Presentation suggestions:

Discuss the material presented in *Career Choices*, using Bert's story as an example. Ask the class to add to the answers provided if they can. Then break the class into small groups and assign each to discuss Juan, Vincent, Sara, or Rose's story answering the questions that follow. Bring the class back together, and have the groups summarize the story, and report their answers to the questions. Allow discussion time for other students to disagree with a group, or to add to its answers. In summing up, be sure to emphasize how important it is for each student to evaluate his or her own values in conjunction with the careers presented. Students should see that, depending on a person's values, some sacrifices would be devastating, others not too hard to accept. Similarly, some rewards would be well worth any sacrifice for certain individuals, while for others the same rewards would be less than satisfying.

Activities:

Ask students to write a paragraph about the situation of a well-known professional person in a postion they know something about and to answer the questions from this exercise for that individual. Suggested individuals might be the President of the United States, the Governor of your state, or the Mayor of your city.

Have a panel of people in different professions discuss the rewards and sacrifices involved in their jobs and what values are reflected in both areas. Be sure to let your guests know what you want them to talk about ahead of time. They may not have given this much thought.

Have students interview a parent or other adult on this topic.

Encourage students to watch some of the celebrity interview shows on TV, or bring in tapes if you can. In-depth interviews of the Barbara Walters or Mike Wallace variety often bring out this kind of information.

You Win Some,
You Lose Some

Page 111

Page 49

Learning objective:

To help students recognize the rewards and sacrifices of specific careers as they relate to their work values.

Presentation suggestions:

Have students complete the exercise individually, or break the class into small groups to discuss and come to an agreement concerning which work values would be rewarded and which would be sacrificed in each of the careers listed. Follow with class discussion.

Then have students go back and circle any careers that are compatible with their own work values. A compatible career would be one in which at least one of their top values matches the rewards, while none of their top three is listed as a sacrifice.

Students are now beginning to relate their own work values to specific career choices.

Activities:

Have students list five careers they have considered for themselves in recent years, identifying which work values would be rewarded or sacrificed in each job.

> *The students are beginning to see that a career offers more than just an income. The psychological rewards are a new concept for many of them.*
>
> — Linda L. Poznanter
> Careers Teacher
> Oasis High School
> Fallbrook, California

After-Hours Rewards

Page 112–113   Page 50

Learning objective:

To demonstrate that values not satisfied on the job can be met with appropriate after-hours activities. This is an important concept, since few careers will be a perfect fit with a person's top work values.

Presentation suggestions:

After presenting the materials and going over the examples, have students—individually or in pairs—complete the exercise. Discuss as a class. There is likely to be some disagreement. That's okay. The individual's perceptions are likely to be valid for her- or himself.

In the examples presented, a social worker would, of course, meet her or his need to help others. Creativity, too, would come into play through creative problem-solving in crisis situations. To meet a need for power, a social worker might consider being an officer in a community organization or political group.

A computer assembly worker might feel secure about working in the high tech industry. He or she is likely to work with many potential friends. A need to help others might be met through community volunteer work.

As for the rest of the exercise —

A carpenter might satisfy a need for adventure with vacations in the wilderness or with hang gliding or similar sports as hobbies.

A traveling sales representative would need to make a point of being available to his or her family when home, calling in nightly from the road, and perhaps taking family members along on a trip from time to time.

A homemaker might satisfy a need for power by taking a leading role in community activities.

A museum guide might find adventure spending a vacation working on an archaeological dig.

A professor might get recognition from publishing books and articles.

A farmer might find friendship in his or her community or religious groups.

A psychologist might satisfy a need for aesthetics by collecting art or find adventure learning to pilot an airplane.

An accountant might find power by starting his or her own firm or find a creative outlet in painting or piano lessons.

A chemist might gain recognition by giving demonstrations (*á la* "Mr. Wizard") to groups of school children.

A writer might find friendship in a writers' group or workshop.

A veterinarian could find power by taking a leading role in a campaign to save an endangered species.

Activities:

Perhaps the same panel that spoke about rewards and sacrifices could address the question of how they meet some of their other values outside of the work setting.

Discuss the concept that leisure activity is really work—unpaid work perhaps—but nonetheless work. These endeavors meet the human need for meaningful work when that need isn't fully realized in paid employment.

When we were talking about a balanced lifestyle, we talked about hobbies. Students brought in pictures or examples of their hobbies and did a quick five-minute presentation. The kids really enjoyed this. We talked about what needs or values their hobbies satisfied.

— Deb Plantz
Language Arts Teacher
South Tama County High School
Tama, Iowa

An Investment in Education
Yields Dividends for a Lifetime

Page 116–119   Page 51–53

Learning objective:

To demonstrate the financial payoff—over a lifetime—of an investment in education.

Presentation suggestions:

Review the chart on page 116. Does a common thread run through the data presented? One obvious theme is that more education usually means increased earning potential. Be sure to remind the students that this is not a hard and fast rule—there are lots of exceptions—but, in the majority of circumstances, education and training usually correlate with earnings.

Ask students to complete the math on page 117. What is their response to these figures?

A student who expects to be in the workforce 38 years, between the ages of 18 and 65 (taking time out for schooling and raising a family), would have a chart like this:

How many years do you plan to work between the age of 18 and 65?

<u>38</u> years in workforce

Multiply the number of years you plan to be in the workforce by each of the annual salaries listed below to find out how much you would earn over the course of your working life.

$10,000 x <u>38</u> years in workforce = <u>$380,000</u> lifetime earnings

$15,000 x <u>38</u> years in workforce = <u>$570,000</u> lifetime earnings

$20,000 x <u>38</u> years in workforce = <u>$760,000</u> lifetime earnings

$30,000 x <u>38</u> years in workforce = <u>$1,140,000</u> lifetime earnings

$50,000 x <u>38</u> years in workforce = <u>$1,900,000</u> lifetime earnings

What is the difference between a $10,000 and $15,000 annual salary over a lifetime? <u>$190,000</u>

What is the difference between a $10,000 and $20,000 annual salary over a lifetime? <u>$380,000</u>

What is the difference between a $10,000 and $30,000 annual salary over a lifetime? <u>$760,000</u>

What is the difference between a $10,000 and $50,000 annual salary over a lifetime? <u>$1,520,000</u>

Beginning the Planning Process

Learning objective:

To help students recognize that education and training pays off in life satisfaction. This awareness is a critical first-step to their education and training plan.

Presentation:

Have the students complete the Bar Graph on page 118. What do their graphs show? Comments should suggest that time spent on the remainder of their education is short compared to the years they'll spend in the workforce.

Ask the students to complete the worksheet on page 119 using the information from the chart.

Discuss the ratio between years spent in post-high school training, education and years in the workforce. Do the energy and time spent in training seem worth it in the long run?

Portfolio Follow up:

The charts found on pages 116–119 begin a process that will continue through the rest of the course. The information students are gathering and analyzing will culminate in completion of the charts on pages 270–273. These charts show each student's education and training plan from high school through post secondary education and training programs.

Now is a good time to begin talking about education and training alternatives, particularly if you sense your students will struggle getting into college or trade school directly after high school (for financial or academic reasons). Students can take different paths to their ultimate career choice as long as they keep their eye on the goal (vision) and are willing the do what is necessary to achieve that goal (energy).

On page 227 of *Career Choices*, students will have the opportunity to create a chart for a career they find of interest. This chart will detail various careers within their area of interest based on the education and training levels. This alternative career ladder will graphically demonstrate how commitment to education and training pays off.

Careers are listed on index cards along with wages. Students are to calculate how many hours/weeks/months they must "work" to afford something on a "wish" list that they brought to class from the previous day. Later they learn that the cards were color coded by education levels. They quickly see that wages are directly proportional to education.

Optional

Lifestyle Math

Pages 98–99

— Judy F. Miller
Teen Living Teacher
Clinton Middle School
Clinton, Tennessee

Ask Someone Who's Been There

Page 120

Page 54

Learning objective:

To help students gain specific information about the costs and rewards of various careers from people they know through the interview process. This is likely to be more meaningful and to stick with them longer than any information they read in a book.

Presentation suggestions:

While making the assignment, be sure to remind students of the etiquette of interviewing. When asking for the interview, they should clearly indicate its purpose and how much time it will take. If they are interviewing people outside their immediate family or visiting people on the job, it is essential to be punctual, and not to stay any longer than they said they would. After the interview, they should send a brief, handwritten thank you.

As in all interviews, the questions asked by the interviewer will usually solicit responses from the interviewee that take the conversation to other topics or areas. For instance, journalists are always looking for a new lead so they listen and let people talk. This type of interview provides the best and richest information. Encourage your students to ask each question on page 120 and then listen carefully, allowing the interviewee to go off on tangents if they choose. Remind students that the interviewee should be doing 90% of the talking. Because of the nature of these questions, they'll unearth information about a particular job or career that they wouldn't normally find in a book.

When students have completed their interviews, ask them to share what they have learned and add their written notes to their *Career Resource File*.

Career Resource File—Have students create a *Career Resource File* for the careers they investigate throughout this course. In a binder or expandable accordion-style file (8½" X 11") they'll include clippings from newspapers, popular magazine articles, assessments, listings of local resources, notes from interviews, web sites and printouts, industry literature, etc. At the end of the course, ask students to bring in their file to share with the rest of the class.

Follow-up:

Encourage students to keep these questions in mind and to continue to ask them of adults working in other fields as they proceed with their career planning process.

Easier Said Than Done

Page 121

Page 55

Learning objective:

To help students realize that, in order to meet long-term goals, they will have to make some short-term sacrifices, and to provide a decision-making model that will help them keep their goals in mind.

Presentation suggestions:

As a class, discuss long-term and short-term goals in relation to the examples presented. In each case, ask students to circle the long-term goal and underline the short-term goal, and then to make a decision about the best course of action for each individual. Complete the chart at the bottom of the page.

Then ask students to turn back to Chapter 3 and identify two or three of their own long-term lifestyle goals. Have them use the model provided to make some decisions about their own current activities.

Activity:

In class, consider what might have happened if certain historical figures had sacrificed their long-term goals in favor of the short term. First you must decide what those long-term goals were. For example, what if Thomas Jefferson had decided to stay home and work in his garden instead of going to Philadelphia and writing the Declaration of Independence? (His long-term goal: to help his country gain independence. His possible short-term goal: to get rid of the crab grass.)

I have students write a lifestyle/budget essay to be shown to parent(s) at conference time after completing chapters 1–4 in **Career Choices.** *The essays are saved and taken home, to be kept and re-read in 20+ years.*

— Kathy Andersen
Journalism/Language Arts Teacher
Central High School
Aberdeen, South Dakota

Optional

Pages 103–107

A Legacy for My Daughter
by James Webb
Read after completing pages 114–121 in *Career Choices*

Career Pathways

One way of integrating career/technical education and academics is through career pathways. The U.S. Department of Education has outlined 16 pathways or clusters that "encompass virtually all occupations from entry through professional levels." We've listed the 16 clusters below, along with a few sample occupations within each cluster.

Agricultural & Natural Resources Veterinary Assistant Environmental Engineer Biochemist	*Architecture & Construction* Plumber Architect Heavy Equipment Operator	*Arts, A/V Technology, & Communications* Actor Journalist Graphic designer	*Business and Administration* Accountant International Trade Manager Entrepreneur
Education and Training College Professor Teacher Assistant Corporate Trainer	*Finance* Tax Preparer Tax Attorney Banker	*Government & Public Administration* Urban Planner Recreation/Parks Director Legislator	*Health Science* Doctor Physical Therapist Hospital Administrator
Hospitality & Tourism Chef Hotel Manager Travel Agent	*Human Services* Child Care Worker Social Worker Psychotherapist	*Information Technology* Web Designer Software Engineer Technical Writer	*Law & Public Safety* Paramedic Attorney Police Officer
Manufacturing Machinist Automated Process Technician Production Engineer	*Retail/Wholesale Sales & Service* Customer Service Representative Interior Designer Marketing Director	*Scientific Research/Engineering* Oceanographer Laboratory Technician Chemical Engineer	*Transportation, Distribution & Logistics* Truck Driver Pilot Automotive Technician

Students can locate information about occupations within each of the pathways listed above using the *Occupational Outlook Handbook*. The online version of this book is available through the Bureau of Labor Statistics web site. Students can browse the "A-Z Index" and locate information using the pathway name.

Pathways are not "tracks" designed to steer students into specific careers. Rather, they are a means by which academics and work-related activities can be integrated using a shared theme—that of a specific area of interest. All students in pathways study the same core academic subjects; however, the information is taught in context, demonstrating how academics are relevant to the world of work.

The emergence of pathway programs makes the surveys in Chapter 5 all the more vital. As your students explore what is important to them in a career (i.e., flexibility vs. security) they will be better able to identify a career with the characteristics they desire. Understanding who they are and what they want before they make a pathway selection will help to reduce "lateral movement" between offerings because students will already know how to get where they want to go.

Chapter 5

Your Ideal Career

It's important for students to take a look at the general characteristics they hope to find in a job before they begin considering a specific career. Since there are more than 12,000 job titles to choose from, narrowing down those choices at the outset will save a great deal of time. In this chapter students are asked to identify some important factors: the physical setting of a job; the working conditions; the kinds of relationships they would like to have in their career; the psychological rewards they hope to achieve; how they want their career to relate to their family responsibilities; the financial situation they would find most comfortable; and the type of work they can do or are capable of learning.

Preparing for a career takes a great deal of dedication and energy. Young people who can identify career choices that meet their personal needs, values, interests and aptitudes are more likely to commit the time and resources to staying in school and getting the education and training required.

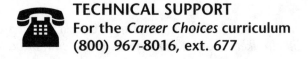

TECHNICAL SUPPORT
For the *Career Choices* curriculum
(800) 967-8016, ext. 677

Your Ideal Job

Page 126–134   Page 57–62

Learning objective:

To help students narrow their career choices by first considering the general job characteristics that are most important to them, and then being creative in thinking of jobs that meet their requirements.

Presentation suggestions:

In class, discuss each of the general classifications presented in this exercise to make sure everyone understands what is involved. Then have students individually go through the lists, checking *all* the items they find appealing.

Once they have completed this process, ask them to go over their lists again, this time choosing only one or two items from each classification, those they think are most essential to career satisfaction.

Circle the boxes in front of these statements. When they have narrowed down their lists, have students enter their preferences on the chart on page 134, as illustrated by Gena's chart. Remind the class that this chart is important and that they should refer to it often as they consider different career options.

After your students have completed their charts, begin brainstorming possible careers that meet their most essential career characteristics.

To get the class in a creative mood, discuss Gena's chart. Try to come up with as many other job titles as possible that fall within the range of her preferences (architect? advertising copy writer? public relations specialist?).

Depending upon the population of your classroom, encourage students to brainstorm careers from many educational training levels. Categories would include:

> Master or Doctorate Degree
>
> College Degree
>
> Vocational school
>
> High school graduate
>
> Blue collar
>
> White collar
>
> Professional/Certified

Example:

> *Gena: furniture refurnisher, antique restorer, art appraiser, cabinetmaker, or office manager of a museum or gallery*

Break the class into focus groups of four or five students each. Have each student share his or her chart. Then, instruct the group to brainstorm possible careers for each member. Students will always come up with the obvious, but encourage them to be as creative as possible. Bring the class back together and ask students to share their most creative ideas.

Energizer:

Offer a prize, extra credit points, or privileges to the group that comes up with the most creative ideas that fall within the range of its participants' charts. Let the class vote. This should encourage energy and creativity.

Resource:

Edward de Bono, *Lateral Thinking: Creativity Step by Step*. New York: Harper & Row, 1973.

A previous student, now at the community college, started the program wanting to be an auto mechanic but realized he didn't want the lifestyle and environment, so he has gone into computers because of the class.

— Jean Anne Conlon
English Teacher
South Tahoe High School
South Lake Tahoe, California

Consider Your Options

Page 135–137   Page 63

Learning objective:

To help students explore the employment options available in the changing workplace and analyze how best to match these with their personal levels of anxiety tolerance.

Presentation suggestions:

Review the terms defined in the text to make sure students understand them. Then, as a class, list examples of jobs that fit each definition. Can the class think of individuals who have had composite careers? Sequential careers? (Examples: Emma Thompson has a composite career. She has won Academy Awards for her work as an actor and as a screenwriter. Former President George H. Bush's political career was sequential. He was a Congressman from Texas, Ambassador to China, Head of the CIA, Vice President, and President.)

Then ask students to circle the most appealing job characteristics on the chart provided. When they finish, bring up the topic of anxiety tolerance. This is an important issue, although students may never have thought about it. Since anxiety is a part of everyone's life, learning to deal with and tolerate it is essential. That is not possible, however, until students can identify anxiety as a normal emotion. Unless they can do that, they are likely to see this uneasy feeling as something to be avoided at all costs. Point out that running away from anxiety means denying themselves many of the things they hold most important in life. If something isn't important to a person, he or she is unlikely to feel anxious about it. For example, someone with low anxiety tolerance who dreams of attending a highly selective college probably would not even bother to apply for admission because the fear of rejection would be so great. Similarly, the aspiring actor or actress will not audition for the school play if he or she thinks a knot in the stomach means it would be wise to stop and reconsider that goal.

Discuss these and other examples with the class to make sure they thoroughly understand the topic. Then relate anxiety tolerance to job selection. As the chart shows, the most flexible careers, the ones offering the greatest amount of control and freedom, also call for more anxiety tolerance. Students need to be able to judge how comfortable they are with ambivalence and ambiguity in order to make a satisfying career choice in this regard. Point out, though, that with practice they can hope to increase their tolerance levels. Again, assure them the feeling is normal, but they must learn to trust themselves enough to go after what they really want.

Activities:

Ask a school counselor or psychologist to talk with the class about anxiety tolerance.

Employee or Employer?

Page 138–139   Page 64–65

Learning objective:

To help students evaluate whether their attitudes, characteristics, and skills are more consistent with those of an employer or of an employee.

Presentation suggestions:

Have students mark the checklist, score, and then discuss. Directions are on page 139 of *Career Choices*.

Point out that this is not a question of whether it is "better" to be an employee or an employer. It is simply a matter of what fits an individual's personality. Students should understand, too, that an employer can be anything from a self-employed individual to the owner of a huge corporation. Self-employed people don't necessarily have to invest a huge amount of money (another common misconception). Anyone with a skill that fills a need for someone else can do it. (*Examples*: carpenters, writers, childcare providers, housekeepers, gardeners, hair stylists, caterers, plumbers, electricians, and physical trainers.)

Brainstorm the *pros* and *cons* of entrepreneurship. Out of this activity should come the realization that most people first entering the workforce do not have the money or experience to start their own business. Point out that owning your business might be a future goal.

Activities:

Invite an entrepreneur to talk with the class. It's best if this is someone whose achievements are realistic enough for your class to identify with him or her.

The Small Business Plan—Ask students to complete this sentence in writing.

> *If I could start a business it would be a* _____.

After reviewing the responses, form "entrepreneurial teams" of students with similar interests. Ask students to imagine they are partners and to write a business plan for a fictional business that they create.

They can start by writing a description of their business and naming it. They'll want to describe how their idea is unique and why it will succeed against the competition. How will they market their product or services? What are the start-up costs? Ask them to formulate a budget for the first six months of operations. How will they raise the capital?

See pages 4/102–4/105 of this guide. The entrepreneurial committees will have a structured opportunity to write their job descriptions after they complete the activities on pages 162–165 of *Career Choices*.

What about Status?

Page
140–141

Page 65

Learning objective:

To help students sort out their own feelings about status as it relates to job selection.

Presentation suggestions:

Review the material presented and discuss the questions on pages 140–141. Then have students decide individually how they feel about the statements on page 141.

English/Language Arts:

First, debate in class: Who should have more status, a teacher or a rock star?

Then ask your students to write an essay on why they would or would not consider teaching as a career.

Point out that in Japan teaching is one of the highest paid and most respected professions. Also point out that until recent decades, teachers and professors were given high status in the United States.

Reading assignment:

Goodbye, Mr. Chips, by James Hilton

> *My students interviewed a person who doesn't like his/her job so that they understand [the effect on a worker's morale and] what that can do to one's spirit over the years.*
>
> — Lynn Porter
> Coordinator of High School Diploma Program
> Santa Monica-Malibu Unified School District
> Santa Monica, California

Optional

I Decline to Accept the End of Man
by William Faulkner
Read after completing Chapter 5 in *Career Choices*

Pages 108–111

Chapter 6

Career Research

In this chapter, students complete a three-step process in order to arrive at a career decision they will use for the remainder of the book. Be sure to emphasize that this is a *tentative* selection, one that will probably be changed a number of times. There is no one perfect occupation. Today's youth will change occupations several times during their years in the workforce.

The process we present here is based on the old saying "Tell me, I forget; show me, I remember; involve me, I understand." For many of us, career research involved only step one of this process. That stops far short of the goal: allowing students to get a real feeling for a career before they invest years of their lives preparing for it. Therefore, it is important to not only research a career with print or online resources, but to also experience it. Encourage students to take this extra step and visit, volunteer or work within their career interest areas.

TV Worth Watching

It's not often we can recommend a TV show without reservation, but CBS's award-winning *Sunday Morning* is a treasure trove of materials you can use in your classroom. You'll find wonderfully written and produced segments on exceptional individuals working in the humanities and sciences. These are excellent resources for career exploration. Or, you might use John Leonard's weekly critique of the popular media as a source for new vocabulary words. Segments on social issues can help launch lively and meaningful debates and discussions.

Check your local TV listing for the broadcast time in your area. The show runs for 90 minutes each week. Videos of selected segments from particular shows can be purchased by calling (800) 242-7747.

Career Interest Areas

Page 145–146 No Workbook
Page

Learning objective:

To help students understand the twelve career interest areas and the types of jobs in each area. This will assist them in matching their own interests and aptitudes to specific career opportunities.

Presentation suggestions:

Review each of the career interest groups presented and ask the class to think of additional careers that might fit each category. It would be a good idea for you to have a copy of the *Guide for Occupational Exploration.* If your library doesn't have one, it can be ordered from any government bookstore for about $15. Or better yet, you'll find a copy of the *Occupational Outlook Handbook* online through www.careerchoices.com.

Resource:

William Hopke. *Encyclopedia of Career & Vocational Guidance.* J.G. Ferguson Publishing Co., 1987.

Students enjoyed interviewing adults in the community
who were already working in a career field of interest to them.
Some were even offered part-time jobs or the opportunity to
"shadow" an adult.

— Mary Turella
8th grade English and Communications teacher
North Royalton Middle School
North Royalton, Ohio

Optional

The Boys' Ambition, excerpt from
Life on the Mississippi
by Mark Twain
Read after reading page 146 in *Career Choices*

Pages 112–117

www.careerchoices.com

At the time of publication of this manual, the following activities were available on our web site, www.careerchoices.com for chapter 6.*

Page 145–146—Career Clusters and Groups

- *Database:* Research career titles chosen from occupational clusters

Page 148–149—Career Research

- *Database:* Search for careers that fit your interest area or school major
- *Database:* Overview of occupational information (i.e., wages, trends) searchable by job title and state
- *Database:* Find the careers with the most promising future in your state
- *Database:* General outlook of the United States job market by wages and education required
- *Database:* Employment trends of the major cities in the United States including unemployment rates, major employers, cost of living, etc.
- *Article:* Highest-paying jobs in the United States

Page 150—Career Interest Survey

- *Database:* Career research online using the Occupational Outlook Handbook

Page 158—The Shadow Program

- *Research Project:* Students learn how to use search engines to locate specific types of businesses near their home

Page 159—Arranging for a Shadow Experience

- *Narrative/Instructional:* How to write a business letter

Page 160—Intern and Volunteer Opportunities

- *Directory:* Finding volunteer opportunities in your community

Page 209—Calculating retirement dividends

- *Calculator:* How much could you save today & what would it be worth in 10, 25, or 50+ years?
- *Calculator:* Factoring the amount of retirement savings expected when using an individualized savings plans
- *Interactive Quiz:* Help with learning basic investing terms and concepts

For detailed information and fee schedules, see pages 7/6–7/14 of this manual, or go online to the Visitor Section of www.careerchoices.com.

* You'll want to go online to see the most current index because of the growing and changing nature of the Internet. As we find new and better resources, we'll include them or substitute them for current lessons.

Bring in Your Identity

Page 147

Page 67

Learning objective:

To help students make some tentative career choices based on their own interests and aptitudes discovered in chapters 2, 3, 4 and 5 of *Career Choices.*

Presentation suggestions:

At this point, students are ready to select some specific careers for more in-depth examination. Before they complete the exercise, make sure they understand that all of the work they have done up to this point must be considered in making these choices. A quick review of Chapters 2 to 5 might be helpful now. In particular, have students review their bull's eye chart (page 27), their required annual salary (page 93), and their job characteristic chart (page 134).

Career Exploration Brainstorming Session (see page **10/5** for details)

You may want to contact a community service organization and solicit their help. There are helpful strategies on pages **10/2–10/4** of this guide. Better yet, turn the organization of this session over to a committee of motivated students. This venture will look great on their college applications.

Optional

Lego
from The New Yorker Magazine
Read after completing page 147 in *Career Choices*

Pages 118–123

Career Interest Survey

Page 150–155   Page 68–73

Learning objective:

To help students begin an in-depth study of careers that match their aptitudes and interests. Students will learn to locate, analyze and apply career information using print and online resources. They'll also gather preliminary education and training information specific to their chosen careers.

Presentation suggestions:

Discuss basic career research methods and review the questions on the career interest survey to make sure everyone understands. Students can do their research in the career center, at the library and/or online. Allowing students to do their research and complete their surveys during class time should take at least three hours.

This is an ideal opportunity to demonstrate different research techniques. Recruit your career center technician or school counselor to assist with this. In particular, the Internet is an excellent research tool for career information. Spend at least one or two class periods in the computer lab.

As noted on page 4/87, you'll find some of the best online resources through www.careerchoices.com.

As your students gather materials (articles, pamphlets, etc.) about each of their career choices, remind them to place the information in their Career Resource File.

The three completed surveys on pages 150–155 of *Career Choices* should be copied and placed in the student's **Career Portfolio** notebook (see pages **4/13–4/14** of this guide).

Activities:

Guest speakers can be very helpful at this point. Before choosing them, however, consider the careers of greatest interest to students. If no one seems to be a potential electrical engineer, for example, there's not much point in bringing one in to speak. Also, try to have an appropriate mix of blue- and white-collar speakers, depending on the class's aspirations. Students seem better able to relate to younger presenters.

Ask speakers to discuss not only the tasks involved in their jobs, but also what they like and dislike about them, how they got interested in them, the necessary training, and so on. Allow time for questions from the class.

If you decide against having guest speakers, you might form committees of students interested in a particular career area and ask them to report their research findings regarding this area to the class.

Tomorrow's Jobs

"Making informed career decisions requires reliable information about opportunities in the future. Opportunities result from the relationships between the population, labor force, and the demand for goods and services.

Population ultimately limits the size of the labor force—individuals working or looking for work—which constrains how much can be produced. Demand for various goods and services determines employment in the industries providing them. Occupational employment opportunities, in turn, result from skills needed within specific industries. Opportunities for computer engineers and other computer-related occupations, for example, have surged in response to rapid growth in demand for computer services.

Examining the past and projecting changes in these relationships is the foundation of the Occupational Outlook Program. This chapter presents highlights of Bureau of Labor Statistics projections of the labor force and occupational and industry employment that can help guide your career plans."

Occupational Outlook Handbook 2002–2003 (online version)

At the end of each Career Interest Survey, students are asked to develop a timeline depicting the changes in that career over the last ten years and possible changes over the next ten years.

In our rapidly changing society, this is a critical step in the career exploration process. Technological advances are changing the way we work. Jobs titles popular today may be very different in format or even defunct by the time your students complete their education and training.

The best place to start this research is at the Bureau of Labor Statistics web site (www.bls.gov) using the online version of the *Occupational Outlook Handbook*. Once in the handbook, students will want to click on the link to Tomorrow's Jobs (sidebar) and study the general societal trends affecting the workplace and employment.

Activity:

Form groups with three students each. Using the data from the online article *Tomorrow's Jobs* mentioned above, ask each group to list the five most "startling" statistics they found. Then ask each group to present their list, explaining why they found these statistics either intriguing or troubling.

Each group should review the three careers for which each member completed a career interest survey. Ask the group to relate the information in the article to that particular career area or industry.

Using the complete *Occupational Outlook Handbook* online, each student should research each of the three careers in their survey in order to create the timeline. For each career, they'll find specific labor market information, societal and economic trends and projections for the future. Remind students to print out the data and articles and include the information in their **Career Resource File** (page 4/76). Once students complete their timelines they can be added, along with the *Career Interest Surveys*, to the **Career Portfolio** (page 4/13–4/14).

Given their research, ask each student to rank their three choices, placing the one most likely to have the best future at the top of their list. While this may not be the career they ultimately choose when completing their plan (chapter 12), at least students have evaluated this issue. By completing this step of the career exploration process they understand how of future workforce projections relate to job opportunity and job security.

Did any of your students discover their career choice might not be around by the time they finish their education and training? If so, work as a class to brainstorm some alternative careers with a strong prognosis for the future (taking the student's interests and aptitudes into account).

Resources:

Recommended Reading:

Jeremy Rifkin, *The End of Work, The Decline of the Global Labor Force and the Dawn of the Post-Market Era*. Tarcher/Putnam Books

Rifkin's work is very interesting, well-written, and easy to read. This book will prepare you to answer your students' questions about the possibilities of the future workplace. It is an outstanding historical perspective of the transition of the worker from pre-industrial revolution, through the era of machines and mass-production, to the advent of the information age in which he predicts there will be fewer and fewer workers required. Anyone interested in the dynamics of technology and globalization of the workforce will find this a fascinating read. His analysis seems hard to refute, yet he also offers some sensible ways in which society can adapt.

> *Jeremy Rifkin addresses boldly and expertly a most important problem facing contemporary society, a problem most economists are reluctant to discuss. This is a very readable and important book.*
>
> — Wassily Leontief, Nobel laureate
> Professor of Economics, New York University

Seeing in the Mind's Eye*

Page 156–157   Page 73–74

Learning objective:

To help students begin thinking about—and actually experiencing—what it would be like to spend a typical day at the job of their choice.

Presentation suggestions:

Review the concepts of visualization and "seeing in the mind's eye"* (SCANS) with the class. Then take them through the exercise.

Allow an entire class period for this exercise. Ask them to choose one of the careers they researched for the career interest survey. Have your students open their books to the exercise on page 157 and have a pen on their desks before you begin.

Turn down the lights and close the doors and windows. If your room is unavoidably noisy, try to find a quieter one.

Speak slowly and quietly, pausing where indicated. Read the following script aloud.

> Relax and settle into your chair. Place your feet flat on the floor. Close your eyes. Clear your mind.
>
> Pay attention to your breathing. (Pause) Inhale slowly, filling your lungs with air. (Pause) Exhale slowly. (Pause)
>
> Take a few slow, deep, deliberate breaths. As you exhale, tell yourself to relax and let go. (Pause long enough for three or four deep breaths)
>
> Feel your body relax (Pause) from your face all the way down to your legs and toes. (Pause) Feel the pleasant warm and tingly feeling of relaxed muscles. (Pause)
>
> Now project yourself into the future. (Pause) You've completed your education. (Pause) You've found a job in the field of your choice. (Pause) This is the beginning of a typical working day. (Pause) How do you feel as you get ready for work? (Pause) What are you wearing? (Pause) Are you looking forward to the day? (Pause)
>
> You're on your way to work. (Pause) Are you in a car or some type of public transportation? (Pause) Is it a long commute? (Pause) Or do you work at home? (Pause)
>
> You walk into your office. (Pause) What does it look like? (Pause) Who else is there? (Pause) How do they greet you? (Pause) How does your morning pass? (Pause) This is a typical day. What kinds of tasks do you see yourself doing? (Pause) Take a minute and do those tasks (Pause for two minutes).
>
> It's lunch time. (Pause) Where are you eating lunch? (Pause) Who is with you? (Pause)

Back at work, you find some special challenges. What are they? (Pause) How do you deal with them? (Pause)

Work with those challenges for a few minutes. (Pause) As you finish your day on the job, how do you feel? (Pause) What are you thinking about? (Pause) Do you have plans for this evening? (Pause) What are they? (Pause)

Now open your eyes and pick up your pen. Without saying anything, complete the exercise on page 157 in your book. Begin now. (Don't say anything more.)

Follow-up:

You might ask students to share any revelations they had during the exercise. For example, a future waiter or waitress may have realized how tired he or she would be by the end of the day.

Suggest the students complete this type of exercise for each of the three careers they researched.

* One of the foundation skills recommended by SCANS is "seeing in the mind's eye." This skill is used by many successful people as they visualize how to complete a project at work or develop a new product.

The Shadow Program

Page 158–159   Page 75

Learning objective:

To give students practice in writing a business letter and conducting an interview, and to allow them to see firsthand what it might be like to spend a day at a particular job.

Important Note: In order to complete this exercise, students will miss an entire day of school. Check with your administration office and the students' parents for permission before proceeding. Solicit the support of your career counselor.

Presentation suggestions:

This is an extremely valuable exercise, but it requires a great deal of research to locate people who will consent to being "shadowed." We strongly urge that you get help from a volunteer. Many community professional associations (Kiwanis, Lions, Soroptimists, Business and Professional Women) are supportive of such projects. These organizations are also a good starting point for locating the individuals who will take part in the exercise. Your Chamber of Commerce should have a list and contact phone numbers of all the groups active in your community.

Don't be shy about calling. This is exactly the kind of program most professional and community organizations love to support. The secret is to ask up-front for a liaison to organize and monitor the project. The right person will take 95 percent of the responsibility. All you need to do is supply him or her with complete copies of the student survey that follows, beginning on page **4/97**.

Over 150 students participated in Shadow Day at WRHS. Each student completed student profiles, wrote thank you notes, interviewed mentors, and conducted on-site evaluation forms ... Students wrote reports on why people work and compiled graphic charts on their results.

— Marilyn D. Gattuso
English Teacher
Wahconah Regional High School
Dalton, Massachusetts

Activity:

Make sure students understand that this is called the Shadow Program for a reason: shadows do not say anything, they do not do anything, they are just there. Emphasize the need for students to be as unobtrusive as possible, except during the agreed upon interview time.

Energizer:

If appropriate, some students could shadow their mentor beginning early in the morning at breakfast. It is a valuable lesson to observe a working parent and see how he or she mixes career and family.

English/Language Arts:

Use this exercise as an opportunity to review the components of a good business letter. Make the letter itself an assignment that will be graded on the basis of correct form, grammar, spelling, and neatness.

Ask students to write a short essay on what they learned from their day as a shadow and include it in their *Career Resource File*.

> *One girl (in our* **Career Choices** *program) shadowed a medical surgeon into surgery, looked through a scope, then held some tissue.... She's still talking about it two years later and has been accepted to nursing school!*

— Megan Schroeder
Vocational/Workplace Readiness Teacher
Cascade High School
Leavenworth, Washington

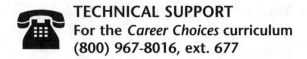

TECHNICAL SUPPORT
For the *Career Choices* curriculum
(800) 967-8016, ext. 677

How to Find Your "Director of Mentors"

Call the president of one of the service organizations whose members are career-oriented. Explain your project and ask for names of individuals who might be interested, or suggest you come and give a presentation at one of their meetings. This is ideal. You can generate a lot of interest and meet prospective volunteers. Be sure to take a couple of copies of *Career Choices* to pass around the audience as you speak. This visual prop will help them better understand what you are doing.

What to Look for in Your "Director of Mentors"

1. *Someone who has lived in your community long enough to have plenty of contacts.* A senior member of one of the professional service organizations mentioned above is ideal. A recently retired professional may have more time.

2. *Someone who likes to be responsible and follow through on a project from beginning to end.* The more the Director of Mentors does, the less responsibility you will have to assume. But remember that you have to let this person do his or her job. Give your director of mentors the necessary tools (completed, legible student surveys) and turn him or her loose. Provide support, praise, and appreciation!

This person could become a community liaison to your class. He or she could assist in finding guest speakers or perhaps be a guest speaker. Your volunteer might even be willing to mentor students with special needs. Many community members are vitally interested in working with young people. You can give them the opportunity to get involved. Be sure to share this *Instructor's Guide* and a copy of *Career Choices* with your volunteer. She or he might have great ideas.

Permission is granted to photocopy the survey on page **4/97** of this *Guide*. Have each student complete it. Pass these on to the director so he or she can begin the process of finding appropriate mentors.

Supply your volunteer with a copy of the Mentor Survey on pages **4/98** and **4/99** of this guide to use in locating mentors and matching students.

Hint: Ask the volunteer to share the completed Mentor Surveys with you. Keep a growing file for future years, along with a file of guest speakers.

Shadow Program Student Survey

Name _____ Age _____

High School _____ Grade _____

Teacher _____

Class Title _____ Period _____

Three careers of interest:

    1st choice _____

    2nd choice _____

    3rd choice _____

When I can shadow: (circle any restrictions)

    Any time   Evenings only

    Weekdays only   Weekends only

    Other _____

Explain any time restrictions such as employment or after-school activities from which you cannot be excused:

_____

_____

Do you plan to attend college?	Yes	No	Maybe	Undecided
Do you plan to attend trade school?	Yes	No	Maybe	Undecided

Why are you interested in these career areas? _____

_____

_____

_____

Shadow Program Mentor Survey

We are seeking volunteers for a Student Career Shadow Program. This important activity links young people with someone in a career field in which they have expressed an interest. For a day or a portion of a day, the student will "shadow" that individual. They have been coached not to be obtrusive or to interrupt your work time. All we ask is that you grant 15–30 minutes for an interview at the end of the day.

If you are interested in allowing a student to "shadow" you for a day or a portion of a day, please complete the following survey and return to:

_____

_____

The student assigned to you will contact you directly by email, letter and phone, so the two of you can arrange a convenient time.

Profession _____ Title _____

Name _____

Address _____

_____

Day phone _____ Email _____

Evening phone _____ Fax _____

Company _____

Address _____

_____

A brief description of your job/duties _____

_____

_____

Your educational background _____

_____

(Over)

Restrictions on shadowing times (days, times, etc.) _____

_____

_____

Any preference on ability and motivation of student?   (check one)

_____ Please send me only motivated students.

_____ I am willing to work with an at-risk or undermotivated student.

_____ I am willing to work with a handicapped/learning disabled student.

_____ I would be especially good with _____

_____

_____ Undecided

Are you a working parent?   Yes   No

Optional: Would you consider allowing a student to come to your home an hour before you leave for work to observe how you mix career and family?   Yes   No   Perhaps

Optional: Would you consider speaking to a high school class on your area of career expertise or other professional experience?   Yes   No   Perhaps

Comments:

Shadow Program Referral Form

Referral for _____

Profession _____ Title _____

Name _____

Address _____

_____

Day phone _____ Evening phone _____

Email _____ Fax _____

Company _____

Address _____

_____

Restrictions on shadowing times _____

_____

Comments _____

_____

_____

_____

_____

If you have questions contact:

_____   _____
              Name   Phone

Involve Me and
I Understand

Page 160–161 Page 76

Learning objective:

To allow students, through paid or unpaid employment, to observe people working in their chosen career field over a period of time.

Presentation suggestions:

Review the material presented in the text and, as a class, try to think of paid and unpaid jobs for people wanting to work at the careers listed on page 160. Add to the list the careers students in your class are considering. Emphasize that the jobs may not be especially fun or interesting, and may offer little or no pay. The purpose is simply for the students to get into a position where they can observe people performing jobs that interest them. Instruct students to be especially observant—both of what is happening around them, and of how they *feel*.

Have your students write a critique of each interview and experience (shadowing, interning, volunteering, beginning employment). They should be incorporated into their *Career Resource File*. They can use the questions on page 161 of *Career Choices* to stimulate their thinking. At the end of each critique they need to answer an important question: Is this a career that I should continue researching and pursuing? If they feel excited and stimulated by what they observe, then the answer should be yes!

Follow-up:

Some students may want to do volunteer work with their shadow mentors. Please advise the students that it is not appropriate for them to do this on the day of their shadow assignment. Suggest that they follow up their visit with a thank you letter and a request for a volunteer position. It is not appropriate for them to request a paid position unless it is offered by the mentor.

Again, your Director of Mentors can help. Finding these types of jobs, both paid and unpaid, usually takes someone with business or professional contacts.

We used most of Chapter 6 during our Career Research paper assignment. In addition to writing a research paper, students are also required to present with a computer-generated multimedia presentation.

— Sharon Hurwitz
English Teacher and Technology Facilitator
Bethel High School
Hampton, Virginia

The Chemistry Test

Page 162–165   Page 77–78

Learning objective:

To help students decide whether the careers they are considering are good matches for the personalities and working styles. Also to help them understand that matching individual strengths with job duties is an important step in effective teambuilding.

Presentation suggestions:

As a class read the story on page 162 and discuss the four personality styles described. This might be a good time to turn back to Chapter 2, pages 38–43 for a quick review. Students might be interested in a more complete personal profile. For more information, see page 4/23 of this manual.

Ask students to recall any occasions in the past few years when they've worked on a committee like this one. How did things work out? Can the students relate the results (either good or bad) to the personality styles of the people involved and the jobs they were assigned?

Have students complete the rest of the exercise individually or in small groups. Encourage students to come up with their own solutions before they look at the answers provided.

Energizer:

Have students identify their work behavioral styles either from the exercise on pages 38–43 or by using the actual Personal Profile Instrument. See page **10/19** for ordering information.

Forming heterogeneous groups that include at least one of each personality type:

Once they have identified their predominant style, ask all the Dominance (D) to go to one corner of the room, Influencing (I) to another, Steadiness (S) to another, and Compliance (C) to another.

Then ask each group to count off. Each group will have one 1, one 2, one 3, etc.

Ask the ones to form a group, the twos, the threes, and so on until you run out of numbers for the smallest group.

Assign the students who are left to the existing groups (which now have one of each of the DISC's) so that each group has five to seven members. Be sure to have no more than two of each work style in a group.

The assignment for each group:

Design a company and assign job titles to each member of the group based upon the strengths and interests of the group.

Ask the group to review the exercises on pages 163 and 164. As a warm-up, choose one of the companies, for example, a factory, and list other jobs that each of the work styles might find matches their personality.

> *Example:*
>
> dominance (D) — union organizer, office manager, head custodian, plant manager.
>
> influencing (I) — salesperson, trainer, personnel director, childcare director, marketing director
>
> steadiness (S) — mechanic, heavy equipment operator, clerical worker, department specialist, computer technician
>
> compliance (C) — auditor, bookkeeper, research and development director, software author

Once you feel the groups understand the process, let them begin brainstorming their company. Provide them with an overview of the points they need to cover to best describe their business (see The Business Plan, page 4/83 of this guide). At the minimum they'll need to describe the business, it's products and services, and how they'll market and deliver their goods. This could take one to three class periods depending upon the enthusiasm of the group.

It may be easiest to outline the assignment for them this way:

First — Identify an industry or company that everyone in the group finds of interest. The larger the company or industry, the better.

Second — Brainstorm all the possible job titles for each of the predominant work behavioral styles—Ds, Is, Ss, Cs—in that company or organization.

Third — Have each person choose a job title based on the charts they completed on pages 27 and 134 in *Career Choices.*

Fourth — As a group, write a job description for each person. Use the form on page 4/105 of this *Guide*. The job description should include the following:

> Job title:
> Experience, skills, and training required:
> Job duties:
> Hours and working conditions:
> Annual salary:

Ask the students to make the conditions as realistic as they can. For example, there should be no inflated salaries just to meet personal budget requirements.

Groups may need to spend one day in the library or online researching

Once the assignment is completed, ask the groups to present their projects to the class.

After they have introduced their company and staff, open up the brainstorming to the rest of the class to complete the lists of possible job titles in that company.

Then ask all members of the staff to make a presentation about their job, why they chose it, and how it fits their personality.

English/Language Arts:

Writing job descriptions is a communication skill that will come in very handy later in life. Those that have some experience in writing job descriptions will impress their supervisors and, therefore, move up the ladder to supervision themselves. This career move brings more autonomy, responsibility, and higher pay. Ask all students to rewrite their job description from their notes.

Remind them that spelling, grammar, punctuation, and neatness are important.

Follow up:

Small Business Plan

If your students are working on their own small business plans (as outlined on page 4/83 of this guide) they can use the information from this activity to write each "partners" job description. Because their team was set up based on interest in an industry rather than work behavioral styles, they may find that all the members of the team have the same work behavioral style (i.e., they are all Ds or dominance). The challenge will be designing job descriptions that fit their styles, especially when they are all the same.

If you have a group in which this is the case, ask them to share with the class what they learned about teambuilding.

A sophisticated concept? Most definitely! Is it important for effective teams to understand this concept? You bet! Can your students grasp the nuisances? You'll be pleasantly surprised.

After reading and discussing "I Hear America Singing," the students, in groups of 3 to 4, rewrote the poem using occupations of today. They also made a collage to accompany their vision of the poem.

— Pam Wieters
English Teacher
Stratford High School
Goose Creek, South Carolina

Optional

I Hear America Singing
by Walt Whitman
Read after completing page 165 in *Career Choices*

Pages 124–126

Job Description for:

Name _____

Predominant work behavioral style is: (circle one)   D   I   S   C

Company/Industry/Organization: _____

Job title: _____

Experience, skills, and training required: _____

_____

_____

Job duties:

1. _____

_____

2. _____

_____

3. _____

_____

4. _____

_____

5. _____

_____

6. _____

_____

7. _____

_____

8. _____

_____

Hours and working conditions: _____

Annual salary: _____

Instructor's Notes:

Chapter 7

Decision Making

The final step in choosing what you want is making a decision. As Anne Morrow Lindbergh said, "One cannot collect all the beautiful shells on the beach." Making a decision is difficult because choosing one thing inevitably means saying "no" to something else. For teens, this can be especially painful. It is essential, therefore, that they understand two points: that not making a decision is making a choice, and that most decisions can be changed.

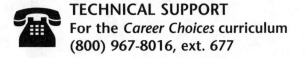

TECHNICAL SUPPORT
For the *Career Choices* curriculum
(800) 967-8016, ext. 677

Identifying Choices

Page 170   Page 80

Learning objective:

To help students discern the difference between long- and short-term goals and learn to take their hopes for the future into account when making daily decisions.

Presentation suggestions:

Ask a student to read Joyce's story aloud. Then have the class identify her two goals:

> Becoming a doctor someday

> Buying a car

What is Joyce's long-term goal? *Becoming a doctor.*

Right now, she is faced with deciding among three alternatives: getting a job so she can buy a car, becoming a candy striper to get medical experience, or spending more time on her studies.

Activities:

List on the board and discuss the choices students face every day to help them realize that they are already quite adept at making short-term decisions. Students usually have no trouble identifying at least ten decisions they make every day: what time to get up, what clothes to put on, what to eat, whether or not to go to school, what friends to call, what music to listen to, what subject to study first, what TV show to watch, whether or not to exercise, what time to go to bed.

Ask them to list some longer term decisions they will face in the next twelve months: what classes to take next year; whether to go out for a sport or school activity; when, and if, to date.

Brainstorm some really long-term (five years to life) decisions students need to start making.

Do I want to take classes to qualify me for college or trade school?

Am I going to be sexually active (risk parenthood)?

Am I going to stay in school?

Am I going to work or give priority to my studies?

Am I going to take as much math as I can?

Am I willing to learn the technology to keep up with current trends?

Am I willing to say "no" to drugs and alcohol?

Am I willing to start saving for the big expenses in life? (i.e. college)

Ask students to discuss what kinds of choices are easiest to make and which are hardest. Why?

Gathering Information

Page 171   Page 80

Learning objective:

To help students understand that before they can evaluate their choices, they need to discover the facts and determine the effect of these realities on the outcome for any of the options being considered.

Presentation suggestions:

Review the material in the text and discuss in class. Other information that might be helpful to Joyce could include: whether the hospital would be willing to write a letter of recommendation to the college of Joyce's choice; whether her parents would let her use the family car several times a week in return for doing extra chores around the house; whether her hours on the job or at the hospital would be flexible enough to let her study when she needs to; and how much time she needs to study each week in order to keep up her grades.

Emphasize the importance of being resourceful when making decisions. Thinking beyond the obvious choices often results in win/win solutions. If Joyce could negotiate the use of the family car, for example, she could satisfy her short-term goal without putting her long-term hopes at risk.

After reading and discussing pages 168–169, students need to see how decision making and problem solving are important in the business world as well as in their personal world. I split the class into small groups and assign them a section of the teachers' parking lot to examine. They are to identify the number of cars and their make so we can eventually determine how many are American-made, German-made, British-made, etc. Then the small groups share their numbers with the whole group until we know how many cars total were in the parking lot and how many are from other countries. We do a math lesson so students can create percentages! (Not a small feat in a Communications class!)

Next, we talk about the problems associated with so many cars being non-American. Then, students write a paragraph about their findings, including the importance of solving this problem in the marketplace. As students word process their paragraphs, they are also being taught how to convert their information into a spread sheet (we use the integrated package Microsoft Works), which will turn their percentages into a pie chart or bar graph. When students finish, they have a paragraph complete with pie chart showing the importance of companies solving problems in the workplace.

— Sharon Hurwitz
English Teacher and Technology Facilitator
Bethel High School
Hampton, Virginia

Evaluating Choices

Page 172–175   Page 81–82

Learning objective:

To help students evaluate the *pros* and *cons* and the likelihood of success of different choices.

Presentation suggestions:

Continuing Joyce's story, have the class list the *pros, cons,* and *probability of success* if she doesn't work at all. (*Pros:* more time for study, more flexibility. *Cons:* no money, no car, no experience. *Probability of success:* moot point.)

After the class has worked through Joyce's example, break into groups of two or three to consider Jessica's and John's stories.

Jessica

Choice 1: To take Algebra I. *Pros:* keeps options for college and future career open. *Cons:* more work, less time for other things. *Probability of success:* reasonably high, since she has done well at math in the past.

Choice 2: To take basic math. *Pros:* easier, less work. *Cons:* fewer future options. *Probability of success:* very high, since she has done well at math in the past.

Choice 3: Not to take math. *Pros:* easy way out. *Cons:* future options severely limited. *Probability of success:* moot point.

John

Choice 1: Quit school and go to work. *Pros:* no more school, earn money. *Cons:* little chance for advancement, fewer options for future. *Probability of success:* could probably get the job.

Choice 2: Graduate and go to vocational school. *Pros:* good chance for rewarding work and good pay. *Cons:* more school. *Probability of success:* good, since he already knows a lot about graphic design.

Choice 3: Graduate and join the army. *Pros:* training with pay. *Cons:* must commit several years to military service. *Probability of success:* good, if he can receive written assurance from the recruiter that he will get the training he wants.

Choice 4: Graduate and go to college. *Pros:* better prospects for high future earnings. *Cons:* must work very hard to bring up high school grades, must commit time and money to future education. *Probability of success:* depends on how hard he's willing to work.

Bring the class back together and, as a group, brainstorm Jessica's and John's decisions. You might make a chart for each story on the board, listing all the alternatives thought of by students. Ask the students what they think are the best decisions for Jessica and John.

Review with your students the steps of the decision-making process listed on page 175 of *Career Choices*. Explain that these steps will become second nature to them over time. In the meantime it is wise to memorize them, so they can make sure they've addressed each of these when making important long-term decisions.

Activities:

As a class, work through the decision-making process for the following goal, using the model on pages 176 and 177 of *Career Choices*. By lottery, choose one student's personal scenario to provide the data required. Explain and analyze each step so everyone is comfortable with the process. Emphasize that the final decision is up to the student involved, but that it's good to get input from others when you are gathering information and evaluating choices.

Goal: To prepare for a career that will support the financial requirements of the lifestyle I envision for myself.

Decision to be made: How much effort do I want to put into my education and training?

We showed the video **Forrest Gump** *to help students explore how choices depend on personal values. We asked students to recall three values that were held by characters in the film. One student focused on Forrest's love of life, and commented, "If you put love of life above all the bad things that can happen in life, you'll probably never commit suicide." He was thinking about a rock star (who recently committed suicide) and concluded that if the rock star had had Forrest's perspective, he would probably be alive today.*

— Doug Campbell
Communication Department
San Gabriel High School
San Gabriel, California

Optional

The Monkey's Paw
A play based on the story by W.W. Jacobs
Read after completing pages 168–174 in *Career Choices*

Pages
127–138

Gloria's Chart/Your Chart

Page 176–177   Page 82–83

Learning objective:

To show students how their own resources, wants, and needs should enter into the process of making major life decisions.

Presentation suggestions:

As a class, discuss Gloria's chart. Note that a new element has been added to the process: considering Gloria's resources, wants, and needs. This is a step to take when making major decisions, such as what career to pursue, whom to marry, and where to live. Can the class think of anything to add to Gloria's chart? What do they think Gloria should do?

Once they have completed the process for Gloria, ask students to review their own resources (strengths, skills, and passions), values, wants, and needs. Have them enter these on the chart on page 177, where their goal is to identify and evaluate four possible career choices. Ask them to complete the chart as best they can. Then break the class into small groups. Students can help each other evaluate their choices and think of other options based on the person's resources and desires. Students should then make a choice (individually, not based on the group's decision).

Activities:

Using the format of the chart on page 177 of *Career Choices,* ask students to complete the same process, this time making a decision about education and training for their future career indicated on page 177. For example, someone who wants to be a hotel manager might decide whether he or she wants to go to trade school, go to college, or get a job in the field and work his or her way up.

> *When using "The Road Not Taken" we had students writing stories looking ahead into their own futures with two different scenarios.*
> — Suzanne M. Reese
> Teacher/Gifted Liaison
> R.L. Turner High School
> Carrollton, Texas

Optional

The Road Not Taken
by Robert Frost
Read after completing page 177
in *Career Choices*

Pages 139-141

Make a Decision

Page 178   Page 84

Learning objective:

To help students evaluate their decision-making strategies, their strengths, and their weaknesses.

Presentation suggestions:

Review the text on page 178, and ask students to check the box on the scale that best represents their decision-making behavior. There are no right or wrong tendencies. The purpose is to help students identify a range of decision-making characteristics and learn to recognize how and when they use them.

English/Language Arts:

Ask students to write a fictional short story about three siblings (à la "The Three Little Pigs") who must make an important decision. Their choices could be autobiographical, about facing an important decision. Each sibling has a different decision-making style. One tends to avoid decisions, another tends to make decisions too quickly, and the third has a more considered or moderate approach. Suggest that students review the words on page 178 and, perhaps, use them in their story. They might also review page 20 of *Career Choices*.

To reinforce the decision-making process, the following value exercise was used: The students were asked to choose between two groups. In one they would get $5 a day just to show up to class. In the other, the first person who showed up would get $50, the second got $45, and so on down to zero for the 10th person and all those who followed.

Fifteen students chose the $5 group because they didn't want to compete. When asked what time the second group would arrive to class, one student said, "I'll show up an hour before to make sure I get in." The next said, "I'll show up two hours before." And a third said, "I'll sleep in the hallway!" They learned that if you pick a competitive field, someone will always "sleep in the hallway."

— Doug Campbell
Communication Department
San Gabriel High School
San Gabriel, California

Career Fair

Now that your students have narrowed their career interests to one career, it might be time to facilitate a student-directed career fair to be held later in the school year. The whole school should be invited. This can be a one-class or multiple-class project.

Have students divide into committees by career interest areas. Each committee will choose a chairperson. Then they'll determine how to operate and communicate with each other. The following tasks will need to be assigned to members.

1. Inviting one or more appropriate representatives in their career interest area

2. Gathering additional information about the career area with pamphlets from professional organizations, books, etc.

3. Designing and writing a fact sheet about the career that can be passed out at the fair

4. Display setup and cleanup

In addition, form an organizational committee of students. This committee should include an event chair or co-chair(s), school publicity chair, a facility chair, and the chair of each career interest committee (mentioned above).

After the Career Fair, ask each committee to meet and evaluate not only the success of the fair, but also the success of the committee. From this evaluation, brainstorm the traits of an effective team member. Then ask the group to brainstorm the strengths each person brings to a team. From this brainstorm each student can prepare an inventory for inclusion in their *Career Portfolio.*

After reading **Julius Caesar** *by William Shakespeare, I ask, "Does Brutus make the right decision?" This is used as the culminating literary piece after studying the complete process of making decisions. Students then have to decide how they would have made a different decision than he did.*

— Sharon Hurwitz
English Teacher and Technology Facilitator
Bethel High School
Hampton, Virginia

Optional

To Build a Fire
by Jack London
Read after reading page 179
in *Career Choices*

Pages 142–163

Instructor's Notes:

Chapter 8

Setting Goals and Solving Problems

Chapter 8 is the first of the "How to Get It" chapters that make up the remainder of the book. As they move through this final section, students will be making the plans, learning the skills, and acquiring the tools they will need to realize their dreams.

Solving problems and setting goals are two of the most important skills a person can learn. Fortunately, because new problems keep coming along and because there are always new goals to be set and achieved, everyone will have ample opportunities to practice these skills!

Optional

Pages 164-165

Uphill
by Christina Rossetti
Read before beginning Chapter 8

Tools for Solving Problems

Page 183–185   Page 86

Learning objective:

To help students identify and apply the problem-solving techniques as presented in the text.

Presentation suggestions:

Discuss the way Hubert's problem relates to the four problem-solving tools: delaying gratification, accepting responsibility, dedication to truth or reality, and balancing. Then ask students to complete the exercise on page 185 individually or in small groups. Follow up with a class discussion.

Activities:

For further small group discussion, ask students to consider the following situations.

Jon has offered to lend his car to Pat for a weekend if Pat will let Jon copy his homework. Pat knows it's wrong to cheat, and that he could be suspended from school if he's caught. But, he rationalizes, Jon isn't as good a student as he is, and the teacher really didn't explain the assignment well enough for him to understand.

> What sacrifices or risks is Pat taking if he gives Jon his homework?
>
> What sacrifices or risks is he taking if he refuses?
>
> Who is responsible for solving Pat's problem? Jon's?
>
> What are the facts in the situation?
>
> What wishful thinking might enter into Pat's decision-making process?
>
> What do you think Pat should do?

Lucy has been asked to go out drinking with a new group of friends on Friday night after work. Her friend, Debbie, plans to drive. Lucy knows it is illegal and dangerous to drink and drive, but Debbie assures her that she knows when she's had enough. Lucy doesn't want to be left out.

> What sacrifices or risks is Lucy taking if she goes with her friends?
>
> What sacrifices or risks is she taking if she stays home?
>
> Who is responsible for Lucy's safety?
>
> What are the facts of the situation?
>
> What kind of wishful thinking could enter into Lucy's decision-making process?
>
> What do you think Lucy should do?

Assign the movie *Apollo 13* for your Video Book Club (see listings beginning on page 6/41). It includes excellent examples of problem solving and has the added advantage of demonstrating that jobs in math, science, and technology can be exciting, dramatic, and even heroic.

Resources:

M. Scott Peck, *The Road Less Traveled*. A Touchstone Book, Simon and Schuster, Inc.

Reading assignment:

Romeo and Juliet by William Shakespeare

Romeo and Juliet exemplifies the theme of fate versus free will. Did the lovers bring about their fate through their actions or was it just meant to be?

Once students have completed their reading ask them to rewrite the ending to *Romeo and Juliet* using Peck's four problem-solving components.

Optional

Possibilities

The Myth of Sisyphus
by Albert Camus
Read after completing pages 182–185 in *Career Choices*

Pages 166–171

Setting Goals
and Objectives

Page 186–190   Page 86

Learning objective:

To introduce students to a process for writing quantitative goals and objectives.

Presentation suggestions:

Setting goals and objectives is an extremely important skill, especially for teens who tend to think in vague generalities. Make a presentation from the text, carefully working through the examples. It is essential that students become familiar with the three questions every goal statement must answer:

> What will be different?
>
> By how much or how many?
>
> By when?

Portfolio

Ask students to complete the exercises on pages 188 and 189 alone or in small groups. Ask a few volunteers to write and diagram on the board their goals and objectives from page 189.

You may want to provide additional practice by listing incomplete goal statements and having students indicate what component is missing. Examples:

Get a good job this summer.	*What will be different?*
Learn to speak Italian.	*By when?*
Get some new school clothes.	*How much or how many? By when?*
Learn to use a computer program.	*By when?*
Make some new friends.	*How many? By when?*

Activity:

Have students choose their most important goal for the next two weeks. Then ask them to write objectives for it. Ask them to keep this assignment at the front of their binder so they can glance at it over the next two weeks.

At the end of two weeks, have students share their goals and objectives in class discussion and report on how successful they were at meeting them.

When students have finished reporting, take a poll to see how many believe writing their goals and objectives down was helpful.

Note: If students are having trouble writing objectives for their goals, have them first identify the steps for reaching their goals. Then translate each step into quantitative objectives, with the three different components. It is helpful to list them in chronological order based on the date of completion.

Follow-up:

Encourage students to practice this skill by setting daily, weekly, and monthly goals and objectives. Suggest that they reward themselves for achieving their goals with small indulgences, such as a new music CD or tickets for a special event.

The students... are asked to set a personal goal for each day for 3 weeks. We discuss if they reached their goals, why or why not. As the year progresses, they are asked to make weekly, monthly, etc. goals. Most of my students stated that this has helped them to improve their grades and also strengthen their organizational skills.

— Dee Herrmann
English Teacher
Sandia High School
Albuquerque, New Mexico

Optional

Pages 102–110

Optional

Pages
178–211

Excerpt from *The Prince of Tides*
by Pat Conroy
Read after completing pages 182–191
in *Career Choices*

Instructor's Notes:

Chapter 9

Avoiding Detours and Roadblocks

The fact that everyone has some degree of difficulty in his or her life comes as a surprise to most people. We tend to think that things should run smoothly—and that they do for everyone else. That idea makes it easier to give up when problems present themselves, or to turn to drugs or alcohol for relief from these difficulties. In this chapter, students should learn that problems are facts of life that must be faced head-on if they are to be overcome. Since they are responsible for their own lives, it is up to them to overcome any limitations they perceive.

In dealing with the issues of teen parenting, dropping out of school, and using drugs, we ask students to imagine how short-range "solutions" can affect their lives in the long run. A number of exercises in this chapter, in fact, give students a chance to think about long-range planning.

Students may also feel pressured to give up their dreams. This pressure can be external (from parents, friends, society) or internal (based on irrational fears, anxiety, inability to take risks). Young women are especially prone to feelings of this sort. Review this material carefully, bringing in a school counselor or outside speaker if necessary. Remind students to turn back to this section any time in the future when they are discouraged and think they want to give up on a dream.

Optional

Mother to Son
by Langston hughes
Read after completing pages 196-197
in *Career Choices*

Pages 214-215

What's Your Excuse?

Page 197–199   Page 89

Learning objective:

Students examine some of the reasons people use for not doing what they want to do, or can do, evaluate those excuses, and determine what might be done to avoid using them.

Presentation suggestions:

Review the material on pages 197–199 Then ask students to check any "I can't do it because" statements which apply to them. After they have completed their charts, turn to page 199 and ask students to take turns reading items from the "They did it in spite of" chart. Discuss any additions that might be made to the chart.

Activities:

Invite someone who has overcome a significant handicap to address the class. Ask your guest to speak about both the physical and emotional processes experienced: not just the physical obstacles encountered in not being able to walk, for example, but how the debilitation affected attitudes and self-esteem.

Assign online or library research on others who have overcome handicaps. Have students write a one-paragraph summary of the research to share with the class.

One excuse area not covered in the text is the "social excuse." Brainstorm with students different social excuses such as:

> I don't have time.

> None of my friends do it.

> My peers would object.

Evaluate those excuses. How inflexible are they? Are there situations where these excuses should not stand in the way?

If you are dealing with a population with a temporary problem (curable physical or emotional problems, incarceration, or chemical dependency), encourage students to carry or display photos of themselves before the problem developed. It is helpful for them to be able to see themselves as healthy, functioning, changing, free individuals.

Reading assignment:

Ask students to read a biography or an autobiography of an individual who overcame an adversity. Brainstorm other individuals in addition to those mentioned on pages 198–199. One obvious choice is the biography of Helen Keller.

To add an element of fun to the class and to control excuse-making, we made a list of excuses—some of them wild ("bad hair day")—posted them, and point to them when students haven't finished an assignment, are late, etc. This was a humorous extension of the activity on page 197.

— Lynn Porter
    Coordinator of High School Diploma Program
    Santa Monica-Malibu Unified School District
    Santa Monica, California

Optional

Pages 172–177

Hope
by Emily Dickinson
Read after completing pages 194–199
in *Career Choices*

Taking Responsibility

Career Choices

Page 200

Workbook and Portfolio

Page 90

Learning objective:

To help students evaluate excuses and reframe them so that they are accepting the responsibility for their problems and at the same time opening new avenues for solving them.

Presentation suggestions:

Ask students to write some excuses they've recently used to absolve themselves from responsibility for solving their problems. Then, individually or in small groups, ask them to reframe the excuses, this time *accepting* the responsibility.

As practice, it may be helpful to reframe the following examples in a class brainstorming session:

I can't take a job because I don't have any way to get there.

I can't do my homework because it's too noisy at home.

I can't go to the party because my parents won't buy me a new outfit.

I didn't make the team because the coach is out to get me.

I failed the test because the teacher expects too much.

Reframed examples:

I can't take a job because I haven't taken the time to investigate bus schedules or car pooling opportunities.

I can't do my homework because I don't want to go to the library.

I can't go to the party because I'm not imaginative enough to come up with something appropriate to wear.

I didn't make the team because I didn't practice hard enough.

I failed the test because I didn't seek out the extra help I need.

Be sure to remind your students that, although they are responsible for their own actions and decisions, many sources of help are available. Another step to solving problems should be to identify those sources of help and support, and determine when to use them. Refer to page 226 of *Career Choices*.

Startling Statement Quiz

Page 201–202   Page 91

Learning objective:

To expose students to some of the statistics regarding teen pregnancy, dropping out of school, and substance abuse.

Presentation suggestions:

Quizzes such as this seem to have a lasting impact on students. Statistics that might be easily dismissed or forgotten in a text or lecture loom much larger in this context. Have students answer the questions to the best of their ability, then turn the page and review the correct statistics. When students have answered correctly, their impressions are reinforced. If they were wrong, the correct answer often has a deep impact. Follow with group discussion.

Activities:

Instead of having students take the quiz individually, divide the class into groups of three students and give them time to come to a consensus about which are the correct answers. The ensuing discussions can be valuable as students examine their own thoughts and where they came from, as well as those of their classmates. Follow with large group discussion.

Offer a prize to the group that gets the most correct answers to the quiz. This approach further reinforces the learning process; students will try even harder to come up with the right answers. And if they don't answer correctly, the right answer is more likely to make a lasting impression.

For extra credit, have students research a topic of interest to the class. Ask them to write their own startling statement quiz using the statistics they uncover.

Energizer:

Have students create a startling statement quiz using the statistics they uncovered regarding the future trends of the workplace. Using the startling statistics each group found in the activity on page **4/90** of this guide, have each group write three or four startling statement questions (like those on page 201 of *Career Choices*), complete with the corresponding answers (as on page 202). Compile a quiz combining the best questions and answers of each group.

This quiz can be shared in a variety of settings. The class can take the entire quiz, because they only know the answers to three or four of the questions. Teams from the class can present it to other class(es) during the same period. Why not have parents take it at the next open house? The students can submit it to the local newspaper for publication. Editors like quizzes that open their readers' eyes to societal trends.

Detours and Roadblocks

Page 203–206   Page 92–93

Learning objective:

To allow students to examine some common problems and then project into the future to consider the possible long-term consequences of present actions.

Presentation suggestions:

Ask the class to read the three stories aloud, or have students complete the exercise on their own. Follow with a discussion in class. Another alternative would be to break into groups of three students each and assign one of the problems to each group. Bring the class together and have the groups present their conclusions. If you have more than one group considering a particular story, compare answers to see how they differ and how they are alike.

Activities:

If you know an adult who actually dealt with one of the problems presented here in their youth, you might invite him or her to talk with the class. Ask them to explain what they would do differently if given the chance to go back in time.

> *The section on roadblocks and detours was very rewarding because the students realized they were using some of those excuses now.*
>
> — Hattie Burns
> Business Education Teacher
> Chesterfield Middle School
> Chesterfield, South Carolina

Is It Worth Staying in School?

Page 207   Page 94

Learning objective:

To help students personalize the effect dropping out of school will have on their eventual job satisfaction.

Presentation suggestions:

If members of your class are at high risk of dropping out of school, you should spend considerable time on this activity. Complete the steps outlined in the text. Revisit the library or career center or have your students go online so they can complete the Career Interest Survey on page 150 for jobs not requiring a high school diploma.

How many students found three careers that met all their personal requirements? There probably aren't many.

After the students finish answering the two questions at the bottom of page 207 of *Career Choices*, ask volunteers to share their responses.

Ask for a show of hands to the question: Which would you find more satisfying— a career from your first list (requiring at minimum a high school degree) or a career from your second list? Continue the discussion on why the majority (if not all) would choose a career that required at least a high school education.

Using their budget requirements (page 92-93) and the salaries of the "no high school diploma required" careers they researched, have students factor their cash short fall per month and per year.

Activity:

Invite a panel of adults who dropped out of high school to speak to the class. One member of the panel should be someone who then went back to school to realize his or her dream.

This exercise is important even if your students are all college-bound. Dropping out of college can have devastating effects on their career and life satisfaction.

> *Students finally understood the cost of an upscale lifestyle and, most importantly, that education plays a major part in determining lifestyle.*
>
> — Dan Somrock
> Social Studies Teacher
> Cass Lake-Bena High School
> Cass Lake, Minnesota

The Economics
of Bad Habits

Page 208–209

Page 95

Learning objective:

To enable students to comprehend the financial costs of bad habits. The concrete evidence presented in this exercise may be more readily grasped than information about the physical or emotional costs, which can seem abstract.

Presentation suggestions:

Review the material and then have students complete the exercise at the bottom of page 208 (mathematical answers are on page 209). What each student would do with the money, of course, will vary. Bring the class together for a group discussion. This is a good time to talk about retirement accounts, guaranteed incomes, and other investments. It may be difficult for most students to imagine that they will ever be of retirement age. You might ask them to think about some older people they know, preferably someone who has enough money to live comfortably and someone who just gets by. How do the lifestyles of these individuals differ? Who has more options for enjoying life? Who has more worries?

Break the class into small groups to consider the daily, weekly, and lifetime costs of nonproductive or even destructive habits. Use the chart at the bottom of page 209. Discuss the proactive nature of turning a negative activity (bad habit) into a positive one (saving for the future). How would that make them feel?

Activities:

Invite a guest speaker to discuss pensions and retirement accounts. Ask her or him to share charts that show how much income will be generated with different savings plans.

Ask a panel of senior citizens to speak to the class about their retirement planning and their current lifestyles. If possible, invite persons whose experiences range from satisfactory to struggling.

After they have calculated the costs per day and per year of their "bad habit," students can go to www.careerchoices.com. There are several online calculators available to help students factor their own savings over a lifetime using the formula at the top of page 209. Moving from abstract totals (someone else's habit) to their own figures should have a strong impact on their motivation to quit. On the next page see an sample portion of the lesson for this activity.

Our class completed the lesson on the economics of bad habits. One "hardcore" smoking student was so astounded by the overall cost of this habit that he quit! Health warnings and legal regulations had not fazed him—it was the money issue presented in this lesson that helped this student!

— Sara L. Carter
Business Education Teacher
Garden City High School, Garden City, Michigan

Lesson Objective:

To demonstrate quickly that there are economic costs tied to bad habits.

Directions:

After your students have completed the activity on p. 209 of *Career Choices,* have them use the money they would spend monthly on smoking as the amount deposited monthly into a retirement account and link to the online calculator. The figure that is computed will be VERY motivating. Do they want this amount to go up in smoke?

Extension Ideas:

Class activity: Is it reasonable to assume that a person would smoke one pack of cigarettes a day? Many people have a tendency to smoke more and more as the years go by. Why not rework the computations in *Career Choices* as a class using an ever-increasing number of packs?

Next, have your students brainstorm the average monthly costs of other detrimental habits (e.g., drinking). Encourage them to consider habits that aren't necessarily as costly physically, but that can take a toll financially.

- Shopping sprees at the mall
- Gambling
- Excessive driving (bad for your car and your wallet)
- Daily Extra Value Meals instead of packing a lunch
- Morning visits to Starbucks for your caffeine habit

You could throw some critical thinking at them, too. Are there physical downsides to any of these other habits?

- High cholesterol from too many french fries
- Stress from unpaid bills
- Broken legs because you can't pay your bookie
- Poor air-quality from too much pollution
- The shakes and irritation from too much caffeine

Do your students know any adults with bad habits they are trying to kick? Suggest the student runs the numbers for them, given the yearly cost of the habit, their age, and the time until they are 65 (retirement age). The student, armed with the printout of the savings, should make a presentation to that individual. Take a poll three months later. Did any of the adults kick their habit?

Over the Hill to the Poor-House
by Will M. Carleton
Read before completing pages 208–209
in *Career Choices*

Optional

Pages 221–224

4/131

If You're a Woman

Page 211–213   Page 96–98

Learning objective:

To help students understand how flexibility and higher salary relate to mixing career and family, and to have young women consider how nontraditional careers may be the best option.

Presentation suggestions:

Young women who hope to have families often think that the best career options for them are the so-called traditional women's jobs: nursing, teaching, clerical work, retail sales, waitressing. On the surface, these choices seem reasonable. Nurses and secretaries can usually drop in and out of the workforce if they want to spend a few years at home with their children, and they can find work almost anywhere to accommodate a husband who may be transferred from place to place. Teachers share the same vacations as their children. Waitresses and sales clerks needn't think too much about their jobs when they're off duty.

Upon closer examination, however, this reasoning falls apart. Today, most women work outside the home even when they have small children. In fact, more than half of all women with children under the age of one year are in the workforce. A staggering number of women are the *sole support* of their families. We have reached a point where it is less important to be able to move into and out of the workforce. Today's priorities are to earn a sufficient salary and to have the day-to-day flexibility required for responsible parenting, such as being able to take a few hours off to attend a school play or parent-teacher session.

The jobs that offer these benefits are likely to be those traditionally held by men, whether blue collar or professional. This exercise should help young women see that preparing for this kind of career is as important for them as it is for the young men in the class.

Review the instructions carefully, then have students complete the exercise on their own.

The amount needed for a woman and three children to live in minimum comfort will vary greatly from community to community. It might be a good idea to bring the class together to try to determine an appropriate figure for your community.

Activities:

Invite a woman who is successfully mixing career and family to talk with the class. Ask her to address her job, her training, and the reasons for choosing that field. Consider blue-collar workers as well as professionals.

On the board, list a number of jobs traditionally held by women (see above) and an equal number most often held by men. Discuss. What are the advantages and disadvantages of each? Which usually pay more? Which usually require more training? Is there anything about the work itself that makes it unsuitable or impossible for someone of the other sex to perform?

For a couple in which either partner is capable of supporting the family, brainstorm possible benefits: taking time off, going back to school, taking a lower-paying job that is more emotionally rewarding, and feeling less pressure. Discuss ways in which employers might make life easier for all working parents through job sharing, flexible hours, parental leave, childcare facilities, and allowing people to work at home.

Resource:

For more information, exercises, and activities, see *More Choices: A Strategic Planning Guide for Mixing Career and Family*, by Bingham and Stryker, Advocacy Press. See pages **10**/17–19 for ordering information.

I think in the exploration of non-traditional careers, the female students have realized that there is a whole "new" world that is open to them!

— Catherine M. Fitzpatrick
Family and Consumer Science Teacher
Humbolt Secondary Complex
St. Paul, Minnesota

I have seen former students enroll at Tech College because of what they learned in class.

— Janet Richards
Equity Teacher
Johnson High School
St. Paul, Minnesota

Optional

Pages 100–101

Before You Give Up
Your Dream

Page 215   Page 99

Learning objective:

To help students learn an evaluation technique to be used before acting rashly in abandoning a dream or plan.

Presentation suggestions:

Ask for a volunteer to identify a dream he or she is considering giving up. Then in "fishbowl" fashion (see page 6/30 of this guide), work through the questions with that student. Ask the rest of the class to share problem-solving ideas they have with the student.

After reading "All I Really Need to Know I Learned in Kindergarten" and discussing it with students, they were allowed to illustrate one scene. They really enjoyed drawing the horror of walking into a spider web. Putting their words into picture form was a nice reverse activity.

— Rebecca Dunbar
Lead Teacher
Crossroads
Leavenworth, Washington

One class made quilt squares using muslin and markers, illustrating their creeds. I stitched the squares to make a wall hanging.

— Nancy S McKinney
English Teacher
Trigg County High School
Cadiz, Kentucky

Optional

A Dream Deferred
by Langston Hughes
Read after completing pages 214–215 in *Career Choices*

A Noiseless Patient Spider
by Walt Whitman

Pages 212–220 **All I Really Need to Know I Learned in Kindergarten**
by Robert Fulghum
Read after completing pages 216–217 in *Career Choices*

Developing
Anxiety Tolerance

Page 216–217

Page 100

Learning objective:

To help students overcome fears by seeing themselves be successful at whatever makes them anxious through the process of guided visualization.

Presentation suggestions:

Refer to page 4/41 and 4/92–93 in this guide for an example of guided visualizations and how they are administered.

Refer to page 4/82 for a review of the topic of anxiety tolerance.

Brainstorm with students a list of the kinds of situations that cause anxiety and, therefore, stop individuals from pursuing a desirable activity or goal. Without naming names, can they relate a story about someone whose anxiety stops them from being successful.

Ask students to identify an activity that makes them feel anxious and then, like Carlotta, break that activity down to its elements. Write a guided visualization that will help them become comfortable with the feeling, thereby defusing it.

A note on guided visualization: This technique is being used more and more by the established medical profession to control pain and anxiety and to promote healing and behavioral change. Yet it should also be pointed out to students that this technique is powerful and in the wrong hands can be used for brainwashing and manipulation.

Reading assignment:

The Tell–Tale Heart, by Edgar Allen Poe

A wonderfully gruesome tale of fear controlling and destroying a man's sanity. This can lead to excellent discussion on fear and anxiety! Good reading with excellent film and tape available.

Optional

Pages 6–9

One Step at a Time

Page 218–221   Page 101

Learning objective:

To expose students to a hierarchical approach to conquering anxieties.

Presentation suggestions:

Read Sally's story aloud; discuss what she did and how she did it. How might her life have been different if she had not taken these steps? After brainstorming, ask the class to think of common fears and list them on the board.

Ask students individually to list some of their own fears, and then to rank them from the easiest to deal with to the hardest. Can they come up with a plan to overcome these fears? Some students may want to discuss this in small groups. Others may prefer to do this project privately. Respect those wishes. This might be a good time to bring in the school counselor for a class discussion.

Emphasize the importance of identifying the stress response and learning to tolerate that feeling. It helps to start with stress responses of lesser degree and work up to stress responses of greater degree.

A word of caution: While some phobic (severe stress reaction) responses can be cured in this fashion, it should not be attempted without the help of a trained professional. If you identify this potential in a student, be empathetic and supportive. Suggest that he or she seek help from the school counselor or community counseling service. Check with your administration on school policy.

Reading assignment:

I Am the Cheese, by Robert Cormier

This is a story of a boy seemingly lost in a circle of memories and forgetfulness resulting from a traumatic experience. As he continues his symbolic trip, he comes closer and closer to discovering the truth and, thereby, freeing himself from the prison of his own mind and his surroundings. To do this, he must face his fears. This book leads to important discussions on self-discovery, overcoming fears, perseverance, and the freedom of self-knowledge.

Optional

George Gray
by Edgar Lee Masters
Read after completing pages 216–221 in *Career Choices*

Pages 225–227

Yorik's Story

Page 222–223   Page 102

Learning objective:

To give students an opportunity, in a third-person situation, to make long-range plans for the success of someone who could reasonably be expected to fail. Since this is the classic American dream, we hope the exercise will allow students who see themselves as outside the mainstream of American society to view their own situation with more optimism and determination.

Presentation suggestions:

This exercise could take up to two class periods. Point out that this is in preparation for the final exam (Chapter 12). You may decide to complete the exercise in small groups or as a class.

If you choose to do the exercise in class, begin with a review of setting goals and objectives. Remind students, too, that Yorik has both a vision (his goals) and the energy to realize it (his objectives, or action plan). Vision plus energy equals success.

Hint: It's often helpful to start with year ten and work backward.

Ask individual students or teams to present their plan for Yorik in class. It will become obvious that there are a variety of ways for Yorik to meet his goal. On the board write a chart of the alternative education and training paths available to Yorik based on the different plans presented in class.

Discuss why having alternative plans is a good idea, particularly when preparing for a career through education and/or training.

Student will find the following time frames helpful as they compete their plans.

    Doctorate or Highest Degree (MD, LLD, etc) — 2 to 6 years beyond bachelor degree

    Masters Degree — 1 to 3 years beyond bachelor degree

    Post Bachelor Certification — 1 to 3 years beyond bachelor degree

    Bachelor Degree — 4 years or equivalent training/experience beyond high school

    Associate degree, technical certification, or equivalent training — 1 to 3 years beyond high school

    High School Diploma — 4 years (on average)

Taking Risks

Page 224–225 No Workbook Page

Learning objective:

To help students see that taking calculated risks is an important skill.

Presentation suggestions:

Although the text contains no exercise on this topic, it's important to discuss it thoroughly. As the text states, taking a risk is a sort of cross between overcoming fears and making decisions. Review these concepts as part of your presentation.

Ask the class for examples of things they believe many people are afraid to do that are not life-threatening, such as public speaking, applying for a job, asking for a date, and introducing yourself to a stranger at a party. List these on the board. Discuss possible outcomes for someone taking these risks. What is the worst that could happen? The best thing? Could it be worthwhile to take this risk?

Activities:

Ask students how they would complete the sentence "If I could do anything I wanted, I would..." Is this action desirable? Is it risky? Have the class evaluate the risks involved.

Ask students to give examples of times they took a risk. Did it pay off?

Brainstorm ways in which students could motivate themselves to take a calculated risk. They might break the action down into more manageable parts, for example, or offer themselves a reward.

Invite someone who has taken a major risk to address the class.

Getting Back on Track
If You've Been Derailed

Page 226–227   Page 101

Learning objective:

To help students understand how to find education and training alternatives, particularly if they have to take a less-than-direct path toward their career and life goals.

Presentation suggestions:

Your students will leave your class with a comprehensive plan for achieving their education and career goals (see Chapter 12 of *Career Choices*). They'll feel empowered, energized and focused; encourage these feelings.

However, the path to success is often a winding one. Even people with the most comprehensive plans sometimes get sidetracked. The causes are varied: financial, health, family or personal problems, societal changes, etc. Any of these can derail your young students during the next six to ten years. Therefore, it is important they develop contingency plans before they are needed. If something happens that takes a person off track, a contingency plan gives them confidence in knowing that, with time and energy, they can continue to follow their dream. The chart on page 227 will help them develop a vision of what is possible.

Before you talk about these issues, assign the completion of the chart on page 227. Students will classify employment opportunities based on the education and training requirements of jobs within their chosen career interest area or industry. At the same time, this chart outlines median salaries based on the varying educational and training requirements. Students will research and fill in the final columns using their own career interest area. This can be assigned to individuals or to teams of students interested in the same industry.

We gathered the data for the first two industry columns using online versions of the *Occupational Outlook Handbook* and the *Career Guide to Industries*. Your students will need some help coming up with enough jobs in their interest area to fill each of the education/training level categories. Suggest they start with these rich reference guides as they complete the columns for their career interest area(s).

Our search began with the *Career Guide to Industries*. This resource from the Bureau of Labor Statistics provides data on careers grouped by industry. In addition to information about working conditions and employment outlook, the *Career Guide to Industries* lists job titles within each industry. The seven industry categories are fairly broad (i.e., Manufacturing), but there are sub-categories within each group (i.e., Aerospace Manufacturing). We found information under the Services category about the Health Services and Educational Services industries.

Using the section within each industry entitled "Occupations in the Industry," we generated a list of job titles. Then we turned to the *Occupational Outlook Handbook*, looking up each job title in search of in-depth information about education/training requirements and earning potential.

Students could create their own electronic spreadsheets, allowing them to update their plans and add additional columns (industries or interest areas) as they and the workforce changes. To start, use the first column printed in the book, along with the top two rows. This document should be added to their **Career Portfolio** notebook and updated periodically.

Once completed, ask students to interpret the data on their chart. Their responses may include:

a) Generally, the more education and/or training, the higher the salary.

b) There is a substantial jump in wages between on-the-job training and vocational certification.

c) With each increase in education level attained, salaries rise substantially.

Ask students to consider the job they listed as their ideal. Given the information gathered, have they changed their plans? If so, how? Some students may decide to make a commitment to more education and/or training. Others may discover they can qualify for a desirable job primarily through training with little or no classroom requirements.

This activity can help students whose vision may be limited. By researching and reviewing the opportunities in a career interest area or industry they find intriguing, especially as it relates to the commitment to education and training, they just might realize a few more years of preparation is worth it for a lifetime of satisfaction (review the exercise on pages 118–119 of *Career Choices*).

Ask students to look back at their salary requirements on page 93. Have them indicate the jobs that meet those requirements. If their ideal career does not pay enough to meet their desired lifestyle projections, have them list a variety of strategies to address this situation. These should include:

a) Reworking their budget to bring it in line with their future salary range

b) Dual earner families—their spouse will work as well (if they get married)

c) Continuing education throughout their working life to increase skills and wages

d) Committing to higher educational goals following high school

Activity:

Create a *"What will I be doing when I'm 30"* timeline

As your students are fine-tuning their vision of the future, this activity provides another opportunity for them to graphically demonstrate the planning process. Have them tape three pieces of paper (8½" x 11") together lengthwise. They will have a strip of paper 33 inches long. Ask them to draw a line down the length of the paper, dividing it proportionately starting with their age today and terminating the line at age 30. Given the plans they are starting to develop, outline their education/training and career plans along the timeline. Alternative plans can be added on additional lines running the length of the page. You may want to provide extra credit for students who include more than one plan for a specific career or interest area.

Include the time frames on page 4/137 of this guide on the board for reference.

Chapter 10

Attitude Is Everything

Attitudes can be empowering—or limiting. To paraphrase the old adage, "You are what you think you are." In this chapter, we try to instill the attitudes that lead to success, as defined by each individual.

We have identified four areas of attitude for discussion here: attitudes toward excellence; toward the work ethic; toward a changing world; and, most important, attitudes that make any chosen career a dignified and noble pursuit.

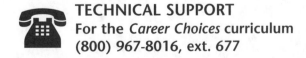

TECHNICAL SUPPORT
For the *Career Choices* curriculum
(800) 967-8016, ext. 677

Affirmation

Page 231   Page 104

Learning objective:

To help students understand the power of affirmations in changing self-limiting attitudes.

Presentation suggestions:

Affirmations have been shown to be a powerful tool in changing attitudes. Ask students to think of attitudes they have that may damage their potential for future success: I'm too shy. I'm too dumb. I'm too lazy. I'm too poor. I'm too uncoordinated. Then have them write affirmations to help change these attitudes: I *(their name)* am a confident person, I *(their name)* am a good student, I *(their name)* am willing to work hard for what I want.

Activities:

Provide 3 × 5 cards on which students can write their affirmations. Instruct them to take these home and tape them to their bedroom or bathroom mirror so they can be repeated every time they comb their hair or brush their teeth.

Follow-up:

Periodically, remind students to keep repeating their affirmations. Several weeks after they've begun, ask if any have noticed a difference in their behavior or thought patterns about themselves.

The Six Es of Excellence

Page 232–235   No Workbook
Page

Learning objective:

To recognize and evaluate the characteristics and attitudes of excellence in themselves or as part of a team.

Presentation suggestions:

Discuss the concept of excellence with the class. This idea goes beyond the "vision plus energy equals success" equation; excellence requires added effort. Ask students if they can recall an instance in which they truly excelled at something, or can think of some part of their lives for which they must meet particularly high standards (playing a musical instrument or sport, for example). Then discuss the six Es as presented in the text, asking students to consider what part each of these characteristics plays in their own interest area. Emphasize that, although performance is often judged by others, only the individuals concerned know for sure whether they gave it their best shot.

Activities:

Ask students to write a paper about something they have done or would like to do, relating how each of the six Es plays a part in this activity.

Or ask the class to write about different activities in which they display each of the six Es of excellence (expecting to be a good student, having enthusiasm for basketball, putting energy into making friends).

Choosing the task of being a first-rate student, ask them to write affirmations that support excellence. For instance:

I, _____*(their name)*_____, am enthusiastic about math; it is fun.

I, _____*(their name)*_____, put my best energy into my schoolwork.

This activity is especially important for young people who do not view themselves as particularly good students. If you get resistance have them, turn back to their charts and plans from page 227 and review their findings.

Using your class' experience with teamwork over this course (see pages 4/25–26, 4/102–105, 4/115, 4/127, 4/137 of this guide for examples of team projects), discuss how the six characteristics and attitudes of excellence are beneficial to a group accomplishing a task. Add these to the list of effective team member traits begun in the activity explained on page 4/25 of this guide.

Ask volunteers to share stories about individuals they know who exemplify excellence, giving examples of how that person personifies each of the six traits. Then ask each student to write a thank you note to one or two individuals they know who they feel embody the traits of excellence. In their letter have them comment on specific instances where each trait was demonstrated. It will be one of the most substantial thank you notes they have ever written. Encourage them to send it; they'll make someone's day.

Reading assignment:

To Kill a Mockingbird, by Harper Lee

This classic novel opens up many wonderful areas of discussion on overcoming adversity and striving for what is right. The book deals with prejudice in a small Southern town and one man's courage to do the right thing. The excellent movie based on the novel can be shown.

The Necklace by Guy de Maupassant

A young woman dooms herself to years of hard labor and poverty because of her inability to admit to her friend that she lost a necklace she borrowed to attend a special ball one evening. Years later, she meets her friend and explains to her that she appears old and worn out "because of her." Ironically, the friend reveals that the necklace had been a fake. Excellent story, excellent departure point for a discussion on "facing up to the truth" and dealing honestly with problems.

I teach the steps of proper negotiating (Communications 2000, module 8 & module 7). Then I have the students read "The Necklace" . . . [and] write an essay on how negotiating could have saved Madame Loisel years of grief. [The students] must include some of the steps of negotiating when they discuss Mme. Loisel's problem.

— Lela Fay Roy
English Teacher
Somerset High School
Somerset, Kentucky

Optional

The Necklace
by Guy De Maupassant
Read after completing pages 232–235 in *Career Choices*

Pages 228–239

Going for It. . .Work Is an Aggressive Act

Page 236–237   Page 104

Learning objective:

To help students realize that action is necessary to achieve any goal. They will also learn to evaluate positive and negative behaviors on the job.

Presentation suggestions:

This is a good exercise to have students read aloud. The correct answers are obvious, and class reaction should help reinforce the lesson to be learned. Young women especially should be assured that aggressive acts are often required at work in order to achieve excellence.

Activities:

Ask students to suggest aggressive words and phrases often used in the context of work, listing them on the board. Examples: organize, manipulate, control, wrestle, grapple, make a killing, break a leg, knock 'em dead, sock it to 'em, whip into shape, take a beating, make a pitch, score a point.

Repeat the same activity with words which connote excellence, noting how they also imply aggression. Examples: superiority, supremacy, advantage, the height of, unsurpassed, overriding, transcending, unequaled, paramount, preeminent, above the mark.

There is no *work* without *effort*—and *effort* requires aggressiveness.

Be sure to point out that the word aggressive, when used in the context of work, does not mean overbearing, uncivil, cruel, arrogant, domineering, rude or dictatorial. If an individual is described as any of these adjectives, they are unlikely to hold a job for long. They'll be fired.

Ask students to write workplace scenarios (similar to those on page 236) about employees they've worked with or about customer service experiences they've encountered where:

a) an individual who personified the positive trait of aggressiveness and

b) an individual embodied the negative traits discussed above.

After completing the next activity, *You're the Boss*, come back to their scenarios. How might they deal with the individuals with negative behaviors?

You're the Boss

Page 238–241   Page 105–107

Learning objective:

Through job scenarios, interviews and activities, help students understand the importance of a positive work ethic, productive work habits and a can-do attitude. They will also learn how to recognize negative behaviors and develop plans to change those behaviors.

Presentation suggestions:

Read the introductory paragraph to the class. Help students identify with Chris so, as they evaluate the employees, they can understand the employer's point of view. This person has made a large personal and financial investment in the business. If students were the employer, how would they feel about the people described in this exercise? Discuss individual employees in small groups. Have students identify the problem exhibited by each employee and design an objective to help him or her overcome it. What about Tim? What productive work habits does he exhibit? (Examples: dependable, helpful, creative, easy to get along with, honest and thoughtful, hard working.)

Brainstorm other productive work habits:

1. Doing your best

2. Finishing a task that you've begun

3. Cooperating with fellow employees

4. Respect for authority

5. Teamwork toward the common goal

6. Promptness

Activities:

Ask students with jobs whether their co-workers exhibit any of these negative or positive work traits (no names, please). Which type of co-worker is the most enjoyable to work with? In teams, ask students to write scenarios (similar to those on pages 238 – 240), choosing two of the negative work traits and two of the positive work traits around which to build their stories.

Discuss the phrase *Puritan work ethic*. The term *work ethic* refers to something you do because you feel obligated to do so. In contrast, the term *work values* implies something you choose to do.

We tried to make our work environment in class as much like a work situation as possible. We used teams, projects, due dates set in advance, bonuses, etc.

— Linda Neef
9th grade English teacher
Pardeeville High School
Pardeeville, Wisconsin

Have students interview three local employers to find out what they expect of their employees. Once the interviewee has shared their thoughts on this topic, have the students then ask them to rank the characteristics they look for in the order of importance. Students will want to include their findings in their *Career Resource File*.

As a class, compile the employers' responses into a report: What employers in our community look for in employees. Suggest your class publish their findings in the school newspaper.

Now ask your students to evaluate their own work habits. Those that don't have jobs should apply these concepts to their schoolwork and other responsibilities.

A Word about Interviewing:

Although face-to-face interviewing is ideal, employers are busy and may not be able to devote more than 10 or 15 minutes to meet with a student. Phone interviews may be the best option.

Email is also another alternative, especially for an individual who uses this medium as part of their regular work. Recommend that students offer email as an option. If the interviewee is enthusiastic about this option, advise students to send only two or three questions at a time rather than the whole interview. Otherwise it may be overwhelming and the responses less thought out. One of the advantages of email is the student can save the text responses in a word processing program. They then have a written record for their *Career Resource File*.

For safety, advise students not to meet with someone they don't know outside of that person's place of employment, unless accompanied by a parent or other adult.

When students look at situations involving others, it helps them to address those same problems with themselves.

> — Karen Michael
> English Teacher
> Bronson Junior-Senior High School
> Bronson, Michigan

Optional

Pages 249–251

To Be of Use
by Marge Piercy
Read after completing pages 238–241
in *Career Choices*

The Employee of the Twenty-First Century

Career Choices

Page 242–245

Workbook and Portfolio

Page 108–109

Learning objective:

To discuss and analyze the workplace attitudes most in demand. This will help students understand how workers can more readily change and grow as technological advances, globalization and advances in the workplace dictate.

Presentation suggestions:

After reading the introduction, ask students to take the self-evaluation quiz and score their answers. Follow with class discussion, brainstorming objectives that can be used to adjust attitudes.

Activities:

Discuss the technological advances most responsible for bringing about change in the way people work today (jet travel, online conferencing, fax machines, wide area networks, cell phones, PDAs, etc.)

Team project: Divide the class into groups of three to five. Ask each group to invent an item or service that doesn't exist today and present their design to the class. They should answer the following questions:

Why is it needed? Will it create new career opportunities or jobs? If so, what types of jobs? What skills will the workers need? What impact will it have on the future?

Some examples include:

- Interactive videos for at-home education
- Cure for the common cold
- At-home desalination machines
- Servant robots
- Gasless automobiles
- Nylon stockings that don't run

Energizer:

Read to the class *Tonia the Tree*, by Sandy Stryker, the 1989 winner of the Merit Award of Friends of American Writers. This charming allegory about a tree that must be uprooted and moved in order to grow, will launch great class discussion concerning dealing with change.

Writing assignment:

Divide the class into small groups to brainstorm possible story lines about the following concepts and then write an allegory based on one of these concepts
  1. Embracing change
  2. Valuing people different from you
  3. Curiosity and valuing learning

An International Perspective:

Invite a panel of individuals who have lived and worked in a foreign country to speak to the class about their international perspective of the workplace. Ideally, you'd like people representing three or four large countries or major continents.

Ask your guests to address the following questions:

> How are the employment opportunities the same and different in this country when compared to the United States?

> What is this country doing to prepare their citizens to compete in the international marketplace? What are the educational and training priorities of this country's government?

> Do the citizens of this country have the same opportunities we have to choose our own careers, or does their educational system direct a person's educational options from an early age?

> How are employment laws the same or different in this country when compared to the United States?

> Projecting ahead ten years, will this country be more or less competitive with the United States? Why?

You can also assign student teams to research the above questions as they relate to a particular country, reporting their findings to the class. They can do this research through interviews, at the library or online.

Ask students to prepare a Venn Diagram comparing and contrasting the employment opportunities of our free enterprise system and the economic systems of the international job market.

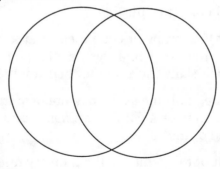

United States Workplace   International Workplace

Optional

Pages 240–248

Tonia the Tree
by Sandy Stryker
Read after completing pages 242–245 in *Career Choices*

Be the Best of Whatever You Are
by Douglas Malloch
Read after reading page 246 in *Career Choices*

Managing Change

Page 246   Page 109

Learning objective:

To help students learn to recognize and manage the inevitable changes in the workplace.

Presentation:

In class, review the points made on page 246. Stress that technological and global changes cause shifts in the workplace. As a job changes so do the skills required to remain competitive in that occupation. Because technology will make certain tasks redundant, students may even have to completely change careers.

Activities:

Brainstorm with students to create a list of the workplace changes they've learned about during this course. You'll want to review material covered in:

Career Choices, pages 135–137, 150–155, 211–213, 242–246

Activities found in this guide on pages 4/90–4/91 and 4/127

In groups of two or three (or individually) compose a report explaining the positive and negative aspects of one example of societal change. Encourage your students to interview friends, relatives and mentors, asking their opinions on the pros and cons of their chosen topic.

Students should keep the planning documents recommended on page 246 in their **Career Portfolio** notebook. They include:

a) An inventory of the computer equipment and software they master along with any and other high tech equipment. They should add these skills to their skills chart and to their resume.

b) A periodic update of all the skills they are acquiring. Remind them to review the list on page 48 of *Career Choices* and update their skills inventory started at that time.

c) An annual audit of the health of the industry and job title they are pursuing. They will want to update their ten-year timeline periodically (see page 151 of *Career Choices* and **4/90–4/91** of this guide).

d) The *Transferable Skills Chart* (as explained on page 31 of *Career Choices* and shown on page 109 of the *Workbook and Portfolio* for *Career Choices*). By using an electronic spreadsheet program, they can easily update this chart as their skill list expands and their career choices change. This will become an important planning document, so they'll want to keep it in their **Career Portfolio** notebook.

Chapter 11

Getting Experience

This chapter introduces students to some of the most basic job-hunting skills: writing resumes, locating jobs, research interviews, filling out applications, job interviews. Because so much information is already available on these topics, we have not covered them in depth. You may want to refer students to other publications or library research if the materials are not sufficient for the needs of your class.

You'll want to visit www.careerchoices.com for a variety of in-depth resources. See pages **4**/153–154 for a sampling of what is available.

If you are using the adult version, *Career Choices and Changes*, turn now to page **4**/171 of this manual for the lesson suggestions for the additional chapter in that version. Upon completion of that chapter, you'll return to page **4**/151 for lesson suggestions for the balance of the *Career Choices and Changes* text.

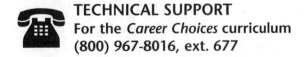

TECHNICAL SUPPORT
For the *Career Choices* curriculum
(800) 967-8016, ext. 677

Your Resume

Page 250–253   Page 111

Learning objective:

To give students experience in writing a personal resume.

Presentation suggestions:

Review the information and example in the text before students complete and turn in their own resumes. If the school has a computer lab, you may suggest that resumes produced by the laser printer will look the most professional.

Activities:

Using a job chosen from the local classified ads, students practice writing a cover letter for that position.

Cover letter checklist:

1. Title of position identified

2. How you found out about the vacancy

3. Brief highlights of your resume related to the job requirements

4. How and when you can be contacted

5. Closure

If you know someone who works in a personnel office, see if you can get copies of about twenty resumes, ranging from very good to very bad. Black out all personal information to assure privacy. Divide the class into small "Personnel Department" groups to evaluate the resumes and decide on five to interview. Ask them to evaluate reasons for their choices.

When they are finished, ask these very important questions: "What impact did the neatness and correctness (spelling, grammar, punctuation, and so on) have on your impression of the applicant? Did you eliminate anyone from the interview process because their resume was not neat, complete, and readable?"

At this point, it should become clear to students how writing skills can have an impact on their lives and their futures.

> *I had the students watch* **Indiana Jones and the Temple of Doom** *and fill out a complete resume for the main characters.*
>
> — Tammy T. Schofield
> Social Studies Teacher
> Walterboro High School
> Walterboro, South Carolina

The type of resume students prepare for this activity (page 250–253 of *Career Choices*) is ideal for a student applying for their first job or volunteer position in an industry in which they are interested.

A Resume for the Future

To give students a chance to prepare a more professional resume (even though they haven't had a lot of experience yet), have students craft their "ideal" resume for their current career choice. This will be the resume they'd have if they could wave a magic wand. For this exercise they need to create a fictional resume that assumes they:

a) Have completed their education and training for the position they are seeking,

b) Have acquired all the skills required for their chosen career, and

c) Have had internships, entry-level jobs and/or volunteer experience in this field.

Resources available on www.careerchoices.com and other web sites.

After students create their first draft using the outline on page 251 of *Career Choices*, they'll want to access resources to help them create their first "professional" resume. There are many online resources available, and this is probably the most direct way to accomplish the task. If Internet access is not available, have students get books and pamphlets on how to write a resume from the library or career center.

Online they can also view resumes of individuals who are currently applying for positions in their chosen area of interest. This will provide ideas for their own "ideal" resume.

To gather the data required, ask students to review their *Career Interest Survey* and ten-year timeline for the career they've chosen. If the position requires specific education or training, skills, attributes, etc, be sure those are listed on this new resume.

a) Once they determine what kind of education and/or training they require, they need to decide what school(s) or apprenticeship programs they are going to attend.

b) What are the skills that would demonstrate to an employer that the student would be an excellent candidate for this job?

c) Next, they'll want to fabricate some experiences—whether paid or volunteer—and list those along with their specific duties...all made up, of course.

They'll continue visualizing their ideal resume as they work through the topics required. Once complete, suggest students include this futuristic resume in their **Career Portfolio** notebook. It will function as a "check list" as they create their plans for the next four to ten years and prepare for their chosen career.

www.careerchoices.com

At the time of publication of this manual, the following activities were available on our web site, www.careerchoices.com for Chapter 11 of *Career Choices* (Chapter 12 of *Career Choices and Changes*).* See pages 7/6–7/14 for detailed information about www.careerchoices.com.

Page 253—Your Resume

- *Interactive Writing Activity:* Building your resume
- *Instructional:* Writing a cover letter
- *Instructional:* Tips on giving your resume international appeal

Page 254—Finding a Job (online)

- *Database:* Search for job opportunities and examples of career specifics
- *Database:* Search for a job in any state in the United States
- *Database:* Search for job listings by company, industry, function and location
- *Database:* Search the federal government's job listing database
- *Database:* Search the free job listings of the largest Internet search engine

Page 255—Conducting an Informational Interview

- *Instructional:* How to write a thank-you note

Page 256—Job Applications

- *Downloadable Form:* Print a Social Security application along with the application directions
- *Directory:* Locate your nearest Social Security Office
- *Directory/Instructions:* How to order a copy of your birth certificate by state and by county

Page 258—The Job Interview

- *Informational:* Skills and strategies for successful job interviews
- *Virtual Job Interview:* Interactive interview practice sessions
- *Informational:* Why a simple thank-you note might mean the difference between getting the job and getting the cold shoulder

Page 261—Accepting a Job

- *Tutorial:* Information on federal tax withholding and completing Form W-4

Page 262—Making Connections (Finding Mentors)

- *Instructional:* Suggestions for developing successful mentoring relationships
- *Directory: Organizations who support mentoring opportunities for students (For teachers only)*

Finding a Job...Conduct an Informational Interview

Page 254–255   No Workbook Page

Learning objective:

To give students experience in the various methods used to find an entry-level job and also familiarize them with techniques for conducting informational interviews.

Presentation suggestions:

Review the information on pages 254–255 in *Career Choices* in class.

Ask for a student volunteer and brainstorm as a class the kinds of workplaces in your community affiliated with that particular student's chosen career. Review the information on page 160–161 of *Career Choices* with your class to facilitate the generation of ideas

See page 4/94–100 in this guide, the Shadow Program, for hints on finding people willing to be interviewed. Review the information in the text before students conduct their interviews. Be sure to review the etiquette involved, along with the tips on page 4/174 of this guide.

Activities:

Ask students to write a paper about what they learned from their interviews.

Our 10th graders do a "Career Portfolio"—complete with actual resume and model application form—to present to parents at our Spring Open House. Its purpose is for students to use when applying for summer jobs, as well as to demonstrate growth and achievement toward personal goals over the course of the year. It begins with a student letter to parents about "me in 1 to 5 years."

— Andree Liscoscos
English Department Chair
Santa Maria High School
Santa Maria, California

We do take field trips to the Workforce Development Center (Job Service) to see what jobs are available.

— Jean Granger
Careers Teacher
School Age Parents Program
Waukesha, Wisconsin

4/155

Job Applications

Page 256–257   Page 112

Learning objective:

To give students experience in filling out job applications.

Presentation suggestions:

Review the material in *Career Choices*. Ask students to get any information they need and then to answer the questions on page 256. Remind them to bring this information along whenever they apply for a job.

Activities:

Go to a local bank or other large employer in the community. Ask for copies of their application forms so students can have experience filling out an actual application. When they have completed the forms, break the class into small groups, asking students to evaluate each other's applications. Would they hire this person? Since most won't have much job experience to relate, the evaluations should center around neatness and completeness.

For practice students can write to an employer in their career interest area and request a copy of their standard job application.

Note: Small businesses rarely use an application form. They rely on the information provided on the resume.

The Job Interview

Page 258–259   Page 113

Learning objective:

To provide students with information and practice, in the form of role-play, regarding the job interview process.

Presentation suggestions:

Review the information in this activity and have students gather the data required for the questionnaire on page 257. They'll use this information for any interview they do in the future, so remind them to update it periodically and include it in their *Career Portfolio* notebook.

Have students role-play the interview process by taking turns "interviewing" for an entry-level job in their area of interest. You can also invite a local employer to conduct mock interviews with student volunteers as the class watches and critiques.

Energizer:

If your school has video recording equipment, tape the interviews and play them back so individuals can judge their own performance. Perhaps a professional interviewer will be willing to watch with the students and offer hints for improvements. This is a frightening experience for most students, but it can be very valuable. You may want to get assistance from the vocational counselor or someone else in the school who has had experience with this type of activity.

Job Interview Night — Turn to page **10/6** of this guide. You may want to contact a community service organization in your community and solicit their help. (See pages **10/2**–**10/4** of this guide for strategies.) You can also turn the project of organizing this session over to a committee of motivated students or a parent/student committee. Ask students if any of their parents belong to the groups listed (or similar groups) on page **10/2** of the guide.

The interviewing helps them to realize how important it is to present themselves appropriately for an interview.

> — Ann Barber
> Business Education Teacher
> Lenox Memorial High School
> Lenox, Massachusetts

Optional

Pages 254–261

Looking for Work
by Gary Soto
Read after completing pages 250–259
in *Career Choices*

Dealing with Rejection
and Accepting a Job

Page 260–261 No Workbook
Page

Learning objective:

To help students gain information on how to deal with these two facets of a job search.

Presentation suggestions:

Review the materials in the text. Share your experiences and those of individuals you know. Some students may wish to share their experiences.

Activities:

Invite a Human Resources Director or owner of a small business to speak on these topics. Roleplaying with an expert would also be helpful.

This chapter is most effective when I take at least two weeks. My students are required to fill out job applications and compose a working resume. After this is accomplished, we set appointments for a mock interview. The students are required to dress professionally and prepare for their interview. The interviews are videotaped. After completion, we view the results in class. Students can see their strengths as well as get tips on how to improve. Everyone learns something; it is a very positive experience.

— Stephanie Born-Mathieu
Business teacher
Edison High School
Minneapolis, Minnesota

Making Connections

Page 262–263   Page 114

Learning objective:

To help students gain an understanding of mentoring and encourage them to watch for opportunities to have or be a mentor.

Presentation suggestions:

Discuss the material in the textbook. Then review the questions on page 263, either individually, in small groups, or as a class. Ask students to relate their own experiences as mentors.

Activities:

When guest speakers come to class, ask them about their own mentors.

You might have students write a paper about an experience they've had as a mentor. If they don't think they've ever been a mentor, try to jar their memories. Have they ever instructed a younger brother or sister? Helped a new student find his or her way around? Tutored a classmate?

Reading assignment:

Ask each student to read and report on a book whose major theme centers around one of their career interest areas. It could be fiction, biography, or autobiography. This is an ideal time to reinforce library research skills. Be sure to demonstrate the use of *Books in Print: Subject Directory*, along with the web site search engines of large online bookstores.

Dance students were mentored by our community dance companies and students founded their own dance companies. They worked on grants, budgets, jobs, dates, etc.

— Jeannette Van Dorn
STW Implementor
Milwaukee High School of the Arts
Milwaukee, Wisconsin

We had students write thank you notes to someone who helped mentor them after reading "The Bridge Builder."

— Suzanne M. Reese
Teacher/Gifted Liaison
R.L. Turner High School
Carrollton, Texas

Optional

Pages 262–269

The Bridge Builder
by Will Allen Dromgoole
Thank You, M'am
by Langston Hughes
Read after completing pages 262–263 in *Career Choices*

Instructor's Notes:

Chapter 12

Where Do You Go from Here?

We've now reached the point in the course where students use the information they've gained and the skills they've developed to write their own plan of action. As they begin, remind them again that this is a tentative plan. It can—and probably will—be changed. The process, however, can be repeated as often as necessary.

This material can also be used as school counselors advise individual students. Recommend that students take their *Workbook and Portfolio for Career Choices* or their personal **Career Portfolio** notebook to any counseling appointments.

This whole chapter could be assigned as a take-home final examination. Allow at least one week; several assignments require research and contemplation to be completed accurately and thoroughly.

My students worked in groups to produce bulletin boards throughout the school depicting themes learned in their class.

— Janet Richards
Teacher
Johnson High School
St. Paul, Minnesota

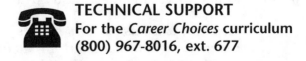

TECHNICAL SUPPORT
For the *Career Choices* curriculum
(800) 967-8016, ext. 677

Getting the Education or Training You Need

Page 267–269

No Workbook Page

Learning objective:

To help students understand the various education and training alternatives available to them. This will enable them to complete a comprehensive education and/or training plan based upon the student's career interest area.

Presentation suggestions:

Review and expand on available education and training opportunities. This is also a good time to bring in various speakers: career counselors, vocational technical counselors, college placement officers, employment development workers, and military recruiting officers.

Ask students to refer to their Career Alternative Ladder from page 227 of *Career Choices* and review the education and training alternatives in their career interest area. Suggest that students go online to investigate in more detail the options they are considering.

Activity:

Ask students to imagine a point in the future when they have completed all education or training necessary for their chosen career. They have worked in this career for five years when the occupation suddenly becomes obsolete. They are forced to make a career change.

Begin by identifying career alternatives. Using the *Transferable Skills Chart* (explained on page 31 of *Career Choices* and shown page 109 of the *Workbook and Portfolio*), create a five- to ten-minute presentation detailing what skills from their now-defunct career would be transferable to their new career. How were these skills used in their former career? How will they be applied to their new career? They will also want to explain what skills they will need to acquire in order to qualify for their new career. Will there be additional education or training involved?

Resources:

Review the list on page 4/163 of this guide that details the resources available on www.careerchoices.com. These web sites will provide your students with up-to-date information for most major education and training institutions within the United States. If students are planning on industry specific accreditation or certification, they'll want to start by visiting the industry association's web site.

> *One student, when asked why he was flunking math even when he said he needed it for his future job, paused then said, "Because I never thought of it like this before, that it would help me for my career."*

— Debra Kuperberg, Special Education Teacher
San Gabriel High School, San Gabriel, California

www.careerchoices.com

At the time of publication of this manual, the following activities were available on our web site, www.careerchoices.com for Chapter 12.*

Page 267—Getting the Education or Training You Need

- *Question and Answers:* Overview of the GED requirements

Page 268—Community or Junior Colleges

- *Directory:* Links to all the community and junior colleges in the United States

Page 268—Four-year Colleges and Universities

- *Directory:* Links to all the college and university homepages in the United States
- *Inventory Survey:* Important questions students need to ask themselves when choosing a college or university. This valuable questionnaire will help students narrow the list of the schools to fit their ideals and majors
- *Calculator:* What total amount of college loans will your proposed career support?
- *Article:* Which schools will give you the most for your money?
- *Table:* Top 100 schools in the United States based on quality and cost

Page 269—Public and Private Vocational Schools

- *Commentary:* Why should you consider attending a community college?
- *Directory:* Listings of vocational schools throughout the country by state

Page 269—The Military

- *Directory:* Home pages for all branches of the Armed Services
- *Directory:* Home pages for all the U.S. Military Academies

Page 271—Where is it You Want to Go (Educational Plan)

- *Registration:* SAT testing schedule and online registration
- *Registration:* Register for the ACT online
- *Instructional:* Preparing for the SAT
- *Instructional:* ACT Preparation Strategies

Page 279—Your Plan

- *Calculator/Comparison:* Cost of living comparison by city and state
- *Commentary:* Top 20 areas to live and work in the United States—2002

Internet Tutorial

- The basic tutorial
- Everything you wanted to know about the Internet

* You'll want to go online to see the most current index because of the growing and changing nature of the Internet. As we find new and better resources, we'll include them or substitute them for current lessons.

Where Is It You Want To Go?

Page 270–273   Page 116–118

Learning objective:

To help students select high school and post-high school courses that relate to a specific career choice in the student's interest area. As they finalize their future plans, they should consider alternative education and training paths.

Presentation suggestion.

Your Education and Training Plan: Ask students to indicate their career choice in the space provided, detailing the kind of education and training they need and the duration of that training. Some careers have several options, such as vocational school, apprenticeship, military and/or college. Urge students to consider the advantages and disadvantages of each alternative course of action before making a decision.

The chart on page 270–271 will require additional research; it is essential you allow time for this important activity. Suggest students review their *Career Interest Surveys* (on pages 150–155) and the various charts or exercises where they contemplated education and training options. Students may want to visit their counselor at this point to complete a chart of their high school classes. Once complete, this chart will be added to their **Career Portfolio** notebook.

Activity:

Knowing exactly what they need to do in order to accomplish their career goals will help students set priorities and make plans. They may be overwhelmed, however, by the thought of spending another ten to fifteen years preparing for and getting established in a job. To help them visualize this commitment as it relates to the normal lifespan (about eighty years), use the following exercise: Give each student two pieces of 8½ x 11 graph paper (¼--inch blocks), and ask them to tape them together lengthwise. Assuming that each block represents one year, have them label each five-year segment, from age one to eighty. Now have them fill in the blocks representing the years they will need for their education or training. In this context, and considering the financial and emotional rewards involved, the investment of time should now appear more justifiable.

You might consider recommending that students reproduce the charts on pages 270 and 271 and complete them for at least one other job. This will enable them to compare the education and training requirements for each alternative career.

Optional

Pages 270–272

If
by Rudyard Kipling
Read after completing pages 270–273 in *Career Choices*

Delaying Gratification

Page 274–275 Page 119–120

Learning objective:

To personalize the issue of delaying gratification by identifying the sacrifices and commitments required.

Presentation suggestions:

Break the class into small groups based on individual career plans, type and duration of training required, or general career field—whatever seems most appropriate. Since training for any career involves some type of delayed gratification, it should be fairly easy for groups to identify the types of sacrifices they will probably need to make. Having done this, they can help each other complete the questions on page 275.

Facing Fears and Anxieties

Page 276–277 Page 120–121

Learning objective:

To personalize the issue of facing fears and anxieties so students can take this into account when they write their own plan.

Presentation suggestions:

Ask students to review the material on overcoming anxieties in Chapter 9 before completing the exercises on pages 276 and 277. You might use yourself or a student volunteer as an example and run through the exercise as a class.

When we read "25th High School Reunion," it inspired the students to create a scrapbook that could be carried throughout their high school years so that they would have it for their 25th reunion. Also, they began work on a time capsule.

— Janet Sinclair
English I Teacher
Hancock High School
Kiln, Mississippi

Your Plan

Page 279–280   Page 121–123

Learning objective:

The student prepares an education and career plan for an occupation within the student's interest area. The student's plan begins where they are in school at this time, continuing through postsecondary education or training and into their first job. The total plan will cover at least ten years.

Presentation suggestions:

Depending upon the level of the class, this segment of the chapter might be used as the final exam. A more advanced or gifted class should be given the whole chapter as an exam. A class with lower abilities may need the assistance of class discussion in the previous exercises.

If you choose to use this as the final, we suggest making it a take-home exam, and allowing at least a week for its completion. Statements should be written as measurable objectives with all three components: What will be different? By how much or how many? By when? Review this material in class, if necessary. You should also evaluate the plans according to how realistic they are, as well as the amount of time and thought students have given them and the accuracy of planning.

You'll want to suggest students review the key planning documents listed the charts on page 125 of their *Workbook and Portfolio of Career Choices.* This data will help them make their plans with confidence.

Many of my students got really excited about creating their plan. I even received a few letters from parents.

— John Fishburne
Teacher
Cascade High School
Leavenworth, Washington

Optional

Ex-Basketball Player
by John Updike
Read before beginning to work on "Your Plan" in *Career Choices*

25th High School Reunion
by Linda Pastan

Pages 273–283   Read after completing "Your Plan" in *Career Choices*

Mission in Life

Page 282   Page 124

Learning objective:

To experience the task of re-evaluating and clarifying a personal mission statement and understanding the importance of this valuable process.

Presentation:

It might be a good time to re-do the guided visualization on page 4/41 of this guide. Preface this with a simple statement that, given their experience articulating their dreams and goals during this course, it makes sense to look at what is important to them now.

Once they've completed their new letters and vision, ask them to re-write their mission statement based on any new feelings or thoughts. Have they changed their mission from what they indicated earlier on page 61 of *Career Choices*?

If students are willing to share their mission statements, you might want to post them around the room or provide the information to the yearbook editor. Be sure to respect any wishes for privacy.

Assessment and Evaluation:

If assessment and/or evaluation is a critical element of your program, be sure to review your options on the following pages of this guide:

Pages in this guide	Description of Assessment
4/169	Post Assessment Activity using *Envisioning Your Future* activity
6/10 – 6/17	Assessment and Evaluation
6/18 – 6/22	Teacher Survey and Evaluation
9/7	Sample Measurable Goals and Objectives for the *Career Choices* Curriculum

As a Portfolio assignment at the end of the year, students read "We Are a Success" and wrote about how they have been successful over the year.

— Suzanne M. Reese
Teacher/Gifted Liaison
R. L. Turner High School
Carrollton, Texas

Back to the Future

Letters Remembering Your Dreams and Goals

Students will have a clearer sense of themselves and their dreams for the future as they finish their *Career Choices* course. This vision should be captured for a future time when it might trigger renewed enthusiasm.

Have your students write two letters to themselves about their dreams and goals for their future. Tell them they will receive one letter in two years and the other in five years. Ask them to attach a copy of their 10-year plan and with a copy of the letter written from the activity "Seeing in the Mind's Eye", **4**/92–93 in this guide.

Ask each student to bring two self-addressed envelopes to school, each bearing double first class postage (to take into account any rate increases). The envelopes should be addressed to the students, in care of someone in their family who they feel is not likely to move. The return address should be that of a second relative who is also likely to stay at the same address. This doubles their chances of receiving the letters.

After they have written and sealed their letters, box them up and store them for mailing. You'll want to label the boxes with the year they are to be sent. Then each year (perhaps with the new year) you'll deliver the appropriate envelopes to the post office.

Your students' letters just might arrive at a critical moment when they are considering giving up a cherished dream or goal. It could rekindle a passion or remind them of the benefits of staying on course and pursuing a goal.

> *We do graduate surveys two years and five years after graduation. Students consistently rank this class as one of their favorites.*
>
> — Steve Rzeka, Counselor
> South Park High School
> Fairplay, Colorado

An Important Reminder

The materials in the *Career Choices* series are copyright-protected and cannot be photocopied, digitally reproduced/stored on computers, servers, intranets, or the Internet, or illegally adapted at any time.

Post Assessment

At this time, the exercise "Envisioning Your Future" on page 14 of *Career Choices* should be administered again. Compare this version with the one completed at the beginning of the course. Do you see any growth in the students? Have their horizons been broadened? Perhaps their goals are more realistic for their capabilities and commitment. Have young women considered non-traditional careers? Do you sense better self-knowledge? Do their plans include post-secondary education?

If appropriate, share these two assessments with the school counselor. They could also be included in the students' school files, if appropriate and legal.

Turn back to the exercise "Defining Success" on page 4/10–12 of this guide. You may be interested in doing the course wrap-up activity recommended there.

> During the last ten minutes on the final day of the course, we recommend reading aloud *Oh! The Places You'll Go!* by Dr. Seuss. This is a wonderful book for people of all ages, filled with many of the messages imparted in *Career Choices*. Published by Random House, New York, ISBN 0-6779-80523-3, it should be available in most bookstores. The summary provided by the Library of Congress is as follows: Advice in rhyme for proceeding in life; weathering fear, loneliness, and confusion; and being in charge of your actions.

Instructor's Notes:

Career Choices and Changes

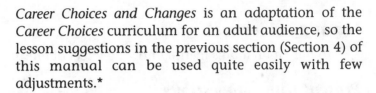

Chapter 11

Making Changes: The inevitable process

Career Choices and Changes is an adaptation of the *Career Choices* curriculum for an adult audience, so the lesson suggestions in the previous section (Section 4) of this manual can be used quite easily with few adjustments.*

Dealing with change is an important component in the career or life planning process for most adults. To address the issues surrounding change, *Career Choices and Changes* has a chapter not found in *Career Choices*. The reader may be contemplating a change in career, lifestyle, economic status, or location. As part of the planning process they may change from student to worker or worker to student. They may even dream of making the change from employee to business owner.

The probability of making a successful change is determined by how individuals manage and plan for that change. Whatever changes readers are considering, the process outlined in this chapter will help.

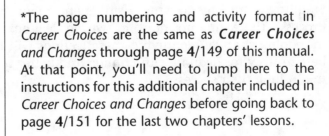

*The page numbering and activity format in *Career Choices* are the same as **Career Choices and Changes** through page **4**/149 of this manual. At that point, you'll need to jump here to the instructions for this additional chapter included in *Career Choices and Changes* before going back to page **4**/151 for the last two chapters' lessons.

How Do You Feel about Change?

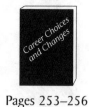

Pages 253–256

Attitude and...Experience

Learning objective:

To help individuals identify how they feel about the change process.

Presentation suggestions:

Different personality types embrace change with varying degrees of enthusiasm and approach changes at different paces. Knowing the pace at which change is most comfortable and identifying feelings about change helps an individual understand how to proceed. For instance, the individual who marked mostly "A" on the survey must be careful to gather data and study their plans; they may over react and move too quickly. Those resistant to change (they marked mostly "D") may find themselves stuck in situations, unable to move forward to a more satisfying circumstance.

Activity:

Once your students have taken the survey on page 253 of *Career Choices and Changes*, ask them to read the explanation on page 254. This will help them analyze their feelings.

Ask them to complete the chart on page 255, listing changes they've made in the last three to five years, how they felt about those changes, and the success of the change.

Once they complete this chart individually, ask volunteers to share a couple of their changes with the group. Do they or the class see any consistency in the feelings expressed about change over this time period? If so, do these feelings match the individuals survey answers on page 253?

Finally, ask students to write a statement about their feelings about the change process. There are no right or wrong feelings, only different strategies for managing change. Identifying these feelings will help your students choose the best strategy for dealing with change and better recognize stumbling blocks that might limit their success.

Recognizing the Need
for Change

Pages 257–258

Objective:

To analyze an individual's situation in relationship to work and personal values; the economic realities of their life; and understanding how lack of congruence can impact the need or desire to change.

Presentation suggestions:

After reviewing the points made on page 257 of the text, ask the class to brainstorm other possible scenarios for the bottom of page 258. Write these on the board. A group with experience in the workforce should have several examples to contribute.

Activities:

Ask each student to write a short statement describing why they might want to change either their current employment or another personal situation in their life (similar to those listed on page 258). When they're done, ask your students to analyze their circumstances. Do they *need* to change or do they *desire* a change?

If a student can't think of a current situation, have them choose one of the statements listed on page 258 that relates to an event or employment predicament earlier in their life. Ask them to re-evaluate whether they had to change or were driven to change.

What differentiates a needed change from a desired change? Break into small groups to brainstorm that question.

You might assign this topic as a short paper or journal entry.

What happens when an individual needs to change, but deals with the situation as if they have a choice? Ask students to share situations known to them of that circumstance. What was the outcome?

Getting Ready for Change

Pages 259–261

Objective:

To recognize that:

- Change takes energy

- Change sometimes takes money

- Support makes change easier

Presentation suggestions:

It is easier to make a change when you are physically, emotionally, and financially prepared. This often requires taking the time to plan and prepare for a change. Review the topics in this section.

Activities:

Ask each student to choose one of the personal or work related changes identified in the preceding activity (preferably a desired change). Using that situation as their point of reference, have students complete the questions and survey on pages 259–261.

Once they have completed the above, ask students to write a statement explaining why making the change does or does not make sense right now. If changing right now doesn't make sense, does it make sense in the future? If so, what preparations can they make to be physically, emotionally, and financially ready?

Break into small groups (three to five individuals per group). Ask each group to create a scenario where change is required—thrust upon them by no doing of their own. Have each group create a plan taking into account energy, money, and support available. Each group will create a fictional situation (probably based upon their consensus experiences). Upon completion ask each group to share their scenarios, stories, and plans.

If one student is willing to share their personal change dilemma, have the class interview the student, brainstorming strategies to prepare for change using the three areas noted.

Mentors

Pages 262

Objective:

To help students identify individuals in their lives who can provide support during the change process.

Presentation suggestions:

Talk about mentors and individuals in your own life who lend support. Ask your students to make a list (page 262) of the individuals most likely to support their change process. You might suggest they go through their personal address books page by page so they are sure to consider all friends and family. Also suggest they think about their work, school, religious, and fraternal affiliations.

Activities:

After their list is complete, ask your students to list family and close friends who might not support their change process. Next to the individual's name (you will not want to share names in class), students should write the reason they think support is unlikely.

Without connecting any names to reasons, ask the students to call out a variety of reasons those closest to them may not support them in their change process.

Once you've got a list of four or five reasons, ask the class to brainstorm strategies for breaking down the support barrier and turning the situation around.

Is Your Job the Real Problem?

Pages 263

Objective:

To understand how outside pressures can impact job satisfaction, and to help students learn to identify the "real" culprit before changing jobs or careers.

Presentation suggestions:

Review topics and the list of possible reasons outside the work environment that might impact work satisfaction. Ask the class to brainstorm other situations that impact job satisfaction, but have nothing to do with position or career choice. Note them on the lines provided.

Activities:

For each of the situations listed and new ones added, brainstorm remedies in small groups. Come back together and share the possible remedies. How many included changing careers or jobs?

Changing Your Life
Often Means
Changing Your Priorities

Objective:

To learn that with change comes the need to reprioritize life goals and daily responsibilities.

Presentation suggestions:

After you present the concepts noted in the text, ask the class to share individual situations that required reprioritization when a change was made. For instance, how did they reprioritize their lives when they returned to school? For those re-entering the workforce, how did their daily priorities change? What about their long-term priorities?

Activities:

As a warm up, ask students to complete a list of their current priorities for the following week. Use the "A, B, C" format described in the text.

Ask each student to make a list of their current life priorities. Draw two columns next to the list of life priorities. Have your students indicate in the first column if that priority is currently an "A," "B," or "C." Once they complete that task, ask students to contemplate one of the changes they've been working on throughout this chapter. Have students write that change above the second column and reprioritize their life priorities given that change. Finally, with that change in mind, they should review the list. Are there any other situations not currently listed that must be added?

For example:

A woman returning to work after years outside the workforce may indicate that the presidency of the PTA is currently an "A" priority. With a return to work full-time, that priority may be relegated to a "B" or even a "C".

An individual who changes careers from a high paying stressful position to a lower paying more satisfying one, may have to add finding time to shop at the wholesale warehouse stores to their list of priorities.

So What Do You Want?

Pages 265–266

Objective:

To build the ability to objectively analyze the career change components and develop a plan, increasing the probability of success for the desired or needed career change.

Presentation suggestions:

You'll first want to brainstorm the scenarios on page 265. Encourage your students to stretch their imaginations. It may be helpful to bring in a career counselor or human resources professional to help with this process.

Once each student has a list of potential careers that match each of the scenarios, encourage them to try to visualize themselves in those positions (page 266).

Does any one career "feel" right? Which one would provide the most satisfaction and match their personal and work values?

Activities:

Once students have written their career change goals (bottom of page 266), have them each develop a plan for changing careers. Be sure to remind them to review their work throughout this chapter, keeping all the components of change in mind as they develop their plan. How do they feel about change? What adjustments will they need to make because of those feelings? Is this a desired or required change? How ready are they are change: physically, emotionally, and financially? Who will be their support team? How will they have to rearrange their priorities?

You'll want to give your students at least a week to complete this activity; they'll need time for reflection and contemplation. Encourage them to brainstorm with each other and with the people they've identified as mentors in their lives.

Once your students complete this activity, ask each individual to make a presentation about their plan and change process.

Once Chapter 11 from *Career Choices and Changes* is completed, turn back to page 4/151 of this manual for lesson suggestions for the balance of *Career Choices and Changes*. Chapter 12 of *Career Choices and Changes* is an adaptation of Chapter 11 of *Career Choices*. Chapter 13 of *Career Choices and Changes* is an adaptation of Chapter 12 of *Career Choices*.

Instructor's Notes:

SECTION FIVE

Specialized Lesson Plans

How Do I Choose?

All the activities and exercises outlined in this guide could easily fill a one-year course, but perhaps you want to be more selective. Let's say you can only devote a nine-week quarter to this topic. We suggest you photocopy this sample worksheet on pages 5/2–5/3 for your planning process.

As you tailor your plan to meet the needs of your particular population of students, keep these points in mind.

1. The text has been written in a sequential order with activities building on skills learned earlier in the unit. You will need to follow the chapters in order, although you may choose to use only a portion of the curriculum (for example: Section One or Sections One and Two).

2. If you complete the text using only the presentation suggestions in this guide and exclude most of the supplemental activities, you should be able to complete this unit comfortably in a nine-week quarter.

At Bethel High School, and most of the high schools on the Virginia Peninsula, Career Choices is used in both the 9th grade and 10th grade Tech Prep Communications classes as a supplemental text. Since every city/division has its own adopted texts for literature, grammar, and writing, Career Choices became the one in-common text for everyone.

— Sharon Hurwitz
English Teacher and Technology Facilitator
Bethel High School
Hampton, Virginia

WORKSHEET FOR LESSON PLAN WEEK OF _____

Monday's Objective(s) _____

_____

Text assignment page(s) _____ Workbook assignment(s) _____

Class discussion _____

Activity _____

Resources _____

Homework assignment_____

Comments _____

Tuesday's Objective(s) _____

_____

Text assignment page(s) _____ Workbook assignment(s) _____

Class discussion _____

Activity _____

Resources _____

Homework assignment_____

Comments _____

Wednesday's Objective(s)_____

_____

Text assignment page(s) _____ Workbook assignment(s) _____

Class discussion _____

Activity _____

Resources _____

Homework assignment_____

Comments _____

Thursday's Objective(s) _____

_____

Text assignment page(s) _____ Workbook assignment(s) _____

Class discussion _____

Activity _____

Resources _____

Homework assignment _____

Comments _____

Friday's Objective(s)_____

_____

Text assignment page(s) _____ Workbook assignment(s) _____

Class discussion _____

Activity _____

Resources _____

Homework assignment _____

Comments _____

Follow-up _____

_____

_____

_____

_____

_____

_____

_____

Making Your Job Easier

The following pages provide two complete optional lesson plans for the *Career Choices* curriculum.

The Sample Nine-Week Interdisciplinary Lesson Plan (pages 5/5–5/14) can save your teaching team hundreds of hours of planning time. This plan, which tracks vertically and horizontally, demonstrates how instructors from different disciplines can work together to present a relevant thematic, academically based curriculum.

The 180-Hour (one full school year) Lesson Plan (beginning on page 5/15) is designed to be used when one instructor is presenting a comprehensive career guidance experience grounded in the academic subjects. Even if you don't have two semesters for your course, you'll want to study this plan to see how the different textbooks fit together. You'll also note the activities that are considered the most important by the authors and other instructors using the curriculum (starred in the last column).

We have a number of other specialized sample lesson plans available for the *Career Choices* curriculum. Give our Technical Support Department a call to see if one fits your needs.

Research Online

 In-Depth Interviews with Innovative Educators   http://www.academicinnovations.com/indepth.html

You'll want to visit our web site and read the stories of innovative educators who use the *Career Choices* curriculum. You may want to build some of their strategies into your lesson plan.

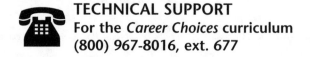 **TECHNICAL SUPPORT**
For the *Career Choices* curriculum
(800) 967-8016, ext. 677

A Sample Nine-Week Interdisciplinary Lesson Plan

The following lesson plan is an example of what could be accomplished if an English/language arts, math, social studies and career, guidance, business or family and consumer science instructor form a cluster unit to teach a quarter class.

This nine-page example demonstrates the scope and sequence of the *Career Choices* curriculum in a multidimensional fashion. Not only does this plan work vertically, which is the traditional way to create lesson plans, but it also relates horizontally. What the guidance component is discussing (column one) relates thematically to what the English, math, and social studies teacher is presenting. Therefore, what is being discussed in English will enrich the discussion in the math and guidance class. The problems worked on in math class will reinforce the dialogues in the social studies, English and guidance components. It is our hope that this sample lesson plan will stimulate you to create similar interdisciplinary lesson plans for not only your *Career Choices* experience but other themes you present in your school.

It is important to note that this lesson plan is just one of many ways to organize the course. Teachers from various disciplines have taught from the different texts. For instance, column one, using primarily the *Career Choices* textbook, might be taught by a career or guidance professional, a business teacher, or family and consumer science instructor. Another possibility would be for the social studies instructor to teach this vertical lesson plan and, therefore, the teaching team would eliminate the last column in this lesson plan.

Perhaps the English/language arts instructor wants to teach from both the *Career Choices* and *Possibilities* texts. Using this format, the first two columns would be combined and the course would be expanded to an 18-week semester unit. The "team" math teacher would then teach a thematic unit from *Lifestyle Math* at the appropriate times while working on other math lessons in between.

If you are working with an at-risk population or one that is performing below grade level, you will probably want to take more time on the individual lessons and, therefore, expand from a nine-week class to an 18- week class.

As you have seen from the comments and quotes of educators using the curriculum, the possibilities of combinations are vast. The *Career Choices* curriculum provides the foundation and you provide the creativity and organization. Here is your chance to be innovative and meet the special needs of your population of students.

Note: You will want to have a copy of each of the textbooks available as you study this plan.

WEEK ONE

CAREER/GUIDANCE CURRICULUM

Text: *Career Choices: A Guide for Teens and Young Adults* and the *Workbook and Portfolio*

The following page examples correlate with those in the *Instructor's and Counselor's Guide* or *Career Choices*. Following each exercise is a definition as to what depth to explore the topic; what discussions, activities and ideas you will have time for.

Monday
Introduction, page 4/2
Presentation suggestions, Activities

Tuesday
Vision Plus Energy Equals Success, page 4/4
Presentation suggestions, Activities
Envisioning Your Future, page 4/6
Presentation suggestions

Wednesday
Defining Success, page 4/10
Presentation suggestions, Activities
Making Career Choices, page 4/13
Presentation suggestions

Thursday
Bull's Eye Chart, page 4/16
Identifying Your Passions, page 4/18
Presentation suggestions, Activities,
English/Language Arts

Friday
Work Values Survey, page 4/20
Presentation suggestions
Homework: Follow-up, page 4/21

ENGLISH/LANGUAGE ARTS

Text: *Possibilities: A Supplemental Anthology for Career Choices*

Assign reading, journal entries and compositions as homework. Each day share themes of journal entries and proceed with discussions and activities in class.

Monday
Introduction
Explanation of journal writing

Tuesday
The Secret Life of Walter Mitty by James Thurber
Discussion: Questions 1 - 5
Quick write: Question 6
Homework: Question 7, Envision Your Future

Wednesday
A Psalm of Life by Henry Wadsworth Longfellow
Discussion: Questions 1, 4, 5, 6
Homework: Antonyms and Synonyms

Thursday
Dreams by Langston Hughes
Discussion: The Formal Debate, pages 21 - 22

Friday
I Have A Dream . . . by Dr. Martin Luther King, Jr.
Discussion: Questions 1, 2, 3

MATH

Text: *Lifestyle Math: Your Financial Planning Portfolio: A Supplemental Mathematics Unit for Career Choices. Unless otherwise noted, all page numbers correlate with the Lifestyle Math text.*

Monday
Introduction and discussion, pages 3 - 4
What Is Your Attitude About Math, page 6
Math Anxiety, page 7

Tuesday
Your vision of being competent in math,
Career Choices, pages 216 - 217
Writing Affirmation about Math
Career Choices, pages 230 - 231
Getting Help, page 8

Wednesday
What Cost this Lifestyle?
Debate from page 12
Read pages 76 - 77 in *Career Choices*
Complete page 12 in *Lifestyle Math*

Thursday
Housing Budget, pages 14 - 16

Friday
Renting or Owning, pages 18 - 20
Property Tax, Insurance, Association Fees, pages 21 - 22

SOCIAL STUDIES

Instructional materials: To be researched and developed. Use *Career Choices* textbook and *Workbook and Portfolio* weeks seven, eight and nine.

Instruction through use of lecture, video, readings, dialogue, activities.

Monday
Introduction

Tuesday
Visionaries in Our Culture, motivational videos

Wednesday
Characteristics of Visionaries
How each of us is a visionary

Thursday
The Societal Movements of the Last 30 Years

Friday
The Societal Movements of the Last 30 Years

WEEK TWO

CAREER/GUIDANCE CURRICULUM

Monday

Strengths and Personality, page 4/22
Presentation suggestions

Tuesday

Your Strengths, page 4/24
Presentation suggestions, Activities,
Energizer

Wednesday

Name That Skill, page 4/27
Presentation suggestions
Skills Identifications, page 4/28
Presentation suggestions, Activities

Thursday

**Roles, Occupations, and Vocations,
page 4/30**
Presentation suggestions, Activities,
Follow-up

Friday

Message Center, page 4/32
Presentation suggestions, Activity,
Debate

ENGLISH/LANGUAGE ARTS

Monday

Excerpt from *The Prophet* by Kahlil Gibran
Richard Cory by Edwin Arlington Robinson
Discussion: Questions 1, 2, 3, 4
Discussion: Question 5
Homework: Question 4

Tuesday

Sonnets From the Portuguese by
Elizabeth Barrett Browning
Discussion: Question 2 and Figurative
Language

Wednesday

Excerpt from *Alice in Wonderland* by
Lewis Carroll
Discussion: Acrostic Poetry #3

Thursday

**Excerpt from *I Know Why the Caged Bird
Sings*** by Maya Angelou
Discussion: Characterization and
Autobiographical Incident
Homework: (extended) Writing
Directions

Friday

Sympathy by Paul Dunbar
Discussion: Questions 2, 4
Personification
Life by Nan Terrell
Discussions: Questions 1, 2, 6

MATH

Monday

Utilities and telephone, pages 23 - 24
Make Your Choice, page 24
Rental Move-In Costs, page 25
Small group activity, page 26

Tuesday

Where Do You Want to Live?, pages 27 - 30
Home Ownership on One Income, page 31
Small group discussion: Last question

Wednesday

Transportation - Buying a Car, pages 32 - 33
Trade-In Time, page 34
Gasoline costs, pages 35 - 37

Thursday

Small group problem, page 38
Insurance and maintenance, page 41
Case Study, page 42

Friday

Yearly Clothing Budget, pages 43 - 44
Spouse and Children's budget,
pages 45 - 47

SOCIAL STUDIES

Monday

Cultural Values
How they change
How they impact our lives

Tuesday

Individual Freedoms;
America's Foundation

Wednesday

Community and Shared
Responsibility

Thursday

Prejudice:
Ethnic, racial, gender, age,
disability

Friday

Diversity:
What is it and why is it important?

WEEK THREE

CAREER/GUIDANCE CURRICULUM

Monday
Maslow's Triangle, page 4/38
Presentation suggestions, Activity
Read "How Do You Want to Be Remembered"
Homework: Complete Mission Statement

Tuesday
How Do You Want to Be Remembered, page 4/39
Presentation suggestions; Panel of self-actualizers

Wednesday
Looking into the Future, page 4/41
Components of Lifestyle, page 4/42
Presentation suggestions

Thursday
Happiness is a Balanced Lifestyle, page 4/43
Presentation suggestions
The Modified Maslow Triangle, page 4/44
Presentation suggestions
Homework: Interview adult on his/her location on triangle

Friday
What About Your Life?, page 4/45
Presentation suggestions, Activity
(parent's triangle)

ENGLISH/LANGUAGE ARTS

Monday
Excerpt from *Self-Reliance* by Ralph Waldo Emerson
Discussion: Share and debate responses to journal entry, Questions 2, 8, 9

Tuesday
***Growing Older* by R. G. Wells**
Discussion: Questions 1, 2 and journal entries

Wednesday
I Shall Not Pass This Way Again
Discussion: Questions 3, 6

Thursday
***Red Geraniums* by Martha Haskell Clark**
Discussion: Questions 1 - 4
The Writer's Notebook

Friday
The Mills of the Gods
Discussion: Journal entries, Questions 1, 4, 6
Discuss extra credit quote

MATH

Monday
Food Budget, pages 48 - 52
Planning Your Weekly Meals, pages 53 - 55
Homework: Grocery shopping, pages 55 - 57

Tuesday
Monthly Entertainment Budget, page 64
Recreation is More than Just Fun, page 65

Wednesday
Saving Plan for Vacation, pages 68 - 69
Creative Planning, small group, page 70

Thursday
Childcare Budget, pages 71 - 73
Health Care Budget, pages 74 - 75

Friday
Furnishing Expenses, pages 76 - 77
Depreciation, Group Brainstorm, pages 78 - 79
Saving for Long-Term, page 80
Percentage you must save, page 81

SOCIAL STUDIES

Monday Appreciating Diversity

Tuesday Cultural Diversity
A historical perspective

Wednesday Cultural Diversity
Today's multicultural society

Thursday Gender Diversity

Friday Age Diversity
Diversity of Ability

WEEK FOUR

CAREER/GUIDANCE CURRICULUM

Monday
Budget Exercise, pages 4/47–64

Tuesday
Budget Exercise, pages 4/47–64

Wednesday
Hard Times Budget, page 4/65
Presentation suggestions

Thursday
Some Sample Budgets, page 4/66
Presentation suggestions

Friday
A Few Words About Poverty, pages 4/67
Presentation suggestions

ENGLISH/LANGUAGE ARTS

Monday
The Savings Book by Gary Soto
Discussion: Questions 1, 2, 3

Tuesday
Activity from **The Savings Book**
Activity a: Group

Wednesday
Miss Rosie by Lucille Clifton
Discussion: Journal entry,
Questions 3, 4, 5

Thursday
Christmas Day in the Workhouse by
George Simms
Discussion: Questions 2, 3
Group activity: Question 5

Friday
The Gift of the Magi by O. Henry
Discussion: Journal entries, Question 4

MATH

Monday
Miscellaneous Expenses, page 84
Group Think, **Saving Strategies**,
pages 82 - 83

Tuesday
Your Total Budget Profile, page 85
What Ends Up in Your Pocket,
page 86

Wednesday
Your Annual Salary Requirement,
page 87
Now Find a Job, page 88

Thursday
Group Project: **Hard Times Budget,**
pages 93 - 94

Friday
Charting Statistics, pages 95 - 97

SOCIAL STUDIES

Monday
Capitalism
How it works

Tuesday
Capitalism vs. Socialism

Wednesday
The Free Enterprise System: Small
Business to Corporations

Thursday
Poverty in the U.S.

Friday
Poverty in the U.S.

WEEK FIVE

CAREER/GUIDANCE CURRICULUM

Monday
Money Isn't Everything, page 4/69
Presentation suggestions
Psychological Cost: Sacrifices Versus Rewards, page 4/70
Presentation suggestions

Tuesday
You Win Some, You Lose Some, page 4/71
Presentation suggestions
After-hours Rewards, pages 4/72–3
Presentation suggestions

Wednesday
An Investment In Education, page 4/74
Presentation suggestions
Homework: **Ask Someone Who's Been There, page 4/76**

Thursday
Easier Said Than Done, page 4/77
Presentation suggestions
Report out from homework assignment

Friday
Your Ideal Job, pages 4/80-81
Presentation suggestions

ENGLISH/LANGUAGE ARTS

Monday
Creative Writing, page 101

Tuesday
A Legacy For My Daughter by James Webb
Discussion: Questions1 - 5, 7, 8

Wednesday
I **Decline to Accept the End of Man** by William Faulkner
Discussion: Questions 1, 5 - 10

Thursday
The Boys' Ambition by Mark Twain
Discussion: Questions 1 - 3, 8, 9

Friday
Lego
Discussion: 1 - 6, 9 - 11

MATH

Monday
Group presentations, pages 95 - 97

Tuesday
Group presentations, pages 95 - 97

Wednesday
Comparing with National Average, page 92

Thursday
Group Project: **What Is Your Math Education Worth To You?,** pages 98 - 99

Friday
Group Project: **What Is Your Math Education Worth To You?,** pages 98 - 99

SOCIAL STUDIES

Monday
The Changing Workforce/Workplace

Tuesday
Changing Demographics

Wednesday
Changes in Laws Affecting the Workplace

Thursday
Changes in the Family Structure and the Workplace

Friday
Technology and the Information Age

WEEK SIX

CAREER/GUIDANCE CURRICULUM

Monday

Complete Your Ideal Job, from previous day
Consider Your Options, page 4/82
Presentation suggestions
Homework: **Employee or Employer, page 4/83**

Tuesday

Employee or Employer, page 4/83
Activities
What About Status?, page 4/84
Presentation suggestions

Wednesday

Career Interest Areas, page 4/86
Presentation suggestions
Bring In Your Identity, page 4/88
Presentation suggestions

Thursday

Career Interest Survey, page 4/89
Presentation suggestions
Go to career library

Friday

Career Interest Survey, page 4/89
Presentation suggestions
Go to career library

ENGLISH/LANGUAGE ARTS

Monday

Essay on Fantasy Job, page 123

Tuesday

Presentation on Fantasy Job

Wednesday

To Build a Fire by Jack London
Discussion of journal entry

Thursday

To Build a Fire by Jack London
Discussion: Questions 1 - 8
Review Observational Writing

Friday

To Build a Fire by Jack London
Share observational writing assignment

MATH

Monday

Investment in Education, page 113,
Career Choices

Tuesday

Math Problem in More Choices, pages 144 - 147 *

Wednesday

Math Problem in More Choices, pages 144 - 147 *

Thursday

Job Research at career center on computers

Friday

Job Research at career center on computers

* From *More Choices: A Strategic Planning Guide for Mixing Career and Family* by Bingham and Stryker.

SOCIAL STUDIES

Monday

The history of vocations/work in the U.S. Colonial days to mid-1880's

Tuesday

The history of vocations/work in the U.S. Industrial Revolution

Wednesday

The history of vocations/work in the U.S. post-World War II to 1970

Thursday

The history of vocations/work in the U.S. the last 20 years

Friday

Predicting the future

WEEK SEVEN

CAREER/GUIDANCE CURRICULUM

Monday
Seeing in the Mind's Eye, pages 4/92–93

Tuesday
The Shadow Program, pages 4/94–95
Explain and write letters
Long-term homework: Arrange for Shadow Experience

Wednesday
Involve Me and I Understand, page 4/101
Presentation suggestions
The Chemistry Test, page 4/102
Presentation suggestions

Thursday
Identifying Choices, page 4/108
Presentation suggestions
Gathering Information, page 4/110
Presentation suggestions

Friday
Evaluating Choices, pages 4/111
Presentation suggestions
Gloria's Chart, 4/113
Presentation suggestions
Make a Decision, page 4/114
Presentation suggestions

ENGLISH/LANGUAGE ARTS

Monday
I Hear America Singing by Walt Whitman
Discussion: Questions 1 - 4
Copy Change

Tuesday
The Monkey's Paw, a play adapted from W. W. Jacobs' short story
Discussion: Question 4
Writing Dialogue

Wednesday
The Monkey's Paw, continued
Share dialogues and run survey of class choices

Thursday
The Road Not Taken by Robert Frost
Discussion: Questions 1 - 7

Friday
Hope by Emily Dickinson
Discussion: Questions 3, 5, 6, 8

MATH

Monday
Group Discussion: **Salary Estimation,** pages 89 - 91

Tuesday
Group Energizer: **Planning a Party**
Spreadsheet lesson at the computer lab

Wednesday
Group Energizer: **Planning a Party**
Spreadsheet lesson at the computer lab

Thursday
Group Energizer: **Planning a Party**
Spreadsheet lesson at the computer lab

Friday
Party with **Math Baseball game,** pages 66 - 67

SOCIAL STUDIES

Monday
The Six E's of Excellence
Career Choices, pages 232 - 235

Tuesday
Work is an Aggressive Act
Career Choices, pages 236 - 237

Wednesday
Work Ethic
You're the Boss exercise
Career Choices, pages 238 - 241

Thursday
Work Ethic
You're the Boss exercise
Career Choices, pages 238 - 241, continued

Friday
The Employee of the Twenty-first Century
Career Choices, pages 242 - 245

WEEK EIGHT

CAREER/GUIDANCE CURRICULUM

Monday
Tools for Solving Problems, page 4/118
Presentation suggestions
Setting Goals and Objectives, page 4/120
Presentation suggestions
Homework: Activities

Tuesday
Goals and Objectives, page 4/120
More practice
What's Your Excuse?, pages 4/124
Presentation suggestions
Taking Responsibility, page 4/126
Presentation suggestions

Wednesday
Startling Statement Quiz, page 4/127
Presentation suggestions, Activities
Detours and Roadblocks, page 4/128
Presentation suggestions
Homework: **Is It Worth Staying In School?, page 4/129**

Thursday
Is It Worth Staying In School?, page 4/129
Activities

Friday
Before You Give Up Your Dream, page 4/134
Presentation suggestions
Developing Anxiety Tolerance, page 4/135
Presentation suggestions

ENGLISH/LANGUAGE ARTS

Monday
Uphill by Christina Rossetti
Discussion: Questions 1 - 9

Tuesday
The Prince of Tides by Pat Conroy
Discuss journal entry

Wednesday
The Prince of Tides by Pat Conroy
Vocabulary
Group Activity B

Thursday
The Prince of Tides by Pat Conroy
Character Development Activity

Friday
Dream Deferred by Langston Hughes
Discussion: Questions 1, 6
Mother to Son by Langston Hughes
Discussion: Questions 3, 5 - 10

MATH

Monday
Group Think: **Savings**, pages 82 - 83

Tuesday
Economics of Bad Habits
Career Choices, page 208

Wednesday
Saving for Retirement, page 100

Thursday
Economics of Women and Work,
Career Choices, pages 211 - 213

Friday
Economics of Women and Work,
Career Choices, pages 211 - 213

SOCIAL STUDIES

Monday
The Employee of the Twenty-first Century
Career Choices, pages 242 - 245, continued

Tuesday
Finding a Job in Today's World
Resume writing
Career Choices, pages 250 - 253

Wednesday
Conducting an Informal Interview
Career Choices, pages 254 - 255

Thursday
Job Applications
Career Choices, pages 256 - 257

Friday
The Job Interview
Career Choices, pages 258 - 259

WEEK NINE

CAREER/GUIDANCE CURRICULUM

Monday

One Step At a Time, page 4/136
Presentation suggestions

Tuesday

Yorik's Story, page 4/137
Presentation suggestions

Wednesday

Taking Risks, page 4/138
Presentation suggestions
Getting Back on Track If You've Been Derailed, page 4/139
Presentation suggestions

Thursday

Homework: Write their own poem: "WE ARE A SUCCESS." Use the poem by Robert Louis Stevenson on page 283 of *Career Choices* as a model.

Friday

Defining Success, page 4/12
Follow-up at the end of the course
Energizer
During the last ten minutes of class, read *Oh! The Places You'll Go!* by Dr. Seuss

ENGLISH/LANGUAGE ARTS

Monday

Excerpt from *All I Really Need to Know I Learned In Kindergarten* by Robert Fulgram
Discussion: Questions 3 - 5, 7, 8

Tuesday

Over the Hill to the Poor-house by Will M. Carleton
Discussion: Questions 3, 5 - 7
Writing assignment

Wednesday

George Gray by Edgar Lee Masters
Discussion: Questions 1 - 4

Thursday

Ex-Basketball Player by John Updike
Discussion: Questions 1 - 3
Writing assignment

Friday

25th High School Reunion by Linda Pastan
Discussion: Questions 1 - 5
Write your essay to be included in your 25th High School Reunion Booklet

MATH

Monday

Developing an Action Plan, pages 102 - 103

Tuesday

Developing an Action Plan, pages 104 - 106

Wednesday

Developing an Action Plan for Your Dream, pages 107 - 109

Thursday

Developing an Action Plan for Your Dream, pages 107 - 109

Friday

A new vision of yourself as math competent
Writing Affirmations, *Career Choices,* page 231

SOCIAL STUDIES

Monday - Friday

Chapter 12, *Career Choices*
Complete pages 266 - 282 as in-class and take-home final.

Career Choices Curriculum

180-Hour Lesson Plan

Designed for:

- one instructor
- using all four textbooks
- in daily 50-minute periods
- for one complete school year

Ideal for:

- Freshmen orientation programs
- A careers course
- Academic classes with a self-discovery theme
- Motivational courses for at-risk students

This specialized lesson plan augments the material of the *Career Choices* curriculum and assists you in your daily planning. In detailed format it shows how the textbooks work together, some of the activities to use, and the order of the activities. It is our hope that this lesson plan will save you hundreds of hours of planning time and present proven strategies for classroom success.

Career Choices: A Guide for Teens and Young Adults: Who Am I? What Do I Want? How Do I Get It?

Workbook and Portfolio for Career Choices

Possibilities: A Supplemental Anthology for Career Choices

Lifestyle Math: Your Financial Planning Portfolio

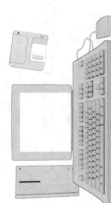

<u>careerchoices.com</u>

Online correction at <u>lifestylemath.com</u>

The Goals of This Lesson Plan

This plan was written for instructors whose goals include facilitating the student guidance and planning process. Students will leave this class with an understanding of the importance of education and the role it plays in their future satisfaction. They will have a strong sense of direction for the balance of their educational experience and the skills to change plans if circumstances dictate.

This is a competency-based course. Students will soon understand the necessity of acquiring basic skills if they hope to have a satisfying adult life. Never again will they ask, "Why do we have to learn this?" While the activities in this lesson plan will give students daily practice in reading, writing, speaking, and mathematical computation, the self-exploration activities of the curriculum are the focus, not the academic drill and skill exercises. More of these exercises may be added at the instructor's discretion.

Because this curriculum teaches an important decision-making process that students will use throughout their lives, it has a strong scope and sequence (curriculum lingo for 'order'). Therefore, skipping around is not recommended. Particular activities may be deleted or substituted, but it is important to note that some exercises are critical to the success of the course. The awareness and skills learned earlier in the course are used as the students finalize their plans. Essential lessons have been noted in the far right margin with a star ☆.

This lesson plan requires each student to have a copy of:

- *Career Choices: A Guide for Teens and Young Adults: Who Am I? What Do I Want? How Do I Get It?*

- *Workbook and Portfolio for Career Choices*

- *Possibilities: A Supplemental Anthology for Career Choices*

- *Lifestyle Math: Your Financial Planning Portfolio*

- Optional: Internet correction key for *Lifestyle Math*

- www.careerchoices.com

As the instructor, you will use the *Instructor's and Counselor's Guide for Career Choices* on a daily basis.

Getting Started

You'll need a copy of each textbook and the *Instructor's Guide* handy so you can turn to the pages and exercises noted in the lesson plan.

It is strongly recommended that, as the instructor, you actually work through your own copy of the main textbook, *Career Choices*, completing the activities for yourself. This will help you integrate the total process, understand the scope and sequence, and provide you with discussion material and examples for your class based on your own experience. Students love to hear teachers' responses! You might want to pretend you are searching for a second career when you retire from teaching. As an adult, this task should take 20 hours or less. Most educators find this an enjoyable and enlightening experience.

How to Use This Lesson Plan

- You'll note the lesson plan is set up in an hour-by-hour format. (Column one)

- The second column notes which textbook(s) the students will use for that lesson, along with the specific pages. This is the reading material for the day. In the case of *Career Choices*, you may want to assign all or a portion of the next day's reading as homework. Students will come to class somewhat familiar with the topic and ready to discuss and complete the activities.

- The third column shows the title of the activity or exercise in the texts. If the title is in parenthesis, it is a description of the lesson.

- The fourth column directs the instructor to the pages in the *Instructor's and Counselor's Guide* for that particular lesson. It also notes what exercises are suggested for that page. For example, if it says "Presentation suggestions" you will read and execute the directions under that topic on that particular page. The same is true for other topics such as Activities, Energizers, Resources, etc. This does not mean you shouldn't use other topics on the page if you have the time or inkling.

- The last column presents Special Directions that complete this special lesson plan and are not included elsewhere in the *Instructor's and Counselor's Guide*. You will want to combine the information in this column with the directions detailed in the fourth column.

- In the right margin, some lessons are starred (☆). We consider these critical to the success of the program. We suggest you not delete these if you decide to do other activities not noted on this lesson plan. You may want to, or need to, spend more time on some of the required lessons.

Hour	Textbook	Lesson	Instructor's Guide	Special Directions (beyond those given in *Instructor's Guide*)	
20	*Career Choices*, p. 30 *Career Choices*, pp. 31-37 *Workbook*, pp. 13-16	(James and Letitia) Work Values Survey	p. 4/20, Presentation suggestions	Dramatic Reading Review the survey together, discuss any words or concepts they don't understand. It is important to be very non-judgmental about statements read. Note the suggestion of the "value totem" on page 4/21.	☆

Example

Career Choices Curriculum
180 hours of instruction

Hour	Textbook	Lesson	Instructor's Guide	Special Directions *(beyond those given in Instructor's Guide)*	
1	*Career Choices*, pp. 6–7	Introduction	p. 4/2, Presentation suggestions Activities	Give students a piece of 8½ × 11 white paper and ask them to "create" something that flies. Responses will vary greatly. Optional: Let students decorate the outside of their *Workbook and Portfolio*. Perhaps allow them to decoupage their books, using pictures they find meaningful or their names in decorative art forms.	☆
2	*Career Choices*, pp. 10–13 *Workbook*, p. 5	Vision + Energy = Success	p. 4/4, Presentation suggestions		☆
3	*Career Choices*, pp. 10–13 *Workbook*, p. 5	(Visualizer activity)	p. 4/7	Divide students into groups of three to develop, design and build their visualizer. Have groups "model" and explain their visualizers to the rest of the class. Leave visualizers hanging in the room with permission to use if needed at any time.	
4	*Career Choices*, pp. 14–17 *Workbook*, p. 6	Envisioning Your Future	p. 4/6, Presentation suggestions	Visual Assessment: Videotape students presenting their Envisioning Your Future essay during the first week of class. Then, during the last week of class, have students rewrite their essays and videotape the new responses. Compare the two videotapes. Share the final production not only with the students but with administrators and funders. This is powerful!	☆
5	*Career Choices*, pp. 15–16 *Career Choices*, p. 17 *Workbook*, p. 7	Why People Work Everybody Works	p. 4/8, Presentation suggestions p. 4/9, Presentation suggestions		☆
6	*Career Choices*, pp. 18–21 *Workbook*, pp. 8–9	Defining Success	p. 4/10, Presentation suggestions		☆
7	*Career Choices*, pp. 18–21 *Workbook*, pp. 8–9	Defining Success *(continued)*	p. 4/10, Activities	Have students write the first of their success statements: p. 21 of *Career Choices*.	☆
8	*Possibilities*, pp. 37–39	"Richard Cory" by Edwin Arlington Robinson		Have the Simon and Garfunkel song "Richard Cory" playing as the students enter the classroom. Read story aloud. Have students discuss journal entry and question 5.	
9	*Possibilities*, p. 38	"Richard Cory" *(continued)* Question 7 How to gather data and conduct an interview		Present the project: Choose an outcome. For example, present findings to the school newspaper or submit to a community paper's editorial page. Where to find people to interview. How to take notes. Homework: Conduct interviews.	
10	*Possibilities*, p. 38	"Richard Cory" *(continued)* Question 7 How to analyze data		Students report out on findings from their interviews. Group decides how to composite findings.	
11	*Possibilities*, p. 38	"Richard Cory" *(continued)* Question 7 How to summarize data		Summarize findings: Discuss and brainstorm ideas. Record findings. Invite school news reporter to sit in on discussion to write an article for the paper [or have a class member(s) write and submit the article]	

Hour	Textbook	Lesson	Instructor's Guide	Special Directions (beyond those given in *Instructor's Guide*)	
12	*Career Choices*, p. 20 *Workbook*, p. 9	Making Career Choices	p. 4/13, Presentation suggestions	After you've discussed as per *Instructor's Guide*, make a chart for classroom wall with the characters' names and a descriptive title. For example, Eric/wishful thinker, Louisa/escape artist, etc. Throughout the course, let students identify the decision-making patterns of friends, characters in stories and even themselves. "Today I'm reacting like Harold (procrastinator) when I wait until the night before to start my social studies report."	☆
13	*Possibilities*, pp. 11–18	"The Secret Life of Walter Mitty" by James Thurber		Read Thurber's story aloud. Use dramatic inflection of voice or invite a senior drama student to do the reading. As a class, discuss question 8 in *Possibilities*.	☆
14	*Possibilities*, p. 17	"The Secret Life of Walter Mitty" *(continued)* Question 9		Break into groups of three to discuss and complete chart. Share charts as a class. As a class, discuss question 5.	☆
15		(Identity activity)	p. 4/6, Activity	Personal Collage: Who am I? What do I want? What are my dreams? On a very large sheet of paper, mark off a quarter section to be used for this assignment. Other parts of the collage can be added later, after they complete other activities that help them identify their dreams and goals.	
16		(Identity activity)	p. 4/16, Activity	Personal Collage: Time to complete. Ask each person to explain his or her collage.	
17	*Career Choices*, p. 24	(James and Letitia)		Choose three students who are able to confidently read aloud to be (1) a narrator; (2) James and (3) Letitia. Their story is told throughout chapter 2 of *Career Choices* (pp. 24–50). Each time the class arrives at a portion of their story, ask the "actors" to read their parts.	☆
	Career Choices, pp. 25–27 *Workbook*, p. 11	(Your Personal Profile) (Bull's Eye Chart)	p. 4/16, Presentation suggestions, Energizer	On their own, create the "first draft" of their charts.	
18	*Career Choices*, p. 28 *Career Choices*, pp. 28–29 *Workbook*, p. 12	(James and Letitia) Identifying Your Passions	p. 4/18, Presentation suggestions, Activities	Dramatic Reading Show the film clip of Dr. Martin Luther King presenting his *I Have a Dream* speech. Discuss King's passion and vision.	☆
19	*Career Choices*, pp. 28–29 *Workbook*, p. 12	Identifying Your Passions *(continued)*	p. 4/18, English/language arts lesson	Break into small groups and have each group member help the others describe their ideal day. Ask each person to report out. Note: Follow-up statement on p. 4/19 of *Instructor's Guide*.	☆
20	*Career Choices*, p. 30 *Career Choices*, pp. 31–37 *Workbook*, pp. 13–16	(James and Letitia) Work Values Survey	p. 4/20, Presentation suggestions	Dramatic Reading Review the survey together, discuss any words or concepts they don't understand. Be non-judgmental about statements read. Note the suggestion of the "value totem" on p. 4/21.	☆
21	*Career Choices*, pp. 31–37 *Workbook*, pp. 13–16	Work Values Survey *(continued)*		Students take the survey. They must take it alone, not in groups. Note: Follow-up suggestion on p. 4/21 of *Instructor's Guide*.	☆

Hour	Textbook	Lesson	Instructor's Guide	Special Directions (beyond those given in *Instructor's Guide*)	
22	*Career Choices*, pp. 31–37 Workbook, pp. 13–16	Work Values Survey (*continued*)		Students score the survey. Discussion of each category.	☆
23	*Career Choices*, pp. 31–37 Workbook, pp. 13–16	Work Values Survey (*continued*)		As a class, brainstorm careers for each student, given his or her top three work values. Ask each student to write his or her top three values on the board. Open the discussion up to the floor so classmates can make suggestions. This is an introductory activity and will need a lot of support from teachers and adults. You might even invite two or three other individuals (career counselor, guidance counselor, principal, etc.) to help brainstorm.	☆
24	*Career Choices*, pp. 31–37 Workbook, pp. 13–16	Work Values Survey (*continued*)	p. 4/20, Gender Equity Activity	Reading and discussion of the story *My Way Sally*. Invite a special guest to read (drama student or teacher, favorite adult or teacher, principal). Call (800) 967-8016 to order.	☆
25	*Career Choices*, p. 38 *Career Choices*, pp. 38–42 Workbook, pp. 17–19	(James and Letitia) Strengths and Personality	p. 4/22, Presentation suggestions	Dramatic reading. Review the definitions on p. 39 of *Career Choices* before students complete the activity. Complete the activities individually.	☆
26	*Career Choices*, p. 43	(How personality impacts career choices)	p. 4/22, Presentation suggestions	Discussion of styles. Brainstorm the types of careers in which each style might be happiest.	☆
27	*Career Choices*, pp. 44–45 Workbook, p. 20	Your Strengths (Developing your strengths)	p. 4/24, Presentation suggestions, Activities		☆
28	*Instructor's Guide*, p. 114	(Contributing your strengths to the team)	pp. 4/25–26, Energizer		
29	*Possibilities*, pp. 43–46	Excerpt from *Alice in Wonderland* by Lewis Carroll Question 3		Have students form editorial teams to help each other write their poems. Two students can choose to work together. Each will complete a poem with the other's help and input. Discussion: Acrostic poetry, question 3.	☆
30	*Possibilities*, pp. 43–46	Excerpt from *Alice in Wonderland* (*continued*)		Have the students make their acrostic poem into a poster (art project) and hang them around the room.	☆
31	*Career Choices*, p. 46 *Career Choices*, pp. 46–48 Workbook, p. 21	(James and Letitia) Skills and Aptitudes, Name That Skill	p. 4/27, Presentation suggestions	Dramatic reading	☆
32	*Career Choices*, p. 48 Workbook, p. 22	Skills Identification	p. 4/28, Presentation suggestions		☆
33	*Career Choices*, p. 48 Workbook, p. 22	Skills Identification (*continued*)	p. 4/28, Activities	You may want to break into small groups to brainstorm and then ask each group to report out. Energizer: Name That Skill toss. Using a ball, have the students sit in a circle and, when tossed the ball, call out a skill they have as they throw to the next person.	☆
34		(Interest Inventory)	p. 4/29, Resources	Work with the Guidance Department and administer the interest inventory of choice.	

Hour	Textbook	Lesson	Instructor's Guide	Special Directions (beyond those given in *Instructor's Guide*)
35		(Work behavioral style inventory)	p. 4/23	Optional: Administer the Carlson Personal Profile System Assessment. For ordering information, call (800) 967-8016.
36 ☆	*Career Choices*, p. 49	Roles, Occupations, and Vocations	p. 4/30, Presentation suggestions, Activities	Energizer: Using a "family tree" format, ask students to research their family tree (through great grandparents), including the roles, occupations and vocations of these people. This may be a long-term project.
37 ☆	*Career Choices*, p. 49	(Who Am I? — Becoming identity achieved)	p. 4/31, Chapter Follow-up	Chapter follow-up: Complete chart on p. 27 of *Career Choices* with information discovered from activities on pp. 28–49. Post charts around the room for all to see.
38 ☆	*Career Choices*, p. 49	(Who do I want to become) (Character analysis)	p. 4/31, Chapter Follow-up p. 4/34–35	Compare bull's eye chart of hero/heroine with their own bull's eye chart. Activity and discussion. Complete a bull's eye chart for one of the following people in their future: Employer, best friend, business partner, spouse.
39 ☆	*Career Choices*, p. 50 *Career Choices*, pp. 50–53 *Workbook*, pp. 23–24	(James and Letitia) The Message Center	p. 4/32, Presentation suggestions	Dramatic reading
40 ☆	*Possibilities*, pp. 61–62 *Career Choices*, pp. 50–53	"Life" by Nan Terrell Reed Message Center Debate: Does Society Give Girls and Boys Different Messages?	p. 4/32, Activity p. 4/32, Debate	Discuss the messages which society gives individuals based on their gender, race, age, physical appearance, physical ability, social status, intellectual capacity, educational achievement, and so forth. See p. 22 of *Possibilities* for a description of a Formal Debate. Energizer: Break students into teams of four or five. Give each team a large piece of art paper. Have students draw a box with lines dividing it into quarters (two rows, two columns). Along the horizontal axis, write "Good Messages" above the left-hand quadrant and "Bad Messages" above the right-hand quadrant. Along the vertical axis, write "Female" next to the top quadrant and "Male" next to the bottom quadrant. Have each group brainstorm the good and bad messages given to them by family, peers and society. You can also have them use magazine pictures to illustrate the messages.
41 ☆		(Projecting into the future)		Divide into triads and ask the student teams to project into the future and write the script for James and Letitia. Describe their lives at age 20, 25, 30, 40 and 50. Keep in mind their described passions, values, strengths, etc.
42 ☆	*Possibilities*, p. 24	(Long-range planning) "Dreams" by Langston Hughes		Have each group report on how they saw the lives of James and Letitia unfolding. Read the poem "Dreams" and discuss the journal entry question.
43 ☆	*Career Choices*, pp. 56–59 *Workbook*, p. 26 *Career Choices*, pp. 60–61 *Workbook*, p. 27	(Maslow's Triangle), Where Are You Now? How Do You Want to be Remembered?	p. 4/38, Presentation suggestions p. 4/39, Presentation suggestions	Ask students to complete Mission Statement over the next two or three days.

Hour	Textbook	Lesson	Instructor's Guide	Special Directions (beyond those given in *Instructor's Guide*)	
44	*Career Choices*, pp. 60–61 Workbook, p. 21	How Do You Want to be Remembered? *(continued)*	p. 4/39, Activity	You'll want to look for this panel a few weeks ahead and lend them a copy of *Career Choices* so they can read chapter 3.	
45	*Possibilities*, pp. 69–71	"Growing Older" by R.G. Wells Discussion Questions 1, 2 and Journal Entry	p. 4/41, Looking Into the Future	After reading the poem aloud and discussing questions, follow directions on p. 4/41 of the *Instructor's Guide* for a guided writing assignment. Make copies of the letters to be used with lesson "Remembering Your Dreams and Plans" (Hour 177).	☆
46	*Possibilities*, pp. 72–73	"I Shall Not Pass This Way Again" Discussion: Questions 3 and 6		Use as art project (optional).	
47	*Career Choices*, pp. 62–63 Workbook, p. 28	Your Lifestyle, Components of Lifestyle	p. 4/42, Presentation suggestions		☆
48	*Career Choices*, pp. 64–69	Happiness is a Balanced Lifestyle, The Modified Maslow Triangle	p. 4/42, Presentation suggestions		☆
49	*Career Choices*, pp. 70–71 Workbook, p. 30	What About Your Life	p. 4/44, Presentation suggestions		☆
50	*Possibilities*, pp. 76–79	"The Mills of the Gods" Discussion: Journal entries, Questions 1, 4, 6 Quote	p. 4/45, Presentation suggestions, Activity (parents' triangle)		
51	*Career Choices*, pp. 74–77 *Lifestyle Math*, p. 12	(Ivy Elm's story, Family Profile)	pp. 4/48–54	Read and discuss Ivy's story. Have students complete their own family profile. Then have them share their plans with the class.	☆
52	*Career Choices*, p. 78 *Lifestyle Math*, pp. 14–16	Housing Budget (Do you want to own or rent?) Presentation suggestions — Real estate professional	p. 4/55	Hand out copies of classified ads and real estate booklets. Be sure to have scissors and glue. Ask a professional if he or she can arrange a shadowing opportunity for class members. Saturday or Sunday is best.	☆
53	*Lifestyle Math*, pp. 18–19	Renting or Owning	p. 4/55, Activity	As a class, figure at least one fictional example of a mortgage using steps on pp. 18–19 of *Lifestyle Math*. Use calculators if necessary.	☆
	Lifestyle Math, p. 20	Your Mortgage Payment		Have students figure their own mortgage payment for house and condo chosen. Check on computer.	
54	*Lifestyle Math*, pp. 21–22	Property Taxes Insurance Home Owner's Association Fees		Find out ahead if your state has a special formula for property taxes. Explain each of these "hidden costs" of owning a home. Check figures on computer. Homework: Bring in copies of utility bills from home.	☆
55	*Lifestyle Math*, pp. 23–24	Utilities Telephone		Ask students to total and share their families' utility costs for a month. Brainstorm ways to save on utilities. Complete calculations and check on computer.	☆

Hour	Textbook	Lesson	Instructor's Guide	Special Directions (beyond those given in *Instructor's Guide*)	☆
56	*Lifestyle Math*, p. 25	If Renting is Your Choice… How Much will it Cost to Move In?		Brainstorm pros and cons of renting. Explain move-in deposits and terms. Have each student complete p. 25 of *Lifestyle Math* and check on computer.	☆
57	*Lifestyle Math*, p. 26	How Numbers Can Help You Make the Best Choices		As a class, complete questions 1–3. Divide into three to four groups (no more than five per group) and answer question 4. Make sure there is at least one capable math student in each group. Ask each group to share final choice and tell why.	
58	*Lifestyle Math*, pp. 27–30	Home Affordability Across the Country Where Do You Want to Live?		Discuss topic. Practice formula on board using fictional example. Ask students to complete the first two problems on p. 30 of *Lifestyle Math*. Check on computer.	☆
59	*Lifestyle Math*, pp. 31	Affording Home Ownership on One Income		Discuss relocation. Ask students to share experiences. Brainstorm pros and cons. Complete An Affordable Location (bottom of page 30 and the exercise on page 31) of *Lifestyle Math*.	
60	*Lifestyle Math*, p. 31	(Reasons to move to a more affordable location)		Brainstorm this list (last question at bottom of page) in small groups. Report out. Optional: Conduct Internet searches of four or five cities students identified. Go to search engine such as Yahoo. Search (name of city) + "real estate" (see *Making It Real*).	
61	*Lifestyle Math*, p. 31	(Reasons to move to a more affordable location — *continued*)			
62	*Lifestyle Math*, pp. 32–34	Transportation — Buying a Car Trade-In Time	p. 4/56	See *Instructor's Guide*. Check on computer.	☆
63	*Lifestyle Math*, pp. 35–36	Planning Monthly Gasoline Costs		Ask students to break into pairs and make a weekly and monthly log detailing the mileage they think they'll travel on average under these headings: Weekly Trips — type of trip, how many times per week, how many miles per trip; Monthly Trips — type of trip, how many times per month, how many miles per trip. After they multiply their weekly trips by 4 and add their monthly trips, they'll have the miles per month they plan to travel. Complete p. 36 in *Lifestyle Math*. Check on computer.	☆
64	*Lifestyle Math*, pp. 39–40	Transportation, Insurance and Maintenance		Invite an insurance agent to speak to the class or ask an agent to give you charts to help students estimate costs. Review the insurance laws in your state. Ask students to interview parents to find monthly maintenance budget of their cars. Good chance for discussion of savings by doing your own tune-ups.	☆
65	*Lifestyle Math*, pp. 41–42	Public Transportation Case Study		Ask students to research bus fares. Divide into groups of three to five classmates and complete Case Study and presentations.	☆
66	*Career Choices*, p. 82 *Lifestyle Math*, pp. 43–47	Yearly Clothing Budget	p. 4/57	Students may have to complete as homework if they projected several children. Divide into groups of two or three students to brainstorm column C of each worksheet if you sense some students don't know average costs. Check on computer.	☆

Hour	Textbook	Lesson	Instructor's Guide	Special Directions (beyond those given in *Instructor's Guide*)	
67	*Lifestyle Math*, pp. 43–47	Yearly Clothing Budget (*continued*)			☆
68	*Lifestyle Math*, pp. 43–47	Yearly Clothing Budget (*continued*)			
69	*Career Choices*, pp. 84–85 *Lifestyle Math*, pp. 48–52	Preparing a Food Budget	p. 4/58	Prepare students to complete weekly meal cost by reading and discussing the noted pages in *Career Choices* and *Lifestyle Math*.	☆
70	*Lifestyle Math*, pp. 53–54	Planning Your Weekly Meals (Consumer of the Week award) (*optional*)		Advise students that an award will be given to the student whose weekly plan is judged most nutritious *and* economical (recruit home ec teacher to judge). Prize: lunch or dinner with you, the instructor. Collect weekly grocery ads for numerous weeks to be used for reference. Allow students to work in teams if you like.	☆
71	*Lifestyle Math*, p. 55	Sample Grocery List		Once they decide on the meal plan, they can make a grocery list.	☆
72	*Lifestyle Math*, pp. 56–57	Find Your Weekly Grocery Costs		Either assign a trip to the grocery store for homework (to investigate the costs of their list) or have resources in the classroom such as food advertisements from grocery stores or inventory price printouts from the stores. Check on the computer.	☆
73	*Lifestyle Math*, p. 64	Monthly Entertainment Budget	p. 4/59	Be sure to advise students they don't need a figure in each line item. Newspaper entertainment sections, catalogs, and brochures for health clubs and the YMCA would be good to have as resources. You may want to brainstorm column B as a class. Check on the computer.	☆
74	*Lifestyle Math*, p. 65	Recreation is More Than Just Fun		Review topic with students. Ask students to choose a hobby they'd like at age 29. Divide class into groups of individuals who have similar ideas so they can brainstorm their budget/start up cost together. Share your hobby with them. Include your start up costs and strategies.	
75	*Career Choices*, p. 87 *Lifestyle Math*, pp. 68–70	Saving and Planning for a Vacation / Creative Planning	p. 4/59	Have teams of students first complete p. 70 of *Lifestyle Math*, Creative Planning, and make a presentation to the class. Begin research for pp. 68–69 of *Lifestyle Math*. Use Sunday travel section from the newspaper.	☆
76	*Lifestyle Math*, pp. 68–70	Saving and Planning for a Vacation (*continued*)		If students have similar plans, suggest they form research teams to figure costs. Check on the computer.	☆
77	*Career Choices*, p. 88 *Lifestyle Math*, pp. 71–73	Child Care Budget	p. 4/60	Divide into groups of three to complete p. 71 of *Lifestyle Math* and brainstorm other child care options.	☆
78	*Lifestyle Math*, pp. 71–73	(Raising a Child on Your Own)	pp. 4/36–40	Invite a panel of single mothers (from teen to adult) to present the challenges of single motherhood. One (widowed or divorced) should be successful due to education and career planning.	
79	*Lifestyle Math*, pp. 71–73	Child Care Budget (*continued*)		Either individually or in groups, complete questions and chart. Check on the computer.	☆

Hour	Textbook	Lesson	Instructor's Guide	Special Directions (beyond those given in *Instructor's Guide*)	
80	*Career Choices*, p. 89 *Lifestyle Math*, pp. 74–75	Health Care Budget Savings for Medical Deductibles	p. 4/60	Using classified ads and medical bills, work through pp. 74–75 of *Lifestyle Math* as a class. Most students will have little knowledge of health care costs. If one student has had extensive medical experience within their family, ask if he or she would like to share the story. Discuss generic medications vs. regular, HMOs, and other health insurance options. This can be overwhelming so present gingerly. Check on computer.	☆
81	*Career Choices*, p. 89 *Lifestyle Math*, pp. 76–77	Furnishing Expenses	p. 4/61	Have merchandise catalogs available for research. Divide into groups to complete chart on p. 77 of *Lifestyle Math*. Check on computer.	☆
82	*Career Choices*, p. 89 *Lifestyle Math*, p. 80	Saving for the Long Term	p. 4/61	Review each line item and, as a class, brainstorm Savings Plan on p. 80 of *Lifestyle Math*. Check on computer.	☆
83	*Lifestyle Math*, p. 100	Saving for Retirement		Ask a retirement specialist to come in and present growth potential on annual deposits in IRA if begun early. Ask students to complete graph on p. 100 of *Lifestyle Math*.	☆
84	*Lifestyle Math*, p. 81	What Percentage of Your Salary Must You Save per Month?		This is an important concept to understand. You may want to use the figures of a couple of students and work through this formula. Discuss the question at the bottom of the page as a class. If you are willing, share your savings philosophy and compare it to your parents' philosophy.	☆
85	*Lifestyle Math*, p. 84	Miscellaneous Expenses	p. 4/62	First complete a fictional example on the board. Then ask students to complete their own annual and monthly costs. Check on computer.	☆
86	*Lifestyle Math*, pp. 85–87	Your Total Budget Profile What Ends Up in Your Pocket Your Annual Salary Requirement	pp. 4/63–64	You'll want to talk briefly about payroll deductions and gross pay versus net pay. It is important that your students understand that their salary requirement will be higher (by at least 20%) than what they expect to spend each month. You may want to share copies of payroll stubs (from your older students) so they can see what is taken out of a paycheck. Check on the computer.	☆
87	*Lifestyle Math*, p. 88	Find a Job That Will Support Your Lifestyle		Resources: *The American Almanac of Jobs and Salaries* can be ordered from a full service bookstore.	☆
88	*Lifestyle Math*, p. 88	Find a Job That Will Support Your Lifestyle *(continued)*		Ask students to share what they found and which occupations they starred. As a class, brainstorm the last question: If you have trouble finding appropriate careers that would support your desired lifestyle, what other options do you have?	☆
89	*Possibilities*, pp. 80–86	"The Savings Book" by Gary Soto Discussion: Questions 1, 2, 3		After you read Gary Soto's story (autobiographical) as a class, brainstorm answers to questions 1, 2 and 3 on p. 84 of *Possibilities*.	
90	*Possibilities*, pp. 80–86	"The Savings Book" *(continued)* Activity A: Group		Break students into groups of three and ask them to write a 30-second spot as described in the Activity. At the end of class, ask each group to "present" their spot.	

Hour	Textbook	Lesson	Instructor's Guide	Special Directions (beyond those given in *Instructor's Guide*)	
91	*Career Choices*, pp. 95–96 *Workbook*, p. 43	In Over Your Head?, Hard Times Budget	p. 4/65, Presentation suggestions	You'll need to research ahead-of-time the amount for AFDC and unemployment in your state. Complete this activity either in small groups or as a class.	☆
92	*Possibilities*, pp. 87–89	"Miss Rosie" by Lucille Clifton Discussion: Journal entry, Questions 3, 4, 5		Before reading the poem, discuss the journal entry on p. 87. Break into small groups and ask each group to describe Miss Rosie's life at age 15 (question 4) and then report on their ideas. As a class, discuss question 5. For homework, ask students to write a first-person narrative of a day in a homeless person's life.	☆
93	*Possibilities*, pp. 90–94	"Christmas Day in the Workhouse" by George R. Sims Discussion: Journal question, Questions 2, 3, 4, Group activity 5		Before reading the poem, discuss the scenario in the journal entry. Let students break into teams and choose to complete one of the following questions: 3, 4 or 5.	
94	*Career Choices*, pp. 97–101 *Workbook*, pp. 44–45	Some Sample Budgets	p. 4/66, Presentation suggestions	Break the class into four groups and assign each group a different budget on pp. 98–101 of *Career Choices*. Once the groups debate and decide on their budget, ask each group to report on their budget and justify their choices.	☆
95	*Career Choices*, p. 102 *Workbook*, p. 46 *Career Choices*, p. 103	A Few Words About Poverty Could You Become a Poverty Statistic?	pp. 4/67–68, Presentation suggestions	After discussing the points on p. 102 of *Career Choices*, ask students to individually complete the questions at the bottom of p. 103. Inviting a panel of single parents is also an option here.	☆
96	*Lifestyle Math*, pp. 95–97	Statistics — Developing Charts and Graphs		As a class or in small groups, complete the activities on these pages. Spend time discussing what the students found shocking about their graphs.	
97	*Career Choices*, pp. 104–110 *Workbook*, pp. 46–48	Money Isn't Everything (Psychological costs – sacrifices vs. rewards)	p. 4/69, Presentation suggestions p. 4/70, Presentation suggestions	After discussing these two topics, choose one of the activities listed in the *Instructor's Guide*.	☆
98	*Career Choices*, pp. 106–110	(Individual's stories)		Break into groups of three or four and assign each group a story. Ask each group to first read the story and then report on their conclusions. Do class members have anything to add?	☆
99	*Career Choices*, pp. 111–113 *Workbook*, pp. 49–50	You Win Some, You Lose Some After-Hours Rewards	p. 4/71, Presentation suggestions, Activities pp. 4/73–73, Presentation suggestions	As a class, brainstorm the possibilities on p. 111 of *Career Choices*. Break into groups of three and have each group help its members list the rewards and sacrifices of one or two careers each student is considering. As a class, discuss and brainstorm points on pp. 112 and 113.	☆

Hour	Textbook	Lesson	Instructor's Guide	Special Directions (beyond those given in *Instructor's Guide*)	
100	*Possibilities*, pp. 95–102	"The Gift of the Magi" by O. Henry Discussion: Journal entry Creative Writing		Before reading the story, discuss the journal entry questions. Ask individuals to give examples. If you can, arrange for a dramatic reading of this story. Break into groups of four or five and ask each group to brainstorm the creative writing assignment. Give extra credit to any group that wants to complete the Creative Writing assignment over the next week.	
101	*Career Choices*, pp. 116–117 Workbook, pp. 51–53	An Investment in Education …Yields Dividends for a Lifetime	p. 4/74, Presentation suggestions	Ask students to study the chart on p. 116 of *Career Choices* and interpret what it demonstrates. Then ask them to individually complete computations on p. 117.	☆
102	*Career Choices*, pp. 118–119 Workbook, pp. 51–53	An Investment in Education …Yields Dividends for a Lifetime *(continued)*	p. 4/74	Help students as they individually complete their bar graph on p. 118 and worksheet on p. 119 of *Career Choices*. Ask students to share their findings.	☆
	Career Choices, p. 120 Workbook, p. 54	Ask Someone Who's Been There	p. 4/76	Assign homework: *Career Choices*, p. 120.	
103	*Career Choices*, p. 121 Workbook, p. 55	Easier Said Than Done	p. 4/77, Presentation suggestions,	Give a report on homework and follow directions on p. 4/77 of the *Instructor's Guide*.	☆
104	*Career Choices*, pp. 124–134 Workbook, pp. 57–62	Your Ideal Career	pp. 4/80–81, Presentation suggestions	Ask students to complete pp. 124–134 in *Career Choices*. They will need to work individually on this assignment. You'll want to follow procedure outlined in the *Instructor's Guide*.	☆
105	*Career Choices*, pp. 124–134 Workbook, pp. 57–62	Your Ideal Career *(continued)*	pp. 4/80–81	After students have completed their charts, begin brainstorming possible careers that meet their essential career characteristics (see *Instructor's Guide*, p. 4/80). If you have a career technician or counselor, you might ask him/her to attend this class to assist.	☆
106	*Career Choices*, pp. 135–137 Workbook, p. 63	Consider Your Options	p. 4/82, Presentation suggestions		☆
107	*Career Choices*, pp. 138–139 Workbook, pp. 64–65	Employee or Employer?	pp. 4/83, Presentation suggestions	After completing the activity as outlined in *Instructor's Guide*, you may want to debate the question "Which worker would have the most options for parenting, someone in a structured job or someone who is self-employed?"	☆
108	*Possibilities*, pp. 118–123	"Lego" Discussion: Journal entry, Questions 1–6, 9–11		Discuss the Mark Twain quote before reading the story. After reading this true story, discuss questions 1–6 and 9–11. Spend the most time on question 11. This is an important concept for students to understand. Then present the project described in the Writing Assignment so students can ponder it that evening.	☆
109	*Possibilities*, p. 123	"Lego" *(continued)* Essay on fantasy job		Have students spend the class time designing their fantasy job and writing a description of it. Encourage their imaginations to run wild.	☆
110	*Possibilities*, p. 123	Presentation on fantasy job		Ask students to give a short presentation on their fantasy job.	☆
111	*Career Choices*, pp. 144–147 Workbook, p. 67	Career Interest Areas Bring In Your Identity	p. 4/86, Presentation suggestions p. 4/88, Presentation suggestions	After completing these activities, ask students to write down three careers that they may want to pursue.	☆
112	*Career Choices*, pp. 148–149	Career Research		Review text. Take a tour of the career center/library.	☆

Hour	Textbook	Lesson	Instructor's Guide	Special Directions (beyond those given in *Instructor's Guide*)	
113	*Career Choices*, pp. 150–155 *Workbook*, pp. 68–73	Career Interest Survey	p. 4/89, Presentation suggestions	You'll want to recruit the assistance of your career librarian or career technician and spend the next three days in the library or career center.	☆
114	*Career Choices*, pp. 150–155 *Workbook*, pp. 68–73	Career Interest Survey (*continued*)	p. 4/89, Presentation suggestions		☆
115	*Career Choices*, pp. 150–155 *Workbook*, pp. 68–73	Career Interest Survey (*continued*)	p. 4/89, Presentation suggestions		☆
116	*Career Choices*, pp. 156–157 *Workbook*, pp. 73–74	Seeing in the Mind's Eye	pp. 4/92–93, Presentation suggestions		☆
117	*Career Choices*, pp. 158–159 *Workbook*, p. 75	The Shadow Program	pp. 4/94, Presentation suggestions	Explain and write letters. Long-term homework: Arrange for Shadow Experience. Optional: This project will be completed over a period of time and require outside work on your part (either finding job shadowing placements or better yet, a Director of Mentors), but the added effort is well worth it. This is an impressive activity for a high school student! See pp. 4/94–100 in the *Instructor's Guide*.	
118	*Career Choices*, pp. 160–161 *Workbook*, p. 76	Involve Me and I Understand	p. 4/101, Presentation suggestions	Optional Energizer: "What's My Line" guest panel. Invite in three individuals from the community who have unique jobs. Divide the class into two teams and have each team take turns asking questions and guessing their professions.	☆
119	*Career Choices*, pp. 162–165 *Workbook*, pp. 77–78	The Chemistry Test	pp. 4/102, Presentation suggestions	Read the story on p. 162 aloud. After discussing the topic as a class, work through the questions on pp. 163–164. Ask students to individually answer the questions on p. 165 of *Career Choices*.	☆
120	*Career Choices*, pp. 168–170 *Workbook*, p. 80	Identifying Choices	p. 4/108–109, Presentation suggestions, Activities		☆
121	*Career Choices*, p. 171 *Workbook*, p. 80	Gathering Information	p. 4/110, Presentation suggestions		☆
	Career Choices, pp. 172–174 *Workbook*, pp. 81–82	Evaluating Choices	pp. 4/111–112, Presentation suggestions	After the class has worked through Joyce's example, break into groups of three to consider Jessica and John's stories and complete their charts on pp. 173–174 of *Career Choices*.	
122	*Career Choices*, pp. 176–177 *Workbook*, pp. 82–83	Gloria's Chart	p. 4/113, Presentation suggestions	As a class, discuss and vote on Gloria's choice. Then have each student complete the chart on p. 177 of *Career Choices*, using the three careers researched earlier as their choices.	☆
123	*Possibilities*, pp. 127–135	*The Monkey's Paw* by W. W. Jacobs		A theatrical reading. Assign parts to students.	
124	*Possibilities*, pp. 127–135	*The Monkey's Paw* (*continued*) Question 4 Writing Dialogue		Discuss question 4 as a class. Break into groups of three and ask each group to write the dialogue for Morris (described in Writing Dialogue). Then have each group share their scenes.	

Hour	Textbook	Lesson	Instructor's Guide	Special Directions (beyond those given in *Instructor's Guide*)	
125	*Career Choices*, p. 178 *Workbook*, p. 84 *Possibilities*, pp. 139–141	Make a Decision "The Road Not Taken" by Robert Frost Homework: Question 7	p. 4/114, Presentation suggestions	Brainstorm a list of important choices you might make as a working parent. Using the Edward De Bono exercise—Plus, Minus, Interesting—ask the students to brainstorm what is positive about each choice, negative about each choice and interesting about each choice. After discussion of decision-making styles and a review of the terms on p. 178 of *Career Choices*, ask each student to complete the chart at the bottom of p. 178. Discuss the topic on p. 179. End the class with the Robert Frost poem, "The Road Not Taken" in *Possibilities* and assign question 7 for homework.	☆
126	*Career Choices*, pp. 182–185 *Workbook*, p. 86	Tools for Solving Problems	pp. 4/118–119, Presentation suggestions, Activities		☆
127	*Career Choices*, pp. 186–190 *Workbook*, p. 86	Setting Goals and Objectives	pp. 4/120–121, Presentation suggestions	Energizer: Hand out a paper clip and a one-foot piece of thin string to each student. Folding the string in half, slip a paper clip until half-way through and then, holding the two ends of the string, dangle the paper clip. Ask students not to move their hand but to think about the paper clip swinging. It will. The point: What we focus on will eventually happen.	☆
128	*Career Choices*, p. 190 *Workbook*, p. 86	Setting Goals and Objectives *(continued)*	pp. 4/120–121, Activities	If you have time, you'll want to have your students complete pages 102–106 of *Lifestyle Math*. This exercise demonstrates how to use goals and objectives to develop a timely, quantitative plan.	☆
129	*Career Choices*, pp. 197–199 *Workbook*, p. 89	What's Your Excuse?	pp. 4/124–125, Presentation suggestions, Activities		☆
130	*Career Choices*, p. 200 *Workbook*, p. 90	Taking Responsibility	p. 4/126, Presentation suggestions	Break into small groups of three students. Write the excuses found in the *Instructor's Guide* on the board and ask the groups to reframe them. Bring the class together and have groups present their conclusions.	☆
131	*Possibilities*, pp. 178–206	*Prince of Tides* by Pat Conroy		Because Pat Conroy's stories are so beautifully written, read this story to the class or ask a drama student to read it.	
132	*Possibilities*, pp. 178–206	*Prince of Tides (continued)* Group Activity B		Break into small groups or use the Fish Bowl technique described on p. 85 of the *Instructor's Guide*.	
133	*Career Choices*, pp. 201–202 *Workbook*, p. 91	Startling Statement Quiz	p. 4/127, Presentation suggestions, Activities, Energizer		☆
134	*Career Choices*, pp. 203–206 *Workbook*, pp. 92–93	Detours and Roadblocks	p. 4/128, Presentation suggestions, Activities		☆
135	*Career Choices*, p. 207 *Workbook*, p. 94	Is It Worth Staying In School?	p. 4/129, Presentation suggestions, Activities		☆
136	*Career Choices*, p. 207 *Workbook*, p. 94	Is It Worth Staying In School? *(continued)*	p. 4/129, Presentation suggestions, Activities	Energizer: Break class into teams to build a tower. Each team gets two sheets of card stock, 10 paper clips and one pair of scissors. The point: the need for a good foundation.	☆

Hour	Textbook	Lesson	Instructor's Guide	Special Directions (beyond those given in *Instructor's Guide*)	☆
137	*Career Choices*, pp. 208–209 Workbook, p. 95	Economics of Bad Habits	p. 4/130, Presentation suggestions		☆
138	*Career Choices*, pp. 208–209 Workbook, p. 95	Economics of Bad Habits (*continued*)	p. 4/130, Presentation suggestions, Activities	Panel: Senior citizens	
139	*Career Choices*, pp. 211–213 Workbook, pp. 96–98	If You're a Woman	pp. 4/132–133, Presentation suggestions		☆
140	*Career Choices*, pp. 211–213 Workbook, pp. 96–98	If You're a Woman (*continued*)	pp. 4/132–133, Activities	Guest speaker: Mixing career and family	
141	*Career Choices*, p. 215 Workbook, p. 99	Before You Give Up Your Dream	p. 4/134, Presentation suggestions		☆
142	*Possibilities*, pp. 212–215	"Dream Deferred" by Langston Hughes Discussion: Question 6 "Mother to Son" by Langston Hughes Discussion: Questions 3, 8–10		At the beginning of class, have a dramatic reading of "Dream Deferred." Discuss the journal entry question as a class. Ask students to complete individually the activity described in question 6 on p. 213 of *Possibilities*. Then have a dramatic reading of "Mother to Son" followed by a class discussion of questions noted.	
143	*Career Choices*, pp. 216–217 Workbook, p. 100 *Lifestyle Math*, pp. 6–7	(Developing anxiety tolerance)	p. 4/135, Presentation suggestions	Have students complete the inventory on p. 6 of *Lifestyle Math* and review the text on p. 7. Then read pp. 216–217 of *Career Choices* and help students write a guided visualization to overcome math anxiety.	☆
144	*Career Choices*, pp. 218–221 Workbook, p. 101	One Step at a Time	p. 4/136, Presentation suggestions		☆
145	*Career Choices*, pp. 222–223 Workbook, p. 102	Yorik's Story	p. 4/137, Presentation suggestions		☆
146	*Career Choices*, pp. 222–223 Workbook, p. 102	Yorik's Story (*continued*)	p. 4/137, Presentation suggestions	Extra Credit: Create a rap song around the theme of "I Hear America Singing," pp. 124–125 in *Possibilities*.	☆
147	*Career Choices*, pp. 224–225	Taking Risks	p. 4/138, Presentation suggestions, Activities		
148	*Career Choices*, p. 226	Getting Back on Track If You've Derailed	p. 4/139, Presentation suggestions	Invite a guest speaker who can review the resources and services available in the community to help an individual get back on track. An optional homework assignment would be to have each student volunteer three to four hours at a social service agency (such as serving at a soup kitchen, assisting at a daycare center for children of the homeless, helping at a church/synagogue fund raiser to assist the less fortunate, or planning a class fund-raiser to help with a particular family or agency).	☆
149	*Lifestyle Math*, pp. 93–94	Hard Times Budget		Brainstorm reasons as a class. Divide into groups of three students each and have groups complete pp. 93 and 94 of *Career Choices*.	☆

Hour	Textbook	Lesson	Instructor's Guide	Special Directions (beyond those given in *Instructor's Guide*)	
150	*Lifestyle Math*, pp. 93–94	Hard Times Budget (*continued*)		Finish work and ask each group to report out their plans and strategies.	☆
151	*Career Choices*, pp. 230–231 *Workbook*, p. 104	(Affirmations)	P. 4/142, Presentation suggestions, Activities		☆
152	*Career Choices*, pp. 232–235	The Six E's of Excellence	p. 4/143, Presentation suggestions, Activities	Energizer: The Seventh E — Entrepreneurship. Have students play the game An Income of Her Own. To order a copy, call National Resources for Girls and Young Women at (800)360-1761.	☆
153	*Career Choices*, pp. 236–237 *Workbook*, p. 104	Going For It…Work Is an Aggressive Act	p. 4/145, Presentation suggestions, Activities		☆
154	*Career Choices*, pp. 238–241 *Workbook*, pp. 105–107	You're the Boss	pp. 4/146–147, Presentation suggestions, Activities	As a class, read and discuss this section. Then break into small groups and assign each group one of the employees to evaluate, and then diagram their objectives.	☆
155	*Career Choices*, pp. 242–245 *Workbook*, pp. 108–109	The Employee of the Twenty-first Century	p. 4/148, Presentation suggestions, Activities	You will probably want to give each group inventing a new item or service a couple of days to think about their invention. Once presentations are made, you may want to ask the class to vote for the best idea.	☆
156	*Possibilities*, pp. 240–247	*Tonia the Tree* by Sandy Stryker Questions 4–8		The full color picturebook of *Tonia the Tree*, winner of the Friends of American Writers Merit award is available from Academic Innovations at (800) 967-8016. Adults as well as children delight in this book.	☆
157	*Career Choices*, pp. 2250–253 *Workbook*, p. 111	Your Resume	p. 4/152, Presentation suggestions		☆
158	*Career Choices*, p. 256 *Workbook*, p. 112	Job Applications	p. 4/156, Presentation suggestions, Activities	As outlined in the activity section, you'll need to arrange to get copies of actual résumé/application forms prior to this class.	☆
159	*Career Choices*, pp. 258–259 *Workbook*, p. 113	The Job Interview	p. 4/157, Presentation suggestions, Energizer	If you want to expand this into a community project, see pp. 10/2–5 of the *Instructor's Guide*. The Job Interview Night described on p. 126 is an excellent year-end project.	☆
160	*Career Choices*, pp. 262–263 *Workbook*, p. 114 *Possibilities*, p. 262	Making Connections	p. 4/159, Presentation suggestions, Activities	At the beginning of class, read the poem "The Bridge Builder." After discussing text on p. 262 of *Career Choices*, ask students to break into pairs and answer questions on p. 263 of *Career Choices*.	☆
161	*Possibilities*, pp. 264–268	"Thank You, M'am" by Langston Hughes Questions 1, 2, 3 and 5		After reading the story (either aloud or individually), discuss questions as a class. Break into groups of three and brainstorm question 5. Report out.	☆
162	*Lifestyle Math*, pp. 89–91	Computing Salaries In Your Head — Quickly! Numbers to Memorize		Break into groups of four or five students and ask them to discuss these problems and formulate group answers. Then have each group report their findings problem by problem. Review formula. Have students team up and practice computing annual salaries quickly.	☆

Hour	Textbook	Lesson	Instructor's Guide	Special Directions (beyond those given in Instructor's Guide)	
163	*Lifestyle Math*, pp. 66–67	Energizer – Math Baseball		Using the Math Baseball format on pp. 66–67 of *Lifestyle Math*, create flash cards for hourly wages for careers and use for game. Objective: Students compute annual salaries from hourly wages. Ask each correct respondent to write the title and salary on the chalkboard so the class can review the annual salaries. Use the *American Almanac of Jobs and Salaries* (see p. 88 of *Lifestyle Math*) for research.	
164	*Career Choices*, pp. 260–261	Dealing with Rejection, Accepting a Job	p. 4/158, Presentation suggestions	Review with class the text on pp. 260 and 261 of *Career Choices*. Here is a chance to invite a personnel manager of a large business to discuss employment issues.	☆
165	*Career Choices*, pp. 266–269	Getting the Education or Training You Need	p. 4/162, Presentation suggestions, Activity	During the last two weeks of school, arrange for students to spend time with their counselor or advisor to map out the classes that meet their career and educational goals for the balance of their high school years. Students will want to incorporate those classes into their 10-year plan.	☆
166	*Lifestyle Math*, pp. 98–99	What is Your Math Education Worth to You? Working As a Team	SCANS	Following the directions and format on p. 99 of *Lifestyle Math*, ask each team to develop their project. As a class, discuss possible strategies, resources and production aids.	
167	*Lifestyle Math*, pp. 98–99	Working As a Team *(continued)*		Goal for today: Complete first, second and third steps.	
168	*Lifestyle Math*, pp. 98–99	Working As a Team *(continued)*		Goal for today: Work on fourth step — data collection.	
169	*Lifestyle Math*, pp. 98–99	Working As a Team *(continued)*		Goal for today: Analyze data and produce graph.	
170	*Lifestyle Math*, pp. 98–99	Working As a Team *(continued)*		Report out: Groups report not only on their findings but their process. Ask math department chair, principal and economics instructor to attend presentations. Showcase graphs in your school display area, school newspaper or community newspaper.	
171	*Career Choices*, pp. 270–273 Workbook, pp. 116–118	Where is it You Want to Go?	p. 4/164, Presentation suggestions, Activity	Hang their charts around the room once completed.	☆
172	*Possibilities*, pp. 270–271 *Career Choices*, pp. 274–275 Workbook, pp. 119–120	"If" by Rudyard Kipling Journal question Delaying Gratification	p. 4/165, Presentation suggestions	Open the class with a discussion of the journal question. Then read "If" aloud, giving each student two lines from text. Line up in order for the reading.	☆
173	*Possibilities*, pp. 252–253 *Career Choices*, pp. 276–277 Workbook, pp. 120–121	"Be the Best of Whatever You Are" by Douglas Malloch Facing Fears and Anxieties	p. 4/165, Presentation suggestions	At beginning of class, read poem on p. 252 of *Possibilities* aloud to class. Ask students to individually complete pp. 276 and 277 in *Career Choices*. If students have built up their level of trust, ask some to share their concerns and their goals.	☆

Hour	Textbook	Lesson	Instructor's Guide	Special Directions (beyond those given in *Instructor's Guide*)	
174	*Career Choices*, pp. 278–281 Workbook, pp. 121–123	Your Plan	p. 4/166, Presentation suggestions	Everything they have been doing in this class leads to this 10-year plan. Include a copy in their school folder. Also provide a copy for the student's next year's academic teachers. A parent-student meeting to present their plans would also be advantageous. It is important that students' plans and dreams are reinforced by everyone with whom they work and play.	☆
175	*Career Choices*, pp. 278–281 Workbook, pp. 121–123	Your Plan *(continued)*	p. 4/166, Presentation suggestions		☆
176	*Possibilities*, pp. 277–283	25th High School Reunion		After reading the poem aloud, ask students to write their "contribution" to their booklet for their 25th high school reunion. Make into a booklet for high school archives or bury as a time capsule to be unearthed by the group the day before their 25th reunion.	☆
177		(Remembering your dreams and plans)	p. 4/168	Project: Ask students to write two letters to themselves detailing their dreams and plans. One will be mailed to them in two years and the other in five years. Attach a copy of their 10-year plan along with a copy of the letter (written in Hour 45). Then ask each student to address two envelopes to themselves using the address and return address of two different relatives who are likely to be at the same address over the next five years. You will keep these letters together, labeled, to be mailed after the first of the year of each appropriate year.	☆
178	*Career Choices*, p. 282 Workbook, p. 124 *Possibilities*, p. 283	(A mission in life) "We Are a Success…" by Robert Louis Stevenson Course wrap-up	p. 4/167, Presentation suggestions p. 4/12, Energizer	You may want to share the art pieces at the next school staff meeting or even the next school board meeting.	☆
179	*Instructor's Guide*, p. 100	Course Wrap-Up		Energizer	
180	Graduation party	*Oh! The Places You'll Go* by Dr. Seuss		Have a spaghetti dinner potluck using recipes from *Lifestyle Math*, p. 60. Read Dr. Seuss book aloud.	☆

Course Follow-Up

Guidance Portfolio

Upon completion of this course, you will want to collect the students' *Workbook and Portfolio* and photocopy the following **completed** pages to form the students' guidance portfolios. This list is found on page 6 of the *Workbook and Portfolio* and permission is granted to photocopy these students' pages for inclusion in their school files.

Pages: 6, 11, 28, 42, 62, 68–73, 83, 109, 111–113, 116–118, 121–124

We also recommend that you give a copy of this guidance portfolio to *each* of their academic teachers for next year. You will probably want to write a brief cover letter to introduce the long-range educational and career plans of the student. This document will provide crucial data to each instructor so there can be continuity of support for that student's plans and dreams. This is very important!

Career Portfolio Notebook

Once students completed their work for the course, they'll want to create a dynamic record of their career exploration and job history. They can use this portfolio throughout their lives. See page 4/13–4/14 of this guide for a detailed description of how to assemble this *Career Portfolio notebook*. Students can also refer to their *Workbook and Portfolio for Career Choices* on pages 125–126. Encourage students to take their *Career Portfolio* notebook when they meet with counselors, mentors and teachers.

Instructor's Notes:

SECTION SIX

Special Teaching Tips and Strategies

Tips from Teachers

Classroom teachers have been very generous in sharing their *Career Choices* tips with us. You'll find their suggestions sprinkled throughout this guide, but the majority are with the lesson suggestions (Section Four, page **4/1**). Here are some additional ideas you might want to try.

Linda Neef, English Teacher, Pardeeville, Wisconsin

Working in teams is a big part of today's workplace, so Linda Neef uses a variety of cooperative learning strategies. Groups change every few weeks. This demonstrates the need to be able to work with all kinds of people and helps teach students this valuable skill. Students are graded individually on weekly vocabulary tests; however, if everyone in a group scores 85 or higher, additional points are awarded. The message is clear: Everybody wins when everyone is encouraged to excel. Linda also issues each group "work orders," indicating what needs to be accomplished. Once the group feels it has met the goals, another group evaluates their achievements.

Cathy Miles and Rosann Lauri, English Teachers, Richmond, Ohio

During their 12-week class, students receive a checkbook with a starting balance. They then "earn" a salary for attending class and completing assignments. Using the budget exercise, individuals choose their own lifestyle and make necessary payments from their "checking account." Every few weeks, quarterly taxes must be paid. Students who run out of money can apply for loans, but loan payments are automatically deducted from future checks. Periodically, Cathy and Rosann announce an unexpected bill, such as a new water heater.

Phyllis Stewart, Family and Consumer Science Instructor, Vincennes, Indiana

Phyllis' career fairs aren't just people lecturing about their jobs. Instead, local business people decide what students need to know to be successful in the workplace. They break into small groups and use role-playing and other interactive methods to deliver their message. For instance, to teach about interviewing for a job, adult participants play applicants and display a variety of behaviors and attitudes. When they're finished, students decide whom they would hire.

To help students relate to the budget exercise, Phyllis sometimes asks them to make up a prom budget assuming they can only spend $200. They can't get everything they want. Are there less expensive alternatives? What are they willing to sacrifice?

Linda Hubbs, Home Economics Teacher, Lone Pine, California

Linda photocopies the completed pages from the students' workbooks (where permission is given on page 6 of the *Workbook and Portfolio*) and sends them to the school guidance counselor. This enables the counselor to provide more appropriate advice in counseling sessions.

Linda Fisher, English Teacher, Jackson, California

Linda's favorite assignment is writing an autobiography titled "Your 70th Birthday". Since this activity involves thinking about the life students hope to have as adults, she assigns this when they are working through the budget exercise and choosing a career.

Dave Major, Lead Teacher, Fallbrook, California

Career Choices is a major component of Dave's elective career course, part of an independent study program for grades 9 to 12. Students sign contracts agreeing to do a certain amount of work in return for a designated number of credits. Most students complete the course in 8 to 10 weeks working at their own pace. Contracts might also include work experience, career research, shadowing, or other projects.

Christine Remmen and Karen Aronowitz, Miami, Florida

Christine and Karen use the traditional game of BINGO in several new ways to enhance their use of *Career Choices*. In Occupation BINGO, students fill their BINGO card with job titles (no free space allowed—nothing in life is free). Then, job titles are read from a rather long list of occupations (compiled from a resource such as the *Dictionary of Occupational Titles* or the *Occupational Outlook Handbook*). The first student to accomplish BINGO wins. This is a great way to expose students to the vast array of jobs. These two creative teachers have also developed Job Application Bingo. In this variation of the classic game, students fill the spaces with information required on a job application (first name, social security number, etc.). *Call our Curriculum Support Department for a copy of the Occupation Bingo activity.*

Ruby Takebayashi, Career Counselor, Honolulu, Hawaii

Ruby has been using *Career Choices* since it debuted in 1990. To keep things fresh she supplements the text with a wide variety of her own activities. One that is wildly popular and functions as a great object lesson is the Group Juggle. When Ruby's class discusses balancing different aspects of life (Chapter 3, *Career Choices*), this activity gets students in a juggling act, of sorts. Students stand in a circle and Ruby tosses in different objects, each representing something—school, work, family, etc. The class has to keep all objects in the air. Ruby may throw a full water balloon (representing drugs, alcohol addiction, divorce, or gossip) into the fray. Students quickly realize that their energy is focused on the water balloon and other things get dropped. Should the water balloon break, everyone in the circle gets wet. *Call our Curriculum Support Department for a copy of the Group Juggle activity.*

In-Depth Interviews
with Innovative Educators

We've conducted in-depth interviews with educators to learn how they use and adapt the *Career Choices* curriculum to fit the needs of their unique programs. Their approaches are insightful and creative. Visit our web site to learn more about these successful programs or, if you are not already online, call our Curriculum and Technical Support department for hardcopies of specific interviews.

Hint: Before you even begin lobbying, we recommend you call our office for technical support. Not only can we give you ideas and examples of how other schools with your demographic profile are using the curriculum, we can provide you with resources such as overheads and slides that might make your presentation planning easier.

  In-depth Interviews with Innovative Educators

www.academicinnovations.com/indepth.html

Phyllis Stewart—Vincennes, Indiana

www.academicinnovations.com/int11.html

Phyllis Stewart, Vocational Coordinator and award-winning teacher, worked with the English and computer instructors to deliver her original *Career Choices* program. She shares her observations on why integration works.

www.academicinnovations.com/int11b.html

Phyllis retired after 39 years in the classroom, but the Career Education class she built using the *Career Choices* curriculum is still going strong. See how a program's longevity pays off for students.

Jerry Anderson—Clinton, Tennessee

www.academicinnovations.com/int21.html

Jerry Anderson's very first semester teaching a brand-new state mandated class (Career Management Success) was itself a huge success. See how Jerry used the *Career Choices* materials to help students make better selections as they plan their high school curriculum and better choices as they plan their life beyond high school.

If you would like to share how you structure your *Career Choices* program on our web site, call our Curriculum and Technical Support Department at (800) 967-8016 ext. 677 to arrange an interview.

Doug Campbell—San Gabriel, California

www.academicinnovations.com/int12.html

Doug Campbell and his colleagues implemented a yearlong interdisciplinary class using the *Career Choices* curriculum in the communications department. This class is now required for all 9th graders. Doug has good ideas for anyone restructuring.

Mary Ellen Fowler—Broward County, Florida

www.academicinnovations.com/int13.html

English teacher Mary Ellen Fowler's class, Career Decision-Making and Critical Thinking Skills, is part of her school's Tech Prep/School-To-Work program. She shares some ideas—an exemplary speakers program and parent orientation.

Roberta Freed—Little Falls, Minnesota

www.academicinnovations.com/int14.html

English teacher Roberta Freed and On-the-Job teacher Ron Hanenkamp created an integrated "Transitions" class for special education students. Roberta's detailed explanation is sure to help any teacher.

Priscilla Gregory—Vonore, Tennessee

www.academicinnovations.com/int15.html

English teacher Priscilla Gregory uses a career guidance theme with all her students, college and non-college prep alike. Her unique community outreach program is worthy of replication.

Scott Hess—Tumwater, Washington

www.academicinnovations.com/int16.html

English teacher Scott Hess explains how an interdisciplinary team of six instructors put together a remarkable program, winner of the 1994 Washington Educators Association's "Leaders in Restructuring Award" for innovative programs. Scott also shares their ideas for "Keys to Successful Teamwork."

Dr. Jim Campbell—Delaware State Tech Prep Consortium

www.academicinnovations.com/int17.html

Dr. Campbell, 1993 winner of the Parnell Award for exemplary Tech Prep programs, reveals his secrets for successful Tech Prep programs. His discussion of the need for comprehensive guidance is complete with relevant statistics.

Barbara Larson and Peg Slusarski—Columbus, Nebraska

www.academicinnovations.com/int18.html

Business teacher Barbara Larson and English teacher Peg Slusarski explain how an integrated class called BECI (Business and English Curriculum Integration) was created. See how their detailed planning process fostered cooperation among teachers and support from administrators.

Teri Redl—Medina County, Ohio

www.academicinnovations.com/int19.html

School-To-Work Site Coordinator Teri Redl developed a class for potential dropout. This interview gives details of how she organized her lesson plans. Her strategies clearly demonstrate the potential success when academic skill improvement is combined with individual support and guidance.

Lorraine Rippey and Wendy Hanslovan—St. Marys, Pennsylvania

www.academicinnovations.com/int20.html

Why did guidance counselors Lorraine Rippey and Wendy Hanslovan develop a classroom-based program where students get "ten months, instead of ten minutes of comprehensive guidance?" This interview will enlighten you.

Pat Marabella—Havre, Montana

www.academicinnovations.com/int01.html

Pat Marabella instilled a love of learning in his multi-cultural, at-risk group of students. Thirty percent of his students were Native American and he developed some unique ideas for working with this population. Pre- and post-tests found significant increases in math and reading abilities.

Nancy Carter—Denver, Colorado

www.academicinnovations.com/int02.html

Nancy Carter's Summer Youth Program helped students make significant gains in learning. One motivating factor was that each student who successfully completed the program, received a unit of credit toward graduation. You don't have to take our word for it. Read what an external evaluator said.

Zora Tammer—Berkeley, California

www.academicinnovations.com/int03.html

Zora Tammer's highly structured, eight-week JTPA program turned reluctant learners into motivated students.

Ron Eydenberg—Boston, Massachusetts

www.academicinnovations.com/int04.html

Ron Eydenberg brought academics to the worksite for his 500 summer JTPA participants—to the benefit of all.

Eric Stephens—Los Angeles, California

www.academicinnovations.com/int05.html

Eric Stephens was able to adjust his curriculum to fit the different learning styles of his at-risk population.

Deb Mumford—Denver, Colorado

www.academicinnovations.com/int06.html

An external evaluation of this academic enrichment program for at-risk students found great results. Staff members also share their insights on why they think this program worked.

Anne Swygert—Greensboro, North Carolina

www.academicinnovations.com/int07.html

Anne Swygert's seven-week summer JTPA program involved some creative activities and approaches. She was able to expose her students to a world they had never known.

Jessy James—Marshall, Minnesota

www.academicinnovations.com/int08.html

Jessy James' students made significant gains in math and reading. What does he credit for these post-testing gains? Find out!

Joe Werner—Monterey, California

www.academicinnovations.com/int09.html

Joe Werner's program for very high-risk youth "puts the needs of the students first." The strength of this program is the individualized attention each of his 78 students received. You'll want to review Joe's strategies for success.

John Gill—Hempstead, New York

www.academicinnovations.com/int10.html

John Gill adapted *Career Choices* and *Possibilities* to work with the varying abilities of his population of 700 at-risk students. Find out how.

If you'd like to share how you structure your *Career Choices* program, call our Curriculum and Technical Support Department at (800) 967-8016, ext. 677 to arrange an interview.

Grading

There are several different grading strategies that can be used with this course.

In language arts classes, grades may be based on reading comprehension and composition skills, along with exams on other reading assignments for the course.

Some exercises can be graded on the basis of how much effort went into their completion. You may wish to offer points for class participation or for attendance, if that is a problem at your school.

The 10-year plan in Chapter 12 of *Career Choices* makes a good final exam. We recommend it be a take-home exam and that you allow the students at least a week to complete it. Grades can be based on how thoroughly the plan is completed and how well goals and objectives are defined.

It's always helpful to let the class know how they will be graded and what they must do to earn an A, B, C. Hand out a grading sheet on the first day of class. This sheet should outline the total graded assignments for the class and how the points are broken down. Students can then keep their own running tally and know exactly how they are doing. Following are sample grading forms for a nine-week quarter class.

Since the main goal of this course is to get students actively involved in planning a satisfying future for themselves, anyone who shows enthusiasm, participates in classroom activities, and completes the assignments should do very well.

My students' semester exam grade was their career research papers. Each unit complemented the stage of their paper. For example, Chapter 5 helped them make their choices of topic; a unit on using resources helped them with their bibliography cards; Chapter 6 helped them with their rough draft and composition; Chapter 7 helped them process their information and decide if it was a good **Career Choices** *for them; Chapters 8 and 9 helped them implement a proper plan.*

— Julia S. Forbus
Occupational Specialist
Fort Pierce Westwood High School
Fort Pierce, Florida

Sample Grading Form

	Total Points Possible
Attendance – You will earn 5 points per day for 45 days (or a total of 255 points). To receive points for the day's attendance, you must also participate in the class discussion, complete appropriate assignments in the workbook, and be supportive of the class goals and rules.	225

Text assignments – Complete all assignments for a total of 150 points.

Complete Chapter 2 and the chart on page 27 =	30 points	
Budget Process *(pages 77–96)* =	30 points	
Your Personal Chart of Job Characteristics = *(pages 126–134)*	10 points	
Career Interest Surveys *(pages 150–155)* =	30 points	
Decision Chart *(page 177)* =	10 points	
Goals and Objectives *(pages 189–190)* =	10 points	
One Step at a Time *(pages 218–221)* =	10 points	
You're the Boss *(pages 238–241)* =	10 points	
Writing Your Resume *(page 253)* =	10 points	150

Your journal –	75 points	75

Writing – Three writing projects at 25 points each for a total of 75 points.   75

Reading assignments – Two outside reading assignments and book reports at 50 points each for a total of 100 points.   100

Exams – Five vocabulary quizzes at 10 points each and the final exam at 100 points for a total of 150 points.   150

775

> TOTAL OF 775 points
> A = 698 points
> B = 620 points
> C = 543 points
> D = 504 points

Sample Student Grading Form

	Total Points Possible	Your Points
Attendance	225	
Text assignments —		
Complete Chapter 2 and the chart on page 27	30	
Budget Process *(pages 77–96)*	30	
Your Personal Chart of Job Characteristics *(pages 126–134)*	10	
Career Interest Surveys *(pages 150–155)*	30	
Decision Chart *(page 177)*	10	
Goals and Objectives *(pages 189–190)*	10	
One Step at at Time *(pages 218–221)*	10	
You're the Boss *(pages 238–241)*	10	
Writing Your Resume *(page 253)*	10	
Your journal —	75	
Writing projects —		
a.	25	
b.	25	
c.	25	
Reading assignments —		
a.	50	
b.	50	
Exams —		
Vocabulary One	10	
Vocabulary Two	10	
Vocabulary Three	10	
Vocabulary Four	10	
Vocabulary Five	10	
Final Exam	100	
	775	

Assessment and Evaluation

A frequently asked question: "How do we know if we're succeeding?" There are many ways to measure progress; we've listed some possibilities throughout this section.

Before you begin, review the sample goals and objectives on page 9/7, and evaluative criteria on the following pages. If you are using the language arts component and/or the math program, you'll find additional learning objectives in Section Two.

With these in mind, consider behavioral and attitudinal changes, such as:

- **Retention rates.** Are more students staying in school and graduating? Is the dropout rate for students who have completed the curriculum lower than for students with similar backgrounds and ability in your school? Do the students who go on to college stay there and graduate? (Remember, only 50 percent of those who start college complete their course of study.)

- **Setting higher or more realistic goals.** Upon completion of the course, do students' 10-year plans reflect higher or more realistic personal, educational, career, and life goals?

- **Engagement.** Do students become more engaged with their education? Are they more motivated? Do they seek out new opportunities and ways to better prepare themselves for the future? Are they signing up for special programs such as School-To-Work and Tech Prep? Are they actively seeking assistance with getting into college? Are they giving the process more attention and energy?

- **Academic achievement.** Are test scores and/or grade point averages rising? As students understand the relevance of reading, writing, speaking, and computing, are they becoming more proficient in these important academic areas?

- **Self-esteem and self-reliance.** Is self-esteem high enough for students to cope with challenges as they enter adulthood? Do they feel competent to move into the adult world as emotionally and economically self-sufficient individuals?

For the really adventurous, you may wish to do a more thorough class evaluation. If so, you will also need to:

- **Survey students:**
  (1) as they go through the course and
  (2) for the remainder of their high school career

- **Survey each student's teachers** for as long as he or she is a student at your school

- **Get feedback from students' parents**

- **Document the education and career histories of students** for several years or even a decade beyond high school

This long-range evaluation would take a great deal of time and effort. But what you discover could have a major impact on your school's educational focus. Perhaps the education department of a local university would be interested in undertaking this project. If you are working toward an advanced degree, this evaluation might function as a portion of your thesis or dissertation.

Innovative Assessment of Students' Progress

Madeline Noakes of Patrick Henry High School in San Diego, California, has developed an innovative way to measure her students' growth. During the first week of her semester-long "Introduction to Careers" class, students complete the Envisioning Your Future exercise (page 14, *Career Choices*). Then, as students are working on other assignments, Madeline videotapes individual students as they read or present their papers.

At the end of the course, she videotapes each student again, this time as they present their 10-Year Plan and Mission Statement (pages 278-81). When the first video is compared with the second, Madeline reports, the differences are astounding. Not only are the students more grounded in realistic expectations and plans by the end of the course, but even their demeanor and attitude have changed. The students present themselves in a more professional and serious fashion once they understand how critical a professional image is to their future success and satisfaction in life.

This project is one you might like to try. School Improvement Committees and School Boards would undoubtedly be interested in and impressed by seeing the before-and-after results.

Pre- and Post-Testing/Surveys

Here is an example of a student survey that can be administered in class to evaluate how your student's attitudes, aptitudes and plans have changed in relation to what they have learned in their *Career Choices* course. While this is qualitative data, it should give you a clear measure of important growth and learning among your students.

Timing

Give the *pre-class survey* during the first day or two of class. It is important to administer the survey before any of the material is covered in class.

Give the *post-class survey* after all work in *Career Choices* is completed.

Explanation of Survey and Results

Last name:_____ First name:_____ Teacher:_____ Period:_____

1. Circle the one statement that best reflects your attitude about school.

   a. I really could care less about school. The sooner I get out the better.
   b. My parents and society require I go... otherwise I wouldn't be here.
   c. All I want to do is graduate from high school. I do only what I have to in order to get by.
   d. I want to go to college, so I will do what it takes to get there.
   e. A good education is important to my future; therefore, I strive to learn as much as I can.

   > **In the post-class survey at the end of the course, each student's responses will be compared to evaluate any change in attitude about the importance of school.**

2. Thinking about your future, circle the highest grade level you plan to achieve before leaving school.

   a. I plan to leave school before I graduate from high school.
   b. I plan to graduate from high school and then enter the workforce.
   c. I plan to complete at least two years of college or trade school.
   d. I plan to graduate with a four-year degree from college.
   e. I plan to get an advanced degree (something beyond a four-year college degree).

   > **In the post-class survey at the end of the course, each student's responses will be compared to evaluate whether educational aspirations have increased.**

3. Imagine you are 30 years old. If you could wave a magic wand and have any career, what would it be?

4. *Complete this sentence with a number.* Between the ages of 18 and 65, I expect to work _____ years at a full-time job outside the home.

5. Describe the life you envision for yourself when you are 35 years old. (Use the back of this paper for more room).

6. What are your plans to make the life you just described a reality?

The above four questions will be evaluated after the post-class survey based upon:

   a. **Appropriateness of career plans in relation to educational plans. Are their career goals realistic given their educational goals?**
   b. **How has their vision of their future been expanded? Students completing the *Career Choices* curriculum should be able to write in detail about the adult life they envision.**
   c. **How close is their fantasy career (pre-class survey) to the one they've now chosen for themselves (post-class survey).**

Pre-Class Survey

Last name:_____ First name:_____ Teacher:_____ Period:_____

1. **Circle the one statement that best reflects your attitude about school.**

   a) I really could care less about school. The sooner I get out the better.
   b) My parents and society require that that I go . . . otherwise I wouldn't be here.
   c) All I want to do is graduate from high school. I do only what I have to in order to get by.
   d) I want to go to college, so I do what it takes to get there.
   e) A good education is important to my future; therefore, I will strive to learn as much as I can.

2. **Thinking about your future, circle the highest grade level you plan to finish before leaving school.**

   a) I plan to leave school before I graduate from high school.
   b) I plan to graduate from high school and then enter the workforce.
   c) I plan to complete at least two years of college or trade school.
   d) I plan to graduate with a four-year degree from college.
   e) I plan to get an advanced degree (something beyond a four-year college degree).

3. **Imagine you are 30 years old. If you could wave a magic wand and have any career, what would it be?**

4. *Complete this sentence with a number.* **Between the ages of 18 and 65, I expect to work _____ years at a full-time job outside the home.**

5. **Describe the life you envision for yourself when you are 35 years old. (Use the back of this paper if necessary).**

6. **What are your plans to make the life you just described a reality?**

Post-Class Survey

Last name:_____ First name:_____ Teacher:_____ Period:_____

1. **Circle the one statement that best reflects your attitude about school.**

   a) I really could care less about school. The sooner I get out the better.

   b) My parents and society require that I go . . . otherwise I wouldn't be here.

   c) All I want to do is graduate from high school. I do only what I have to in order to get by.

   d) I want to go to college, so I do what it takes to get there.

   e) A good education is important to my future; therefore, I will strive to learn as much as I can.

2. **Thinking about your future, circle the highest grade level you plan to finish before leaving school.**

   a) I plan to leave school before I graduate from high school.

   b) I plan to graduate from high school and then enter the workforce.

   c) I plan to complete at least two years of college or trade school.

   d) I plan to graduate with a four-year degree from college.

   e) I plan to get an advanced degree (something beyond a four-year college degree).

3. **Imagine you are 30 years old. What career do you plan to have at that time?**

4. *Complete this sentence with a number.* **Between the ages of 18 and 65 I expect to work _____ years at a full-time job outside the home.**

5. **Describe the life you envision for yourself when you are 35 years old. (Use the back of this paper for more space).**

6. **What are your plans to make the life you just described a reality?**

Quantitative Evaluation Criteria

If your school or funding provider requires quantitative data, here are a few suggestions on providing appropriate information. The gathering of this data is more time consuming than conducting the previous surveys. However, the information collected will be very valuable as you plan your best practices for helping your students.

The motivation to learn and the understanding of why education is important is a key factor in predicting how well students will do in school. Change a young person's attitude about the value of school, and you'll see grades rise, dropout rates decrease, and test scores increase.

1. **Comparison of your students' GPAs.** Look at the difference between a student's GPA at the end of the previous academic year and the end of the year they complete their *Career Choices* course.

    a. How many students' GPAs increased during the year they took *Career Choices*?

    b. How many students' GPAs decreased during that year?

    c. How many students' GPAs stayed the same.

2. **Compare dropout rates.** Has there been a decrease or increase in the dropout rates? Use statistics from the prior three years, comparing students from similar backgrounds who did not complete *Career Choices* to your students.

3. **Compare year-end test scores.** Look at English and math test scores for your class members, comparing these with the scores of students from the previous three years with similar abilities and backgrounds.

Sample Guidance Counselor Survey

How would they compare your students with students who haven't taken *Career Choices*? Do your students have more focused education or career goals in comparison with students of similar abilities? Are they willing to take more rigorous classes to meet these goals?

Sample Survey for Guidance Counselors

1. Students who completed the *Career Choices* curriculum were more focused and had a better understanding of why they were in school than students of similar abilities who were not exposed to the curriculum.

                True   False

Please explain your response:

2. Students who completed the *Career Choices* curriculum came to their guidance meetings with a better idea of the courses they required than students of similar abilities who were not exposed to the curriculum.

                True   False

Please explain your response:

3. The *Career Choices* course-completers (particularly average and low achievers) were willing to be scheduled into more rigorous academic classes than students who had not had *Career Choices*.

                True   False

Please explain your response:

4. *Career Choices* graduates articulate their career and life goals more clearly than students who were not exposed to the *Career Choices* curriculum.

                True   False

Please explain your response:

Annual Teacher Survey and Evaluation

We invite your feedback and input. Your suggestions and comments allow us to better serve the educational community. On the following four pages you'll find a copy of the annual survey we provide to teachers we've identified as using the *Career Choices* program.

If you've never received this survey, you may not be on our mailing list. This may be because orders are generated through districts and alternative sources. Please call our office toll free at (800) 967-8016. Identify yourself as a classroom teacher of *Career Choices*, and our customer service representatives will add your name to our list of teachers. You'll then be ready to receive the most current edition of the following survey in the spring of each year.

The majority of the ideas and input in this manual came from completed surveys and interviews triggered by those surveys. Because your input is invaluable to us (and your colleagues using the curriculum around the country), each instructor completing our survey receives a thank you gift. Please take time to complete the Teacher Survey.

Go to www.academicinnovations.com/survey.html where you can complete our annual teacher survey online.

CLASSROOM TEACHERS!
Your Comments & Recommendations are Valued by the Publishers of the *Career Choices* Curriculum!

From the Desk of:
Jim Comiskey, President

Dear Colleague,

This is your chance to tell us what you think about *Career Choices!* We welcome your ideas and suggestions —they help us improve the materials and provide students with an even more beneficial learning experience. Photocopy this form (pages 4/19–22) and we'll send you a thank you coupon for a discounted annual license. Thanks for your input!

careerchoices.com

Jim

Your name:_____

Title _____ Discipline _____

School _____

Address _____

City _____ State _____ Zip _____

Day phone ( )_____ Fax ( )_____

E-mail address _____

Principal or Administrator _____

Number of students enrolled in your school _____

Number of students in the class(es) using *Career Choices* _____

Overview

Number of years you've taught *Career Choices* _____

1. Which *Career Choices* books does your program use?
   - ❏ *Career Choices* textbook
   - ❏ *Workbook and Portfolio*
   - ❏ *Possibilities* (language arts anthology)
   - ❏ *Lifestyle Math*
   - ❏ *Lifestyle Math Companion Software*
   - ❏ *Instructor's Guide*
   - ❏ Not currently using books.
     (Please answer questions based on past experience.)

2. In what type of class(es) are you using the curriculum?
   - ❏ Language arts
   - ❏ Career exploration
   - ❏ Freshman orientation
   - ❏ Equity programs
   - ❏ Tech Prep/School-to-Work
   - ❏ Math
   - ❏ Drop-out prevention/At-risk program
   - ❏ Family and Consumer Science
   - ❏ Special Education
   - ❏ Other _____

3. Title of class(es) _____

4. In what grade(s) do you use the curriculum?
   - ❏ 8th
   - ❏ 9th
   - ❏ 10th
   - ❏ 11th
   - ❏ 12th
   - ❏ Other _____

5. How is the curriculum funded?
   - ❏ Tech Prep and/or Perkins grant
   - ❏ School-to-Work grant
   - ❏ General curriculum funds
   - ❏ Grants (what type) _____
   - ❏ Students purchase text (which one) _____
   - ❏ Other _____

IG

Your Overall Impressions

1. What statement best describes the *Career Choices* program in terms of its contribution to your class goals?
   Check one:
   ❑ Made a significant positive contribution   *Reason for your evaluation:*
   ❑ Made a positive contribution
   ❑ Didn't make a positive or negative contribution
   ❑ Made a negative contribution

2. Considering all the curriculum you have used as a teacher, how would you measure *Career Choices*?
   Check one: *Reason for your evaluation:*
   ❑ Significantly better than others
   ❑ Better than others
   ❑ Just as good as others
   ❑ Not as good as others

3. Approximately how many classroom hours per week did you devote to the *Career Choices* program?
   _____ hours per week for _____ weeks

4. During the time you had, how far did your class(es) get in each textbook?
   ❑ *Career Choices*   ❑ most of the book in sequence   ❑ from Chapter ____ to ____
                          ❑ completed book but used less than half of the activities   ❑ used only selected activities

   ❑ *Possibilities*   ❑ most of the book in sequence   ❑ from page ____ to ____
                          ❑ completed book but used less than half of the activities   ❑ used only selected works

   ❑ *Lifestyle Math*   ❑ most of the book in sequence   ❑ from page ____ to ____
                          ❑ completed book but used less than half of the activities   ❑ used only selected activities

   If you used less than half of the book(s), please explain why. Would you like to use more? What are your barriers?

5. Which exercises or activities in *Career Choices* did you find most successful for your students?
   Please briefly explain the benefits of the learning experience.

6. Did you encounter any problems with students or the curriculum that prevented you from having gratifying success with the program? Please explain.

7. If your program used *Possibilities*, the language arts anthology, what selections were most successful and why? Please comment.

8. If your program used *Lifestyle Math*, what was your experience with this text?

9. ❑ Our school is interested in learning more about the *Lifestyle Math correction web site*, *www.lifestylemath.com*

   ❑ I'd like more information. Call me at (   ) _____ between _____ AM/PM and _____ AM/PM.

10. Did you use any unique and creative teaching strategies to enhance your program? If so, please describe and reference the activity in the textbook/anthology.

11. Did you experience any particularly gratifying successes with your students? Please include anecdotes or quotes from students, if any.

(We appreciate the attachment of lesson plans, student work, a syllabus or special lesson extension.)

Some Information to Help Us Plan

1. Will your school continue the *Career Choices* program next year? ❑ yes ❑ no ❑ not sure
   If yes, what are the plans for the future?
   ❑ Maintain program at approximately the same level as this year.
   ❑ Increase the number of students taking *Career Choices* to _____.
   If no or not sure, could you explain why?

2. Please list the names and titles of other instructors teaching *Career Choices* now or next year at your school:
   (Circle next year's *Career Choices* instructors.)

   Name _____ Title _____ Name _____ Title _____

   Name _____ Title _____ Name _____ Title _____

3. Does your school have a Tech Prep or School-to-Work program in place or in development? ❑ yes ❑ no

4. Is your school now using interdisciplinary teaching teams or planning to next year? ❑ yes ❑ no

5. How can our Curriculum Technical Support Department be of service to you? What could we do that would help you present a better course?

6. If you feel other teachers or administrators would benefit from the *Career Choices* newsletter, *Focus on the Future*, please list their name(s) and titles:

   Name _____ Title _____ Name _____ Title _____

   Name _____ Title _____ Name _____ Title _____

7. Are you currently using the sixth edition of the *Instructor's Guide*? ❑ yes ❑ no

8. Computers and technology:
   a. Approximately how many computers are on your school's premises? Number of PCs _____ Number of Macs _____
   b. How many are in your classroom? _____
   c. How many are easily accessible to your classes? _____
   d. Do you have access to a computer with a modem? ❑ yes ❑ no ❑ home ❑ school
   e. Do you use the Internet? ❑ yes ❑ no ❑ home ❑ school
   f. Would you be interested in joining a special online users group of other educators across the country using the *Career Choices* curriculum? ❑ yes ❑ no ❑ tell me more/I don't know
   g. Your e-mail address: _____ ❑ home or ❑ school
   h. Rate your computer knowledge on a scale of 1 to 10 (1 = no knowledge, 10 = very knowledgeable). _____
   i. Your school's web site address: _____

9. ❑ I'd like information on **www.careerchoices.com**, the Internet enhancement for *Career Choices*.

10. ❑ Yes, you may pass on my comments/suggestions/ideas and give me credit.
    ❑ Yes, you can call me for clarification.
    ❑ Yes, I'd like to be interviewed for the newsletter, *Focus on the Future*.
    ❑ Yes, I'd like to be considered for "Master Teacher" status. Call me with details.

    Phone: ( ) _____ (school); ( ) _____ (home/summer); Best time to call _____

11. ❑ I'd like my thank you coupon for a discounted **careerchoices.com** annual license sent to me at

    Location: ❑ home ❑ school Street address _____

    City _____ State _____ Zip _____

Thank you—your ideas and comments are gratefully accepted!

Academic Innovations • 800-967-8016 • Fax 800-967-4027
World Wide Web: http://www.academicinnovations.com   E-mail: academic@academicinnovations.com

Cooperative Learning/Team Building

The success of group discussions can depend largely on the class environment. Every student must feel important, cared for, and supported. It is helpful if students can see each other. Arrange desks in a circle or have students sit around a table, if possible.

Before you begin, set simple guidelines for the class. The essential ones are:

1. Every student must be allowed to give his or her own opinion on a topic.

2. No one is allowed to interrupt or discount anyone else's opinion.

3. Since some topics are extremely personal, everyone is allowed to "pass" if called on in discussion.

You'll want to point out that these same basic ground rules apply when working as a team to accomplish anything.

The personal nature of some discussions may lead students to reveal serious problems requiring professional help. In these situations, show concern; however, avoid giving the impression that anything's "wrong" with the individual. You'll want to suggest where the student can get help and then offer any assistance he or she may need.

Make yourself available after each class or after school, and let students know you are willing to listen and lend support. This allows students who are reluctant to speak before the entire class a more private forum in which to share their concerns. Likewise, if a student seems to be upset during the class discussion period, suggest that he or she see you after class.

Just as there are sensitive subjects, there are sensitive students who may feel uncomfortable sharing their innermost thoughts with the class or even with you. Their privacy should be respected. Those who prefer to hand in written work rather than participate in group discussions should be allowed to do so. On particularly troubling points, they may indicate that you are not to read an assignment by turning it in folded in half or by folding down those pages in the workbook. As you establish an atmosphere of trust in the class, these students should gradually become less fearful.

The curriculum is appropriate for team teaching with the school guidance counselor. You may ask him or her to participate, in particular, with your presentation of Chapters 2 and 9.

An Important Reminder

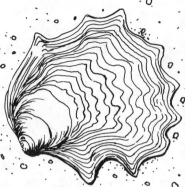

Effective Group Facilitation

For those instructors who have been involved with more traditional, lecture-style teaching in recent years, we offer a brief review of effective group facilitation:

1. Group participation is essential, but students must be motivated to participate. In general, they will be motivated by student input on topics for discussion; seeing the topics of discussion or exercises as relevant to their own lives; solving a problem or making a decision as a group; having an opportunity to voice and hear a variety of opinions; and completing tasks with a definite beginning and end.

2. An informal atmosphere is key. Students should be able to see each other. Desks or chairs should be arranged in a circle rather than in rows.

3. Peer pressure can stifle expression. It is important to build a cohesive group in which others' opinions are validated and accepted.

4. Practice active listening skills and instruct the group to do the same. You may want to devote at least one class session to discussing and practicing this communication tool. In active listening, the person who is not speaking takes an active role in the dialogue. He or she never interrupts the speaker, but paraphrases what's been said when the speaker has finished. In this way, the speaker knows that he or she has been heard.

Example:

Speaker: "I like this book very much. I can really relate to the main character."

Active listener: "You like the book very much because the main character is someone with whom you can identify."

It is also appropriate for an active listener to ask about the speaker's feelings.

Example:

Speaker: "I don't like stories with unhappy endings."

Active listener: "How do they make you feel?"

Effective group facilitation and active listening will involve:

1. Repeating what's been said.

2. Asking how the speaker feels.

3. Letting the speaker complete his or her statement without interruption.

4. Addressing students by name. They need to know that they are important, that you are interested in them. The class might agree to address everyone in the group, including you, in the same way (either by first name, or by Mr. or Ms. Jones).

5. Asking questions rather than lecturing, which often isn't effective with teens. Before offering your opinion, ask students if they want to hear it. Establish a dialogue.

6. Giving students your full attention. Make eye contact with everyone in the group.

7. Using humor in appropriate situations.

8. Establishing an atmosphere of trust within the group. Be consistent. Respect students' privacy. Be honest. If you make a mistake, admit it.

9. Being clear about classroom rules, and insisting that they be honored. State the consequences for breaking these rules and enforce them actively. Threats are not effective.

10. Pointing out cause and effect. Hold students accountable for their actions. Ask them to think of consequences, both immediate and long-term. This will increase their sense of autonomy and responsibility.

11. Asking for and listening to students' opinions. This will help to increase their self-esteem (something that often needs to be done). Use their suggestions when you can. Let students know that you believe in them. A smile or a private word to an adolescent often means a great deal.

12. Celebrating the accomplishments of the group or individuals within the group.

13. Letting the group get to know you. Be aware of your feelings at the beginning of each class period and, if you are angry or distracted about something, let the group know that they are not the cause of your negative feelings.

14. Changing the subject for a while or taking a short break if you sense too much tension in the room.

15. Communicating your approval. When a student does or says something that pleases you let him or her know with a word, look, smile, or nod.

16. Reminding students of the ground rules. If one or more students tend to be judgmental or to try to impose their values and ideas on the group, speak with them outside the group regarding everyone's right to speak without fear of ridicule from others. You might note that learning to get along with others and to work effectively within a group will be a valued skill when they enter the workforce.

17. Mentioning positive traits or behaviors, especially with particularly difficult students.

18. Recognizing students' growing sense of self-identity. Note that they are becoming more mature and independent, that they are developing their own values and plans for the future.

19. Expecting students to be enthusiastic about the course. They will probably live up to your expectations. Attitudes are contagious.

20. Being patient when the inevitable setbacks occur. Group learning often proceeds in a "two steps forward, one step back" fashion.

21. Letting all students know you care. The students with the least apparent skills and positive attributes need your support most.

22. Never concurring with a student's disparaging remarks about parents, siblings, or friends. His or her ties to these people are still very strong, and your remarks will not be well received.

23. Taking advantage of opportunities to have students practice empathy. Encourage them to imagine how other people feel. Through your example as an empathetic facilitator, students will understand the importance of empathy.

Typical Problems and What To Do about Them

No matter how well you facilitate your group, some students are likely to have problems. We've listed a few common difficulties and some suggestions for dealing with them.

If a student doesn't get an opportunity to talk:

To make sure everyone gets an opportunity to be heard, break the group into pairs and have each duo come up with a certain number of ideas, answers, or suggestions. Bring the class back together and have team members take turns stating their responses.

If someone else has already presented a student's idea or answer:

Ask him or her to state the response in another way, or to elaborate.

When self-conscious students are embarrassed to speak:

Again, working in small groups can help these students feel safe enough to speak up. As they gain confidence, they should be able to participate in larger group discussions. Don't push it, but encourage shy students with words, smiles, or nods.

When the class isn't paying attention:

A less formal atmosphere may encourage some students to act up; others will need time to adapt to the new rules. You may confront the problem by stating your own feelings of frustration. You could also help students recognize their behavior as a response to change. Allow students to discuss their feelings and possible ways to make the group feel more comfortable and, therefore, more focused.

When the class is bored:

Boredom can be a sign that students don't understand the material or don't find it relevant. The better you know your group, the better able you will be to tailor the materials. Breaking into smaller groups is another way to get more students active and involved.

When no one seems able to concentrate:

Lack of concentration may be due to tension or fatigue. A short stand-up break might be helpful. Alternatively, ask students to sit quietly, close their eyes, and concentrate fully on the source of their distraction for two or three minutes. When you bring their attention back to the classroom, ask them to note what they see, hear, and feel. This will help them return their attention to the present.

When there are conflicts or bad feelings in the classroom:

Conflicts between individuals should be settled out of class. It might be helpful to place these students in different groups. The student who simply wants to complain about something should be asked to elaborate on his or her feelings and explain what, exactly, should be done about it.

Evaluating Your Group

Is your group operating effectively? Take time periodically to consider this question. The following checklist may be helpful. In an effective group:

- Members participate somewhat equally

- Members are involved and stimulated by group discussions

- The environment is warm and supportive

- Ideas and emotions are effectively communicated and accepted by others

- Stated tasks are completed (or not completed by group agreement)

- Group accomplishments are easily discernible by all members

Group Size

Whatever the size of your class, dividing into smaller groups can be advantageous. The desirable number of students in a group varies with the task to be completed. In general, we've discovered the following:

Pairs of students:

These are ideal for sharing personal information or for encouraging students to voice personal opinions or ideas.

Groups of three:

This is a great size for discussion, especially at first, when some students may feel uncomfortable speaking in front of larger groups. Groups of three feel relatively safe. They are also good at accomplishing tasks. However, if group members are close friends there tends to be too much socializing. If you use trios regularly, assign students to different groups from time to time.

Groups of four or five:

As students become more experienced and confident communicators, they can move effectively into a slightly larger group. This size is good for meetings, making decisions, or completing tasks (make sure the task or goal is clearly understood). It also allows students to practice group problem-solving skills.

Groups of six:

To be most effective, groups of six need an appointed or elected leader, a student who is a good communicator. It might be helpful, too, to have a secretary or recorder. Groups of this size can break down into pairs or trios, resulting in overlooking the assigned task; however, they are good for situations in which personal feedback is required. An easel or oversized pad can help groups of this size to keep on track. Generally, they are most effective as the course nears its end.

Groups of seven or more:

As groups reach this size, they tend to become less effective. It's too easy for individuals to sit back and let others do the work.

Mixing groups:

Depending on the task to be completed, it may be appropriate for group members to know each other well or to be less well acquainted. When you want to mix the composition, you might base groups on numbers or names pulled out of a hat. Or you might give half the class questions written on 3 × 5 cards, and the other half of the class answers to the same. Allow students to mingle until they find the person with the matching question or answer.

Group Strategies and Techniques

Many techniques can encourage learning by stimulating enthusiasm, motivation, and group participation. Some strategies that seem to work particularly well with the *Career Choices* materials are listed below; they can be employed whenever you see fit.

Brainstorming: A topic is introduced to the group using a phrase such as, "Think of as many ways as you can to..." or "What are some possible solutions for..." Class members then make verbal suggestions that are written on the board. There is no comment or criticism from the group. When all ideas have been expressed, class discussion, ranking, or prioritizing may follow.

Buzz Groups: Groups of six or less get together and share their opinions or reactions to a speaker, a book, a question, or a statement. A time limit (short in duration) should be stated at the outset to stimulate participation and competition.

Case Studies: An actual situation that illustrates a point or problem is presented and analyzed. Case studies are often fascinating, easy to relate to, and can be less threatening than dealing with the same topics on a personal level. Cases may come from newspapers, magazines, TV shows, movies, books, or students' past experiences.

Debates: Debates are valuable for allowing students to express their opinions or for giving them experience in seeing the other side of an argument. (This is a valuable job skill. You might set up a debate in which the participants argue the position opposite their own.) A debate can match two individuals or two panels of students. Allow each side to present its case and respond to the other arguments, then follow with class discussion.

Dialogues: Two students discuss a particular topic in front of the class. Class discussion follows.

Exercises: These can be done individually or as a group to stimulate discussion or teach skills.

Fishbowls: A small group of students (six or less) discusses an issue or case study while the rest of the class observes.

Interviews: Asking questions of people outside the class allows students to collect and synthesize data and reach conclusions concerning their topic of investigation.

Journals: This is an important ongoing activity for use with *Career Choices*. By keeping a journal, students can review their growth process now and in years to come.

Lectures or Panels: An outside speaker or group of speakers can offer detailed information, new perspectives, personal experiences, and opinions on a topic. Time should be allowed for questions from the class.

Models: Models aid understanding with visual representations of certain concepts, processes, or events.

Peer Learning Groups: This is an advanced technique utilizing the leadership skills of peer leaders. Leaders must be trained for their tasks. They then lead teams of their peers through an exercise.

Role-playing: Students are asked to act out the roles in a particular situation, saying what they think their character would say under the circumstances. This can be an emotional experience for some individuals, so be sure to ask each role player how he or she feels both before and after the exercise.

Skits: Groups of students prepare, practice, and present short plays dealing with a given situation.

We presented a play based on the **Prince of Tides** *selection in* **Possibilities,** *and the students loved it. Many wanted to be "Luke." While not totally professional, everyone dressed as a character. We even made a dolphin and stuffed it.*

— Julie Delrusso
SLD instructor
Lake Brantley High School
Altamonte Springs, Florida

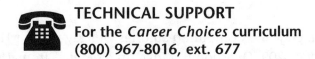

TECHNICAL SUPPORT
For the *Career Choices* curriculum
(800) 967-8016, ext. 677

Examples of Group Learning

To get you started planning cooperative learning experiences for your class, we've listed some examples of activities and exercises that lend themselves to the Group Strategies and Techniques discussed on the previous pages. This list is by no means complete. You may find a different group technique works just as well (or better) for an activity listed below.

What we've heard over and over again is that it is important to use different strategies and techniques to maintain the students' interest. Try not to get stuck in the rut of using only brainstorming techniques and small work groups.

Many of these cooperative learning experiences will also provide your students with opportunities to practice teambuilding. However, this might not be obvious to them. You'll want to remind them periodically that the skills they are honing as they learn to form effective teams with classmates will pay off in the workplace.

Brainstorming

> *Lifestyle Math*: page 31, Raising a family on one income
> *Possibilities*: page 213, Question 6, How not to give up your dreams
> *Career Choices*: page 4/145 in the *Instructor's Guide*

Buzz Groups

> *Lifestyle Math*: page 38, Questions 4 & 5, Would you pay cash or use
> your savings?
> *Possibilities*: page 224, Questions 1, 2, 3, & 4
> *Career Choices*: page 4/118-119 in the *Instructor's Guide*

Case Studies

> *Lifestyle Math*: page 42, Case Study
> *Possibilities*: page 85, Menu of Activities
> *Career Choices*: pages 204-205, Detours and Roadblocks in *Career Choices*

Debates

> *Lifestyle Math*: page 83, Making Choices
> *Possibilities*: page 22, Formal Debate
> *Career Choices*: page 4/32 in the *Instructor's Guide*

Dialogues

> *Lifestyle Math*: page 89, Computing Salaries Quickly in Your Head
> *Possibilities*: page 209, Question B. Make up dialogues from *The Prince of Tides*
> *Career Choices*: page 4/33 in the *Instructor's Guide*

Exercises

Lifestyle Math: page 60–63, Planning a Party
Possibilities: pages 279–283, Your 25th High School Reunion Booklet
Career Choices: page **4**/26 in the *Instructor's Guide*

Fishbowls

Lifestyle Math: page 26, Question 4, Would you choose Los Angeles or
Oklahoma City?
Possibilities: page 88, Question 4
Career Choices: page **4**/20 in the *Instructor's Guide*, Gender equity activity

Interviews

Lifestyle Math: page 52, Stretching Your Food Dollar
Possibilities: page 215, Question 10, Overcoming Obstacles
Career Choices: page **4**/30 in the *Instructor's Guide*

Lectures and Panels

Lifestyle Math: page 92, Budget Comparisons
Possibilities: page 31, Question 10
Career Choices: page **4**/67 in the *Instructor's Guide*

Models

Lifestyle Math: pages 102–106, Developing an Action Plan
Possibilities: pages 44–45, Acrostic Poetry
Career Choices: page 27, Bull's Eye Chart in *Career Choices*

Peer Learning Groups

Lifestyle Math: pages 98–99, What is Your Math Education Worth to You?,
Working As a Team
Possibilities: page 248, Writing a Children's Story
Career Choices: page **4**/118 in the *Instructor's Guide*

Role Playing and Skits

Lifestyle Math: pages 95–97, Developing Charts and Graphs
Possibilities: page 269, Create a Dialogue
Career Choices: pages **4**/102–105 in the *Instructor's Guide*

Project-Based Learning

Today, many educators are experimenting with project-based learning models. They've found that students retain learning better when tied to a project. The more relevant to their students' lives, the more enthusiasm exhibited and, therefore, the more the student retains the information and skills experienced.

Life is one big project! It is important that we de-compartmentalize learning, particularly for the adolescent. Students can experience problem solving and project management within the context of project-based learning. These models also provide students with opportunities to function as effective team members.

You'll find a variety of activities in the *Career Choices* curriculum that are ideal for group projects. For example:

Career Choices:

On page 4/26 of this *Instructor's Guide,* you'll find four scenarios that challenge student teams to develop creative solutions.

On page 4/102–105 of this manual is a format for helping students develop a company and design the jobs within the company that match each team member's aptitudes and work profiles.

Possibilities:

Your students will enjoy projecting into the future and developing their own 25th High School Reunion Booklet. Details on this project are found on pages 279–283 of *Possibilities*. Team members will learn important workplace skills along with organizational skills.

For your creative thinkers and future authors, review the project on page 248 of *Possibilities*, Writing a Children's Story.

Lifestyle Math:

Everyone loves to plan a party. Do your students know how much math this entails? On pages 60–63 of *Lifestyle Math*, students will find a spreadsheet for planning a great spaghetti feed.

On pages 98–99 of *Lifestyle Math*, you'll find the project: "What is Your Math Education Worth to You?" Developed as a project that demonstrates the use of SCANs skills, the results will be a real eye-opener.

Getting Acquainted

If most of your students are unacquainted, you may want to use a group warm-up exercise on the first day of class, or even daily for the first week. We suggest dividing students into pairs and having them interview each other for a total of five minutes. Bring the class back together and have students introduce their interview subject to the others. If the group seems unsure of what to ask, you might suggest some of the following questions:

If you could have any job in the world, what would it be?

If you could be any age, what would it be, and why?

Where would you most like to live, and why?

What would you consider the ideal vacation?

Who is your hero, and why?

What do you like most about school? What do you like least?

What are your favorite hobbies? Books? Movies? Sports?

Speakers Bureau

Many of the discussion topics in *Career Choices* provide great opportunities for guest speakers to come into the classroom. It is up to the individual instructor to decide who to use and how to use them. However, it is unlikely you will be personally acquainted with experts and resource people in all these areas. To make tracking down appropriate guest speakers a bit easier, we have compiled a chart listing general speaker descriptions for the entire course. The list can be easily tailored to reflect community needs or the needs of your students. Use this chart to get some help; you might:

- Make photocopies of the chart and pass them around to friends and co-workers who might be able to supply some names and phone numbers

- Pass a chart around at the next meeting of a community organization, such as the Kiwanis, Soroptimists, or the Rotary, especially if you are a member

- Make a brief presentation about your class to some of these community organizations, asking for help from the members

- Get other community people involved by bringing your request before the school improvement team

On page 4/96 we have outlined a description of a "Director of Mentors." Perhaps, the person who holds this volunteer position could be enlisted to assist in locating and scheduling guest speakers.

If you conduct this class many times throughout the day, it may be difficult to find individuals who can devote that amount of time. We suggest scheduling your guest speakers in the morning—a half-hour to forty-five minutes before the school day begins. Most working adults are used to breakfast meetings, so the early morning should not interfere too much with their workday.

Arrange for the presentations to be held in the school theater so many classes can be accommodated. While students may groan about the earlier hour, you could point out that schedule adjustments are common in the work world and flexibility of time is a mandatory requirement of most jobs. The expectations should be clear and this should be seen as part of their homework.

Be sure to advise the other faculty members of your scheduled presentations. Perhaps they would like to attend. If the school has a video recording service, arrange for a student to videotape the presentations. This way you can keep the better ones on file and can share them with the counseling office for individual counseling situations.

It might be helpful to lend each speaker a copy of the *Career Choices* text. This will allow your speaker to review the appropriate section and be familiar with the concepts the students are studying.

Guest Speakers Make Career Planning More Real

At Plantation High School in Broward County, Florida, the guest speakers are the most popular part of English teacher Mary Ellen Fowler's Career Decision-Making class.

When asked which element of the class was most beneficial, students responded unanimously: meeting real people who work in careers in which students had expressed an interest. Using the *Instructor's and Counselor's Guide for Career Choices* to set up a Speaker's Bank, Mary Ellen invited over 30 people from the community to address the class.

"I tried to include people from all walks of life, and that race, color, gender are not necessarily limiting factors," she says. The guest list included a professional soccer player, a 28-year-old journalist who had traveled all over the world, a woman mortician, a goalie on the Women's National Water Polo Team, a Navy Seal, and a lawyer.

"It was amazing—there were no absences!" Mary Ellen told us. "Students actually like coming to school because they find the material relevant and are doing something they really want to do: discovering themselves and exploring their opportunities."

Parents came in to speak to classes about how they started in their chosen field. They brought slides, videos, etc. Since many students knew these speakers personally, it was highly relevant and interesting to them.

— Mary Turella
   8th grade English and Communications teacher
   North Royalton Middle School
   North Royalton, Ohio

Speakers Bank Recruitment Form

Please list resource people below who could be contacted to make a presentation to a

class on careers at _____.

(name of school)

Speaker required	Name	Day phone	Evening phone
Successfully retired individual			
Real estate professional			
Travel agent			
Insurance agent			
AFDC parents			
Person who gave up an opulent lifestyle to do something meaningful			
Psychologist			
Entrepreneur			
Physically-challenged individual who has persevered			
Individuals who overcame adversity: High school dropout			
Teen mother			
Recovering substance abuser			
Individuals still struggling: High school dropout			

Speaker required	Name	Day phone	Evening phone
Teen mother	_____	_____	_____
Recovering substance abuser	_____	_____	_____
Women successfully mixing: Career and family	_____	_____	_____
Professional	_____	_____	_____
Blue collar	_____	_____	_____
Immigrant entrepreneur	_____	_____	_____
Community social service resource specialist	_____	_____	_____
United Way staffperson	_____	_____	_____
Bank manager	_____	_____	_____
Stockbroker	_____	_____	_____
Personnel specialist	_____	_____	_____
Career counselor	_____	_____	_____
Vocational counselor	_____	_____	_____
College placement officer	_____	_____	_____
Military recruiter	_____	_____	_____
Union director	_____	_____	_____
Employment development director	_____	_____	_____
Owner of recruiting firm	_____	_____	_____

References for Speakers' Bank

* Be sure they meet the criteria of the exercise.

After hearing the insurance speaker, one boy asked, "If I have to pay this much for insurance, how can I afford gas for the car?"

— Phyllis A. Stewart
Vocational Director
Lincoln High School
Vincennes, Indiana

Video Book Club

*Being literate in contemporary society means being active,
critical, and creative users not only of print and spoken language
but also of the visual language of film and television,
commercial and political advertising, photography, and more.*

— "Standards for the English Language Arts"
International Reading Association and
the National Council of Teachers of English

As forms of communication change, our societal focus is shifting from reading, writing, and speaking to include electronic communications—video, audio, computerization. Today's youth must be media-conscious consumers. Therefore, it is imperative that we teach students to transfer the same skills required in analyzing traditional forms to electronic mediums.

To help students gain these skills, we suggest you form a Video Book Club. It may be difficult to get some adolescents to read a book; however, most are willing to watch a movie. Like a traditional book club, the purpose of the Video Book Club is to introduce literary themes, provide practice in analysis, and encourage lively discussion.

You'll want to make sure that all students have access to a VCR or DVD player. You may need to sponsor a showing of the film after school or during the lunch break for those students who do not have access or cannot rent the film. Students could also form groups, meeting at one member's house and splitting the cost of the movie rental.

Assignments should be made far in advance, so all students will be able to see the film. You might pass out a list early in the course with film titles and dates of discussion so students can schedule accordingly.

After discussing several videos, you may assign a novel or play for the next meeting. Students are more likely to complete the assignment enthusiastically and participate in the discussion once they have experienced success in the Video Book Club.

Then, encourage students to watch the movie version of the literary work that was read. At some point you will want to discuss how the book and movie were different. You'll also want to ask student which they preferred. People generally prefer the book; ask students why.

Top Video Suggestions*

The movies we've listed center around the several of the topics raised in the text. Many of these video suggestions came from *Career Choices* instructors and are based on novels or plays that could also be assigned for reading.

* Please preview selections before showing them to your class. You will want to make sure they are appropriate for *your* students and fulfill *your* classroom goals.

Accidental Tourist, The (1988) PG—*Starring William Hurt, Kathleen Turner, and Geena Davis*
Based on Anne Tyler's Pulitzer Prize-winning novel, this film deals with self-definition and self-discovery, changing direction, and learning to take risks.

Air Up There, The (1994) PG—*Starring Kevin Bacon and Charles Gitonga Maina*
Kevin Bacon plays Jimmy Dolan, a restless assistant basketball coach who travels to Africa in search of a new recruit. He finds there are more important things in life than basketball. Good self-discovery movie.

Amadeus (1984) PG—*Starring Tom Hulce and F. Murray Abraham*
Based on a play by Peter Schaeffer, this film about Mozart and rival composer Salieri has much to say about passion, commitment, and the creative process.

American Dreamer (1984) PG—*Starring Jobeth Williams and Tom Conti*
When American housewife, Cathy Palmer, wins a contest for writing a mystery story, she is flown to Paris to accept her award. A car hits her on her way to the ceremony. When she regains consciousness, Cathy believes she is Rebecca Ryan, the fictional detective from her story, and begins to live this dream. This is a film about becoming the person you dream of and about taking control of your own destiny.

Apollo 13 (1995) PG—*Starring Tom Hanks, Kevin Bacon, and Ed Harris*
Based on a real-life adventure in problem solving, this film dramatically illustrates a number of exciting jobs available to those who excel in math and science.

Baby Boom (1987) PG—*Starring Diane Keaton*
When a high-powered businesswoman "inherits" a child, she discovers the challenges of mixing career and family. Along the way she experiences some lifestyle changes and has to reassess her own values. This is a good film to illustrate personal definitions of success, creativity, and entrepreneurship.

Beautiful Mind, A (2001) PG-13 – *Starring Russell Crowe, Ed Harris, and Jennifer Connelly*
Based on a true story, this movie explores the working life of Nobel Prize-winning mathematician John Nash. Although diagnosed with schizophrenia, Nash learns to cope with his illness. The love and support from those closest to him enable him to persist and succeed. This movie can underscore your discussion of Detours and Roadblocks in chapter 9 of *Career Choices*.

Breaking Away (1979) PG—*Starring Dennis Christopher and Dennis Quaid*
Based on the novel by Steve Tesich, this is a story about four working-class boys trying to decide what to do with their lives after high school graduation. One boy's passion for and commitment to bicycle racing helps them all learn to take responsibility, gain self-confidence, and experience success.

Cool Runnings (1993) PG—*Starring Leon, John Candy, and Doug E. Doug*
A warm-hearted comedy based on the true story of the first Jamaican bobsled team. Great obstacles had to be overcome before they could compete in the 1988 Winter Olympics. An excellent film about encouragement and self-esteem.

Captains Courageous (1937) Unrated—*Starring Spencer Tracy, Mickey Rooney, and Lionel Barrymore*
Based on the novel by Rudyard Kipling, this film depicts the warm and appealing story of a rich kid who, through a series of events, is forced to apprentice on a Portuguese fishing boat. In the movie, the rich kid learns self-sacrifice, teamwork, the work ethic, and a love of the sea. He decides he wants to make fishing his life's work even after his rich father finds him again. Should he give up the advantage of money to be a poor fisherman? Would that define success?

Clueless (1995) PG-13—*Starring Alicia Silverstone*
By watching the classic Jane Austen story, *Emma*, and this updated version, students should realize that the problems of youth haven't changed all that much in 200 years. This may make them more open to reading classic literature.

Color Purple, The (1985) PG-13—*Starring Whoopi Goldberg and Danny Glover*
Alice Walker wrote the Pulitzer Prize-winning novel on which this film is based: the story of Celie, a woman who suffers through a brutal childhood and marriage, but goes on to acquire self-worth and build a satisfying life for herself.

D2: The Mighty Ducks (1994) PG—*Starring Emilio Estevez*
Emilio Estevez plays a yuppie lawyer who is "sentenced" to coaching a hockey of kids who were told they could never play hockey. Good motivational movie.

Dave (1993) PG-13—*Starring Kevin Kline, Sigourney Weaver, and Ving Rhames*
Dave Kovic runs a temp agency, impersonating the President in his spare time. When he is asked to play President full-time, Dave finds ways incorporate his own passions and values in his new "job."

Dead Poets Society (1989) PG—*Starring Robin Williams, Ethan Hawke, and Robert Senn Leonard*
Based on a novel by Tom Schulman, this film illustrates the difficulties adolescents face in finding and maintaining their identity. Mr. Keating, an unorthodox English teacher at an exclusive prep school, implores his students to "seize the day," "suck the marrow out of life," and "make your lives extraordinary." If you include this movie, be prepared to deal with the topic of suicide during your classroom discussion. You may even want to invite a guidance counselor or private counselor to class to join the discussion.

Emma (1996) PG – *Starring Gwyenth Paltrow*
By watching this classic Jane Austen story and its updated version *Clueless*, students should realize that the problems of youth haven't changed all that much in 200 years. This may make them more open to reading classic literature.

Finding Forrester (2000) PG-13—*Starring Sean Connery, Rob Brown, F. Murray Abraham, Anna Paquin and Busta Rhymes*
This is the story of Jamal Wallace, an African-American student studying at an all-white prep school. Although recruited for his athletic merit, Jamal dreams of becoming a writer and finds a mentor in a reclusive author.

Forrest Gump (1994) PG-13—*Starring Tom Hanks, Sally Field, Robin Wright, and Gary Sinise*
Tom Hanks stars in this drama about this adventure known as "life." The story's focus is a simple man with a passion for living and an enduring positive perspective. In spite of his low I.Q., Gump becomes an unforgettable hero.

Hoop Dreams (1994) PG-13—*Starring William Gates, Arthur Agee, and Steve James*
This documentary film follows the athletic careers of two promising high school basketball players. Success would provide a means to escape their poverty-stricken environment. They must struggle with academics, coaches, and families along the way. Both players end up in the real world, not the NBA.

Howard's End (1992) PG—*Starring Emma Thompson and Helena Bonham-Carter*
A beautiful film based on the novel by E.M. Forster, this is a story of two sisters living in Edwardian England. They struggle to live independent and worthy lives in a class-conscious and repressive society.

Immediate Family (1989) PG-13—*Starring Glenn Close, James Woods, and*
Mary Stuart Masterson

> *"I have used the movie* **Immediate Family** *in my classes to show the challenges of teenage pregnancy and the difficult choices that follow. You may have to check on district policies on ratings and parental consent. I was using it in an alternative education setting and we had a bit more leeway than others.*
>
> *"The movie is about a girl who is pregnant and plans to give her child up for adoption. She meets the parents before birth and establishes a relationship with them. When the baby is born, she changes her mind and tries to keep the child and care for it herself. That becomes so difficult that she changes her mind again and gives the baby to the parents after all. The film does a very good job of portraying the emotions of all involved."*

— Suggested by Paula Murray, Teacher, Jamison High School
Lemoore, California

In the Army Now (1994) PG—*Starring Pauly Shore, Lori Petty, and David Alan Grier*
Pauly Shore plays a slow-witted sales clerk who joins the Army Reserves to receive money for an electronic venture and ends up going to the Middle East and becoming a hero.

Iron Will (1994) PG – *Starring MacKenzie Astin, Kevin Spacey, and David Ogden Stiers*
After the death of his father, teenager Will Stoneman decides to join a cross-country dogsled race. He and his mother need money, and the winner of the race receives a large cash prize. Will is racing against men with years of experience—men who will stop at nothing to win. Through harsh weather and terrain, the is young man displays courage, character, and a will of iron.
—Suggested by Roseann Reynolds, Teacher, Moreno Valley High School
Moreno Valley, California

Irreconcilable Differences (1984) PG—*Starring Ryan O'Neal and Shelley Long*
A comedy about a child who "divorces" her parents, this film is a provocative starting point for a discussion of the definition of success, both personal and professional. You'll also want to touch on the importance of taking responsibility for the person you become.

It's a Wonderful Life (1946) Unrated—*Starring James Stewart and Donna Reed*

This sentimental Frank Capra film is often written-off as a tearjerker about the rewards of helping others. However, look at it from another point of view. George Bailey, the main character, has sacrificed his passions and dreams to uphold commitments to his family and community. The movie's conclusion is that his sacrifices were noble and that George should be a very happy man. What does the class think? How does one balance responsibility for others with responsibility to oneself? Have the class think of ways that George might have been able to incorporate some of his passions into the life he's created. This movie was made immediately following World War II, which came on the heels of the Great Depression. These major, unforeseen events disrupted that lives of millions of people like George Bailey. You may also want to discuss how such impersonal factors can affect any plans for the future.

Joy Luck Club, The (1993) R—*Starring Rosalind Chao and Tamlyn Tomita*

From the novel by Amy Tan, this wonderful film explores the lives of four Chinese women who immigrated to America. How does identity reflect personal history, and what strengths can be gained through misfortune?

Kramer vs. Kramer (1979) PG—*Starring Dustin Hoffman and Meryl Streep*

Dustin Hoffman plays Ted Kramer, a career man whose work always comes first. When his wife leaves him, Ted is suddenly faced caring for their young son. This is an interesting role-reversal and depicts the very real challenges facing single parents.

Lean on Me (1989) PG-13—*Starring Morgan Freeman*

This story of Principal Joe Clark and his tough-love philosophy of education should lead to some spirited discussions. Does the class agree or disagree with his methods? What motivates students to learn? Who is ultimately responsible for an individual's education?

Little Giants (1994) PG—*Starring Rick Moranis and Ed O'Neil*

Rick Moranis plays the unlikely coach of an underdog football team. He goes up against his brother, a Heisman Trophy winner played by Ed O'Neil, who coaches the town-sponsored team. Good motivational movie.

Mr. Holland's Opus (1995) PG—*Starring Richard Dreyfuss*

This film is about a passionate musician who takes up teaching in order to pay the rent. His true goal is to compose one piece of music for which he will be remembered. As the years go by, Mr. Holland finds his own personal definition of success. A great film to help students understand the concepts discussed with the bulls eye chart activity (p. 27, *Career Choices*).
— Suggested by Julie Gergen, Teacher, Dover-Eyota High School
Eyota, Minnesota

My Left Foot (1989) R (for language)—*Starring Daniel Day-Lewis and Brenda Fricker*

Based on the autobiography of Christy Brown, an Irish writer and painter with cerebral palsy, this film makes a convincing argument for refusing to let real or perceived handicaps stand in the way of living up to one's potential.

Never Been Kissed (1999) PG-13 – *Starring Drew Barrymore*

For Josie Geller, high school was one disappointment after another. Now she works for the *Chicago Sun-Times*, the youngest copy editor ever. She's good at what she does, but she wants to be a reporter. Her chance comes when she is sent "undercover" to write a series of articles on high school. To do that, Josie tries to become part of the "in" crowd. We watch this successful adult struggle with the same identity and self-esteem issues that plagued her as a teenager. You can have some interesting discussions on how unresolved esteem problems can follow us into adulthood, the messages we receive from those around us, and how revisiting the past can be both painful and healing.

October Sky (1999) PG—*Starring Jake Gyllenhaal*

When Sputnik takes flight in October 1957, so do the dreams of Homer Hickman, a boy growing up in a small mining town. Homer is inspired to learn about rockets, hoping to build one of his own. Just about everyone in town, including his father, thinks his efforts are a waste of time. After all, his future is already decided—to work in the local coal mine like his father. Homer and his friends keep working toward their dream anyway, with the encouragement of one of their high school teachers. This movie is based on the memoir *Rocket Boys*.

> ### *"October Sky was GREAT for visions and dreams!! The best yet!"*
>
> — Kim Smith
> Special Resource Teacher
> Ewing Township
> Lawrenceville, New Jersey

One True Thing (1998) R (for language)—*Starring Meryl Streep, William Hurt, and Renee Zellweger*

When her mother is stricken with a serious illness, the heroine is "forced" to quit her job and move back home. As she nurses her mother, she learns a lot about the paths her parents chose and has a chance to rethink her own values and choices. Based on the novel by Pulitzer Prize-winning columnist Anna Quindlen.

Pay It Forward (2000) PG-13—*Starring Kevin Spacey, Helen Hunt, and Haley Joel Osment*

When a young boy is challenged by his teacher to make the world a better place, he comes up with the "pay it forward" concept. You begin by doing a good deed for someone; in turn, they do a good deed for three other people. Rather than paying someone back (for a good or bad deed), they are "paying it forward." If you include this movie, be prepared to deal with the topic of the senseless deaths of young people during your classroom discussion. You may even want to invite a guidance counselor or private counselor to class to join the discussion.

Regarding Henry (1991) PG-13—*Starring Harrison Ford and Annette Bening*

Harrison Ford plays a career-obsessed lawyer who is shot. He survives, only to discover that he remembers nothing of his life...and that's not all bad. The film focuses on his struggle to redefine his life, his priorities, and his idea of success.

Remains of the Day, The (1993) PG—*Starring Anthony Hopkins and Emma Thompson*

This film depicts the story of Stevens, head butler at an English country house. Based on the novel by Kazuo Ishiguro, it explores the personal costs of his extraordinary devotion to his job.

Remember the Titans (2000) PG—*Starring Denzel Washington*

Based on a true story, this movie is a rousing celebration of the human spirit. Set in 1971, you witness how a town torn apart by resentment and mistrust comes together in harmony. A great values video, use it along with the values assessment as well as with Dr. King's speech in Possibilities.

Renaissance Man (1994) PG-13—*Starring Danny DeVito*

Danny DeVito plays a big-time ad executive who loses his job and is recruited by the Unemployment Office to teach a group of "slow learners" in the army. Under his guidance they gain comprehensive skills, discover Shakespeare, and find themselves. Themes include self-esteem, mutual respect, and righting wrongs.

Richie Rich (1994) PG—*Starring Macaulay Culkin*

This is a film about rich kid who has everything money can buy, but still lacks what he most desires—friends. Great film for What Cost This Lifestyle? (*Career Choices*, Chapter 4).

River Runs Through It, A (1992) PG—*Starring Craig Sheffer and Brad Pitt*

Based on the book by Norman Maclean, this is a story of two brothers growing up in frontier Montana, their passion for fly-fishing, and the different paths they take through adult life.

Roman Holiday (1953) Unrated—*Starring Audrey Hepburn and Gregory Peck*

While a modern-day princess is touring Rome, she decides she wants to experience "real life." She meets up with an American reporter, who shows her the sites. As all good things must come to an end, the princess must weigh her personal freedom against her sense of duty—a "Richard Cory" theme with a less-tragic end. What would students have done if they were Princess Anne?

Rookie, The (2002) G—*Starring Dennis Quaid*

In this true story, Jim Morris is forced due to injury to leave a baseball career behind. He becomes a father, teacher, and high school coach, but still harbors a dream. One day Morris makes a deal with his student-players: He'll try out for the majors if his team can go from worst to first. His team makes it and so does Morris, becoming the oldest rookie in the major leagues. This is a heartfelt, uplifting story about not giving up on your dreams, delaying gratification, and goal setting.

Rudy (1993) PG—*Starring Sean Astin and Ned Beatty*

Rudy wanted to play football at Notre Dame, something the folks in the steel town where he grew up thought was impossible. After all, most people in the town ended up working at the steel mill. Rudy had some other barriers: His grades were a little low and he was only half the size of the other players. People told him he'd never play for Notre Dame, but Rudy had drive, spirit, and determination.

> *Rudy [is] great for showing how to pursue a goal, a dream and not letting other say you can't accomplish something.*
>
> — Roseann Reynolds, Teacher
> 9th Grade Foundation Class
> Moreno Valley High School
> Moreno Valley, California

> *For Rudy I have my students write a response to "what would have happened to Rudy if he believed what everyone else though he should do—Quit," and then we have an open discussion.*
>
> — Kim Smith
> Special Resource Teacher
> Ewing Township
> Lawrenceville, New Jersey

Say Anything (1989) PG-13 – Starring John Cusack and Ione Skye

Lloyd Dobler is an intelligent but underachieving recent high school graduate. He has no real plans, unless you count spending as much time as possible with Diane Court. Diane, the class valedictorian, has the rest of her life planned. Lloyd is admittedly confused about the future, but thinks just making Diane happy defines success. This movie can enhance your discussion of success or underscore the concept of rewards and sacrifices. Diane's academic success is the result of sacrifice. Although she is proud of her achievements, she wonders if she has sacrificed too much. Then there's Diane's father. His questionable business practices are being investigated and he may find himself forced to sacrifice his freedom and his relationship with his daughter because of his choices.

Schindler's List (1993) R—*Starring Liam Neeson and Ralph Fiennes*

This Academy Award-winning film about the Holocaust, based on the book by Thomas Keneally, offers a wealth of important topics for discussion. Identity, values, passions, risk taking, problem solving, and anxiety tolerance all come into play.

Sister Act 2: Back in the Habit (1993) PG—*Starring Whoopi Goldberg*

Whoopi Goldberg returns as a former lounge singer hiding out as a nun. She takes a group of disadvantaged, inner-city youth in San Francisco and turns them into an award-winning choir. Themes include the importance of self-esteem and self-awareness.

Sneakers (1992) PG-13—*Starring Robert Redford, Sidney Poitier, David Strathairn, Dan Aykroyd, River Phoenix, and Mary McDonnell*

A group of security system experts are asked by government agents to steal a top-secret black box. Each member must use individual strengths to help the team win this game of danger and intrigue. A fun film to explore work styles, team building, and individual strengths.

Stand and Deliver (1987) PG—*Starring Edward James Olmos and Lou Diamond Phillips*

This is the true story of a remarkable math teacher at a high school in the Los Angeles barrio. A good basis for a discussion of looking beyond familial expectations and societal messages, this film demonstrates how some people must overcome many obstacles; the necessity for hard work; and the importance of mentors.

Thousand Clowns, A (1965) Unrated—*Starring Jason Robards and Barbara Harris*

Based on the play by Herb Gardner, this comedy concerns a single, unemployed writer, Murray Burns, who is the guardian of his nephew. Authorities threaten to take the boy away unless Murray gets a job. However, his philosophy that to "know what day it is, you've got to own your own days and name 'em" makes it difficult for him to stay employed. The film is a good basis for a discussion on identity and compromise, as well as how children can limit your freedom.

To Kill a Mockingbird (1962) Unrated—*Starring Gregory Peck, Brock Peters, and Robert Duvall*

Based on Harper Lee's Pulitzer Prize-winning book, this film tells the story of Atticus Finch as seen through the eyes of his children. Atticus, a lawyer in 1930's rural Alabama, agrees to defend Tom Robinson, a young black man who is accused of raping a white woman. Atticus remains true to his values and passions, even when going ahead with Tom's defense jeopardizes his safety and the safety of his children.

Turning Point, The (1977) PG—*Starring Shirley MacLaine and Anne Bancroft*

A drama about two dances making very different choices for their lives, this film points out that every career involves sacrifices and rewards. It also effectively demonstrates the depth of commitment required for achieving excellence.

I incorporate film as much as possible. For example, after reading "The Secret Life of Walter Mitty" in **Possibilities**, *we viewed the film and then contrasted the two. Before reading "Growing Older," we viewed the first half of* **Driving Miss Daisy**. *We then completed the journal and poem prior to completing the film. The students were very responsive.*

— Kathryn T. Harcum, English Chairperson
North Caroline High School, Ridgely, Maryland

I showed the Australian movie **My Brilliant Career** *at the end of the unit. The movie is hard to find but is about a spirited young girl who is being pushed by her father to get married. She refuses a proposal at the end, from a man she deeply cares about, in order to be a writer. None of my students had seen the movie, and we discussed opportunities for women in the past and present. This worked very well!*

— Tania Lyon, 10th grade English teacher
Pequot Lakes School, Pequot Lakes, Minnesota

Vocabulary Lists and Definitions

Printable lists of vocabulary and definitions are available for classroom use. Visit the Academic Innovations web site: www.academicinnovations.com/vocab.html. You can also call our Curriculum Support Department at (800) 967-8016, ext. 677.

Chapter One

1. **elaborate**: to explain in detail
2. **gamut**: the full or complete range of things
3. **vision**: a dream
4. **realization**: to make something real
5. **frustration**: a feeling arising when hindered in trying to reach a goal
6. **security**: feeling safe and certain; no apprehension or anxiety
7. **discrimination**: wrongful treatment of a person (or group) due to a bias or prejudice
8. **achievement**: accomplishing something rewarding
9. **fanatic**: someone excessively devoted to or enthusiastic about a cause or activity
10. **excess**: more of something than is necessary
11. **flaunt**: to exhibit something (an achievement or prize) a little too proudly
12. **prima donna**: an overly vain person
13. **integrity**: free from corruption or vice; honesty
14. **humility**: a lack of false pride; feeling modest or unassuming
15. **intuition**: instinctive knowing; a feeling that something might happen; second sight
16. **impulsive**: actions typified by a lack of planning or preparing
17. **procrastination**: putting an assignment or task off until a later time; dawdling
18. **compliant**: easily persuaded or swayed; submissive
19. **rational**: logical or sensible
20. **interchangeable**: being able to change places or replace something else

Chapter Two

1. **aesthetic**: relating to beauty; artistic
2. **forthright**: going straight to the point
3. **forceful**: full of force; powerful
4. **authoritative**: official; conclusive
5. **influencing**: to alter something in an indirect or even sneaky way
6. **spontaneous**: an action arising from a whim or sudden impulse
7. **amiable**: friendly; good-natured; sociable; pleasant
8. **methodical**: systematic, following a definite method
9. **analytical**: characterized by division of a problem into separate parts for study
10. **meticulous**: great care shown to details
11. **diplomatic**: using tact, especially in stressful circumstances; smooth
12. **systematic**: methodical thoroughness
13. **submissive**: submitting to others; obedient
14. **charismatic**: exhibiting a dynamic personality
15. **empathy**: having compassion or understanding for the pain or struggles of another
16. **innovative**: on the cutting edge; creative
17. **perseverance**: steadfastness; doggedness
18. **versatile**: able to move from one activity or situation to another easily; adaptable
19. **synthesize**: combine parts or pieces into a whole
20. **negotiate**: bargain; make terms

Chapter Three

1. **self-actualization**: to fully realize your potential
2. **esteem**: worth; value; admiration
3. **survival**: the process of staying alive
4. **capable**: qualified; competent
5. **necessity**: something that is essential or indispensable
6. **satisfaction**: a state of having all your need or want; contentment
7. **hierarchy**: a series of levels or ranks; power structure
8. **legacy**: something passed on from one generation to another; something left behind
9. **acknowledgement**: recognition for a notable deed
10. **epitaph**: an account meant to summarize the life of a dead person; commemoration
11. **lifestyle**: typical way in which someone chooses to live
12. **sociology**: the scientific study of society, its institutions, and the relationships within
13. **psychology**: the scientific study of the mind and behavior
14. **component**: a piece, part, or ingredient
15. **contemplation**: to study in your mind; reflection
16. **spiritual**: relating to sacred things
17. **recuperate**: to get back health or strength; recover
18. **external**: existing on the outside; an external force
19. **internal**: existing inside the mind
20. **priority**: something of the utmost importance

Chapter Four

1. **privacy**: free from unwanted intrusion; seclusion
2. **commitment**: a promise or pledge to do something
3. **profile**: the amount to which someone demonstrates specific traits as arrived at through inventories or tests
4. **widow**: a woman whose husband has died and who, generally, has not remarried
5. **aristocrat**: a member of the aristocracy; a nobleman
6. **affordability**: the point at which a person can manage to buy something
7. **variable**: susceptible to changes; likely to vary
8. **extensive**: having wide or considerable extent
9. **liberal**: generous; ample; full
10. **reallocate**: to designate or earmark again
11. **poverty**: having a shortage of the necessary money or material possessions for comfortable living
12. **conscious**: deliberate; purposeful
13. **traits**: a characteristic or quality
14. **minimum**: the smallest amount possible
15. **windfall**: an unexpected or unforeseen gain
16. **arrogant**: overstating your own importance in a haughty way; egotistical
17. **persistence**: being tenacious; determination
18. **dividends**: a bonus or payoff
19. **inducement**: the stimulus that motivates a person to act
20. **interpretation**: explanation or definition

Chapter Five

1. **category**: a classification or grouping
2. **characteristics**: traits or attributes
3. **environment**: your surroundings; the setting in which you live or work
4. **frequent**: to hang out at a place regularly
5. **acquaintances**: a person you know but who is not a close friend
6. **isolation**: being detached or far removed from others
7. **variety**: many different forms or types of something
8. **compatible**: able to live or work together in harmony
9. **flexible**: adaptable to new, changing, or developing circumstances
10. **potential**: hidden talent or possibility
11. **incentive**: motive; something that provokes action
12. **option**: a choice; an alternative way of arriving at something
13. **composite**: a combination of several different parts
14. **freelance**: a person who works within a profession but with no fixed long-term responsibility to any one company
15. **sequential**: one after another
16. **anxiety**: uneasiness; a feeling of impending doom
17. **tolerance**: open-mindedness; understanding someone else's beliefs even if they are unlike your own
18. **entrepreneur**: someone who establishes and runs a business or company
19. **capital**: the money invested to start or maintain a business
20. **status**: a person's position in relation to others

Chapter Six

1. **artistic**: creative or imaginative skill in the arts
2. **accommodate**: to adjust or adapt
3. **protective**: to guard or shield
4. **humanitarian**: a person working for the welfare of all humans
5. **occupation**: a person's chosen work; vocation
6. **tentative**: not fully developed or worked out
7. **excursion**: a brief trip
8. **attributes**: inherent traits
9. **visualization**: the process of producing visual images in your mind
10. **typical**: regular; normal
11. **mesh**: to fit or function together
12. **consult**: to ask someone for their opinion or advice; confer
13. **accurate**: no mistakes correct
14. **explicit**: clear or specific; leaving no room for misinterpretation
15. **decisive**: resolute; determined
16. **gregarious**: liking to be around other people; friendly
17. **contagious**: catching; arousing the same emotions in others
18. **patient**: dealing with problems without becoming anxious
19. **conscientious**: careful; painstaking
20. **prominent**: well-known; distinguished

Chapter Seven

1. **alma mater**: the school, college, or university someone attended
2. **automatic**: something done without the need for thought; unconscious
3. **issue**: to put out or deliver, usually officially
4. **logical**: capable of reason
5. **evaluate**: to measure the value of something
6. **differentiate**: to distinguish between at least two things
7. **essential**: indispensable; a part so important to a thing that to remove to would destroy the thing itself
8. **gratification**: satisfaction or enjoyment
9. **long-term**: taking place over a long period of time
10. **pro**: an argument for a certain course of action
11. **con**: an argument against a certain course of action
12. **probability**: something that is likely to come to pass
13. **analyze**: to study all the parts of something in order to understand it
14. **apprenticeship**: someone who is learning through work experience with people skilled in an specific art or trade
15. **certification**: being certified, as in a trade or skill
16. **expedite**: to take care of right away
17. **agonize**: struggle or suffer
18. **fret**: to worry
19. **avoidance**: the act of evading something
20. **tendency**: a inclination toward a certain type of action or behavior

Chapter Eight

1. **opportunities**: a good chance for promotion or growth
2. **flatter**: to praise inordinately especially when inspired by self-interest
3. **courage**: bravery; nerve; guts
4. **reputation**: recognition of other people for some quality or characteristic
5. **motivation**: the driving force; incentive
6. **technique**: how details are treated in a certain trade or art; methodology
7. **temporary**: lasting for only a short or limited time
8. **abstract**: theoretical; hypothetical
9. **postpone**: put off the execution of some task
10. **struggle**: to move forward with trouble or against obstacles
11. **joyous**: full of joy
12. **temptation**: enticement; something tempting
13. **wishful**: having to do with wishes and not reality
14. **privy**: being "in on" a secret
15. **discipline**: self-control
16. **destructive**: intended to destroy; ruinous
17. **goal**: the purpose for which effort is exerted; aim
18. **objective**: crucial position to be attained; goal; aim
19. **diagram**: a drawing that explains something
20. **beliefs**: confidence in the truth of something

Chapter Nine

1. **detour**: deviating from the usual or more direct route
2. **challenge**: a task or problem
3. **ironic**: when the expected result is contrary to the actual result
4. **affliction**: great struggling or suffering
5. **paraplegic**: the state of having the lower half of the body paralyzed
6. **debilitate**: to weaken
7. **orator**: a skillful or powerful public speaker
8. **serenity**: being peaceful
9. **solution**: the answer to a problem
10. **median**: being in the middle; as many above as below
11. **consideration**: careful thought
12. **obligation**: something that ties a person to a certain course of action, such as a promise or vow; duty
13. **valedictorian**: the student in a graduating class with the highest rank
14. **ambition**: a strong desire to achieve a certain goal
15. **evidence**: an outward sign; indication
16. **obstacle**: an impediment to progress or achievement
17. **concentration**: focused attention on a single object or task
18. **confront**: to oppose or challenge
19. **confident**: certain of your own skills or capabilities
20. **progressive**: making use of new ideas; broad-minded

Chapter Ten

1. **attitude**: how you feel toward something
2. **pretend**: to make believe; feign
3. **affirmation**: a positive assertion; confirmation
4. **effective**: to accomplish a task in a competent manner
5. **reverse**: to completely turn around
6. **capable**: able to perform a certain task
7. **excellence**: the quality of being exceptional or extraordinary
8. **expectation**: an anticipated result or performance
9. **enthusiasm**: a strong excitement or eagerness
10. **prophecies**: predicting something that is to come
11. **livelihood**: means of making a living or providing financial support
12. **enterprise**: a purposeful undertaking
13. **efficient**: effective; productive; without waste
14. **ethic**: a set of principles or values
15. **aggression**: a forceful action for the purpose of overpowering or conquering
16. **tardy**: late
17. **elapse**: to slip away; expire
18. **global**: involving the entire world
19. **enormous**: extraordinarily big
20. **dignity**: self-respect

Chapter Eleven

1. **principles**: a basic belief or idea
2. **publication**: a published work
3. **resume**: summary of a person's professional or work experience
4. **summary**: an abridgment of something
5. **original**: not a copy or reproduction
6. **chronological**: listed in the order of time elapsed
7. **honesty**: dealing only in the truth
8. **references**: someone who can answer questions regarding your character or ability
9. **draft**: a preliminary version; make a rough sketch
10. **polite**: courteous; respectful
11. **impression**: a striking perception
12. **vaccination**: inoculating someone so as to create an immunity to something
13. **misdemeanor**: a crime that is not as serious as a felony
14. **felony**: under federal law, a crime that is punishable by death or imprisonment for more than one year
15. **appropriate**: fitting; suitable given the circumstances
16. **rejection**: being turned down
17. **mentor**: a trusted tutor, coach, or guide
18. **inspirational**: something that spurs you on
19. **tragedy**: a disastrous event; calamity
20. **negotiable**: open to bargaining or debate

Chapter Twelve

1. **overwhelming**: something so awesome it overpowers your thoughts or feelings
2. **alternative**: a choice or option
3. **misfortune**: an unhappy situation
4. **alienate**: to make unfriendly or cause someone to withdraw
5. **despotism**: a government where the ruler has unlimited power
6. **solace**: to lend comfort; soothe
7. **chasten**: to punish; discipline
8. **virtue**: a good quality
9. **duration**: the length of time that something lasts
10. **perspective**: point of view
11. **patience**: the act of being patient
12. **surmount**: to overcome; to prevail over
13. **muff**: to bungle or fumble
14. **fantasies**: daydreams
15. **impress**: to dazzle; to "blow away"
16. **genius**: someone of extraordinary intellect
17. **niche**: a place, group, or job where a person is best fitted
18. **respect**: high regard or admiration
19. **appreciation**: gratefulness or thankfulness
20. **success**: attainment of an auspicious or desired outcome

Career Choices and *Possibilities* Meet English/Language Arts Standards

The National Council of Teachers of English and the International Reading Association joined forces in a four-year project to develop a set of standards for the English language arts. The standards define what all students should understand about language and be capable of doing with language in order to be literate, functional members of society.

Many years ago literacy was defined simply as the ability to read and write your own name. In our ever-changing society, literacy must take on a much broader meaning. To be truly literate a person must be capable of performing myriad reading, writing, and speaking tasks analogous with day-to-day activities. This modern literacy involves the use of many different forms of print and nonprint literature (e.g., books, magazines, movies) and digital content found on the Internet.

Below we've listed the standards defined by the NCTE and IRA. *Career Choices* and *Possibilities* can help teachers address these standards in their English classroom while providing their students with a critical guidance experience.

1. *Students read a wide range of print and nonprint texts to build an understanding of texts, of themselves, and of the cultures of the United States and the world; to acquire new information; to respond to the needs and demands of society and the workplace; and for personal fulfillment. Among these texts are fiction and nonfiction, classic and contemporary works.*

Career Choices helps students gain greater understanding of themselves. It also prepares students to find their place within society and the workplace. The selections in *Possibilities* expose students to many different cultures within the United States and abroad.

2. *Students read a wide range of literature from many periods in many genres to build an understanding of the many dimensions (e.g., philosophical, ethical, aesthetic) of human experience.*

Possibilities exposes students to a wide variety of writings from many different periods, some commonly found in the canon, others from contemporary writers and leaders.

3. *Students apply a wide range of strategies to comprehend, interpret, evaluate, and appreciate texts.*

The discussion points and questions following the readings in *Possibilities* employ a various interpretive strategies. The use of *Career Choices* inspires class discussions that go beyond the traditional interpretations of the writings and allow students to view literature from a different viewpoint (e.g., personal career advice).

4. *Students adjust their use of spoken, written, and visual language (e.g., conventions, style, vocabulary) to communicate effectively with a variety of audiences and for different purposes.*

5. *Students employ a wide range of strategies as they write and use different writing process elements appropriately to communicate with different audiences for a variety of purposes.*

Career Choices gives students various opportunities to use spoken, written, and visual language to communicate different information to different people or groups of people. Small group discussions allow students to communicate in an intimate setting with peers. Groups then make a variety of written or oral presentations to the teacher or the class as a whole. Students are also encouraged to venture into the community in search of information (e.g., informational interviews) or opportunities. Students find themselves using spoken or written language in these encounters with adult or professional audiences (e.g., writing a business letter to a prospective job shadow mentor).

6. *Students apply knowledge of language structure, language conventions (e.g., spelling and punctuation), media techniques, figurative language, and genre to create, critique, and discuss print and nonprint texts.*

The discussion points and writing assignments in *Possibilities* help to meet this standard. Equally important is the Video Book Club, described on page 6/41 of this guide. The implementation of this activity allows students the opportunity to transfer critical-thinking skills traditionally reserved for books, poems, or essays, to movies, television, and other modern media.

7. *Students conduct research on issues and interests by generating ideas and questions, and by posing problems. They gather, evaluate, and synthesize data from a variety of sources (e.g., print and nonprint texts, artifacts, people) to communicate their discoveries in ways that suit their purpose and audience.*

The career research conducted in *Career Choices* is solely about the individual issues and interests of the student. They are encouraged to use various reference materials and research strategies to gather the information needed—from traditional library research to informational interviews to Internet resources.

8. *Students use a variety of technological and information resources (e.g., libraries, databases, computer networks, video) to gather and synthesize information and to create and communicate knowledge.*

Not only are students encouraged to use the Internet as a source for gathering information, but the implementation of www.careerchoices.com makes that all the easier. There are also several projects mentioned throughout this guide and among the www.careerchoices.com lessons that encourage the use of electronic media to communicate the knowledge gathered.

9. *Students develop an understanding of and respect for diversity in language use, patterns, and dialects across cultures, ethnic groups, geographic regions, and social roles.*

The diverse nature of the selections included in *Possibilities* expose students to myriad ways language is used among different groups, both within our contemporary society and those past.

10. *Students whose first language is not English make use of their first language to develop competency in the English language arts and to develop understanding of content across the curriculum.*

Career Choices reinforces this understanding of the use of English across the curriculum. As students work through the activities in *Career Choices* they also practice basic reading and writing skills—not in the context of the English classroom, but within the context of career and life planning.

11. *Students participate as knowledgeable, reflective, creative, and critical members of a variety of literacy communities.*

The NCTE/IRA project defined a literacy community as "a group of language users who share a common language and a common set of concerns." *Career Choices* affords students many opportunities to explore different literacy communities, giving them practice in communicating with a variety of audiences. Students also learn to become "knowledgeable, reflective, creative, and critical" community members through class and small group discussions.

12. *Students use spoken, written, and visual language to accomplish their own purposes (e.g., for learning, enjoyment, persuasion, and the exchange of information).*

The activities in *Career Choices* and *Possibilities*, and many of the suggestions in this *Instructor's Guide*, encourage students to use all forms of language—spoken, written, and visual—in communicating their dreams, goals, and plans for the future.

The above standards are taken from **Standards for the English Language Arts** by the International Reading Association and the National Council of Teachers of English (1996). To order the NCTE/IRA **Standards for the English Language Arts**, contact:

National Council of Teachers of English
1111 W Kenyon Rd
Urbana, IL 61801

International Reading Association
800 Barksdale Rd
PO Box 8139
Newark, DE 19714

Help Meet Your State-Specific English Standards

Career Choices and *Possibilities* can help you meet the English/language arts standards established by your own state. You can easily integrate vital life-skills practice using a thematic approach to literature to enhance your current curriculum. Teaching goal setting, decision making, responsible risk taking, and the work ethic doesn't mean you'll sacrifice student achievement, academic rigor, or content standards.

California English Language Arts Content Standards
Correlated to
Career Choices, Possibilities and *Instructor's Guide*

Benchmark	Career Choices	Possibilities	Instructor's Guide, 6th Edition
Reading			
1.0 Word Analysis, Fluency, and Systematic Vocabulary Development			
Students apply their knowledge of word origins to determine the meaning of new words encountered in reading materials and use those words accurately.			
1.1 - Identify and use the literal and figurative meanings of words and understand word derivations.	Vocabulary throughout text (see *Workbook & Portfolio*)	pp. 22–23, 67–68, 165, 207, 263	pp. 4/4, 4/18, 6/49–6/54
2.0 Reading Comprehension (Focus on Informational Materials)			
Students read and understand grade-level-appropriate materials. They analyze the organizational patterns, arguments, and positions advanced. The selections in *Recommended Literature, Grades Nine Through Twelve* (1990) illustrate the quality and complexity of the materials to be read by students. In addition, by grade twelve, students read two million words annually on their own, including a wide variety of classic and contemporary literature, magazines, newspapers, and online information. In grades nine and ten, students make substantial progress toward this goal.			
2.1 - Analyze the structure and format of functional workplace documents, including the graphics and headers, and explain how authors use the features to achieve their purposes.	Chap. 4, p. 92; Chap. 6, pp. 158–159; Chap. 8, pp. 186–189; Chap. 11, pp. 250–257	pp. 94, 279–283	pp. 4/58, 4/90, 4/95, 4/97, 4/103–4/105, 4/151–4/160, 6/1
2.3 - Generate relevant questions about readings on issues that can be researched.	Chap. 6, pp. 148–155; Chap. 7, pp. 168–179	Journal entries throughout text	pp. 2/10–2/14, 4/62, 4/68
2.4 - Synthesize the content from several sources or works by a single author dealing with a single issue; paraphrase the ideas and connect them to other sources and related topics to demonstrate comprehension.	Practiced throughout text	pp. 21, 38–39, 62, 140, 164–165, 172–175, 213, 262–269	pp. 2/10–2/14, 3/8–3/12
2.5 - Extend ideas presented in primary or secondary sources through original analysis, evaluation, and elaboration.	Goal of the entire text	Journal entries throughout text	pp. 2/10–2/14, 4/63, 4/121, 5/5–5/14, 6/7
2.6 - Demonstrate use of sophisticated learning tools by following technical directions (e.g., those found with graphic calculators and specialized software programs and in access guides to World Wide Web sites on the Internet).	Use of online activities*	pp. 174–177, 272, 279–283	pp. 2/21, 4/50–4/51, 4/87, 4/153–4/154, 4/163, 7/2–7/14
2.7 - Critique the logic of functional documents by examining the sequence of information and procedures in anticipation of possible reader misunderstandings.	Use of online activities*	pp. 209–211	pp. 7/6–7/14

Benchmark	Career Choices	Possibilities	Instructor's Guide, 6ᵗʰ Edition

3.0 Literary Response and Analysis

Students read and respond to historically or culturally significant works of literature that reflect and enhance their studies of history and social science. They conduct in-depth analyses of recurrent patterns and themes. The selections in *Recommended Literature, Grades Nine Through Twelve* illustrate the quality and complexity of the materials to be read by students.

Benchmark	Career Choices	Possibilities	Instructor's Guide, 6ᵗʰ Edition
3.2 - Compare and contrast the presentation of a similar theme or topic across genres to explain how the selection of genre shapes the theme or topic.	The integration of *Career Choices* with *Possibilities*	pp. 208–211, 213, 216–219, 228–238, 240–248	pp. 2/8–2/14, 4/1–4/170
3.3 - Analyze interactions between main and subordinate characters in a literary text (e.g., internal and external conflicts, motivations, relationships, influences) and explain the way those interactions affect the plot.	Chap. 2, pp. 52–53; Chap. 3, p. 60; Chap. 4, pp. 104–110; Chap. 5, p. 124; Chap. 6, pp. 162–163; Chap. 8, p. 185; Chap. 9, pp. 204–206	pp. 11–18, 47–56, 80–86, 90–94, 95–102, 112–117, 127–138, 142–163, 178–211, 228–239, 254–261, 264–269, 274	pp. 2/10–2/14, 4/11, 4/34–4/35
3.4 - Determine characters' traits by what the characters say about themselves in narration, dialogue, dramatic monologue, and soliloquy.	Chap. 1, pp. 10–13; Chap. 2, pp. 24–53; Chap. 3, pp. 66–69; Chap. 7, pp. 168, 170–171, 173–174; Chap. 9, pp. 194–199	pp. 11–18, 47–56, 62, 80–86, 95–102, 112–117, 127–138, 142–163, 171, 178–211, 228–239, 254–261, 264–269, 274	pp. 2/10–2/14, 4/31, 4/34–4/35, 4/152
3.5 - Compare works that express a universal theme and provide evidence to support the ideas expressed in each work.	Theme of entire text	Self-discovery theme of entire text	pp. 2/8–2/14, 3/1–3/5, 4/1–4/170
3.6 - Analyze and trace an author's development of time and sequence, including the use of complex literary devices (e.g., foreshadowing, flashbacks).	Chap. 1, pp. 10–13	pp. 11–18, 47–56, 80–86, 87–89, 95–102, 127–138, 142–163, 178–211, 228–239, 254–261	pp. 2/10–2/14
3.7 - Recognize and understand the significance of various literary devices, including figurative language, imagery, allegory, and symbolism, and explain their appeal.		pp. 21–23, 25–26, 41, 54, 58–60, 63, 76–78, 171, 238, 240–248	pp. 2/10–2/14
3.8 - Interpret and evaluate the impact of ambiguities, subtleties, contradiction, ironies, and incongruities in a text.	Chap. 9, pp. 203–206; Chap. 10, p. 242	pp. 37–38, 101, 238	pp. 2/10–2/14, 4/115
3.9 - Explain how voice, persona, and the choice of a narrator affect characterization and the tone, plot, and credibility of a text.	Chap. 9, p. 222	pp. 47–56, 80–86, 112–117, 178–211, 254–261	pp. 2/10–2/14
3.11 - Evaluate the aesthetic qualities of style, including the impact of diction and figurative language on tone, mood, and theme, using the terminology of literary criticism.		pp. 22–23, 25–26, 41, 54, 58, 63, 66, 72, 76–78, 87–88	pp. 2/10–2/14, 4/4
3.12 - Analyze the way in which a work of literature is related to the themes and issues of its historical period.	Chap. 4, pp. 74–75	pp. 21–22, 25–26, 36, 41–42, 54–56, 58, 84–86, 103–107, 110–111, 116–117, 124–126, 171, 172–177, 221–224, 238–239, 247, 251	pp. 2/10–2/14, 4/43

Benchmark	Career Choices	Possibilities	Instructor's Guide, 6th Edition

Writing

1.0 Writing Strategies

Students write coherent and focused essays that convey a well-defined perspective and tightly reasoned argument. The writing demonstrates students' awareness of the audience and purpose. Students progress through the stages of the writing process as needed.

Benchmark	Career Choices	Possibilities	Instructor's Guide, 6th Edition
1.1 - Establish a controlling impression or coherent thesis that conveys a clear and distinctive perspective on the subject and maintain a consistent tone and focus throughout the piece of writing.	Practiced throughout text in a variety of essays and exercises	pp. 54–56, 137–138, 261, 275	Practiced throughout entire curriculum
1.2 - Use precise language, action verbs, sensory details, appropriate modifiers, and the active rather than the passive voice.	Chap. 2, pp. 44–45, 53; Chap. 9, pp. 216–217; Chap. 10, pp. 230–231, 236–237	pp. 31–32, 162	pp. 4/24
1.3 - Use clear research questions and suitable research methods (e.g., library, electronic media, personal interviews) to elicit and present evidence from primary and secondary sources.	Chap. 5, pp. 124–141; Chap. 6, pp. 148–159; Chap. 9, pp. 211–213; online activities*	pp. 38, 79, 106–107, 165, 174–177, 253, 261, 272	pp. 4/85–4/106, 7/6–7/14
1.8 - Design and publish documents by using advanced publishing software and graphic programs.	Chap. 12, pp. 278–281	pp. 38, 44–45, 279–283	pp. 4/90, 7/2–7/5

2.0 Writing Applications (Genres and Their Characteristics)

Students combine the rhetorical strategies of narration, exposition, persuasion, and description to produce texts of at least 1,500 words each. Student writing demonstrates a command of standard American English and the research, organizational, and drafting strategies outlined in Writing Standard 1.0.

Benchmark	Career Choices	Possibilities	Instructor's Guide, 6th Edition
2.1 - Write biographical or autobiographical narratives or short stories:			
A - Relate a sequence of events and communicate the significance of the events to the audience.	Chap. 1, pp. 12–13; Chap. 8, pp. 186–191	pp. 54–56, 89, 161–162, 208–211, 224, 226, 261, 275	pp. 4/18, 4/77, 4/93–4/94
B - Locate scenes and incidents in specific places.	Chap. 6, p. 157	pp. 125, 160–162, 208–211	
C - Describe with concrete sensory details the sights, sounds, and smells of a scene and the specific actions, movements, gestures, and feelings of the characters; use interior monologue to depict the characters' feelings.	Chap. 1, p. 14; Chap. 3, pp. 70–72; Chap. 6, pp. 156–157; Chap. 9, pp. 196–199	pp. 42, 44, 54–56, 162, 171, 208–211, 261, 275	pp. 4/9, 4/18, 4/93–4/94
D - Pace the presentation of actions to accommodate changes in time and mood.		pp. 54–56, 102, 208–211, 275	p. 4/114
E - Make effective use of descriptions of appearance, images, shifting perspectives, and sensory details.	Chap. 1, p. 17; Chap. 2, pp. 29, 44–45	pp. 42, 44, 54–56, 162, 208–211	pp. 4/93–4/94
2.2 - Write responses to literature:			
A - Demonstrate a comprehensive grasp of the significant ideas of literary works.		Writing projects throughout text	pp. 2/10–2/14
B - Support important ideas and viewpoints through accurate and detailed references to the text or to other works.		Writing projects throughout text	pp. 2/10–2/14, 4/77
C - Demonstrate awareness of the author's use of stylistic devices and an appreciation of the effects created.		pp. 36, 42, 44, 139–141, 161, 170–171, 173, 215, 216–220, 250	pp. 2/10–2/14, 4/8, 4/113

Benchmark	Career Choices	Possibilities	Instructor's Guide, 6th Edition
2.3 - Write expository compositions, including analytical essays and research reports:			
A - Marshal evidence in support of a thesis and related claims, including information on all relevant perspective.	Practiced throughout text	pp. 31–32, 38, 110, 137–138, 174–177, 275	pp. 4/1–4/106, 4/32
B - Convey information and ideas from primary and secondary sources accurately and coherently.	Practiced throughout text	pp. 31–32, 38, 122–123, 174–177, 253	pp. 4/1–4/106, 4/64, 4/68, 4/144
C - Make distinctions between the relative value and significance of specific data, facts, and ideas.	Chapters 1–6	pp. 38, 84–94, 139–140	pp. 4/1–4/106, 4/42, 4/63
E - Anticipate and address readers' potential misunderstandings, biases, and expectations.		pp. 94, 117, 239, 272, 274–275	pp. 4/1–4/106, 4/84, 4/112
2.5 - Write business letters:			
A - Provide clear and purposeful information and address the intended audience appropriately.	Chap. 6, pp. 158–159; Chap. 11, pp. 250–253, 254–255; online activities*	pp. 38, 85, 94, 263	pp. 4/39–4/41, 4/76, 4/95, 4/151–4/160, 4/168
B - Use appropriate vocabulary, tone, and style to take into account the nature of the relationship with, and the knowledge and interests of, the recipients.	Chap. 6, pp. 158–159; Chap. 11, pp. 250–253, 254–255; online activities*	pp. 38, 85, 94, 263	pp. 4/76, 4/95, 4/151–4/160, 4/168
C - Highlight central ideas or images.	Chap. 6, pp. 158–159; Chap. 11, pp. 250–253; online activities*	pp. 38, 85, 94, 263	pp. 4/39–4/41, 4/95, 4/151–4/160, 4/168
D - Follow a conventional style with page formats, fonts, and spacing that contribute to the documents' readability and impact.	Chap. 6, pp. 158–159; Chap. 11, pp. 250–253; online activities*	pp. 38, 85, 94, 263	pp. 4/12, 4/55, 4/76, 4/95, 4/151–4/160, 4/168, 7/2

Listening and Speaking

1.0 Listening and Speaking Strategies

Students formulate adroit judgments about oral communication. They deliver focused and coherent presentations of their own that convey clear and distinct perspectives and solid reasoning. They use gestures, tone, and vocabulary tailored to the audience and purpose.

Benchmark	Career Choices	Possibilities	Instructor's Guide, 6th Edition
1.1 - Formulate judgments about the ideas under discussion and support those judgments with convincing evidence.	Discussions, presentations, and debates throughout text	Discussions, presentations, and debates throughout text	Activities throughout; pp. 2/10–2/14, 4/1–4/170, 10/5–10/6
1.5 - Recognize and use elements of classical speech forms (e.g., introduction, first and second transitions, body, conclusion) in formulating rational arguments and applying the art of persuasion and debate.		pp. 22, 27–32, 94, 108–111, 239	pp. 4/32, 4/42, 4/68, 4/83–4/84
1.10 - Analyze historically significant speeches (e.g., Abraham Lincoln's "Gettysburg Address," Martin Luther King, Jr.'s "I Have a Dream") to find the rhetorical devices and features that make them memorable.		pp. 27–32, 108–111	p. 4/6
1.14 - Identify the aesthetic effects of a media presentation and evaluate the techniques used to create them (e.g., compare Shakespeare's *Henry V* with Kenneth Branagh's 1990 film version).		pp. 11–18, 44–45, 125, 208, 279–283	pp. 4/6, 4/10–4/11, 4/17, 4/112, 6/41–6/48

SECTION SEVEN

Integrating Technology into Your *Career Choices* Classroom

Integrate Basic Technology Skills into Your *Career Choices* Classroom

It is better to teach skills in context than in isolated situations. This is as true for computer skills as it is for academic skills.

Most employers require that new employees (entry level and beyond) have at least minimal computer skills. If all graduates left your school with basic computer skills and a working knowledge of common programs, they'd have a great advantage entering the job market. Students going directly into the workforce from high school would have the skills necessary to compete for jobs with a career path and a future. Those young people going on to college or advanced training would be able to earn more than minimum wage while working their way through school; they would also have wonderful tools to help them excel in the classroom.

Checklist of Basic Technology Skills Required for the Workforce of the 21st Century:

- ☑ Keyboarding (at least 50 words per minute)
- ☑ Using an Internet browser and search engine
- ☑ Using electronic mail
- ☑ Word processing*
- ☑ Using spreadsheets*
- ☑ Using presentation software*
- ☑ Using simple graphics/design software*

The *Career Choices* curriculum presents a variety of opportunities to practice these very important skills. In addition to the technology enhancements we've developed, there are several successful suggestions from *Career Choices* teachers throughout Section Four and this section.

* These are common applications available in most office suite software packages: Microsoft Office, Corel WordPerfect Office, or Lotus SmartSuite.

> *Since this is a computer/career class, many of the assignments for* **Career Choices** *are done on a computer. For instance, spreadsheets for budgets, word processing and formatting for many of the other assignments.*

— Dee Fay, Computers/Careers Teacher
Ukiah High School, Ukiah, California

Technology Is Most Effective When Integrated

This "integrated, blocked, teamed, and applied English/Technology program" from Tumwater High School in Tumwater Washington, utilizing both *Career Choices* and the anthology, *Possibilities*, received the Washington Education Association's Leaders in Restructuring Award.

"Alarmed by a lack of motivation among freshmen in previous years," the school's application letter reads, "we aimed to develop a comprehensive, student-friendly, motivational, curriculum-intensive block that would begin each student's high school academic course on the very best foundation possible. We believe that we succeeded."

By bringing together English and technology classes, instructors hoped to make both more interesting and relevant to their students. The new program superseded the old freshman English trilogy of grammar, composition, and literature, using *Career Choices* and *Possibilities* as its texts for one trimester (twelve weeks, one hour a day) of the year-long program. The books were funded through general curriculum funds. The model was part freshman orientation, part tech prep, and part language arts. Students completed all exercises in the *Career Choices* text.

The following is taken from the letter of application: "Essentially, the team of six teachers (three from the English department and three from the business department) determined that new technology resulting from a recent bond levy could be of maximum effectiveness only if thoroughly integrated into a core subject area. English was a natural choice due to the extensive writing required of students in that arena. Technology teachers wanted students to work with substantive material while learning essentials of technology. Our goal would be maximum integration—each day's technology lessons would reinforce concepts covered in English. That concept provided the basis for our design, which evolved to include so much more.

"Incoming freshmen were placed into a two-hour morning block to provide a home base where friendships could develop. English and technology rooms were realigned into pairs with a door punched in the adjoining wall to allow a flow of students between rooms in addition to hall access. Freshman lockers were relocated so that students' lockers were near their morning block location. Standard expectations of behavior were developed for all classes, and reality therapy and control theory were taught by counselors early in the year to encourage freshmen to take control of their destiny from their first day at the high school.

"Essays now look and read beautifully. Editing is a snap. Graphics provide a special flair for student-created poetry. Book reports have become tri-fold brochures publicizing the novel. The classroom has become a workplace from which professional looking letters could be drafted and mailed to the editor of the local paper, to the manufacturer of a gender-biased toy, or to a pen pal in a high school across the nation. Using many of the Applied Communications Modules, we dovetail with the objective of our Student Learning Improvement Grant which is to help students experience an effective school to work transition. Students quickly have surpassed their English teachers' knowledge of software and showed their expertise with pride. English is revitalized; technology has substance. Color technology-produced posters, newspapers, and spell-checked and grammar-checked essays replace the drudgery-laden, hand-written daily English assignments.

"Our six-member team churns out creative and meaningful assignments week after week. English teachers accomplished more than ever before, due to the efficiency of technology and the block of time. We still teach traditional material such as *Romeo and Juliet*, and *The Miracle Worker*. We also teach the fundamentals of communication, units on success, units on careers, units on business fundamentals, and units on diversity. Most importantly, the curriculum has cohesive organization based on our three-trimester system. We address personal communication in the fall, business communication in the winter, and creative communication in the spring. The program has re-invigorated the at-risk students due to the hands-on environment and professional-appearing results of their efforts. Next year, portfolio assessment will allow all freshman students to see their tremendous progress and keep their best efforts for posterity.

"Our program brings community members into the classroom to emphasize relevance of the curriculum to the world of work, makes education dynamic and interactive, displays innovation conceptually and on a daily basis, was developed based on district outcomes from the 'bottom up' in a site-based setting, involves integration and teaming, and has been a huge success." (Special thanks to English instructor Scott Hess for allowing us to share this information with you. We thought you'd rather hear from your peers than from us.)

We believe the Tumwater High School program is worthy of its success and can serve as an admirable integration model for other schools. Here is a unique guidance curriculum—competency based, truly interdisciplinary in scope and sequence—that makes integration of technology and academics possible. What's more, using this model will save you hundreds of hours of planning time! We recommend that, like Tumwater, you set up a pilot program to demonstrate the effectiveness of interdisciplinary teams. The *Career Choices* curriculum offers an excellent vehicle for efficiently and effectively doing this. From there, you can expand your efforts, and other grades and departments can also follow your model.

Creative Idea: Students Create Multi-Media Presentations

Not every school is fortunate enough to have a sophisticated media lab, but California's San Gabriel High School has such a facility. Thanks to a state grant, English and Career Education teacher Elizabeth Farris makes good use of it.

When her ninth grade students have worked through a good portion of the *Career Choices* curriculum (in a year-long class), Farris assigns them to use HyperStudio, an authoring software program from Roger Wagner Co., to make a presentation on something they have learned. Some focus on a career of interest, others choose one of the topics from the text, such as Maslow's triangle, personal profiles, "why people work." To develop their projects, they use CD-ROMs, laser discs, clip art, drawings and scanned pictures, all put together in the media lab.

One year's highlight came from several future firefighters who used segments of the movie *Backdraft*, complete with theme music and sound effects.

Later in the year, when the class is writing their resumes (Chapter 11 of *Career Choices*), Farris reminds students, "You all have computer skills." "We do?" they reply. They'd been so involved, having so much fun, that they didn't realize they were also picking up some very high-tech skills along the way!

**Students create a PowerPoint *presentation on a career to teach the rest of the class about the job.*

— Brenda Vatthauer
Family and Consumer Science Teacher
Lafayette High School
Red Lake Falls, Minnesota

After reading and discussing pages 168-169, students need to see how decision making and problem solving are important in the business world as well as in their personal world. I split the class into small groups and assign them a section of the teachers' parking lot to examine. They are to identify the number of cars and their make so we can eventually determine how many are American-made, German-made, British-made, etc. Then the small groups share their numbers with the whole group until we know how many cars total were in the parking lot and how many are from other countries. We do a math lesson so students can create percentages! (Not a small feat in a Communications class!)

Next, we talk about the problems associated with so many cars being non-American. Then, students write a paragraph about their findings, including the importance of solving this problem in the marketplace. As students word process their paragraphs, they are also being taught how to convert their information into a spread sheet (we use the integrated package Microsoft Works), which will turn their percentages into a pie chart or bar graph. When students finish, they have a paragraph complete with pie chart showing the importance of companies solving problems in the workplace.

— Sharon Hurwitz
English Teacher and Technology Facilitator
Bethel High School
Hampton, Virginia

With an "applied" approach to keyboarding, students now practice on reports and exercises generated in English, instead of meaningless keyboarding exercises. They do everything from acrostic poems to reports on careers.

Using the computer program PowerPoint, each student created a series of 12 slides about a chosen career. By incorporating graphics, word processing, and other elements in the process, a colorful, sound and motion "advertisement" was displayed. The programs became personal and interactive when students viewed and evaluated the displays. They then wrote positive comments in a formal business letter to send to the students whose work was chosen.

— Scott Hess
Applied English and Technology teacher
Tumwater High School
Tumwater, Washington

We primarily used the [Possibilities] journal entries and had students keep the entries and their responses in a file on their computer disks.

— Dee Fay
Computers/Careers Teacher
Ukiah High School
Ukiah, California

Internet Integration Made Easy
with www.careerchoices.com

The award-winning *Career Choices* curriculum is now linked to the Internet, with over 80 individualized lessons and web-site links on www.careerchoices.com.

How Does It Work?

Students will find a special logo throughout the current edition of *Career Choices*. The appearance of this logo at the bottom of the page indicates the existence of an optional Internet lesson and link that enhances that particular activity in *Career Choices*.

As students work to complete the exercises on these logo-noted pages, they can visit www.careerchoices.com, signing in with their password from anywhere—home, school, the library. By selecting the textbook page they are working on, they'll be linked to a specific Internet-enhanced lesson.

Once they've read the step-by-step instructions, they jump directly to a specially chosen web site containing resources, calculators, or interactive lessons to enrich their understanding of the *Career Choices* assignment.

Your students can easily access information that is...

- **Current**—The www.careerchoices.com links provide students with some of the most current information and statistics available from federal, state, and private sources.

- **Relevant**—The links on www.careerchoices.com allow students to gather important data that is critical to making informed choices for their life plan.

- **Dynamic**—Because www.careerchoices.com gives students the opportunity to determine the specific nature of the information they gather, the results of their time online will quickly and quantitatively demonstrate how changes in their educational and career plans will affect their lifestyle.

For example, www.careerchoices.com *provides students help with:

- Careers research tools

- Job interview tips and practice

- Information on colleges/post-secondary education opportunities

- Writing a resume

- Calculating a mortgage or car loan

- Applying for financial aid

- Factoring the amount of student loan debt a chosen career can support

- The most current national and state labor market statistics

- Projected job growth for chosen careers

See pages 7/11–7/14 for a detailed index of the lessons at the time of this printing. Better yet, visit www.careerchoices.com for sample lessons for both teacher and student.

www.careerchoices.com *Instructor's* Guide Online:

After a teacher signs on to www.careerchoices.com using their individualized password and user ID number, they'll be immediately directed to a special *Member Teacher* area on the web site. This portion of the site is for instructor's only—students will not see the information you see. In addition to in-depth explanations of each student activity and web link, this restricted area will also include lesson objectives, special directions, presentation suggestions, extension ideas, and how you, personally, might use these web links in your own life.

Benefits of an Internet Curriculum Enhancement

More meaningful: Because the Internet activities correspond to their *Career Choices* course work, students will find more relevance in the information they are researching and the surveys they are taking. Their online activities will be supported by classroom discussion, written assignments, and personal exploration and contemplation.

Easy-to-use: When a student accesses www.careerchoices.com (at school, at the library, or at home) they are linked directly to approved web sites. This process will help reduce indiscriminate or fruitless searching.

Higher academic standards: The information and processes students are exposed to on the Internet sites will challenge them to meet higher standards and, thereby, improve student achievement.

Lifelong skills: The Internet research processes the students learn will help them later in their lives: planning their post high school education, researching careers, finding and interviewing for a job, and planning their financial future.

Meets the mandates for introducing Internet-linked curriculum: In the not-too-distant future, all classrooms will be linked to the Internet. State, district, and federal educational technology mandates will continue to be introduced as a requirement for teaching. www.careerchoices.com will help teachers meet these mandates with solid digital content.

Only the best: Because of the changing nature of the Internet, the web site links and the student and teacher directions found on www.careerchoices.com will be checked and updated monthly.

The time-consuming research and lesson plans have already been done: We know time is a precious commodity for busy classroom teachers. Our team of curriculum developers is specially trained to provide exciting, timely, and relevant lessons. This will save you hours of planning time.

Membership and Fee Policy

www.careerchoices.com is a password-driven membership web site for educators and students currently using the *Career Choices* curriculum. Any school who has ordered a minimum amount of *Career Choices* materials from Academic Innovations within the preceding 12 months qualifies for membership under our licensing fee schedule.

The maximum fee for an annual license at the time of this printing is only $249.00 (subject to change). For most schools who adopt *Career Choices*, this figure will be lower. Our sliding fee schedule is based on a school's largest annual order and their order for the current school year. For schools who have made a significant commitment to using the *Career Choices* curriculum, this fee is reduced until, in some cases, the annual license is complimentary.

To register for membership:

You can register online at www.careerchoices.com, or you can complete the following form and fax it to us at (800) 967-4027. We'll check your school's ordering history and send you a quote for this year's licensing fee within 2 to 3 working days. If you are in need of a quicker estimate, contact us by phone at (800) 967-8016.

To receive your licensing fee quote for this school year, please fax the following form to **(800) 967.4027** or go online to **www.careerchoices.com**. In the **Visitor's section**, complete your request for a quote on-line.

❑ We are already using **Career Choices**. Please review our order history to factor our licensing fee.
❑ We plan to adopt **Career Choices**. Below are **the numbers of each title** so you can factor our licensing fee.　# _____ *Career Choices*　# _____ *Workbook/Portfolio*　# _____ *Possibilities*
　　　　　　　　　# _____ *Lifestyle Math*　# _____ *Instructor's Guide*

First name _____ Last name _____

Title _____ Discipline _____

Email address _____

School/agency name _____

School address _____

City _____ State _____ Zip _____

Phone ( ) _____ Fax ( ) _____

District Office _____

District Address _____

City _____ State _____ Zip _____

❑ Please fax our quote to the school.　　❑ Please email our quote to my email address.
❑ Please call me, as I have questions.
　Best times to call _____ Contact phone number ( ) _____

How To Use the Internet When You Don't Have Access in the Classroom

What can you do if you don't already have your classroom linked to the Internet? Can the average teacher incorporate something as powerful as the Internet without classroom access? Teachers using www.careerchoices.com have found that the activities are so intriguing, students seek out alternatives to classroom access. Here are some suggestions from teachers:

Identify Internet access sites on campus: Make a list of the sites on campus where a student can go online. What hours are the computer labs open for individualized work? Does your school library have Internet connections available for student use?

Locate access within the community: What about locations in the community where Internet access is available? Kinkos is a good place to start, or there may be an Internet café in your city. Does your community library have Internet access? If your students are working as interns, perhaps their job sites will give them permission to use the Internet while not working.

Form homework teams: Phyllis Stewart of Indiana recommends forming homework teams if Internet access is difficult at school. She has enough students with Internet access to create teams in which at least one member has an Internet connection at home. Teams can be given specific assignments to work on collaboratively.

Give extra credit for completing the Internet activities: If every student can get access to the Internet, let them pick and choose the activities that are most meaningful to them. They could complete these on their own time for extra credit. Have students demonstrate their work by printing a hard copy of the calculations and data searches they've conducted using www.careerchoices.com.

Lobby for Internet access: If you don't have classroom access to the Internet, show the *Career Choices* curriculum and www.careerchoices.com to your administrators and school board. Because it is a focused curriculum integrating solid curricular content and technology, it might be the catalyst to getting the Internet in your classroom sooner rather than later.

Index of Lessons on www.careerchoices.com

This index was complete at the time of printing. However, as activities are added, deleted, or changed, the index will expand. For the most current index information, visit www.careerchoices.com, Visitor Section and click on the Index link.

Chapter Four: What Cost This Lifestyle?

Page 78—Housing

- *Table:* Today's home mortgage interest rates
- *Calculator:* Factoring your monthly mortgage payment
- *Calculator:* Factoring how much house you can afford
- *Calculator:* An individualized estimate of the cost of homeowners insurance
- *Calculator:* An individualized estimate of the cost of renters insurance
- *Calculator:* Should you buy a home or should you rent? (basic)

Page 80—Transportation

- *Search:* Finding the "blue book" value of a particular car
- *Calculator:* Finding the current auto loan interest rate
- *Calculator:* Factoring your monthly payments on a car loan
- *Table:* Side-by-side comparisons of any four new car models
- *Commentary:* The pros recommendations among used car models based on vehicle type
- *Informational:* Weigh the pros and cons of purchasing a new vs. used car
- *Table:* Environmental Protect Agency's (EPA) listing of the 20 best models of cars based on miles per gallon (MPG) and the 20 worst
- *Table:* The operating costs of the 10 top selling cars
- *Interactive Quiz:* Help with learning the terms related to auto insurance

Page 83—Clothing

- *Database:* Sample costs from online catalogs of various children's clothing manufacturers
- *Database:* Sample costs from online catalogs of various adult clothing manufacturers

Page 88—Childcare

- *Calculator:* The cost of raising a child to young adulthood based on lifestyle projections (includes childcare figures in the calculations)

Page 89—Savings

- *Calculator:* How much do you need to save to send your child to college (basic)
- *Calculator:* How much do you need to save to send your child to college (advanced)
- *Calculator:* How much do you need to fund your retirement account in order to live the lifestyle you envision at retirement

Page 93—What Salary will Support this Lifestyle?

- *Tables:* Comparison of wages between different occupations
- *Tutorial:* Information on federal tax withholding
- *Calculator:* Calculating take-home pay
- *Tutorial/Calculator:* Estimate taxes due based on income, deductions, etc. Learn important financial terms related to the tax structure (advanced)

Page 116—An Investment in Education . . . Yields Dividends for a Lifetime

- *Tables:* Charts comparing salary levels with education levels
- *Calculator:* How does your earning potential compare with the "power players"

Page 120—Ask Someone Who's Been There

- *Email Interview:* Seek out career information by communicating with an expert in your interest area via email

Chapter Six: Career Research

Page 145–146—Career Clusters and Groups

Database: Research career titles chosen from occupational clusters

Page 148–149—Career Research

- *Database:* Search for careers that fit your interest area or school major
- *Database:* Overview of occupational information (i.e., wages, trends) searchable by job title and state
- *Database:* Find the careers with the most promising future in your state
- *Database:* General outlook of the United States job market by wages and education required
- *Database:* Employment trends of the major cities in the United States including unemployment rates, major employers, cost of living, etc.
- Article: Highest-paying jobs in the United States

Page 150—Career Interest Survey

- *Database:* Career research online using the Occupational Outlook Handbook

Page 158—The Shadow Program

- *Research Project:* Students learn how to use search engines to locate specific types of businesses near their home

Page 159—Arranging for a Shadow Experience

- *Narrative/Instructional:* How to write a business letter

Page 160—Intern and Volunteer Opportunities

- *Directory: Finding volunteer opportunities in your community*

Chapter Twelve: Where Do We Go From Here?
(Writing your plan of action)

Technology Enhancements for
Lifestyle Math

Lifestyle Math is more than a math workbook; it is a covert learning experience—basic math skills training in the guise of *personal* financial dreaming. Once students calculate the projected monthly costs associated with their ideal lifestyle, they will be *blown away* and the importance of math will be abundantly clear.

Lifestyle Math is such a powerful activity because it makes numbers real. It makes the cost of living real. It makes annual earnings real. It makes withholding of income taxes real. Most importantly, it makes finding a job—a good paying job—real!

Lifestyle Math brings this element of reality to the classroom through:

- Real-world computations in *Lifestyle Math*
- Personalized math and easy online correction at www.lifestylemath.com
- Dynamic information using www.careerchoices.com

Lifestyle Math helps students take responsibility for their own learning by demonstrating the value of applying themselves to their math education. It also emphasizes the need for mastering basic skills by showing how math skills are used everyday and exposes students to important mathematical formulas they will use throughout their lives. As it encourages critical thinking and problem solving skills, it also encourages students to enroll in upper division math classes by providing them with reasons to master difficult concepts.

Effective Use of Technology in the Classroom

The implementation of www.lifestylemath.com and www.careerchoices.com contribute something else—effective use of technology in the classroom. Many researchers and experts agree that effective use of technology in the classroom is a critical element in creating a new school model that will prepare students for the information age. Turning a computer on isn't enough. Integrated activities need to focus on three things: content, critical thinking, and computer skills.

Lifestyle Math is a wonderful example of a project-based learning experience, providing content and critical thinking. If you utilize www.lifestylemath.com to check calculations and the links available through www.careerchoices.com to enhance the *Lifestyle Math* activities, you will have all of the elements necessary for effective use of technology in the classroom.

Correcting *Lifestyle Math* Using Technology

Traditionally, math problems have been designed with one unvarying answer for each problem. This allowed instructors to check student work against a static answer key.

www.lifestylemath.com

Because of the individualized design of *Lifestyle Math* and the dynamic nature of student answers, correction and assessment was once challenging at best. However, with the advent of our *optional* Internet correction key, this task is quick and easy. The online correction tool available at www.lifestylemath.com delivers a straightforward and uncomplicated correction tool your students can access at school or home.

Here's How it Works!

Students begin by working through a mathematical problem in their *Lifestyle Math* workbook, completing the calculations themselves the old-fashioned way—with paper, pencil, and their own brainpower.

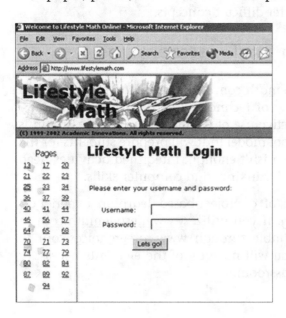

Once students factor each personal budget item, they can go online to www.lifestylemath.com and login using your school's access information.

They'll choose the page they want to correct from a sidebar listing and a web page will appear that looks like the worksheet page in their workbook.

Your Calculations of Gasoline Cost Per Month - Page 36

Pages	
13 17 20	
21 22 23	
25 33 34	
36 37 39	
40 41 44	
46 56 57	
64 65 68	
70 71 73	
74 77 79	
80 82 84	
87 89 92	
94	

A. Miles you plan to drive per week _____ miles

B. Miles per gallon for your car / _____ miles per gallon

C. Gallons of gasoline per week
   (this calculation is A divided by B) _____ gallons per week

D. Cost per gallon of gasoline
   ($1.30 average or research gas costs in your area) $ _____ cost per gallon

E. Total cost of gasoline per week
   (This calculation is C * D) $ _____ gasoline cost per week

F. Multiply by 4 weeks per month   X 4

G. Gasoline expense per month
   (This calculation is E * 4) $ _____ gasoline cost per month

[Check Answers!]   [Clear Form]

Clear All Entries!

Page 36

Students enter their calculations in the appropriate fields and click "Check Answers!" The computer program reviews their work and notes any incorrect figures or incomplete information. Students can then rework their mathematical calculations as many times as needed.

After correcting any errors, students can go back online and enter their amended figures. Once they have successfully completed the assignment, they can print out their work and turn it in to their instructor for credit.

You'll find even reluctant math students are eager to pursue the "correct" answer because the final product—their budget—has meaning to them. What was once drill and drudgery will be attacked with newfound enthusiasm and curiosity. And, because students receive instant feedback on the correctness of their mathematical calculations, the end result is confident students with increased career goals and, therefore, increased educational aspirations!

SECTION EIGHT

Resources and Curriculum Support

Technical Support Department

Academic Innovations provides curriculum support to schools using or considering implementation of the *Career Choices* materials. Choose the means of support that's right for you.

☑ Telephone support   **(800) 967-8016, ext. 677**

☑ Online support   **techsupport@academicinnovations.com**

☑ Web page resource files **http://www.academicinnovations.com**

☑ On-site workshops
  and consulting   **Call or email us for information**

☑ A community of
  Career Choices users   **http://www.careerchoices.com/forum**

Our staff, consultants, authors, and certified trainers can provide a variety of services to help make your *Career Choices* program exciting and productive.

Telephone Support

Academic Innovations has Curriculum and Technical Support Specialists to help you implement your *Career Choices* program.

With their finger on the pulse of career education nationwide and a wealth of experience, our staff can answer your questions on using *Career Choices* in a variety of ways: integration/interdisciplinary models, applied academics, freshman orientation, career guidance, college prep, Tech Prep, or a launching place for a pathway or academy program.

If you are interested in professional development, they can help you determine the best plan for training.

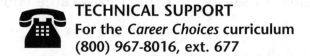

TECHNICAL SUPPORT
For the *Career Choices* curriculum
(800) 967-8016, ext. 677

Online Support

Get the help you need by email: techsupport@academicinnovations.com.

Make sure your message includes your name, question, and return email address. Our support staff will get you an answer or direct you to the resources you need.

Question	Go to URL:	You'll find:	Helpful hints & tips
I have lots of questions about the particular applications of the Career Choices curriculum. Where can I easily find the answers?	http://www. academicinnovations.com/ ccres.html	A list of resources and services offered by our Curriculum and Technical Support Department.	*To request information, email our Tech Support Department using the hyperlink at the bottom of the page or call at (800) 967-8016, ext. 677.*
AND...	http://www. academicinnovations.com/ faq.html	A variety of frequently asked questions and the answers as you scroll down this page.	*Print out for later study. This is a wealth of information. You may want to visit this page several times to hyperlink to other sites referenced here.*

Question	Go to URL:	You'll find:	Helpful hints & tips
I'd like to ask the authors a question about one of the exercises. How can I do this?	http://www. academicinnovations.com/ ask.html	A hyperlink to an email dialog box in which you can type your question.	*Allow up to one week to get a response. If you need help sooner, contact our Tech Support Department by phone at (800) 967-8016, ext. 677.*

www.academicinnovations.com

The Internet has quickly become an "essential" resource. Why all the fuss? Information is power, and the Internet puts that power at your fingertips. The Internet gives us the opportunity to link diverse populations and make information more accessible to everyone. With the advent of the World Wide Web and user-friendly web browsers, people of all ages all over the world are "online."

We've worked hard to provide an Internet site filled with resources for classroom teachers dedicated to improving the lives of their students. Your first surfing expedition will provide immediate rewards.

You'll discover a variety of resources:

- See how other teachers are using the *Career Choices* curriculum

- Review or share specialized lesson plans for the *Career Choices* curriculum

- Become part of an online discussion group of *Career Choices* users and share enrichment ideas

- Meet the authors of our books, and ask them questions online

- Explore funding strategies and review sample grant proposals

- Information on new technology enhancements for *Career Choices*

- Gather information about professional development opportunities

- Learn about the technology enhancements for *Career Choices*

- Find out about new curriculum from Academic Innovations

I am so excited at the discovery of your web page and WONDERFUL links! Thank you so much for providing such wonderful information. Now I have substantial information to be able to deliver to several departments on the campus which is sorely needed. Those departments include Tech Prep directors and the technical/industrial division chair at the college. We have all been working on ways to integrate academia and technical studies. Now at least for me, I have found a source of excellent information (that is CURRENT) and extremely applicable to where we are. Again, thanks so much for providing a wonderful, informative, and well-constructed site for "one-stop shopping" for academic and technical instructors alike!

—Response via email

Career Choices Forum
Online Discussion Group

There's no need for you to feel isolated as you pioneer and innovate new ways of educating and motivating your students. Networking with other teachers is easier than ever. You can become part of a growing community of *Career Choices* educators by joining the *Career Choices* Forum.

The goal of the *Career Choices* Forum is to provide a nationwide medium for educators that will foster open-minded discussion of issues important to the educational community. As a member of this online discussion group, you'll:

- Receive information on new legislation

- Be alerted to possible grant opportunities

- Discuss ideas with other educators using the curriculum

- Share your own innovations—and learn about ideas others have used

- Ask questions of fellow teachers, our support staff, and the authors

Once you have been accepted for membership, you'll be added to our electronic mailing list. Any *Career Choices* Forum messages will be sent to you automatically via email. This format allows you to be as active as you like. You can choose to remain a passive participant by just reading the dialogues delivered to you. You can choose to get actively involved by answering queries from fellow teachers, sharing ideas, and providing resource suggestions.

The possibilities are endless. Help us create a virtual community of *Career Choices* users by sharing your experiences with us. Together we can benefit students across the country.

Joining the Group

You can subscribe to the *Career Choices* Forum through the *Career Choices* web site. Visit www.careerchoices.com/forum and fill out the online form. Your membership will be processed.

Or, join by sending an email message to usrgrp@academicinnovations.com. The message should indicate that you want to join the *Career Choices* Forum. Make sure you include the following information: your name, email address, title, department, school, address, phone and fax numbers, and a brief description of your program.

Professional Development Opportunities

Professional development is always a concern for school systems, but especially as new programs and mandates come along. Staying abreast of changes in the realm of education is one thing; actually implementing all of the new information is the real challenge. Teachers need plenty of opportunities to explore new learning strategies, gain insights, exchange ideas, evaluate approaches, and develop plans. We can provide those opportunities.

Workshop Formats

Sponsor a One- or Two-Day Workshop at Your Site

The most convenient option may be to sponsor a *Career Choices* professional development workshop at your site. Academic Innovations will present a high-quality one- or two-day workshop at your chosen site. You simply invite a group of educators. If you're interested in bringing one of these workshops to your area, call our Curriculum and Technical Support department at (800) 967-8016, ext. 677.

Capacity-Building Workshop for Your School or District

You may be more interested in hosting a *Career Choices* capacity-building workshop for teachers at your school or within your district planning to implement the *Career Choices* materials in their classroom. There are myriad benefits to this option. Your needs are assessed, and the scope and sequence or the training are tailored to fit your specific goals. All participants will gain a clear understanding of the need for comprehensive guidance. They'll also be exposed to the *Career Choices* curriculum in a "hands-on" fashion. Best of all, you'll have a Certified *Career Choices* Trainer to answer specific questions, brainstorm strategies, and help with planning.

Two-Day Workshop Held in Santa Barbara, California

Academic Innovations also sponsors two-day *Career Choices* workshops in our hometown of Santa Barbara, California. Participants gain motivation, valuable information, and concentrated "hands-on" experience. If you need to "train the trainer," this is a great opportunity. Teachers from around the country attend to receive the insight necessary to return to school and make a presentation to other faculty members. This approach is best accomplished by sending a team of at least two teachers.

Borrow a Video of the Two-Day Workshop

Academic Innovations has a six-hour videotape highlighting one of our two-day workshops conducted by author Mindy Bingham. This is a good option for schools with limited time and money. You may even want to preview the videos prior to attending one of our other workshops. These tapes are available for loan. If you wish to borrow a copy, please visit www.academicinnovations.com/wvideo.html, or contact our office at (800) 967-8016.

These tapes are not "studio quality" and are not recommended for use with large groups. They are designed as a "video tutor" for individuals or small groups developing class strategies. Due to demand, please allow up to one month for delivery.

Hold a Phone Conference

For teaching teams with limited resources, this is an excellent option. Award-winning author and curriculum developer Mindy Bingham or a member of our Curriculum and Technical Support staff will gladly "sit in" on your next staff meeting via speaker phone. You set the agenda. We'll answer specific questions about the curriculum, help troubleshoot issues, mediate your team's brainstorming session, and assist in developing your action plan. To arrange for a phone conference, please contact our Curriculum and Technical Support Department at (800) 967-8016, ext. 677.

The workshop was an excellent first step for those of us who will initiate new career programs in our areas.

— Jan Knight
Counselor
Horn High School
Horn Lake, Missouri

The most valuable [aspect] was the practical hands-on modeling of how to present materials and lessons.

— Bonnie Morris
Business/Career instructor
Anacortes High School
Anacortes, Washington

Question	Go to URL:	You'll find:	Helpful hints & tips
I'm interested in attending a Career Choices workshop in my area. How can I get more information?	http://www.academicinnovations.com/wcal.html	A form you can request professional development information.	*Complete the form and submit it online or fax it to (800) 967-4027. Our tech support staff will contact you.*

Professional Development Workshop Themes

Professional development doesn't have to be as big a challenge as you imagine with some guidance from Academic Innovations. With several rousing and relevant workshop modules, we can design a training session that is sure to meet your specific program objectives from any combination of the following modules.

- **A Tour of the *Career Choices* Curriculum** — This introductory module lays the groundwork for your successful workshop.

- **Integrating Career Guidance into the Academic Classroom** — This module demonstrates through lecture and hands-on activities how using a theme of self-discovery and personal planning can motivate students in any academic subject.

- **How to Integrate the Internet into the Academic Classroom** — This online session gives teachers the hands-on experience they need to successfully integrate the power of the Internet.

- **Math, Career Guidance, and Technology: A Winning Combination** — This module explains how a real-world budgeting activity can motivate your students to pursue post-secondary education and training as it gives them basic math practice.

- **Teaching Strategies and Techniques for the *Career Choices* Curriculum** — This module gives you an in-depth look at how other educators have implemented *Career Choices*—so you can replicate their success.

- **How to Integrate *Career Choices* into the English/Language Arts Classroom** — This module exhibits how your English/language arts program can teach vital career and life planning skills while fostering a love of literature.

[A] variety of tools with practical applications . . . I was engaged throughout the training.

> — Nina Whitney
> Community Service Worker
> Lane Workforce Partnership
> Eugene, OR

Print and online resources immediately available for classroom use. Very user friendly.

> — Mary Airhart
> Counselor
> Borden County ISD
> Gail, TX

The No Child Left Behind, Title II-D Professional Development Mandate

Use your NCLB Title II-D funds to bring a workshop to your district.

Districts are required to spend 25 percent of the funds they receive on high-quality professional development in the integration of technology into the classroom.

Now that schools are wired with high-speed access to the Internet, learn how to integrate technology's power and excitement into your daily lesson plans. The Internet intensifies learning by encouraging students to analyze, synthesize and evaluate information.

Learn techniques to integrate the Internet into any curriculum using the award-winning *Career Choices* curriculum and its Internet enhancements. Learning with an existing curriculum model, you'll *experience* each teaching strategy. Rather than listening to theoretical approaches, you'll see exactly how it works, and you'll be ready to utilize the methods in your own classroom.

The hands-on computer lab session is designed for beginning and experienced web surfers alike. Using the *Career Choices* curriculum and the accompanying web sites, www.careerchoices.com and www.lifestylemath.com, as the model, participants learn how to infuse the Internet into their current lessons, making them technology rich.

Participants discover:

- How to choose the best web sites to motivate their students

- The seven characteristics of optimal online learning opportunities

- A replicable model for enhancing current lessons with the Internet's rich resources

- Classroom techniques for managing and monitoring computer lab sessions

- Effective strategies for incorporating the most popular business-based software into academic classes

- How to identify interactive web sites that build language, reading and writing skills and support mathematical skill development

- Proven methods for creating meaningful, real-life, real-world projects critical to the maturation process of adolescents

- Effective ways to add "high touch" (collaboration, group learning, discussion and project-based learning) into the "high tech" classroom

- Strategies to help engage, enrich and excite their students

If you're interested in bringing one of these workshops to your area, call our Curriculum and Technical Support department at (800) 967-8016, ext. 677.

Special Resources

Common Miracles

Correspondents Peter Jennings and Bill Blakemore reveal how we can help students realize their unique talents and learning abilities in the ABC News Special "Common Miracles: The New American Revolution in Learning." The documentary features penetrating interviews with instructors, principals, psychologists, parents, and students, focusing on methods and schools that provide their students with freedom and options through education.

Illustrating several innovative and positive techniques that help young people grasp the "keys to a glorious future," Jennings and Blakemore go on location to schools across the nation. They find that traditional education—including tracking, factory model schools, and IQ-based assessment—is being replaced with cooperative learning, the use of computers, apprenticeships, parent and community involvement, and the philosophy that every child is gifted.

"Common Miracles" exposes the ultimate goal of educational revolution: to "liberate the human potential in all Americans." We recommend showing it at staff and parents' meetings. Copies of this 60-minute program are available for $19.98, plus shipping. Contact MPI Media Group at (800) 323-0442.

Educated in Romance

Why are young women-even those who perform very well in school-less likely to be achievers in the world than their male counterparts? According to Dorothy C. Holland and Margaret A. Eisenhart, authors of the fascinating book *Educated in Romance* (University of Chicago Press), the answer lies not so much in what or how much is learned, but in why they learn. In their longitudinal study, the authors found most females are more interested in pleasing others, attracting males, getting good grades, or just getting by than they are in mastering knowledge or skills. Only those who saw a relationship between their education and future occupations went on to live up to their potential in the workplace.

The authors' findings provide strong support for comprehensive career education programs in secondary schools. By understanding the forces that can lead even gifted young women into dead-end futures, you can take steps to prevent this from happening to your students and your daughters. This book is available through the University of Chicago Distribution Center. Call them to order at (800) 621-2736. We highly recommend it to you.

The Neglected Majority by Dale Parnell

In his visionary book, *The Neglected Majority*, author Dale Parnell champions the cause of those high school students who are too often overlooked: the 75 percent who will not graduate from a 4-year college. For their sake, and for the country's, he argues, it is time for our high schools to develop and implement Tech Prep programs. If you haven't read this easy to understand blueprint for educational reform, you will find valuable strategies and solutions within its pages.

In the book's foreword, Thomas A. Shannon, Executive Director of the National School Board Association, states, "Parnell makes a convincing case for the argument that the complex, technological world of the future is really already here. The emerging truth is that higher and more comprehensive skills must be developed, particularly by the middle two quarters of the workforce." A copy can be obtained through your local bookstore or directly from the Community College Press at (800) 250-6557 for $33.00.

Road Map for Change

If you want to learn how high schools successfully improve, read *Making High Schools Work through Integration of Academics and Vocational Education*. Published by the Southern Regional Educational Board, this 200-page report speaks to reality, not theory, and is based on the experience of using SREB-recommended strategies. Loaded with specific experiences from consortium members in 19 states already restructuring and implementing Tech Prep programs, this book is highly recommended reading for administrators, teachers, and counselors who want to avoid reinventing the wheel. Available for $10.95 per copy from SREB, Publication Orders Dept., 592 10th Street NW, Atlanta, GA 30318-5790, (404) 875-9211, ext. 236. You can print an order form from the SREB website at www.sreb.org/main/Publications/catalog/srebcatalog.asp

Second to None: A Clear Vision

Educational reform and restructuring plans are taking shape across the country. Florida's *Blueprint* and Ohio's *Future at Work* are two excellent examples of action plans to modernize the educational process. California's vision of the future, *Second to None*, written by their High School Task Force, is another exemplary step toward 21st-Century schools.

Second to None begins with a vignette of a student's day at Bayshore High, a fictional school where students want to learn and teachers want to teach. The model program involves clusters, student-centered learning, and teachers who coach and support all students. As one reads this well-crafted description of the state's ambitious educational reform plan, it is not difficult to see how the wheels of educational change can spin more quickly. Seven of California's 30 Investment High Schools (educational reform demonstration sites) chose the *Career Choices* curriculum as an important component of their restructuring projects.

For a copy of *Second to None*, ($9.50, plus shipping and handling), write the California Department of Education, CDE Press, Sales Unit, P.O. Box 271, Sacramento, CA 95812-0271, or call toll-free (800) 995-4099. A 33-minute video highlighting the major themes of the *Second to None* publication is also available ($13.00, plus shipping and handling). Online ordering information available: www.cde.ca.gov/cdepress/presorder.html.

Why Do I Have to Learn This? by Dale Parnell

One of the most frequently asked questions by students is "Why do I have to learn this?" Instead of responding with the typical answer, "You might need it someday," try using the approach that Dale Parnell provides in his first book dedicated primarily to teachers and students of K-Adult education.

In *Why Do I Have to Learn This?* ($16.00, CORD Communications, 1995), Parnell discusses the latest research in learning styles and outlines a common sense but ever-so-important strategy for improving teaching and learning. Previously available as *LogoLogic*, Parnell's book has been updated and re-titled. This book demonstrates the importance of providing a solid philosophical and academic base for the Tech Prep program.

A natural follow-up to *The Neglected Majority*, this insightful and thought-provoking book, by one of the leading educational reformers today, stresses the complexity and effectiveness of learning for meaning. Without meaning, students will continue to search for the answers to why education is relevant to their future. To order, call CCI Publishing at (800) 231-3015 or order online by visiting www.ez.com/cord.

Other Resources Recommended by Teachers

Enter Here

Do you want to bring the world of work into your classroom? The *Enter Here* video-based library is one great way. An encyclopedia of career opportunities, the 100 video vignettes feature real people in a wide variety of real jobs filmed at their actual work sites. The videotapes are organized into 10 occupational clusters, with each lasting approximately 10 minutes. Supplemental print materials are designed for either the middle school or high school level. These videos demonstrate the relationship between school and work, while encouraging continuing education and training. For a product catalog and ordering information, contact: Delmar Learning, (800) 998-7498.

Baby! Think It Over

Many teachers are using *Baby! Think It Over* with *Career Choices* in their life skills classes and/or as part of a pregnancy prevention program. Students are assigned an infant simulator for a given period of time. The infant simulator is anatomically correct, with a lifelike vinyl body measuring 21 inches in length and weighing between 6.5 and 7 pounds. *Baby* is equipped with a recording of a real infant crying, tamper resistant electronics, and different temperament settings.

Just like an infant, the simulator cries at random throughout the day-and night. The student must care for *Baby* by inserting a key into the back of the simulator. Crying will stop when the key is inserted, but it must be held in place for at least a minute—or as long as 30—replicating the time needed to care for an infant. The key is worn on a tamperproof wristband, so only the assigned student can soothe *Baby*.

The electronics driving *Baby* are also tamperproof and record the quality of *Baby*'s care. By reporting total simulation time, neglect, rough handling, and total minutes for crying, *Baby* allows teachers to monitor each student in the role of instant parent.

For more information on *Baby! Think It Over*, visit www.btio.com or contact: Realityworks, Inc., 2709 Mondovi Road, Eau Claire, WI 54701, (800) 830-1416 or (715) 830-2040.

Unlocking Your Potential

Your students have a lot to offer. You know it, but often they don't. Helping them uncover their natural talents can be a challenge, and then they still have to choose to use their abilities? In the motivational video *Unlocking Your Potential*, students learn about building a positive self-image, the importance of goal-setting, and the characteristics of high-performers.

Contact the Edge Learning Institute for more information:, (800)858-1484 or (253)272-3103, 2217 North 30th Street Suite 200, Tacoma, WA 98403, www.edgelearning.com.

In the Mix

A national award-winning PBS television series, *In the Mix* provides a quality viewing experience for teens by teens. *In the Mix* has covered myriad topics of concern to today's young people—making the grade in school; moving into the world of work; violence in dating relationships; preparing for college; and dealing with conflicts at home, to highlight just a few.

A list of episodes is available online, complete with discussion guides. For more information, or to order copies of the program for your classroom, visit www.pbs.org/inthemix/educators/index.html.

> *[T]he* **Enter Here** *career video series is excellent. The series highlights 100+ career titles, job requirements, and what the entry-level job can lead to. It uses real people in the real positions doing the teaching, on the job in their career.*
>
> — Roseann Reynolds
> Moreno Valley High School
> Moreno Valley, California

Freshmen Orientation Class

The following standards are for a state mandated class in Tennessee that is required for all freshmen entering vocational programs. The *Career Choices* curriculum is one of the state-recommended curricula for this course. At the time of printing, Tennessee is considering making this course mandatory for all freshmen.

If your school has or is considering an orientation course for all entering freshmen, you'll want to review this chart, along with the standards for the Texas Career Connections course that follows. Helping 9th graders develop a vision of their future from the very first day of high school will decrease dropout rates and result in higher academic achievement. Students will make the connection between success in school and success in life at a time when they can make positive choices that will impact their futures.

Tennessee Career Management Success Standards

Correlated to
Career Choices, Instructor's Guide, CareerChoices.com, Possibilities and *Lifestyle Math*

Learning Expectations	Career Choices	Instructor's Guide, 6th Edition	Possibilities	Lifestyle Math	CareerChoices.com Internet site
STANDARD 1.0 — Students will display attitudes necessary for achieving personal and academic success. The student will:					
1.1 Examine learning styles and adapt learning strategies to their identified styles.	38–43, 162–165	4/22–4/26, 4/102–4/105			
1.2 Prioritize and manage personal and academic activities using time management strategies.	121	4/77		104–110	
1.3 Use advanced study skills.	148–161	4/89–4/101	Throughout text	4–9	
1.4 Diagram steps required to achieve identified short and long-term goals.	183–185, 186–190	4/117–4/121	182–191	102–110	
1.5 Generate personal strategies for managing stress.	194–227, 274–277	4/123–4/140	172–177, 214–215, 212–220, 221–224, 225–227	6–9	
1.6 Model attitudes conducive to personal success.	231–237	4/141–4/149	38, 240–248, 249–251	93–97	
STANDARD 2.0 — Students will demonstrate attitudes, skills, and strategies necessary for achieving workplace success. The student will:					
2.1 Analyze the role of values and ethics in career and workplace.	238–241, 242–245	4/146–147, 4/148–150	249–251		
2.2 Correlate lifestyle requirements with career	56–59, 62–63	4/38–4/42		12–88	Enhancing activities available online

Learning Expectations	Career Choices	Instructor's Guide, 6th Edition	Possibilities	Lifestyle Math	CareerChoices.com Internet site
2.3 Assess implications of diversity for communities and workplaces.	194–199, 211–213, 242–247	4/124–4/125, 4/132–4/133, 4/148–4/150	69–71		
2.4 Infer relationships between work ethics and organizational and personal job success.	64–71, 238–241	4/43–4/45, 4/146–4/147	64–68, 72–73, 76–79, 270–272		
2.5 Demonstrate attitudes conducive to workplace success.	232–247	4/141–150	240–247, 249–251	6, 98–99	

STANDARD 3.0 — Students will use teamwork skills to accomplish goals, solve problems, and manage conflict within groups. Students will:

Learning Expectations	Career Choices	Instructor's Guide, 6th Edition	Possibilities	Lifestyle Math	CareerChoices.com Internet site
3.1 Analyze the role and functions of teams in the workplace.	162–165	4/102–105, 4/143, 4/146		98–99	
3.2 Perform the functions of various roles within a team.		4/25–4/27, 4/83, 4/105–107, 4/115, 4/148, 6/30–6/35	Team projects throughout text	98–99	
3.3 Use strategies to resolve or reduce conflicts within groups.	183–185	4/118, 6/23–6/28	264–269		
3.4 Give and receive constructive criticism.	196–200	4/124–4/126	208	8–9	
3.5 Achieve solutions as members of a multicultural team.	242–245	4/148–4/150, 6/1–6/2	164–165, 212–213		

STANDARD 4.0 — Students will communicate effectively and comprehend oral and written communication. The student will:

Learning Expectations	Career Choices	Instructor's Guide, 6th Edition	Possibilities	Lifestyle Math	CareerChoices.com Internet site
4.1 Demonstrate effective verbal communication.	Projects throughout text	Projects throughout text	Practiced throughout text	Group projects	
4.2 Demonstrate effective written communication in various business formats.	159, 250–257	4/102–4/105, 4/152–4/153		Practiced throughout text	Enhancing activities available online
4.3 Demonstrate listening skills and oral comprehension.	120, 161, 241, 257–259	4/76, 4/101, 4/147, 6/2–6/27	Practiced throughout text		
4.4 Demonstrate comprehension of written communication.	Throughout text		Practiced throughout text		Throughout

STANDARD 5.0 — Students will demonstrate job-seeking skills and exhibit employability characteristics required for employability and job retention in the workplace. Students will:

Learning Expectations	Career Choices	Instructor's Guide, 6th Edition	Possibilities	Lifestyle Math	CareerChoices.com Internet site
5.1 Plan a job search strategy.	250–263	4/151–4/159	254–261, 273–275	88–91	Enhancing activities available online
5.2 Exhibit positive interview behavior.	258–259	4/155–4/157			Enhancing activities available online

Learning Expectations	Career Choices	Instructor's Guide, 6th Edition	Possibilities	Lifestyle Math	CareerChoices.com Internet site
STANDARD 6.0 — Students will adapt to the requirements of specific business or industry employability and job retention in the workplace. The student will:					
6.1 Model attitudes, actions, and behaviors required for successful performance on the job.	13–21, 232–247	4/4–4/13, 4/141–4/150, 4/146–4/148	19–32, 33–36, 252–253	98–99, 102–107	
6.2 Demonstrate an appropriate workplace appearance.	82–83	4/57, 6/11		43–47	
6.3 Analyze the importance of a wellness program for employees.	64–71, 89	4/43–4/45		74–75	
STANDARD 7.0 — Students will demonstrate leadership, citizenship, and teamwork skills required for success in the school, community, and workplace. The student will:					
7.1 Cultivate positive leadership skills.	232–247	4/141–4/150, 6/23–6/31, 6/32–33	262–263	98–99	
7.2 Participate in a student organization directly related to their program of study as an integral part of classroom instruction.	160–161	4/101, 10/2–10/6			
7.3 Assess situations and apply problem-solving and decision-making skills within the school, community, and workplace.	170–178	4/24–4/26, 4/108–4/115, 4/148	127–138, 139–141, 142–163	95–97	
7.4 Participate as team members.	162–165, 238–241	4/24–4/26, 4/83, 4/102–4/105, 4/115, 4/146		26, 38, 60–63, 82–83, 98–99	
STANDARD 8.0 — Students will integrate multiple roles and responsibilities in family, work, and community settings. The student will:					
8.1 Analyze the contribution of the family to the development of its members individually, as family members, and as members of the community and workforce.	49–53, 66–71	4/30–4/33, 4/44–4/45, 10/7–10/11	44–45, 95–102, 103–107, 214–215	26, 27–30, 92–94	
8.2 Analyze strategies to manage multiple individual, family, work, and community roles and responsibilities.	96–111, 128–130, 211–213, 222–223, 270–282	4/65–4/71, 4/80–4/81, 4/132–4/133, 4/137, 4/164–4/167		30–31, 71–73, 82–83	
8.3 Demonstrate the transfer of employability and other related skills to workplace settings.	46–48, 112–113, 247	4/27–4/29, 4/72–4/73, 4/150	118–123		

Learning Expectations	Career Choices	Instructor's Guide, 6th Edition	Possibilities	Lifestyle Math	CareerChoices.com Internet site
STANDARD 9.0 — Students will perform basic PC operations and file management using appropriate software. The student will:					
9.1 Demonstrate the ability to perform basic PC operations.	Projects throughout text	7/6–7/17	172–177, 279–283	98–99	Projects throughout web site
9.2 Selects the appropriate software for a given problem or task.	226, 247	4/139–4/140, 4/150, 7/1–7/5		60–63	Projects throughout web site
9.3 Perform file management tasks.		4/13–4/14	279–283	60–63	Projects throughout web site
STANDARD 10.0 — Students will explore career opportunities and career paths offered in the local education system. The student will:					
10.1 Explain the titles, roles, and functions of individuals engaged in the career paths offered at their local high school.	120, 144–161, 254–255, 262–263	4/76 4/85–4/101 4/155 4/159			Enhancing activities available online
10.2 Investigate employment and entrepreneurial opportunities.	135–137, 138–139, 150–155	4/82–4/83, 4/89–90, 4/102–105	118–123		Enhancing activities available online
10.3 Evaluate personal characteristics required for working in the various career paths offered at their local high school.	24–48, 126–134, 135–137, 145–147	4/15–4/29, 4/80–4/82, 4/86–4/88			Enhancing activities available online
10.4 Investigate post-secondary education, professional organizations, trade publications, and web sites appropriate for continuing education.	150–155, 227, 267–269, 270–273	4/13–4/14, 4/87–90, 4/139–140, 4/162–4/164			Enhancing activities available online

Career Guidance Course

The following standards are for a high school career education class in Texas. Comprehensive guidance is a vital experience for students to have early in their high school career, especially if they will be entering an academy or pathway program. One way to ensure that all students receive the necessary career guidance is to implement the *Career Choices* materials in this type of required career education or freshman orientation class. A comprehensive class such as this will help students make better selections as they plan their high school curriculum and better choices as they plan their life beyond high school.

If your school has or is considering a career guidance education course for all high school students, you'll want to review this chart along with the standards for the Tennessee Career Management Success course that precedes this chart. Helping students develop a vision of their future from the very first day of high school will decrease drop out rates and result in higher academic achievement. Students will make the connection between success in school and success in life at a time when they are able to make positive choices that will lead to a successful and productive life.

Texas Essential Knowledge and Skills (TEKS) for Career Connections

Correlated to
Career Choices, Instructor's Guide, and CareerChoices.com

Knowledge and Skills	Career Choices	Instructor's Guide, 6th Edition	CareerChoices.com Internet Site
01. The student analyzes the effect of personal interest and aptitudes upon educational and career planning. The student is expected to:			
A. Complete a formal career interest and aptitude assessment	24–27, 28–29, 31–37, 39–43, 4–48	4/15–4/31	
B. Match interests and aptitudes to career opportunities	105–113, 124–141, 144–147, 148–165	4/38–4/45, 4/80–4/84, 4/86–4/105, 10/5	145–150, 158–160
C. Begin a personal career portfolio by conducting an in–depth study of the varied aspects of occupations related to the student's interest areas.	24–53, 57–71, 124–141, 144–165	4/38–4/45, 4/80–4/84, 4/86–4/105	145–150, 158–160
02. The student knows how to locate, analyze, and apply career information. The student is expected to:			
A. Access career information using print and online resources to complete an educational and/or training plan for a career pathway	144–165, 203–207, 222–223, 266–283	4/78, 4/86–4/105, 4/139, 4/162–4/169	145–150, 158–160, 229, 267–269, 271, 279–280

Knowledge and Skills	Career Choices	Instructor's Guide, 6th Edition	CareerChoices.com Internet Site
B. Access career information using interviews with business and industry representatives to create a career resource file	120, 254–255, 262–263	4/76, 4/91–4/101, 4/146, 4/155, 10/5	120, 229, 254–255
C. Complete career critiques gained through a variety of experiences (for example, shadowing, career study tours, guest speakers, career fairs, videos, CD-ROM, Internet, and simulated work activities)	120, 156–157, 158–159, 160–161	4/76, 4/94–4/101, 4/115, 4/157, 6/36–6/40	120, 158–160
D. Use career information to apply entrepreneurial skills by developing a small business plan.	38–43, 138–139, 162–165, 238–241	4/22–4/23, 4/83, 4/103–4/104, 4/146–4/147	

03. The student knows that many skills are common to a variety of careers and that these skills can be transferred from one career opportunity to another. The student is expected to:

A. Compile a list of transferable skills with a corresponding list of possible career options matching the student's interests and aptitudes to be placed in the personal career portfolio	46–48, 132–134, 147, 150, 162–165, 246	4/13–4/14, 4/27–4/28, 4/150	
B. Create a presentation portraying transferable skills within the student's interest area.		4/150	

04. The student knows the process used to locate and secure employment. The student is expected to:

A. Prepare a Venn diagram comparing and contrasting employment opportunities of our free enterprise system and the economic systems of the international job market	242–245, 246	4/149	253
B. Develop a chart classifying employment opportunities based on educational and training requirements of careers in the student's interest area	116–119, 204–206, 207, 211–213, 226, 227, 229	4/132–4/133, 4/139, 4/164–4/166	
C. Complete a job application form for an employment opportunity in the student's interest area	256–257	4/156	256
D. Develop a resume for an employment opportunity in the student's interest area	250–253	4/152–4/153	253
E. Role-play appropriate interviewing techniques for an employment opportunity in the student's interest area	258–259	4/157, 10/5–10/6	258

Knowledge and Skills	Career Choices	Instructor's Guide, 6th Edition	CareerChoices.com Internet Site
05. The student recognizes the impact of career choice on personal lifestyle. The student is expected to:			
A. Prepare a personal budget reflecting lifestyle desires	74–121	4/48–4/67	78, 80, 83, 88–89, 93, 120
B. Use print or online information to determine salaries of at least three career choices in the student's interest area with vary education requirements (for example, no high school diploma, high school diploma, and postsecondary training)	116–119, 148–155, 207, 211–213, 227	4/89–4/90, 4/164–4/166	148–150
C. Select the career most closely matching the student's personal lifestyle budget	93, 131, 148–155, 227	4/64, 4/129, 4/139	
06. The student knows the process of career planning. The student is expected to:			
A. List and explain the steps in the decision-making process	168–179	4/108–4/115	
B. List characteristics of an effective team member	162–165, 229–247	4/24–4/25, 4/102, 4/104, 4/115, 4/118–4/119, 4/143	
C. Identify high school courses related to specific career choices in the student's interest area	266–283	4/129, 4/162–4/169	267–269, 271, 279
D. Select high school courses and experiences to develop a graduation plan that leads to a specific career choice in the student's interest area	150–155, 266–283	4/129, 4/162–4/169	267–269, 271,279
E. List and explain educational and/or training alternatives after high school for a career choice within the student's interest area	116–119, 148–155, 210–215, 227, 266, 272	4/75, 4/90–4/91, 4/137, 4/139, 4/162–4/169	267–269, 271,279
F. Prepare an educational and career plan for an occupation within the student's interest area that begins with entry into high school and continues through a postsecondary educational and/or training program and place this information in the personal career portfolio.	116–119, 227, 266–283	4/139, 4/162–4/169	267–269, 271–279

Knowledge and Skills	Career Choices	Instructor's Guide, 6th Edition	CareerChoices.com Internet Site
07. The student knows the importance of productive work habits and attitudes. The student is expected to:			
A. Conduct interviews with a minimum of two employers to determine the importance of work ethics such as dependability, promptness, getting along with others and honesty	238–241	4/146, 10/4–10/5	
B. List characteristics of an effective team member	38–43, 162–165, 229–247, 232–235, 236–237, 238–241	4/24–4/25, 4/102–4/105, 4/115, 4/118–4/119, 4/143	
C. Work on a team to accomplish an assigned task and complete an "effective team member" profile to place in the personal career portfolio	38–43, 162–165, 232–235, 238–241	4/22–4/23, 4/25–4/26, 4/102–4/105, 4/115, 4/127, 4/137, 4/148	
D. Write job scenarios demonstrating positive and negative employee/customer relations.	232–235, 238–241	4/145–4/146, 4/178	
08. The student knows the effect change has on society and career opportunities. The student is expected to			
A. Cite examples of change in our society	135–137, 211–213, 242–246, 266	4/14, 4/61, 4/90–4/91, 4/139, 4/148, 4/150	
B. Compose a report explaining positive and negative aspects of one of the examples of societal change	135–137, 242–245	4/61, 4/150	
C. Develop a timeline covering the last ten years depicting the change in a selected career choice	150–155, 226	4/90–4/91, 4/139, 4/150, 4/153	
D. Use labor market information, knowledge of technology and societal and/or economic trends to forecast a job profile for a career in the student's internet area ten years from now and add this profile to the personal career portfolio	135–139, 148–149, 150–155, 226, 242–246	4/90–4/91, 4/139, 4/150, 4/153	148–149

4800 West Virginia Youth Benefit from Career Choices at Summer Work Sites

In 1998, Myreeha Randolph, a Senior Employment Programs Specialist for the West Virginia Bureau of Employment Programs, was functioning as the director of the Governor's Summer Youth Program for the state. Obviously, the majority of her job was making sure the goals of the program were met. As Myreeha told us, the main goal was "[t]o meet the federal mandate using a curriculum that would appeal to the kids and help them learn while they thought they were having fun, or at least learn without feeling like it was classroom learning!"

The early part of the year found Myreeha hard at work "casting about for potential vendors." She remembered a letter she had received about the Career Choices curriculum. It seemed worth a shot, so Myreeha sent an RFQ (request for quote) to Academic Innovations, publishers of the Career Choices materials. The RFQ had some very specific challenges that had to be dealt with—even more so than usual.

One challenge was the size of the program: There would be nearly 5,000 youth involved and almost 1,000 instructors. A variety of attitudes, academic levels, and presentation styles would have to be considered. Another challenge presented itself. All instruction would take place at the work sites—there would be no time spent in classrooms. If the students were working as part of a road crew, their instruction may take place on a bus. If students were working on a park crew, they may hold "class" at picnic tables. The program would run from mid-June to the end of July, with students working 5 days a week, 6 hours a day. Of the time spent at work sites, a minimum of 4 hours each week were to be devoted to basic skills instruction. Obviously, flexibility would have to be a key component of whatever curriculum was chosen.

The completed RFQs were evaluated, and Career Choices was chosen as the curriculum for the 1998 summer program. The deciding factor? Myreeha was not only impressed with the textbooks but also with the support offered by Academic Innovations. "I found [the] staff friendly, easy to work with, and they all seemed to place high value on customer support. From what I could tell, the tech support was available and on target. To me, that's just as important as the product!"

Myreeha believes that Career Choices was able to overcome the initial challenges presented—reluctant summer learners, work site teaching, and varying skill levels. "It seemed like a fun book in which to work… [with] a variety of exercises, so most academic skill levels represented by the kids were able to find an appropriately challenging set of exercises."

Was Career Choices well received? So much so that even though the Governor's Summer Youth Program couldn't consider using Career Choices again for 4 years (because of the high return rate of participants year-after-year), a new Academic Innovations' text was chosen to provide the 1999 program materials: Career Strategies: How to Get and Keep a Job, a new text written by Jim Comiskey and Jay McGrath.

SECTION NINE

Start-Up Strategies

Getting Started

Starting a new program offers a variety of challenges. This section will provide strategies and resources that will help with this process.

1. Identify Your Goals

The first step to any new project is to identify your goals and objectives. You might want to review the system presented in Chapter Eight of the *Career Choices* textbook. This tried and true simple format will help you articulate what you want to make different, in what time frame, and by how many. It will be the beginning roadmap that will help you explain your plan to your peers and funding sources.

2. Create Buy-In within Your School and Community

It is critical that you get others within your school to buy-in to your new program. After you identify who they are, review the following pages for some step-by-step strategies that have worked for other educational innovators. See Section Ten for community involvement strategies.

3. Identify and Secure Funding

A critical and important step, pages **9/8–9/18** demystifies the process of getting the funds you require to make your plan a reality. You'll want to review the federal, state and local mandates that support your goals, as funding is probably available through these mandates.

Strategies for Creating Buy-In—
The Student-Centered Model

> **THE TRADITIONAL
> ORGANIZATIONAL MODEL**
>
> **Organization**   The **ORGANIZATION** of education...
>   *(so many "periods" that were so long, 8 am to 3 pm, five days per week, English, math, science, social studies departments, classrooms with desks in rows, lecture format leading to easily scored tests, etc.)*
>
> **Curriculum**   dictated the **CURRICULUM**
>   *(50-minute lessons, broken into specific disciplines for students in a structured classroom studying for a test)*
>
> **Needs of students**   The **CURRICULUM** defined the "**NEEDS OF STUDENTS.**"

In the past, many organizations, including public education, were structured after the above model. Industry and commerce were the first to recognize that the needs of the customers—not the organization—must come first. This concept drove the restructuring many companies experienced in the 1990s. Today, education, too, is finding it must restructure to better serve its "customers"—the students.

> **THE *PROGRESSIVE*
> STUDENT-CENTERED MODEL**
>
> **Needs of students**
>
> **Curriculum**
>
> **Organization**

The first step is to articulate the educational **NEEDS OF STUDENTS**, after which an appropriate **CURRICULUM** can be designed. Once a **CURRICULUM** is designed to meet students' needs, an **ORGANIZATIONAL STRUCTURE** to deliver that curriculum must be put in place (see pp. 9/5 and 9/6 of this guide).

The future of public education is likely to be both exciting and challenging. The more support and information you have in your restructuring efforts, the better your chances of success. Toward that end, we have included a variety of optional resources and suggestions that you may find helpful as you and your colleagues restructure your school and district.

Academic Innovations is committed to helping you provide your students with the best and most relevant education possible. Please don't hesitate to contact our Curriculum and Technical Support Department as you work to implement the *Career Choices* curriculum.

Creating Buy-In for Your Course

Vision and teamwork are critical elements in any restructuring effort. However you plan to use the *Career Choices* curriculum, you will probably have to change some of the things you've done in the past, and change is uncomfortable for everyone.

The first step to a positive and lasting change is creating buy-in from the individuals involved. If you plan a class where you are the only instructor, you will need to get buy-in from the administration and, perhaps, a school improvement committee (parents and community members). If you are planning an interdisciplinary curriculum, you will also need to get active buy-in from all teachers working with you, including the other instructors that touch your students' lives at some level.

You'll need to "lobby" for your project. Studies on the process of change suggest that the best way to get people to accept the transition is through **one-on-one discussions**. Meet with individuals over lunch or coffee and present your idea. Use this time to listen for any discomfort or concern on the part of your colleagues. You will want to address their concerns or provide possible solutions right then. If this isn't possible, get back to the individual with more information quickly. Once you have addressed any concerns and you have a team of individuals willing to explore the possibilities, it is time to call a meeting.

Question	Go to URL:	You'll find:	Helpful hints & tips
I need to convince our administration that the Career Choices curriculum works. How can I print out stories and comments for other schools?	http://www.academicinnovations.com/indepth.html	A listing of programs across the country using *Career Choices* in a variety of settings.	*Scroll through and choose the stories that match your needs. Print them out to share with your administration.*
AND...	http://www.academicinnovations.com/whatsay.html	A list of themes on which other educators have commented.	*Hyperlink to <u>Proven</u> and print out the statements to incorporate into your report. Then surf any other relevant themes/issues to your proposed program.*
AND...	http://www.academicinnovations.com/expert.html	A list of articles on a variety of topics about the special needs of adolescents.	*Read each hyperlink and then download the appropriate articles to include in your report. By downloading, you can later edit the text into your proposal.*

Creating a Shared Vision

Your Meeting

We suggest opening your meeting immediately (after only a word or two of welcome) with the following group discussion:

If you could wave a magic wand and give your students any characteristics, attitudes, or skills, what would they be?

Have a large pad of paper and easel available to write on, so you can hang your notes on the wall for future reference. Following the rules of brainstorming (page 6/30 of this guide), identify the needs of students. Once you have completed this exercise, and perhaps edited and prioritized your list, present the concept of The Progressive Model (page 9/2).

Hint: Before you even begin lobbying, we recommend you call our office for curriculum and tech support. Not only can we give you ideas and examples of how other schools with your demographic profile are using the curriculum, we can provide you with resources such as overhead masters and slides that might make your presentation planning easier. We can even give you a copy of a PowerPoint presentation you can then edit to fit your needs.

Notes from Your Meeting:

This list was created by 36 teachers and administrators during a brainstorming session at the beginning of one of our two-day workshops in Santa Barbara.

Would your list look similar?

Once you have read this list, fold back along the dotted line. →

What characteristics, attitudes and skills do we want for the teens we teach?

Critical thinking skills

Interpersonal skills

Pride in who they are

Adaptability to change

Value the educational system

Enthusiasm

Tolerance of people/cultures

Pride in workmanship

Ability to plan for the future

Setting goals/Planning

Stick-to-itiveness

Follow through

Risk taking

Good decision-making skills

Respect for others and self

Indulge creativity

Ability to handle stress

Initiative

Personal responsibility

Pursuit of excellence

Feeling entitled

Sense of humor

Good role models

Seek out mentors

Find out aptitudes/interests/strengths

Career exploration

Communication skills

Vocational skills

Empowerment

Introspection and self-evaluation

Being in charge of their destiny

Visionary

Access information

9/5

You'll want to evaluate any curriculum materials you choose for your program, based upon the list of "needs of students" you produce at your meeting.

☎ **TECHNICAL SUPPORT**
For the *Career Choices* curriculum
(800) 967-8016, ext. 677

Fold page 9/5 to here →

Where Career Choices Addresses These Issues

Infused throughout activities

Practiced in group activities

Chapter 2

Pages 242–245

Pages 116–119; 266–273

Page 233

Pages 242–245

Pages 238–241

Chapter 12

Chapter 8

Pages 114–121

Chapter 1 on

Pages 224–225

Chapter 7

Chapters 2, 9, 10

Encouraged in all activities

Pages 216–221; 276–277

Chapter 1

Pages 194–200

Pages 232–235

Chapter 1 on

Light-hearted stories

Pages 158–159

Pages 262–263

Chapter 2

Chapter 5 and 6

Practiced throughout

Chapters 5 and 6

Focus of curriculum

Chapters 1, 2, 3 on

A major theme in text

Chapter 1 on

Chapters 6 and 11

"Sample" Measurable Goals and Objectives for the *Career Choices* Curriculum:

The following measurable goals and objectives are the kind funding sources (from private foundations to school boards) require. You may want to choose the most appropriate two or three for your project and edit accordingly. You'll want to include a copy of your assessment tool(s) with your proposal. See pages 6/12–6/16 for a sample pre- and post-survey, along with suggested assessment surveys.

- Upon completion of the *Career Choices* curriculum, ___% of students will have raised their career goals and expectations as demonstrated by pre- and post-surveys.

- Upon completion of the *Career Choices* curriculum, ___% of students who at the beginning of the class had not planned any further education or training after high school will have changed their minds and will be preparing for post-secondary education or training.

- Upon completion of the *Career Choices* curriculum, ___% of the students in the course will have changed their attitude towards and therefore increased their performance in their academic subjects, as evaluated by pre- and post-surveys of their other teachers.

- Upon completion of the *Career Choices* curriculum each student will have a realistic educational and career plan for the next ten years. They will also be able to demonstrate the goal setting, analytical and decision-making skills necessary to adapt that plan as they mature.

- Upon completion of the *Career Choices* curriculum, all females will be able to articulate, in a quantitative way, why becoming a teen parent is not a good plan. Females who were ambivalent about teen pregnancy at the beginning of the course will have a strong opinion and attitude against teen parenting.

- Students completing this course will be less likely to drop out of high school. This will be demonstrated by decreasing the dropout rate among the graduates of this program from ___% (current school average or average of similar ability students) to ___%.

- Test scores within academic subjects (define which ones) will increase by _____ within one year of completing this course.

- In post-class surveys, ___% of graduates' parents will report a positive impact on their child due to this classroom experience.

Getting Funding

From the responses we get via the phone and email, finding funding for a new program is among the most challenging aspects of starting a course. The following pages are included to help you start this process. You'll find information on:

- Federal programs (Carl Perkins funding in particular)

- State funding

- Corporate funding

- Online resources to help with writing your grant

- Information on student-funded workbook purchases

- Funding from community organizations

You probably won't want to stop here. The domain of funding and grants is an ever-changing arena, particularly when it comes to federal programs. You'll want to visit our website periodically to gather the newest information on available grants that will fund a *Career Choices* program. As a member of the *Career Choices* Forum, you'll receive periodic updates on intriguing funding sources.

 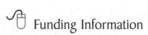 Funding Information   http://www.academicinnovations.com/funding.html

By going online you'll have access to sample text you can download and use for your first draft or as the backbone of your written proposal (see pp. 9/14–16). This will save you hours of research and writing time.

Remember, our Curriculum and Technical Support Department stands ready to help you with this empowering process. Please don't hesitate to call.

Many students commented that this class (vocational studies using **Career Choices***) was their favorite class. The reasons included their ownership of their workbook and questions and activities about themselves.*

— Deborah Back
Vocational Studies Teacher
Carr Creek Elementary
Litt Carr, Kentucky

Carl Perkins Funding Guide

 Carl Perkins Funding Guide <ins>http://www.academicinnovations.com/calperk.html</ins>

To assist you in writing grants for Perkins funds, Academic Innovations has compiled information on the Carl D. Perkins Vocational and Technical Education Act of 1998. This act will be up for reauthorization in 2004 and changes are bound to be made. However, the Act of 1998 addresses the need for career counseling as a recommended program. This allows *Career Choices* to be purchased with Perkins funds. The information found on the above web site will show you how to:

- Develop clear goals, objectives, and outcomes, requirements for most proposals

- Research funding opportunities in your state

- Develop strong proposals

- Eliminate common weaknesses found in many proposals

- Prepare common proposal formats

- Interpret rating criteria

- Find other funding sources

It is important to note that each state allocates Perkins funds differently. Before you spend valuable time writing a proposal, determine whether funds are available for the program you envision. You can do this by contacting your state or school district Perkins Coordinator.

However, the grant writing process described will be appropriate for obtaining funding from a variety of other sources, such as foundations, community organizations, PTAs, and local businesses. Whether you are an administrator, counselor, supervisor, or teacher, this resource will help you write a successful proposal and save you time.

There are many opportunities for funding from community businesses and service organizations. As education becomes more responsive to the needs of the workplace, more groups will respond by funding effective programs. If you can't obtain Perkins funding, review your proposal, change it slightly, and submit it to community sources: Rotary, Kiwanis, or a progressive business owner. If they see that a project can produce results and help young people focus on their future, persuading them to support you won't be difficult.

Unfortunately, many good projects go unfunded because people fear the funding process is far too difficult. In some areas (and for some projects) that may be the case. But in most school districts, developing funding proposals is not overwhelming—if you have a **strategy** and a **fundable program**. This guide will help you with the strategy and *Career Choices* will provide the fundable program.

Career Guidance Funding under Perkins

The main focus of the 1998 Perkins Act is on academic standards and accountability. States develop their own performance measures. However, in developing these performance measures, each state must adhere to four core indicators:

- Student attainment of challenging State established academic and vocational technical, skill proficiencies
- Student attainment of a secondary school diploma or its recognized equivalent, a proficiency credential in conjunction with a secondary school diploma, or a post-secondary degree or credential
- Placement in, retention in, and completion of post-secondary education or advanced training, placement in military service, or placement or retention in employment
- Student participation in and completion of vocational and technical education programs that lead to nontraditional training and employment

With the new emphasis on standards and accountability, career guidance is needed more than ever. If students are able to visualize their future and plan beyond high school, they are far more likely to take an active part in their education, graduate from high school, and pursue some form of post-secondary education or training. Perkins not only requires this, but state's must be able to prove that they accomplish what they set out to do—all while continuing to integrate academics with vocational education and maintain academic rigor.

Career Choices works to help students meet each of the four core indicators. We have reduced each of the four core indicators to one word to make remembering them easier.

- **INTEGRATE:** By integrating academics and career guidance, *Career Choices* bolsters academics. Each activity in the *Career Choices* texts motivates students to sharpen academic skills by demonstrating the relevance of present academic studies to their future lives. At the same time they practice reading, writing, and computation, students learn to identify interests, explore career options, and build decision-making skills.

- **GRADUATE:** Academic success hinges on a student's ability to identify interests, build self-esteem, and gain decision-making skills early in their high school experience—this is what *Career Choices* does best. Completion of *Career Choices* means completion of an individualized education and career plan, ensuring future course planning success for students and simplified assessment for school counselors. The existence of this plan increases the chances of graduating from high school.

- **ARTICULATE:** Students with a plan for the future are more likely to finish high school and pursue post-secondary education. Why? Because they understand the relationship between high-paying jobs and their education.

- **INFILTRATE:** Identifying and investigating their interests and aptitudes helps students (especially young women) realize that myriad careers are open to them. By exploring a variety of career options, students discover careers they'd never thought of—or heard of. A comprehensive career guidance experience will increase the likelihood young men and women alike will investigate and pursue a career in a nontraditional field.

State Funding

How to Research State Funding for your Program

http://www.academicinnovations.com/statefun.html

Each state has different mandates and different priorities for allocating funds to new and innovative programs. The best place to start your research is with your principal. You'll want to be sure to advise him/her of your plans. Ask for the names of individuals at the district office who are responsible for grant writing. Contact them to discuss your project and find out what opportunities there are in your state. Ask what special funding is available for:

1. Career and vocational programs

2. Freshmen orientation

3. Advisor/Advisee programs

4. Tech Prep

5. Guidance and career planning

6. At-risk or dropout prevention programs

7. Gender equity or teen pregnancy programs

8. Juvenile justice programs

Be sure your district grant writers are familiar with your program and its goals. "Requests for Proposals" (RFP—documents soliciting grant applications) come across their desks daily. If the grant writers are familiar with your program and a suitable RFP arrives, they will be much more likely to contact you and write a proposal for your program. It's a good idea to write a brief summary of what you'd like your program to accomplish and send it to the district office.

How to Build a Strong Proposal

http://www.academicinnovations.com/cppropo.html

Funding Decisions are Personal

http://www.academicinnovations.com/cpfun.html

Defining the Need, Purpose, and Goals of Your Program

http://www.academicinnovations.com/cpdef.html

Fundable Projects — Team and Cluster Concept

http://www.academicinnovations.com/cpproj.html

Example of a District Plan and Objectives

http://www.academicinnovations.com/cpex.html

Suggested Narratives for Proposals

http://www.academicinnovations.com/cpnarr.html

Corporate Funding Ideas

🖱 Corporate Funding Ideas

http://www.academicinnovations.com/corpfun.html

Many companies focus their corporate philanthropic efforts on education. Members of the business community are very aware that they need educated and motivated workers—now and even more so in the future. Because *Career Choices* helps students prepare for the workplace, it is a wonderful vehicle for soliciting corporate sponsorship. Here's one plan for researching and executing a corporate funding campaign.

Find out what corporations do business in your community, and what local businesses are prominent. The best place to start your research is with the Chamber of Commerce or the Better Business Bureau. Keep an eye on the local newspaper to see what companies are in the news (for good reasons).

Once you've narrowed your choice to two or three prospects, use your own network of peers, parents, and friends to see if you can get an introduction to the CEO, Director of Public Relations, or Director of Community Relations. If you cannot get an introduction, make an appointment to see the Director of Community Relations anyway.

When you pay your first visit, take along a complete set of the *Career Choices* textbooks. They make a wonderful "prop" for your presentation. Besides talking about the program, be sure to ask questions and listen carefully to what the funder has to say. You'll want to incorporate his or her ideas into your written proposal, which should arrive within a few days of your interview.

In developing your proposal, don't be shy. Remember you are not asking for a lot of money by most corporate standards. Let's say you request funding for 100 copies of the *Workbook and Portfolio*. This costs about $700, or the price of a medium-size display advertisement in a regional newspaper.

Most businesses and corporations make donations to do some good in the community. However, they are also looking for publicity and an opportunity to generate good public will. It is imperative that you solicit media attention for your program throughout the year (newspaper articles, TV news stories, etc.). Anywhere your *Career Choices* program is mentioned, be sure to add the tagline "Funded by the XYZ Corporation." The more you do this, the more likely the business or corporation is to fund your program year after year.

Some of your presentation strategies will parallel what we suggest for Community Service Organizations in Section Nine of this guide.

Student Funding

 Student Funding   http://www.academicinnovations.com/studfun.html

Many states have policies allowing for the student purchase of "consumable" supplies. For instance, art supplies and shop materials are considered consumables. Under such policies some schools have students purchase their own copies of the *Workbook and Portfolio*. If your state has a similar provision, you might use this strategy to fund part of your *Career Choices* program.

You can seek special funding for students who can't afford to buy their own workbook. This is a small project for a Community Service Organization and one that members can decide on quickly.

Online Resources for Your Grant Proposal

The following resources should help as you begin seeking funds for your *Career Choices* program. Review the charts below to find the areas on our web page that best meet your needs.

Besides helping you understand how a variety of funding sources work, these web pages contain a variety of documents that can be downloaded and used as the backbone of your proposal. Naturally, you will want to edit them to fit your school's program methodology, but using some of the text will save you hours of researching, creating, and keyboarding.

If you don't find what you need online or you do not have access to the Internet, be sure to contact our Curriculum and Technical Support Department at (800) 967-8016, ext. 677. They can help you.

Question	Go to URL:	You'll find:	Helpful hints & tips
I've never written a grant proposal for funding before. Where do I start?	http://www.academicinnovations.com/sampgrant.html	In-depth resources to assist you with your grant application.	*Explore the links to find sample grants, documentation of effectiveness, and ideas for program methodology.*
AND...	http://www.academicinnovations.com/cppropo.html	Information that will help you begin your proposal process.	*Explore the other hyperlinks on the Corporate Funding Ideas page. Print out or download appropriate sections.*

Question	Go to URL:	You'll find:	Helpful hints & tips
I'd like to approach a community service organization for help funding our workshops and to recruit mentors the students can shadow. Give me a step-by-step plan.	http://www.academicinnovations.com/cso.html	An extensive plan on how to get funding from your organizations.	*Print out and review this easy-to-follow plan. Return to surf the funding hyperlinks recommended on this page.*
AND...	http://www.academicinnovations.com/comminv.html	Ideas of how to get community members actively involved with your *Career Choices* program.	*Hyperlink to Career Exploration Brainstorming Session and Job Interview Night for details on how to run these community activities.*

Question	Go to URL:	You'll find:	Helpful hints & tips
I need help writing a grant proposal for my Career Choices program. Where can I find sample text?	http://www. academicinnovations.com/ cpex.html	Text of an example of one district's plan.	*Print out the text for future reference or download to your hard drive for later word processing.*
AND...	http://www. academicinnovations.com/ cpnarr.html	Text for a variety of proposals.	*Choose the most appropriate narrative for your program and print or download it for later inclusion in your proposal.*
AND...	http://www. academicinnovations.com/ expert.html	A series of short articles on the special needs of adolescents.	*Choose the articles that help to justify your program. Download that text to your hard drive for later editing, customizing and inclusion into your proposal.*
AND...	http://www. academicinnovations.com/ ccphilo.html	More text that can be partially incorporated into your proposal.	*Download to your hard drive for later editing. You may want to use part of this essay in your cover letter.*

Question	Go to URL:	You'll find:	Helpful hints & tips
How would I approach a business in our community for help with funding our Career Choices program?	http://www. academicinnovations.com/ corpfun.html	A detailed explanation of how to approach the business community for funding.	*Print out this page plus the text from all the hyperlinks in this section. Form a committee to strategize a plan using this information.*

Writing Your Grant Proposal

Why reinvent the wheel? You'll find a variety of resources on our web site, www.academicinnovations.com, that can be downloaded, edited, reformated, customized, and developed into a creditable proposal. You'll find text at the following sites on our web page.

Problem statement and assessment of needs:

www.academicinnovations.com/cpnarr.html
www.academicinnovations.com/expert.html

Goals and Objectives

www.academicinnovations.com/cpex.html
www.academicinnovations.com/goalobj.html

Methodology

www.academicinnovations.com/incorp.html

Sample Proposals

www.academicinnovations.com/jtpapro.html
www.academicinnovations.com/stwpro.html

Program Ideas and research

www.academicinnovations.com/indepth.html
www.academicinnovations.com/ideas.html
www.academicinnovations.com/cpproj.html

Putting Your Funding Proposal Together

Using the standard proposal outlined below, move the text you've gathered, customized, and edited into the appropriate sections:

1. **Introduction** emphasizing your own and your school's credibility
2. **Problem Statement**: Why this program is needed. Provide statistics
3. **Program Goals and Objectives**: Make them measurable.
4. **Program Design**: Your methodology for meeting the goals and objectives
5. **How you plan to access and evaluate** your program
6. **How you plan to fund the program**, once the requested funding is complete
7. Your program budget
8. **Attachments** that support your credibility and claims.

WIA Funding

August 1998 brought with it a big change in the youth employment programs funded by the federal government. The Job Training Partnership Act (JTPA), which had provided youth with educational and work-related opportunities through summer and year-round programs, was replaced by the Workforce Investment Act of 1998 (WIA).

There are seven key principles driving the WIA; among these is a desire to improve the youth services provided. However, the overall goal of the new Act was more far reaching. As stated in the Act, the goal is "To increase the employment, retention, and earnings of participants, and increase occupational skill attainment by participants, and, as a result improve the quality of the workforce, reduce welfare dependency, and enhance the productivity and competitiveness of the Nation."

In working toward this goal, the Workforce Investment Act involves services for adults, dislocated workers, and youth. To effectively provide services to these target populations, WIA mandates the development of a One-Stop service delivery system. These all-encompassing centers will provide, among other things, job training and counseling services. The One-Stop Centers may also provide the formula youth programs required under the Act. However, the decision to integrate the formula youth programs into the One-Stop Center is a local decision.

Funding for summer and year-round youth programs will come from a single funding stream. This means that, although summer employment opportunities are a required element of the WIA youth services, there are no separate appropriations for these programs. To be eligible for participation, youth must be between 14-21 years of age, low income, and meet at least one of the six barriers to employment:

- Basic skills deficient
- School dropout
- Homeless, runaway, or foster child
- Pregnant or parent
- Offender
- Requiring additional assistance to complete education programs, or to secure and hold employment

Up to 5% of the youth served are not required to meet the low-income requirement in order to participant, as long as they meet one or more of the barriers to employment. However, 30% of funds allocated for youth services must go to serve out-of-school youth.

The youth services provided for under WIA retain the JTPA requirements for:

- Individual assessment
- Service strategy

In addition, the WIA requires the following elements:

- Preparation for post-secondary educational opportunities or unsubsidized employment (as appropriate)
- Strong linkages between academic and occupational learning
- Effective connections to the job market and area employers

The other required elements of WIA youth programs are:

- Tutoring, study skills training, and instruction leading to completion of secondary school, including dropout prevention activities
- Alternative secondary school services
- Summer employment opportunities
- Paid and unpaid work experience, including internships and job shadowing
- Occupational skills training
- Leadership development activities
- Adult mentoring
- Supportive services
- Follow-up services for not less than 12 months (as appropriate)
- Comprehensive guidance and counseling

The success of these youth programs will be determined based on Core Indicators of Performance outlined in the WIA. They are broken into two categories: performance indicators for youth 19–21 and performance indicators for youth 14–18.

Basic Performance Indicators for Youth 19–21 (also, adults & dislocated workers)

- Placement
- Retention
- Earnings
- Skill attainment

Basic Performance Indicators for Youth 14–18

- Attainment of basic skills and, as appropriate, occupational skills
- High school diplomas
- Placement and retention in post-secondary education, advanced training, or employment (including the military)

Career Choices was proven to be an effective tool in helping youth involved in JTPA programs gain essential skills; it has been equally effective in WIA programs. You may also find that *Career Choices* or the adult version, *Career Choices* and Changes, are resources that are appropriate for inclusion in your local One-Stop Center. For additional information on how *Career Choices* meets WIA mandates, visit www.academicinnovations.com/wia.html.

Meeting Federal and State Mandates and Plans

Career Choices Meets the NOICC and SCANS Guidelines

"A new effective and integrated approach to career and life planning, **Career Choices** *and the anthology,* **Possibilities,** *give schools a head start in addressing the recommended SCANS competencies and foundations skills."*

— Gloria J. Conn
Member of the SCANS Commission

Responding to concerns about the future of education and employment in America, the federal government established two committees to investigate the problems and make recommendations for solving them. The National Occupational Information Coordinating Committee (NOICC) attends to the occupational information needs of policy makers, vocational education coordinators, and employment and training program managers; they also survey the career development needs of youth and adults.

The purpose of the Secretary's Commission on Achieving Necessary Skills (SCANS), set up by the Department of Labor, is to help teachers understand how curriculum and instruction must enable students to develop the skills needed to succeed in a high performance workplace. Both groups released reports and issued guidelines that greatly influence the direction of career education in the United States.

The NOICC guidelines, comprehensive and competency-based, aim to encourage quality career guidance and counseling programs and to recommend learning outcomes organized around self-knowledge, educational and occupational exploration, and career planning. NOICC officials say that using the National Career Development Guidelines will, among other benefits, provide students with a better understanding of the relationship of education to work and improve career decision-making skills.

On the following pages you will find a chart demonstrating, chapter by chapter, how the *Career Choices* curriculum meets these important guidelines. You will notice that the NOICC initiative calls for a curriculum nearly identical to that of *Career Choices*. For more information on the NOICC national guidelines, contact NOICC, 2100 M Street NW, Suite 156-a, Washington, DC 20037, or call the Curriculum and Instructional Materials Center at (800) 654-4502. Each state has its own SOICC; you may want to check out www.noicc.gov/files/nsoicweb.html to find links to your states' site.

On pages 9/24–25, you'll find information on how *Career Choices* addresses the SCANS competencies. You can order a copy of Teaching the SCANS competencies ($12) from The United States Printing Office, (213) 239-9844.

National Occupational Information Coordinating Committee
High School Student Competencies and Indicators

Self-Knowledge

COMPETENCY I: Understanding the influence of a positive self-concept.

Identify and appreciate personal interests, abilities, and skills.

Demonstrate the ability to use peer feedback.

Demonstrate an understanding of how individual characteristics relate to achieving personal, social, educational, and career goals.

Demonstrate an understanding of environmental influences on one's behaviors.

Demonstrate an understanding of the relationship between personal behavior and self-concept.

COMPETENCY II: Skills to interact positively with others.

Demonstrate effective interpersonal skills.

Demonstrate interpersonal skills required for working with and for others.

Describe appropriate employer and employee interactions in various situations.

Demonstrate how to express feelings, reactions, and ideas in an appropriate manner.

COMPETENCY III: Understanding the impact of growth and development.

Describe how developmental changes affect physical and mental health.

Describe the effect of emotional and physical health on career decisions.

Describe healthy ways of dealing with stress.

Demonstrate behaviors that maintain physical and mental health.

Educational and Occupational Exploration

COMPETENCY IV: Understanding the relationship between educational achievement and career planning.

Demonstrate how to apply academic and vocational skills to achieve personal goals.

Describe the relationship of academic and vocational skills to personal interests.

Describe how education relates to the selection of college majors, further training, and/or entry into the job market.

Demonstrate transferable skills that can apply to a variety of occupations and changing occupational requirements.

Describe how learning skills are required in the workplace.

COMPETENCY V: Understanding the need for positive attitudes toward work and learning.

Identify the positive contributions workers make to society.

Demonstrate knowledge of the social significance of various occupations.

Demonstrate a positive attitude toward work.

Demonstrate learning habits and skills that can be used in various educational situations.

Demonstrate positive work attitudes and behaviors.

COMPETENCY VI: Skills to locate, evaluate and interpret career information.

Describe the educational requirements of various occupations.

Demonstrate use of a range of resources (e.g., handbooks, career materials, labor market information, and computerized career information delivery systems).

Demonstrate knowledge of various classification systems that categorize occupations and industries (e.g., *Dictionary of Occupational Titles*).

Describe the concept of career ladders.

Describe the advantages and disadvantages of self employment as a career option.

Identify individuals in selected occupations as possible information resources, role models, or mentors.

Describe the impact of population, climate, and geographic location on occupational opportunities.

COMPETENCY VII: Skills to prepare to seek, obtain, maintain, and change jobs.

Demonstrate skills to locate, interpret, and use information about job openings and opportunities.

Demonstrate academic or vocational skills required for a full- or part-time job.

Demonstrate skills and behaviors necessary for a successful job interview.
Demonstrate skills in preparing a resume and completing job applications.
Identify specific job openings.
Demonstrate employability skills necessary to obtain and maintain jobs.
Demonstrate skills to assess occupational opportunities (e.g., working conditions, benefits, and opportunities for change).
Describe placement services available to make the transition from high school to civilian employment, the armed service, or post-secondary education/training.
Demonstrate an understanding that job opportunities often require relocation.
Demonstrate skills necessary to function as a consumer and manager of financial resources.

COMPETENCY VIII: Understanding how societal needs and functions influence the nature and structure of work.

Describe the effect of work on lifestyles.
Describe how society's needs and functions affect the supply of goods and services.
Describe how occupational and industrial trends relate to training and employment
Demonstrate an understanding of the global economy and how it affects each individual.

Career Planning

COMPETENCY IX: Skills to make decisions.

Demonstrate responsibility for making tentative educational and occupational choices.
Identify alternatives in given decision-making situations.
Describe personal strengths and weaknesses in relationship to post-secondary education/training requirements.
Identify appropriate choices during high school that will lead to marketable skills for entry-level employment or advanced training.
Identify and complete required steps toward transition from high school entry into post-secondary education/training programs or work.
Identify steps to apply for and secure financial assistance for post-secondary education and training.

COMPETENCY X: Understanding the interrelationship of life roles.

Demonstrate knowledge of life stages.
Describe factors that determine lifestyles (e.g., socioeconomic status, culture, values, occupational choices, work habits).
Describe ways in which occupational choices may affect lifestyle.
Describe the contribution of work to a balanced and productive life.
Describe ways in which work, family, and leisure roles are interrelated.
Describe different career patterns and their potential effect on family patterns and lifestyle.
Describe the importance of leisure activities.
Demonstrate ways that occupational skills and knowledge can be acquired through leisure.

COMPETENCY XI: Understanding the continuous changes in male/female roles.

Identify factors that have influenced the changing career patterns of women and men.
Identify evidence of gender stereotyping and bias in educational programs and occupational settings.
Demonstrate attitudes, behaviors, and skills that contribute to eliminating gender bias and stereotyping.
Identify courses appropriate to tentative occupational choices.
Describe the advantages and problems of non-traditional occupations.

COMPETENCY XII: Skills in career planning.

Describe career plans that reflect the importance of lifelong learning.
Demonstrate knowledge of post-secondary vocational and academic programs.
Demonstrate knowledge that changes may require retraining of employees' skills.
Describe school and community resources to explore educational and occupational choices.
Describe the costs and benefits of self-employment.
Demonstrate occupational skills developed through volunteer experiences, part-time employment, or cooperative education programs.
Demonstrate skills necessary to compare education and job opportunities.
Develop an individual career plan, updating information from earlier plans and including tentative decisions to be implemented after high school.

Where *Career Choices* Addresses Specific NOICC Competencies

Page	Activity / Assignment	I	II	III	IV	V	VI	VII	VIII	IX	X	XI	XII
10–14	Envisioning Your Future					●	●			●	●		●
15–17	Why People Work, Everybody Works			●		●		●			●		
18–19	Defining Success	●		●		●					●		
20–21	Making Career Choices									●			
24–27	Personal Profile — Identity	●	●	●							●		
28–29	Identifying Your Passions	●											
30–37	Work Value Survey	●				●						●	
38–45	Strength and Personality	●	●			●							
46–48	Skills & Aptitudes/Name That Skill	●			●	●							
49	Roles, Occupations & Vocations	●			●						●		
50–53	The Message Center	●	●									●	
56–59	Lifestyle/Maslow Triangle	●		●							●		
60–61	How Do You Want to Be Remembered?	●			●								
62–63	Components of Lifestyle	●		●			●	●	●		●		
64–71	Happiness is a Balanced Lifestyle, etc.	●	●	●		●			●		●	●	
74–76	What Cost This Lifestyle/Ivy Elm's Story			●					●			●	
77–92	The Budget Exercise				●			●				●	
93	What Salary Will Support this Lifestyle							●					
95–96	Over Your Head/Hard Times Budget							●					
97–101	Some Sample Budgets							●	●			●	
102–103	Poverty/Poverty Statistics	●									●	●	
104–105	Money Isn't Everything	●									●		
106–110	Rewards and Sacrifices Stories	●		●		●				●			
111–113	You Win Some… Lose Some/Avocation Choices	●		●		●				●			
114–115	Commitment				●	●							
116–119	An Investment in Education… Yields Dividends for a Lifetime				●	●				●			
120	Ask Someone Who's Been There	●	●		●	●	●	●	●	●	●		●
121	Easier Said Than Done	●			●	●			●	●			
124–125	Your Ideal Career	●					●	●		●	●		
126	Physical Settings	●					●	●		●	●		
127	Working Conditions	●					●	●		●	●		
128	Relationships at Work	●	●				●	●		●	●		
129	Psychological Rewards of Working	●		●		●	●	●		●	●		
130	Mixing Career and Family	●					●	●		●		●	
131	Financial Rewards	●					●	●		●	●		
132–134	Job Skills/Your Chart	●	●	●	●		●	●					
135–137	Change Creates Options	●					●	●	●	●			●
138–139	Employee or Employer	●					●	●			●		●
140–141	What About Status			●		●				●			
144–146	Career Research/Step One						●	●		●			●
147	Bring in Your Identity	●					●	●					●
148–155	Career Research/Survey	●		●	●		●			●			●
156–157	Visualize Your Career				●		●	●		●			●
158–159	The Shadow Program						●	●	●				●
160–161	Involvement: Volunteering/Entry Level				●	●	●	●			●		●

Where *Career Choices* Addresses Specific NOICC Competencies

Page	Activity/Assignment	I	II	III	IV	V	VI	VII	VIII	IX	X	XI	XII
162–165	The Chemistry Test: Work Behavioral Styles	●	●				●						
168–169	Decision Making				●		●			●			
170	Identifying Choices				●		●			●			
171	Gathering Information				●					●			
172–175	Evaluating Choices				●		●			●			
176–177	Your Choices —- Evaluating				●		●	●	●	●			●
178	Making A Decision					●				●			
179	Keeping Your Options Open					●				●			
183–185	Tools for Solving Problems	●	●										
186–190	Setting Goals & Objectives		●		●			●		●			●
191	Change Process Style			●									
194–195	Avoiding Detours and Roadblocks	●		●									
196–197	I Can't Do It Because/What's Your Excuse?	●		●		●				●		●	
198–199	They Did It in Spite of ...	●		●		●				●		●	
200	Taking Responsibility	●	●	●		●				●			
201–202	Startling Statements			●							●	●	
203–206	Detours & Roadblocks Lifestyle Choices			●	●	●					●		
207	Is It Worth Staying in School				●	●		●		●		●	●
208–209	The Economics of Bad Habits	●		●									
210	If You've Decided to Give Up Your Dream	●		●		●							
211–213	If You're a Woman	●		●	●	●		●	●		●	●	
214–215	Support for your Dream/If You Don't Think You Deserve It	●		●	●	●				●			
216–221	Anxiety Tolerance/Overcoming Fears	●	●	●	●	●							
222–223	10 Year Plan for Yorik (remedial plan)		●		●			●	●	●	●		●
224–225	Taking Risks	●		●		●							
226	Getting Back on Track if You've Derailed	●		●	●	●	●		●				●
230–231	Attitude is Everything	●	●	●		●							
232–235	The Six Es of Excellence	●	●	●	●	●		●					
236–237	Going for It ... Work Is an Aggressive Act	●	●	●		●		●				●	
238–241	You're the Boss/Work Ethic	●	●	●		●		●		●			
242–245	The Employee of the Twenty-first Century		●	●	●	●	●	●	●			●	●
247	Managing Change			●	●	●	●	●	●		●		●
250–253	Getting Experience/Your Resume							●					
254	Finding a Job							●					
255	Conduct an Informal Interview		●				●	●	●				
256–257	Job Applications							●					
258–259	The Job Interview		●					●					
260	Dealing With Rejection	●	●					●					
261	Accepting A Job		●					●					
262–263	Making Connections/Mentors		●				●						●
266	Where Do You Go From Here?				●	●				●			●
267–269	Getting the Education or Training You Need				●	●	●	●		●			●
270–273	Where Is It You Want to Go/Life Plan				●	●	●	●		●	●	●	●
274–275	Delaying Gratification		●	●						●	●	●	●
276–277	Facing Fears and Anxieties	●	●	●		●				●		●	●
278–283	Your Plan	●	●	●	●	●	●	●	●	●	●	●	●

Put SPIRIT into Your Classroom with SCANS

Quick, can you rattle off the SCANS Competencies and Foundation Skills? Perhaps you'll want to use the SPIRIT acronym as a mnemonic device to help you remember these very important components as you design your restructured curriculum.

The following chart outlines ways in which the *Career Choices* curriculum addresses the SCANS competencies and foundation skills. You might want to use these points in a funding proposal or presentation.

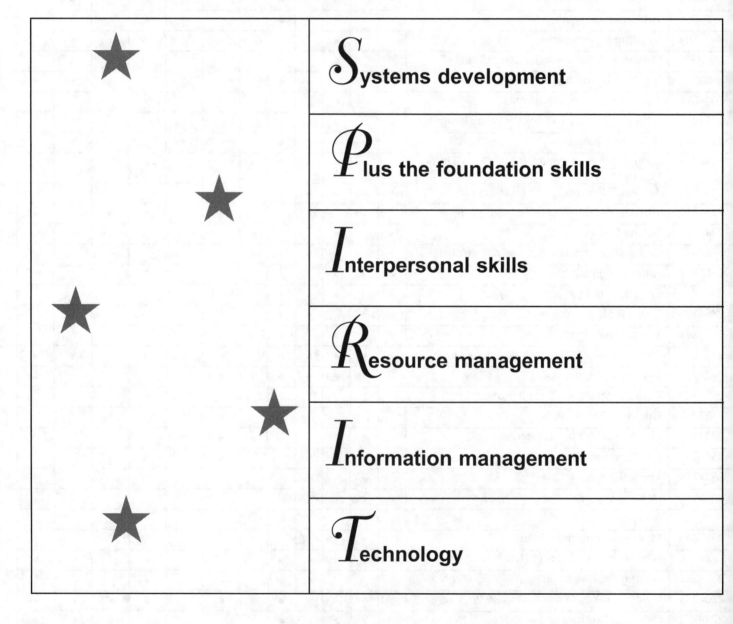

*S*ystems development

*P*lus the foundation skills

*I*nterpersonal skills

*R*esource management

*I*nformation management

*T*echnology

The *Career Choices* curriculum is filled with activities and exercises that help students understand how systems work and why students learn to master the processes that make individuals efficient and effective, beginning with simple tasks that become increasingly complex as they develop comprehensive plans for building a satisfying future.

A competency-based curriculum that offers relevant practice in reading, writing, and mathematics, the *Career Choices* program gives concrete instruction in the areas of creative development, decision making and goal setting, problem solving, and "seeing in the mind's eye." It promotes self-esteem, self-management, accountability, and responsible citizenship.

Because *Career Choices* works best in a cooperative learning environment, students will have an opportunity to practice such interpersonal skills as working in teams, leading, negotiating, and teaching others—all so important in the workplace. Specific activities and exercises help them perfect techniques that are valuable both in and out of the workplace.

Project-oriented activities throughout the *Career Choices* curriculum offer students the opportunity to practice resource management. As they complete their projects or case studies they learn to identify, organize, plan, and allocate time, money, human resources, and technology.

As they work through a life planning process, students gather, evaluate, and organize data and produce a product or thesis based on that idea. A variety of information-gathering strategies are suggested throughout the course.

The value and use of technology is promoted throughout the curriculum. Optional activities offer opportunities for students to use electronic spreadsheets and graphs, desktop publishing and computer graphics, word processing programs, and computerized information systems as they develop their projects.

Career Guidance for All Freshmen

Can anyone teach careers? At San Gabriel High School, an urban school in eastern Los Angeles, the answer is a resounding "yes!" *Career Choices* is used in a required course, "Directions," which is taught in a variety of classes: English, music, art, drama, and communications—even special ed and ESL.

This program was first imagined when Steve Taylor, the Career Education Coordinator, was on staff in the Career Center. In designing a college dissertation study, Steve happened upon a disturbing fact: 70% of students made a career choice after only one week of activity. Students needed more time to explore their aptitudes and dreams, and Steve was determined to provide it. He approached the district several times over the next decade, but always encountered the same objections: No room in students' schedules and no teachers for the class.

In the early '90s, Steve found a curriculum that combined career exploration and guidance—*Career Choices*. He shared the books with Career Center teacher John Holmes, who encouraged him to try again, this time with the Practical Arts and Vocational Education office. The response was positive; San Gabriel got the nod to pilot a class.

With input from Steve and John, two English teachers studied *Career Choices*, assembling a notebook of supplemental materials. But two teachers couldn't teach all sections. They put out a call for help. The first year teachers from special education and ESL joined in. Teachers from other disciplines came on board later.

Fortune smiled, in a rather ironic way. The Board of Education wanted to remove the school's five-credit speech requirement. Speech teacher Doug Campbell had to redesign the class or risk losing support. The Directions teachers had a plan: Keep the speech format and use a career guidance component for the content. Directions had a home.

"The real gift of the Directions class," Steve Taylor concludes, "is that we have an entire 9th grade discovering what it is they want to focus on in high school, and then asking us for—demanding—that we develop the classes, the career pathways to fulfill their goals."

A Case Study—One District's Start-Up Story

How to Integrate Career Development into the English Classroom

"I could have been talking to the wall," said Career Coordinator Liz Lamatrice, referring to her early efforts to infuse a careers theme into the academic curriculum of high schools in Jefferson County, Ohio. "Because until teachers see it for themselves, they don't believe it." And that is exactly what happened in the Jefferson County Joint Vocational District—a model careers program spread from school to school as English teachers taught teachers how to develop lessons and deliver the new subject to 1,500 students in their academic classes.

When Liz, a former English and Social Studies teacher, came on board to develop a K-12 career program for the 33 schools in her five districts, the seeds had already been planted. Earlybird Ohio introduced career development in 1972, but it wasn't until almost 20 years later that enough state money was available through the Department of Education to expand the program to all vocational and academic districts in the state. Liz's new office became the channel for the state funds, as well as federal Perkins dollars and matching money from local sources, earmarked for career development programs in the schools. Each year, Liz wrote a non-competitive request for proposal (RFP), detailing specific areas of coordination, to receive her funding.

As the new Coordinator, Liz approached her Board of Supervisors with the activities she planned to implement to bring about full integration of careers into academic subjects. Yearly teacher training in career education topped the list, followed by the development of a Career Resource Guide, a directory of people in local business and industry who were available to come into the classroom, to be distributed to all five school districts. Another plan was to have career planning teams at each school site, made up of teachers, counselors and parent volunteers who supported the integration effort. These "action committees" would carry out specific tasks such as distributing classroom resources, promoting district-wide career days and fairs, and forming a network to share information with other schools and district administrators.

Today, six years later, Liz's plan is firmly in place and growing. "Our major goal has been to get career development fully integrated into the classroom—math, social studies, English—all the academic subjects," she explained. Her rationale: "When academic learning is related to what students feel is important to them, such as careers and jobs in the future, then 99% will respond to the classroom activities, because it's so much more interesting."

A Perfect Fit

Liz and her husband, Lou Lamatrice, a former Tech Prep Coordinator for the Jefferson County Consortium, attended a one-day Academic Innovations *Career Choices* Workshop in Columbus. They brought back with them the *Career Choices* materials—*Career Choices*, the literary anthology *Possibilities*, the student *Workbook and Portfolio*, *Lifestyle Math* and the *Instructor's and Counselor's Guide*—and passed them on to guidance counselor Elizabeth Truax at Edison High School, where Lou had once taught.

The timing couldn't have been better. Teachers at Edison were looking for a way to support the district-wide Individual Career Plan (ICP), a process that began in the 8th grade for all students, and culminated in the 12th grade with a Senior year exit document, the Career Passport. Each year, students added to their ICP records of their career interest surveys, reports on guest speakers, participation in career day activities, and details of tours of high schools and colleges. In the 11th grade, students worked on their Career Passport by including documentation of part-time work, a basic résumé listing skills, writing samples, goal statements, awards and certificates of community service, a letter of introduction from the principal—all with the aim of supporting students' future employability. In the 12th grade, the document was revised, and upon graduation, the diploma was added.

Teachers felt 10th graders needed to focus on career exploration, decision-making, and self-awareness in preparation for the work they would do in 11th grade. The English Department had been given the responsibility of overseeing this process, and since the *Career Choices* curriculum had a strong literature component that would tie English to career themes, it seemed like a perfect fit. Counselor Truax looked for a teacher who would be willing to take the time to read over the curriculum and flexible enough to try something new. She contacted English teacher Cathy Miles and gave her the materials.

Cathy saw the fit right away. "I didn't want to have to reinvent the wheel," she told us. "Having a proven curriculum like this one gave us a foundation on which to build our own unique program." Cathy and another English teacher, Rosann Lauri, agreed to spend the following summer putting together a set of lesson plans and activities to integrate careers into their Sophomore English classes.

First, the two English teachers wrote a mini-grant proposal to get funds to purchase the 250 copies of *Career Choices*, *Possibilities*, and the student Workbook and Portfolio they needed to run a pilot class, and submitted it to Liz Lamatrice's office. In the grant, they described their plan to include both tech prep and college-bound students in a nine-week, five-days-a-week program. n

Teachers Take the Ball

Liz Lamatrice knew that once a program was in place at one school, it would serve as a benchmark for other schools. She funded the proposal and that summer, Cathy and Rosann went to work. By the end of a summer of numerous volunteer hours, the two teachers emerged with their task accomplished.

"What helped us most to put careers into the English class was the *Career Choices* literary anthology, *Possibilities*," Cathy told us. "Not only were some of the selections ones we'd already been using, but in *Possibilities*, students were being asked to see themselves in the characters—their own motives and goals—rather than just analyze content, as in the older literature books." In previous years, Cathy reported, students were noticeably bored and disinterested by the same selections.

The biggest challenge for Cathy and Rosann was to justify the lesson plans they'd developed with the adopted course of study for English. Without matching specific pupil objectives to each of the activities, they were afraid they might be seen as stepping too far outside the established framework—an image they didn't want. To insure their program would be accepted as an "inside job," the two teachers plugged each lesson into a skill listed in the state-designated objectives: Did a particular activity support the goal of increasing listening skills? They showed exactly how.

Armed with this ammunition, Cathy and Rosann approached their Assistant Superintendent, who presented it to the Superintendent of Schools. Again, the timing was good: A state-wide evaluation was scheduled for Edison High School, and administrators wanted to show their school was on the innovative edge. The teachers got a green light to pilot the program that spring.

But Cathy and Rosann still had hurdles to clear. The district's Curriculum Director, for one, questioned the teachers: Would they be teaching values in such a way that might invade family privacy? "We had to convince him that we were helping our students to develop their own work values," Cathy explained. "Once he realized we were doing career and work values, not family values, he gave us support."

Another concern arose in the English department about using a careers theme in the accelerated classes. Was it really necessary, since these students were already college-bound? Cathy and Rosann argued: These are skills for lifelong learning, and accelerated students need them as well as tech prep students. Everyone will have to deal with the realities of downsizing and disappearing jobs in the future and will need to meet the challenges of changing careers without feeling like failures with no other options.

First Year

Spring came and Cathy and Rosann took their program into the classroom for 250 students. Right away, the teachers could see the light bulbs go on as students began to engage in the creative and critical thinking required by the lessons and activities. Group activities, such as debates or discussion groups inspired by selections from *Possibilities* (see Longfellow's "A Psalm of Life" and Pat Conroy's "The Prince of Tides" in *Possibilities*), took on new focus. "We used to shudder about cooperative learning," Cathy said. "But with *Possibilities*, the students get excited and involved, because the topics are meaningful to them. They're able to stay focused much longer."

Using the *Career Choices* text, Cathy and Rosann wanted to include the extended budget activity from Chapter 4: "What Cost This Lifestyle?", in which students plan for their chosen lifestyle of the future. But they didn't feel they could justify spending three weeks doing math in an English class. So they modified the activity and came up with a "Financial Planner," a group of exercises based on the *Career Choices* budget but slanted more towards the English objectives. Students went to the library to research and write about a chosen career, including salaries, availability of jobs in the field, and educational requirements. Then, they made lifestyle charts based on their chosen career, showing where they would live, whether they'd rent or own a house, where they'd go on vacation, etc. Each student was issued a "salary" packet by the teachers, complete with fake checks and credit cards to pay bills, insurance, utilities, rent and emergencies. "They take it very seriously," Cathy told us. "One student refused to be absent for a dental appointment, afraid he'd miss a day's 'salary'!"

In the accelerated classes, the teachers infused career themes into the students' required curriculum. In one activity, students wrote a paper comparing and analyzing the ambition factor in Mark Antony's speech from Shakespeare's *Julius Caesar* with Martin Luther King Jr.'s "I Have a Dream" speech from *Possibilities*. What were the similarities and differences in the way the two speakers attempted to persuade their audiences? How were they successful and why? To write the paper, the students mapped out a bull's eye chart in *Career Choices*, on page 27 in Chapter 2: "Your Personal Profile," for both characters, comparing their passions, values and motivations. Then, to make the exercise more personally relevant, students compared their own bull's eye chart, which they had done earlier, to both King's and Mark Antony's, gaining further insight into their own motivations.

In a follow-up activity, students viewed the film *It's a Wonderful Life*, starring Jimmy Stewart which explores balancing a sense of responsibility to self with responsibility to others. They then did the bull's eye chart for the main character, George Bailey, and compared it to their own to see where they stood on this issue.

"That's the great thing about *Career Choices*," Cathy commented. "You can pull in movies, other reading materials and outside activities to a lesson and make it richer, more appealing on many levels."

At the end of the first term, students presented a video to the teachers which they had written and produced on their own. In it students gave their testimonials about what they'd learned in the class. "When we saw the video, we cried," Cathy said. "It was so rewarding to see students talking about how the true meaning of success was not only in getting a good job, but in all walks of life." Now, when Cathy and Rosann give talks and workshops for other teachers, they always show the video, and it never fails to move audiences. n

The Program Expands

The following year, teachers and administrators agreed to institutionalize the successful pilot and expand it by adding a third English teacher. The new teacher had never taught careers before and was understandably hesitant to dive into the unfamiliar curriculum. Cathy won him over by sharing lesson plans and providing some one-on-one coaching—"Academic teachers, especially, learn by example."

Since their classrooms were side by side, Cathy could leave her class briefly and enter his to model her enthusiastic delivery style. "I showed him how to be a cheerleader for the students—to get things started and make it fun," she said. "When the teacher is excited about the material, the students will follow." Cathy also invited the new teacher into her class for more in-depth training.

The program also expanded to include cross-disciplinary lessons and activities involving teachers of other subjects. "It's one of the advantages of having an older faculty where everyone knows and trusts each other," Cathy said. When Cathy and Rosann approached social studies teachers about participating in overlapping activities developed by the English teachers, they gladly cooperated. In one such activity, the students did an activity from *Career Choices*, page 14, Chapter 1: "Envisioning Your Future," in which they apply the equation "vision plus energy equals success" to their own lives. Then, Cathy asked the social studies teachers: "Which famous person who you're currently studying would you like to have students write an extra paper about?" Students then applied the same equation to that famous person, answering the following questions: "What was the famous person's vision, and what did he or she do to achieve that vision? Was he or she a success? Why or why not?" Students got credit in history, and then again when English teachers graded their papers, giving them two grades for one project.

"This is where integration is headed," Cathy commented. "Relating the different subjects to each other through a common theme." The same cross-disciplinary spirit, she believes, can be applied to computer classes, music, the developmentally handicapped—all by modifying *Career Choices* activities so they can be shared with teachers of other disciplines. "It's important that students have the careers theme not only in the English class," she emphasized. "They need to see how all their subjects relate to the future, because then it's real for them."

By the end of the second year, Cathy and Rosann had been invited to the Ohio Career Education Association to lead workshops and share the materials and their expertise. They applied to do a presentation at the national American Vocational Association (AVA) in Cincinnati and were accepted. Funds to cover travel expenses and substitute teachers were provided through the local Career Development Council, a part of Liz Lamatrice's office that supported teacher training.

Cathy and Rosann also did a one-day training for all Jefferson County schools—as well as schools in neighboring counties looking at adopting the program—on the use of *Career Choices* in the classroom. "We do it gratis," Cathy told us. "Once we get started, we can't stop sharing our enthusiasm. We tell other teachers to give us a call, because we've been there and can help them."

Success Begets Success: Buckeye High School

A presentation by Cathy and Rosann at a Tech Prep summer workshop caught the attention of English teacher Belinda Boyce of nearby Buckeye High School, also in the

Jefferson County funding territory of Liz Lamatrice. Normally, Belinda wasn't interested in the subject of their talk, "Applied Communications." After all, she'd become an English teacher to teach literature and writing, not business forms and letters! But by the time the Edison teachers had shared sample lesson plans and showed the student-made video, Belinda was sold.

"I was captivated by the hands-on demonstration of how they used literature—which we'd previously used for comprehension, symbolism, theme and main idea—to teach real life," she told us. "It made more of an impression than any statistics, to see how real teachers had actually done it." Also, Belinda saw the program as a way to give students a peek at what opportunities were available, rather than to pigeon-hole them into any one type of job or career. Inspired and encouraged by Cathy and Rosann, she approached Liz Lamatrice, who helped her write a mini-grant and get the funding to buy a few class sets of the books and enough workbooks for the entire 9th grade class.

Right away, Belinda began to enlist the help of other English teachers in bringing the careers theme into their English classes. Her principal, impressed by her enthusiasm, provided the release time for teachers—some of them from the two middle schools that feed Buckeye—to attend an on-site presentation by Cathy and Rosann, which Belinda had organized. Again, the "teachers-teaching-teachers" model worked its magic. Belinda's colleagues were treated to a live demonstration of lessons and activities, as well as the highlights and pitfalls to expect in their own program. "It looked so easy," Belinda told us. "All the work was done, especially covering all the English objectives, which was a concern."

It was decided that individual teachers would pick up the program and try it out for a nine-week unit the next term. Cathy and Rosann had given them some of their lesson plans and, with the help of suggestions in the *Career Choices Instructor's and Counselor's Guide*, teachers were able to come up with many others on their own.

"The program was more than a fit—it really served our purposes!" Belinda commented, referring to the ICP and Career Passport process, which all students, as at Edison High School, needed to complete by their senior year.

"The poetry was especially popular," she reported, "because at this age they're trying to find themselves, and the selections in *Possibilities* spoke volumes to them." Students were encouraged to write poems of their own modeled on selections they'd read from the anthology. "When I stayed away from literary techniques, and put more emphasis on how the selections were relevant to students' lives, they understood the meaning and really enjoyed them," she told us. To teach literary concepts, Belinda followed suggestions in the *Instructor's and Counselor's Guide*, bringing popular music into the classroom and using rock singer Alanis Morisette's hit song, "Isn't It Ironic?" for a lesson on irony. "They'll never forget that lesson because it brought English to their level," she commented.

In spite of the success of her pilot, Belinda felt strongly that 9th grade was too late for students to be thinking about their futures, and that it would be better to start the program at the middle school level. "The decision about college needs to be made before they enter high school, so they can choose what academic courses they'll take over the next four years," she explained.

In this spirit, Belinda approached teachers at the two "feeder" middle schools with the idea of using the first half of the *Career Choices* book—Chapters 1 through 6—in their 8th grade English classes. The second half would then be the focus of the 9th grade class, and the budgeting activities in Chapter 4 could be omitted until the 10th grade, when they would be picked up under a unit on employability skills.

Middle School Joins In

Teachers at both Buckeye North Middle School and Buckeye Southwest Middle School responded positively. They, too, had seen Cathy and Rosann's demonstration, and realized the value of the program in supporting the statewide ICP/Career Passport efforts. In addition, the careers unit could possibly help them with another academic goal. In Ohio, all students are required to pass a series of state proficiency tests in order to graduate, beginning in the 8th grade with reading, writing, math, citizenship and science tests. English teacher Rhoda Thompson at Southeast Middle School was looking for a way to help her students improve their writing skills, and thought that a careers theme might inspire and motivate them to write more. She agreed to do a nine-week unit using the *Career Choices* books for her 8th grade English students.

"I got some excellent essays from my students on topics such as dreams, goals and success," she reported. Students read Martin Luther King Jr.'s speech "I Have a Dream" from the *Possibilities* anthology then watched a video of Dr. King delivering the speech and wrote an essay about their own dreams and goals.

"I taught very little grammar, but my students' writing scores doubled from the previous year." What did she think was responsible for this dramatic increase? "I think it was a culmination of everything we did," she told us, but one technique was particularly effective, suggested in the *Instructor's and Counselor's Guide* on page 4/92, "Seeing in the Mind's Eye." To prepare for a writing exercise, students closed their eyes while listening to instructions about a topic, then visualized what they would write before beginning to write.

Rhoda was amazed by the improvement of her lower-level writers, who were able to avoid distractions and concentrate more easily, she believed, with their eyes closed. "The essay just wrote itself!" one enthusiastic student told her.

Intrigued by these results, Rhoda tried the exercise with her learning disabled students and found it also helped them. She concluded that auditory learners—the majority of her LD students, and perhaps many of her low-level regular students—benefit most when given a chance to "listen" to their thoughts during a period of silence before writing.

Surprisingly, a highlight for the 8th graders was the work values survey in *Career Choices*, Chapter 2: "Your Personal Profile." "The idea that you need to consider what you like to do before picking a career—that was the most important point in the whole program, and they got it," Rhoda said. Lively discussions followed about whether it was more important to have a job you like or to make a lot of money. "Working with *Career Choices* makes my students better thinkers," Rhoda reported. "It offers them something to think about, instead of focusing on memorization and rote learning."

Results Are In

At Edison High School, the first graduating class to go through Cathy Miles and Rosann Lauri's English classes proved the worth of the program beyond a doubt. Of the 221 graduates, 70% went on to pursue further education, generating over $1 million in academic scholarships. The year before, students received one half that amount, an increase Cathy attributes to the rise in ambition and involvement on the part of students who set goals for their future in Sophomore English. "Parents told us they were surprised how their children had learned so much about money and planning for the future," Cathy told us. "These are skills that helped them go after the scholarship money available instead of sitting back as in previous years."

That year's valedictorian read a quote from Robert Louis Stevenson she'd read two years earlier in *Possibilities* (p. 283), but which made a lasting impression: "We are a success when we have lived well, laughed often and loved much..."

"We'd like to think we share in the responsibility for these kinds of results," Cathy commented. Certainly, Liz Lamatrice would agree. "Today, I have commitments from schools in five districts to provide this outstanding program to help students plan for the future," she told us. "We think we are going down the right road to lifelong learning, and the *Career Choices* curriculum has provided us with the perfect vehicle."

Instructor's Notes:

SECTION TEN

Getting the Community and Parents Involved

Getting the Community Involved

Career Choices is an ideal vehicle for getting community members and organizations involved with your school. Many people have a particular interest in helping young people prepare for their future, especially local employers.

Community Help with Funding

More and more, large businesses and corporations are funneling corporate donations into education. Because of the nature of this curriculum, it makes sense to approach a local business, industry, or community service organization for funding assistance. Grant requests might include funding for books; resource materials; Personal Profile System assessments for each student; teacher attendance at a *Career Choices* workshop in Santa Barbara, California; a stipend for the director of mentors; or the cost of organizing a career fair.

Section Nine of this guide (pages 9/8–9/18) has additional ideas and information on finding funding for your *Career Choices* program. If you would like further assistance with your grant request, contact the Curriculum and Technical Support Administrator at Academic Innovations at (800) 967-8016, ext. 677.

Working with Community Service Organizations

Many people in the business community are interested in helping young people prepare for the working world. If you haven't already considered it, why not recruit one of the service organizations in your community to sponsor your school's program?

Finding the Right Service Organization to Approach

If you aren't familiar with the different service organizations in your community, contact your local Chamber of Commerce. They will have the names and phone numbers of the president and the program chairperson for each organization in your community.

Some of the organizations you should consider contacting include:

- Altrusa
- American Association of University Women
- Business and Professional Women
- Kiwanis
- Lions Club
- Rotary
- Soroptimist
- Zonta International

These organizations are made up of professional and career-oriented individuals, people who have a particular interest in readying young people for the workforce.

Do some homework before you contact each organization. Try to find out which organizations are interested in supporting either youth or education. Use your network of friends and professional acquaintances to research this information. If you have an advisory board, ask for help with this task.

Recruiting the Service Organization

Once you have determined which organization(s) might be interested in supporting your school's program, contact the program chair and offer to give a presentation at one of their meetings. Many organizations have weekly meetings (usually at lunch or dinner), and program chairs are constantly on the lookout for interesting presentations about the community. Your call will be most welcome.

Your Presentation

Once you have scheduled a presentation, plan and practice what you want to say. Be sure to ask the program chair how much time you have and be careful not to go over that limit. Leave time for questions. The following suggestions might be helpful as you plan your presentation:

- Tell success stories about students who have graduated. Bring graduates willing to speak in front of groups for a testimonial.
- Give the Startling Statement Quiz (*Career Choices*, p. 201) to warm up the audience.
- If you have display material, supporting videos, or articles, be sure to bring these along and set up a display in the back of the room.
- Take along at least one set of *Career Choices* curriculum to pass around the audience while you are speaking.

Asking for Support

Toward the end of your presentation, be sure to ask for support or assistance from the members. As their name implies, community service organizations are dedicated to giving service to the community. They organize primarily for that purpose and are usually looking for projects in the community that will make a difference. Helping students become productive citizens should have a high appeal for members.

What Kinds of Support Can You Ask for?

Speaker's Bureau

At the minimum, be sure to take a copy of pages 6/38–39 in the *Instructor's Guide*. Ask the audience to help you identify individuals who would be good guest speakers for your group. Pass the form around the room as you speak.

Shadowing Mentors

Have a number of copies of the Shadow Program Mentor Survey form (*Instructor's Guide*, pages 4/98–99) with you. Ask individuals to volunteer as mentors for your program. Be sure to add your name and address at the bottom of the form so people can fill it out and send it to you.

Director of Mentors

If you are looking for a Director of Mentors (*Instructor's Guide*, pages 4/95–96) mention that fact and ask any interested individuals to see you after the meeting. There will probably be retired individuals in the audience who are interested in quality volunteer placement (activities where they see that they are making a difference) and who have good contacts in the business community.

Funding for Books

Most community service organizations raise funds throughout the year for projects in the community. If, after your presentation, you feel there was a lot of interest in your program and the members support the concepts, contact the president of the organization and ask what their procedure is for requesting program funding.

Follow the procedure and suggest that the organization fund a copy of *Career Choices* for each participant. This is something "concrete" that the service organization can take pride in providing.

Once you receive funding for the books, design a sticker. Affix it to the cover of each book. Your local instant print shop can arrange for custom stickers and may be willing to donate their services.

Keeping Your Supporters Involved

Book Presentation Ceremony

You may want to ask representatives of your sponsoring community service organization to attend a ceremony where each participant of your class is presented with their own *Career Choices* book (consider putting a ribbon around each copy). When the students see that people care about them, they will work harder to learn.

At Graduation Time

At a meeting of the service organization, share copies of the students' ten-year plans (*Career Choices*, pp. 279–280) and their mission statements (p. 281). When service organization members see young people making an effort, you'll find they become interested in seeing that these students succeed in getting jobs.

Thank You—Say It Early; Say It Often

Remember to say thank you often. Cards made by students or letters written by students are always appreciated. Solicit media attention for your program throughout the year (newspaper articles, TV news stories, etc.). Anywhere your *Career Choices* program is mentioned, be sure to add the tagline "Graciously funded by the local chapter of the _____." The more you do this, the more likely the organization is to fund your program year after year. A group that knows it is appreciated will become a committed group.

Presentations throughout the Year

If you keep your sponsoring organization informed and involved, it will probably continue to support you in the future. In coordination with the program chair of the community service organization, schedule two or three informative programs throughout the year. Here are some ideas:

Career Exploration Brainstorming Session

A one- or two-week activity, this session could be scheduled after your students have completed Chapter 5 in *Career Choices*.

First half-hour: During the first week, make a presentation about the *Career Choices* career decision-making process to the service organization membership. Include a description of the bull's eye chart, the budgeting process and the career characteristics in Chapter 5. Because you are going to ask them to work directly with students, give them some guidelines and prospective outcomes.

Second half-hour: At the follow-up meeting, bring enough students so that each student can brainstorm career possibilities with a panel of 2 or 3 service organization members. Ask the service organization members to break into panels and assign each student to a panel. The students will provide each member of their panel with a completed copy of the following worksheets from *Career Choices*: the bull's eye chart (p. 27), a copy of their budget (p. 92), and a copy of their desired career characteristics (p. 134). Because these business people have real world experience, they can be helpful in presenting career options and strategies for getting a job.

This should be a noisy and lively session that everyone will enjoy. Allow enough time for the groups to report out. Some of your students may receive offers for shadowing or internships from their group members. You may find that your sponsors enjoy this activity so much they will want to repeat it with more students from your program.

Job Interview Night

Towards the end of the year ask your service organization to sponsor a job interview night. You may want to hold this at the school so you have plenty of classrooms to use for breakout rooms.

The service organization members will break into three-person panels and conduct mock job interviews. Each panel will provide a fictitious job description for the position for which they are interviewing.

Once the 15-minute trial interview is complete, the panel will critique the interviewee and give suggestions of how better to handle the interview.

Students will float between panels and interview with at least three different panels. Suggest that they pay particular attention to the areas that the panel identifies as needing practice and try to improve each time. A social/reception for all participants could be held in the cafeteria at the end of the evening.

You may also want to hold a training session for the interviewers before the activity if you feel they need to be sensitive to certain issues.

Parent-Student Project

Here's a great opportunity to facilitate parent-child communication. After your students have completed the *Career Choices* program, why not sponsor a weekend workshop where the "teachers" are your students and the "students" are their parents?

By popular demand, we have rewritten and re-edited *Career Choices* for the college and adult market. "Even though *Career Choices* was written for secondary schools," explains Mindy Bingham, "we have a number of colleges and adult programs using the materials. After all, the process of making wise life choices is the same no matter the age."

This adult edition, *Career Choices and Changes*, mirrors the original text; however, the examples and stories are geared for a more mature audience.

Take advantage of the fact that in most cases, parents and children experience mid-life challenges and adolescence, respectively, at about the same time. Organize your students to host a workshop for their parents. It could prove to be one of the most powerful experiences of your teaching career.

To receive a 60-day examination copy of the adult edition, *Career Choices and Changes*, call (800) 967-8016, or fax your request to (800) 967-4027.

Sample Parent-Student Workshop

This activity can be accomplished during a weekend workshop—for instance, Saturday and Sunday 9:00 am to 4:00 pm each day. Or why not consider five weekly 2-hour sessions held in the evening from 7:00 to 9:00 pm.

Texts:

For parents—*Career Choices & Changes: A Guide for Discovering Who You Are, What You Want, and How To Get It* by Bingham & Stryker (Academic Innovations)

For students—*Career Choices: A Guide for Teens and Young Adults, Who Am I? What Do I Want? How Do I Get It?* by Bingham & Stryker (Academic Innovations)

For instructors—*Instructor's and Counselor's Guide for Career Choices* (Academic Innovations)

Lectures:

In the following lessons the students are the teachers/lecturers. It is assumed here that the students have completed *Career Choices* and are now introducing their parents to the process of career and life planning. Ideally, teams of students can be assigned different lectures to prepare ahead of time.

Small Group Discussions:

These will be pre-assigned groups that stay together for the whole 10 hours. We recommend that each group consist of three or four parent-student pairs.

Sample Agenda—10 Hours

Hour One and Two

Lecture: Introduction to class, goals, and personal benefits of comprehensive career planning. Make assignments to discussion groups of three or four parent-student pairs.

Small Group Discussion: Begin with an introduction activity. Have the individuals in each group use the "Getting Acquainted" activity described on page 4/30 of the *Instructor's and Counselor's Guide*. As an energizer, hand out whistles to be used when a person describes themselves in relation to what they do or their roles.

Then, ask the parents and students to read the definitions on page 26 of *Career Choices* and individually complete the bull's eye chart (*Career Choices*, page 27).

With this information, go around the group one more time (using the bull's eye chart as a reference) and have each person reintroduce themselves to their group.

> *Note:* In many of the activities/discussion, the students will revisit activities they have already completed in their *Career Choices* class. This will demonstrate how this self-discovery information is fluid and changeable, and how they need to continually re-evaluate their goals.

Lecture: *Do what you love and you will never work a day in your life.*

Small Group Discussion: Individually, have each person in the group complete page 29 in *Career Choices and Changes*. As a group, discuss each person's findings. Review suggestions in *Instructor's and Counselor's Guide* on pages 4/18–19.

Have each participant add the information to their bull's eye chart.

Hour Three and Four

Lecture: *Before you can choose what you want to do you first have to know who you are.*

Activity: Have each participant take and score the Work Values Survey on pages 31–37 of *Career Choices (and Changes)*.

Small Group Discussion: Share each person's findings in their group.

Small Group Discussion: Individually, complete and score the Personal Profile Assessment instrument (approx. 30 minutes: 10 to take and 20 to score). Or use the surveys on pages 38–43 in the textbooks. Share results with members of discussion group.

Lecture: *Interpretations of profiles as it relates to career choice.* (*Career Choices and Changes*, pages 162-165).

See *Instructor's and Counselor's Guide* for a variety of activities that you might want to adapt.

Complete chart on page 27 of *Career Choices* with new data and make six copies, one for each member of the group.

Hours Five and Six

Opening Activity: Complete pages 44–45 in *Career Choices and Changes*. Share findings in small group discussion.

Lecture: *Messages of Expectation or Limitation.* How the messages we receive from parents, teachers, peers, and society impact our choices. Have students arrange for a guest speaker (counselor or psychologist).

Have each group member share their work on pages 52–53 of *Career Choices and Changes* and then, as a group, brainstorm additional messages for each person to counteract the negative or limiting messages they are getting.

Small Group Discussion: One more time, ask each discussion group to come together and share their new, expanded bull's eye chart, giving a copy to each other member of the group.

First Career Brainstorm: Given each person's bull's eye chart, the group will brainstorm for each member of the group a list of 5 to 10 careers that match that person's profile.

Activity: Looking Into the Future (*Instructor's and Counselor's Guide*, page 4/41).

Optional Guest Speakers: Invite two individuals with contrasting lifestyles to speak about how they made their choices.

Small Group Debate: "Which should come first, lifestyle choice or career choices?" Divide each discussion group in two. The first team takes the position that lifestyle choice should come first; the other group defends the position of career choice first.

Individuals share their desired lifestyles with others in the group by completing page 63 from *Career Choices*.

Second Career Brainstorm: Now, adding information from page 63 of *Career Choices*, continue brainstorming possible careers for each member of the group. Adding or deleting from the previous list.

Hours Seven and Eight

Lecture: *What Cost this Lifestyle? The impact of earning power on lifestyle* (pros and cons).

Optional Guest Speaker: Career counselor or financial planner.

Small Group Discussion: Have each member of the group share the description of their ideal house and costs. Next, have the group discuss the following question: "Do you want to own your house or have your house own you?" As a small group brainstorm strategies for sensible home ownership.

Total Group Discussion: Have each group share their strategies for sensible home ownership with the other small groups.

Small Group Discussion: As a group, complete the budget exercise on pages 77–93 of *Career Choices and Changes*. See pages 4/47–64 of the *Instructor's and Counselor's Guide*. Students will facilitate the groups. The task: for parents to come up with the a budget for their ideal lifestyle looking ahead five years or at the age of retirement.

Lecture: *Planning for hard times*. The role of savings and the need to be financially conservative.

Optional Guest Speaker: Financial planner.

Hours Nine and Ten

Activity: Ask each participant to complete page 126–134 of *Career Choices*.

Lecture: *Knowing what you want in a job*.

Optional Guest Speaker: Someone from the career counseling staff.

Third Career Brainstorm: Now, adding information from page 134 of *Career Choices and Changes* and their budget expectation, brainstorm possible careers for each member of the group, adding or deleting from the previous list.

Reporting Out: Ask each participant to report out the most exciting career opportunity they have discovered so far and explain why it sounds so interesting to them.

Celebrate: Allow time for everyone to mingle and share their findings over refreshments. Close your program or weekend with a party or meal.

Bibliography

Bingham, Mindy, Judy Edmondson, and Sandy Stryker. *Challenges: A Young Man's Journal for Self-awareness and Personal Planning*. Santa Barbara, CA: Advocacy Press, 1984.

Bingham, Mindy, Judy Edmondson, and Sandy Stryker. *Changes: A Woman's Journal for Self-awareness and Personal Planning*. Santa Barbara, CA: Advocacy Press, 1987.

Bingham, Mindy, Judy Edmondson, and Sandy Stryker. *Choices: A Young Woman's Journal for Self-awareness and Personal Planning*. Santa Barbara, CA: Advocacy Press, 1983.

Bingham, Mindy, Lari Quinn, and William P. Sheehan. *Mother Daughter Choices: A Handbook for the Coordinator*. Santa Barbara, CA: Advocacy Press, 1988.

Bingham, Mindy, and Sandy Stryker. *Women Helping Girls with Choices: A Handbook for Community Service Organizations*. Santa Barbara, CA: Advocacy Press, 1989.

Bingham, Mindy, and Sandy Stryker. *More Choices: A Strategic Planning Guide for Mixing Career and Family*. Santa Barbara, CA: Advocacy Press, 1987.

Bolles, Richard Nelson. *What Color Is Your Parachute?* Berkeley, CA: Ten Speed Press, 1972.

Chess, Stella, M.D., and Alexander Thomas, M.D. *Know Your Child. An Authoritative Guide for Today's Parents*. New York: Basic Books, 1987.

Comiskey, James. *How to Start, Expand and Sell a Business: A Complete Guidebook for Entrepreneurs*. San Jose, CA: Venture Perspectives Press, 1985.

Crystal, John C., and Richard Bolles. *Where Do I Go from Here with My Life?* Berkeley, CA: 1974.

de Bono, Edward. *Lateral Thinking: Creativity Step by Step*. New York: Harper & Row, 1970.

Dyer, Dr. Wayne W. *What Do you Really Want for Your Children?* New York: William Morrow and Company, 1985.

Erikson, Erik. *Childhood and Society*. New York: W. W. Norton, 1963.

Fritz, Robert. *The Path of Least Resistance: Principles for Creating What You Want To Create*. New Hampshire: Stillpointe, 1986.

Gelatt, H. B., Barbara Varenhorst, and Richard Carey. *Deciding: A Leader's Guide*. New York: College Entrance Examination Board, 1972.

Goldberg, Herb. *The Hazards of Being Male*. New York: New American Library, 1976.

Goldberg, Herb. *The New Male*. New York: New American Library, 1979.

Goldberg, Joan Rachel. *High-tech Career Strategies for Women*. New York: Collier Books, 1984.

Hewlett, Sylvia Ann. *A Lesser Life: The Myth of Women's Liberation in America*. New York: William Morrow and Company, 1986.

Hopke, William. *Encyclopedia of Career & Vocational Guidance*. J. G. Ferguson Publishing Co., 1987.

Horton, Thomas R. *What Works for Me?* New York: Amacom, 1989.

Hoyt, Kenneth B. *The Concept of Work: Bedrock for Career Development*.

James, Jennifer, Ph.D. *Women and the Blues. Passions That Hurt, Passions That Heal*. San Francisco: Harper & Row, 1988.

Jongeward, Dorothy, and Dru Scott. *Women as Winners*. Reading, MA: Addison-Wesley Publishing Company, 1976.

Kanter, Rosabeth Moss. *When Giants Learn to Dance*. New York: Simon Schuster, 1989.

Knowles, M. and H. *Introduction to Group Dynamics*. Chicago: Association Press, Follett Publishing, 1972.

Lenz, Elinor, and Barbara Myerhoss. *The Feminization of America*. Los Angeles, CA: Jeremy P. Tarcher, 1985.

Marston, William Moulton. *Emotions of Normal People*. Minnesota: Persona Press, 1979.

Maslow, Abraham H. *Toward a Psychology of Being*. New York: D. Van Nostrand Company, 1968.

Mitchell, Arnold. *The Nine American Lifestyles: Who We Are and Where We're Going*. New York: Warner Books, 1983.

Morrison, Ann M., Randall P. White, Ellen Van Velsor, and The Center for Creative Leadership. *Breaking the Glass Ceiling: Can Women Reach the Top of America's Largest Corporations?* Massachusetts, 1987.

Naisbitt, John. *Megatrends*. New York: Warner Books, 1982.

Naisbitt, John, and Patricia Aburdene. *Re-inventing the Corporation*. New York: Warner Books, 1985.

Occupational Outlook Handbook. U.S. Department of Labor—Bureau of Labor Statistics. 1988–89 Edition.

O'Neill, Nena, and George O'Neill. *Shifting Gears*. New York: Avon Books, 1974.

Peters, Tom. *Thriving on Chaos: Handbook for a Management Revolution*. New York: Alfred A. Knopf, 1988.

Poynter, Dan, and Mindy Bingham. *Is There a Book Inside You? How to Successfully Author a Book Alone or through Collaboration*. Santa Barbara, CA: Para Publishing, 1985.

Ricci, Larry J. *High Paying Blue-Collar Jobs for Women*. New York: Ballantine Books, 1981.

Rohrlich, Jay B., M.D. *Work and Love: The Crucial Balance*. New York: Summit Books, 1980.

Sanderson, Jim. *How to Raise Your Kids to Stand on Their Own Two Feet*. New York: Congdon & Weed, 1983.

"Saving Our Schools." *Fortune* Magazine. 121, No. 12, Spring 1990.

Schaevitz, Marjorie Hansen. *The Superwomen Syndrome*. New York: Warner Books, 1984.

Scholz, Nelle Tumlin, Judith Sosebee Prince, and Gordon Porter Miller. *How to Decide: A Workbook for Women*. New York: Avon Books, 1978.

Simon, Sidney B., Leland W. Howe, and Howard Kirschenbaum. *Values Certification: A Handbook for Teachers and Students*. New York: A and W Publishers, 1972.

"The New Teens: What Makes Them Different. Who Are Their Heroes?" *Newsweek*. Summer/Fall 1990.

Viscott, David, M.D. *Risking*. New York: Pocket Books, 1979.

Biographical Sketches

Mindy Bingham

Innovative educational approaches have always been a mission for Mindy Bingham. As a part-time college professor, seminar leader for educators, author, publisher, and community activist, Mindy has dedicated herself to improving education. She has traveled around the country conducting workshops for educators and curriculum specialists. In 1985, she was named one of the outstanding women in education by the Santa Barbara County Commission for Women. In 1991, she was named an honorary life member to VEEC, the Vocational Education Equity Council of American Vocational Association. She was honored as the Entrepreneur of the Year for Santa Barbara for 1998 by the South Coast Business Network.

To date, the 17 titles authored or co-authored by Mindy Bingham have sold well over two million copies. Besides the *Career Choices* series of textbooks and software, they include the best-selling *Choices: A Teen Woman's Journal for Self-awareness and Personal Planning*, and *Challenges*, the young man's version, with sales of over 500,000 copies to date. Her children's picture books include the Ingram number one bestseller *Minou*; and *My Way Sally*, the 1989 Ben Franklin Award winner for Best Children's Picture Book. Mindy's most recent release, *Things Will Be Different for My Daughter, A Practical Guide for Building Her Self-Esteem and Self-Reliance from Infancy Through the Teen Years* was published by Penguin.

Tanja Easson

Tanja Easson is a living example of the need for career guidance for all students. Upon graduating from high school with high honors, she entered the University of Utah and, eventually, Weber State University. A member of the Phi Kappa Phi Honor Society, Tanja explored several fields of study—music performance, psychology, criminal justice, education—finally pursuing a major in English and a minor in sociology. Her post-college years found her in the computer software industry. The Curriculum & Technical Support Administrator for Academic Innovations since 1997, Tanja is also a wife, mother, and an amateur musician. She lives and works in Saint George, Utah.

Sandy Stryker

Sandy Stryker is co-author of the best-selling *Choices: A Young Woman's Journal for Self-awareness and Personal Planning*; *Challenges*, the young man's version; *More Choices: A Strategic Planning Guide for Mixing Career and Family*; and *Changes: A Woman's Guide for Self-awareness and Personal Planning*. Her first children's book, *Tonia the Tree*, was the 1988 recipient of the Merit Award from the Friends of American Writers. She is co-author of *The World of Work Job Application File*, and has edited numerous publications. She holds a degree in journalism from the University of Minnesota.

Rochelle S. Friedman

Rochelle S. Friedman received her doctorate in education from the State University of New York at Buffalo. She has been an administrator and teacher in both the public and private sector. Dr. Friedman has served as a consultant to schools in Louisiana and Florida and has served as an adjunct faculty member at both Nova University and Louisiana State University. She has been honored as Outstanding Educator of the Year both for program development and for classroom teaching.

Laura Castle Light

Laura Light is a mother of two daughters and a foster daughter, a professional musician, an artist, and a teacher of literature, French, in Virginia. A graduate of Stanford University in creative writing and literature, she completed her M.Ed. at Ohio University in 1984.

Acknowledgments

We would like to thank the following individuals for their assistance in the production of the manuscript: Shirley Cornelius, Robin Sager, Chas Thompson, Nancy Marriott, copy editing; Michele Julien, layout; Betty Stambolian, Pat Lewis, Linda Wagner, editing; Jim Johnson; Christine Nolt, design and layout; Itoko Maeno, Janice Blair, and Diana Lackner, art; Delta Lithograph, printing.

We would also like to thank the following individuals for contributions to this guide: Kathy Araujo, Kyle Brace, Mikell Becker, Deb Carstens, James Comiskey, Sara Lykken, M.Ed., Shirley Myers, M.Ed., Edward Myers, Susan Neufeldt, Ph.D., Penelope Paine, Robert Shafer, Betty Shepperd, Linda Wagner, and the hundreds of educators who have used the *Career Choices* series over the last several years and shared their ideas.

And finally a very special thanks to Kenneth B. Hoyt, Ph.D., for the hours he spent reviewing the manuscript, giving constructive criticism, and challenging our assumptions. His advice, guidance, and contributions to this *Instructor's and Counselor's Guide* were invaluable. So, to this steadfast pioneer, we dedicate our effort to infuse career education into the core curriculum.

Ordering Notes:

Ordering Information:

Throughout the *Instructor's and Counselor's Guide for Career Choices*, we have noted resources and materials you can order directly through Academic Innovations. Satisfaction is guaranteed. If the resource is not what you need, return the merchandise in re-saleable condition within 30 days of the invoice for a refund. Call (800) 967-8016 for current prices.

SCHOOL ORDERS

For faster and more accurate order processing, please include: the school purchase order number; quantity; full book title; school; district; person placing the order; date the books are needed; and shipping and billing (if different from shipping) addresses.

Career Choices: A Guide for Teens and Young Adults, by Mindy Bingham and Sandy Stryker. 288 pages. Hardcover, ISBN 0-878787-00-4. Softcover, ISBN 0-878787-01-2.

Instructor's and Counselor's Guide for Career Choices, by Mindy Bingham and Sandy Stryker. Softcover, 352 pages. ISBN 0-878787-11-X.

Workbook and Portfolio for Career Choices, by Mindy Bingham and Sandy Stryker. Softcover, 128 pages. ISBN 0-878787-08-X.

Possibilities: A Supplemental Anthology for Career Choices, by Janet Goode and Mindy Bingham. Softcover, 288 pages. ISBN 1-878787-09-8.

Lifestyle Math: Your Financial Planning Portfolio, A Supplemental Mathematics Unit for Career Choices, by Mindy Bingham, Jo Willhite and Shirley Myers. Softcover, 112 pages. ISBN 1-878787-07-1.

Career Choices and Changes: A Guide for Discovering Who You Are, What You Want, and How to Get It, by Mindy Bingham and Sandy Stryker. Softcover, 304 pages. ISBN 1-878787-15-2.

www.lifestylemath.com: Call for membership information.

www.careerchoices.com: Call for membership and licensing information.

SHIPPING

Allow at least four weeks for delivery. Prices quoted are FOB Utah; shipping and handling costs will be added. Regular shipping rates are based on ground shipment. Use of other delivery methods (2nd Day Air, Overnight, etc.) will result in additional shipping charges.

EXAMINATION COPIES

Examination copies are available on a 60-day approval basis. If you find the books requested are not what you need, return them in saleable condition prior to the end of the 60-day examination period. You will be invoiced after 60 days.

Fax written orders to: Academic Innovations
                                    FAX (800) 967-4027
                                    Order a 60-day set of the materials
                                    Online at www.academicinnovations.com/60day.html
                                    Call (800) 967-8016 for more information

Publications Available from Academic Innovations

Career Choices: A Guide for Teens and Young Adults: Who Am I? What Do I Want? How Do I Get It?,
    by Mindy Bingham and Sandy Stryker. 288 pages. Hardcover, ISBN 1-878787-00-4. Softcover,
    ISBN 1-878787-01-2.

Workbook and Portfolio for the text Career Choices, by Mindy Bingham and Sandy Stryker. Softcover,
    128 pages. ISBN 1-878787-08-X.

Instructor's and Counselor's Guide for Career Choices, by Mindy Bingham and Sandy Stryker.
    Softcover, 408 pages. ISBN 1-878787-11-X.

Possibilities: A Supplemental Anthology for Career Choices, edited by Janet Goode and Mindy Bingham.
    Softcover, 288 pages. ISBN 1-878787-09-8. $11.95

Lifestyle Math: Your Financial Planning Portfolio, by Mindy Bingham, Jo Willhite, and Shirley Myers.
    Softcover, 112 pages. ISBN 1-878787-07-1.

www.careerchoices.com. Call for membership and licensing information.

www.lifestylemath.com. Call for membership information.

Career Choices and Changes: A Guide for Discovering Who You Are, What You Want, and How to Get It,
    by Mindy Bingham and Sandy Stryker. Softcover, 304 pages. ISBN 1-878787-15-2.

Career Strategies: How to get and Keep a Job, by Jim Comiskey and Jay McGrath. Softcover, 172 pages.
    ISBN 1-878787-22-5.

Career Strategies Instructor's Edition, by Jim Comiskey and Jay McGrath. Softcover, 172 pages.
    ISBN 1-878787-23-3.

Career Strategies Student Workbook, by Jim Comiskey and Jay McGrath. Softcover, 96 pages.
    ISBN 1-878787-29-2.

Life Strategies: How to Succeed in School and Beyond, by Jim Comiskey. Softcover, 156 pages.
    ISBN 1-878787-25-X.

Life Strategies Instructor's Edition, by Jim Comiskey. Softcover, 154 pages. ISBN 1-878787-26-8.

Career Portfolio. Three-ring binder with insets.

Choices: A Teen Woman's Journal for Self-awareness and Personal Planning, by Mindy Bingham,
    Judy Edmondson, and Sandy Stryker. Softcover, 240 pages. ISBN 0-911655-22-0.

Challenges: A Young Man's Journal for Self-awareness and Personal Planning, by Mindy Bingham,
    Judy Edmondson, and Sandy Stryker. Softcover, 240 pages. ISBN 0-911655-24-7.

Workbook for Choices and Challenges. Softcover, 103 pages. ISBN 0-911655-25-5.

Changes: A Woman's Journal for Self-awareness and Personal Planning, by Mindy Bingham,
    Sandy Stryker, and Judy Edmondson. Softcover, 240 pages. ISBN 0-911655-40-9.

Workbook for Changes. Softcover, 104 pages. ISBN 0-911655-1-7.

More Choices: A Strategic Planning Guide for Mixing Career and Family, by Mindy Bingham
    and Sandy Stryker. Softcover, 240 pages. ISBN 0-911655-28-X.

Workbook for More Choices. Softcover, 104 pages. ISBN 0-911655-29-8.

Instructor's Guide for Choices, Challenges, Changes, and More Choices. Softcover, 272 pages.
    ISBN 0-911655-04-2.

Minou, written by Mindy Bingham, illustrated by Itoko Maeno. Hardcover with dust jacket,
    32 pages with full-color illustrations throughout. ISBN 0-911655-36-0.

My Way Sally, written by Mindy Bingham and Penelope Paine, illustrated by Itoko Maeno. Hardcover with dust jacket, 48 pages with full-color illustrations throughout. ISBN 0-911655-27-1.

Berta Benz and the Motorwagen, written by Mindy Bingham, illustrated by Itoko Maeno. Hardcover with dust jacket, 48 pages with full-color illustrations throughout. ISBN 0-911655-38-7.

Is There a Book Inside You? A Step-by-Step Plan for Writing Your Book, by Dan Poynter and Mindy Bingham. Softcover, 236 pages. ISBN 0-911655-68-3.

Personal Profile System Assessment Instrument, Adult Version. Call or write for ordering information.

Things Will Be Different for My Daughter: A Practical Guide to Building Her Self-esteem and Self-reliance, by Mindy Bingham and Sandy Stryker. Softcover, ISBN 0-14-024125-6. 1995. Penguin.

To order any of the above titles, call (800) 967-8016.

It's too bad more students don't have an opportunity to have this class and use these materials.

— Ann Dabb
Wahlquist Junior High School
Ogden, Utah

Ordering History:

Index

Life is the sum of all your choices.
—Albert Camus